GHOSTLY DEMARCATIONS

RADICAL THINKERS }V

"A golden treasury of theory" Eric Banks, *Bookforum*

"Beautifully designed...a sophisticated blend of theory and thought" Ziauddin Sardar, *New Statesman*

SET 1 ($12/£6/$14CAN)

MINIMA MORALIA
Reflections on a Damaged Life
THEODOR ADORNO
ISBN-13: 978 1 84467 051 2

FOR MARX
LOUIS ALTHUSSER
ISBN-13: 978 1 84467 052 9

THE SYSTEM OF OBJECTS
JEAN BAUDRILLARD
ISBN-13: 978 1 84467 053 6

LIBERALISM AND DEMOCRACY
NORBERTO BOBBIO
ISBN-13: 978 1 84467 062 8

THE POLITICS OF FRIENDSHIP
JACQUES DERRIDA
ISBN-13: 978 1 84467 054 3

THE FUNCTION OF CRITICISM
TERRY EAGLETON
ISBN-13: 978 1 84467 055 0

SIGNS TAKEN FOR WONDERS
On the Sociology of Literary Forms
FRANCO MORETTI
ISBN-13: 978 1 84467 056 7

THE RETURN OF THE POLITICAL
CHANTAL MOUFFE
ISBN-13: 978 1 84467 057 4

SEXUALITY IN THE FIELD OF VISION
JACQUELINE ROSE
ISBN-13: 978 1 84467 058 1

THE INFORMATION BOMB
PAUL VIRILIO
ISBN-13: 978 1 84467 059 8

CULTURE AND MATERIALISM
RAYMOND WILLIAMS
ISBN-13: 978 1 84467 060 4

THE METASTASES OF ENJOYMENT
On Women and Causality
SLAVOJ ŽIŽEK
ISBN-13: 978 1 84467 061 1

SET 2 ($12.95/£6.99/$17CAN)

AESTHETICS AND POLITICS
THEODOR ADORNO, WALTER BENJAMIN, ERNST BLOCH, BERTOLT BRECHT, GEORG LUKÁCS
ISBN-13: 978 1 84467 570 8

INFANCY AND HISTORY
On the Destruction of Experience
GIORGIO AGAMBEN
ISBN-13: 978 1 84467 571 5

POLITICS AND HISTORY
Montesquieu, Rousseau, Marx
LOUIS ALTHUSSER
ISBN-13: 978 1 84467 572 2

FRAGMENTS
JEAN BAUDRILLARD
ISBN-13: 978 1 84467 573 9

LOGICS OF DISINTEGRATION
Poststructuralist Thought and the Claims of Critical Theory
PETER DEWS
ISBN-13: 978 1 84467 574 6

LATE MARXISM
Adorno, Or, The Persistence of the Dialectic
FREDRIC JAMESON
ISBN-13: 978 1 84467 575 3

EMANCIPATION(S)
ERNESTO LACLAU
ISBN-13: 978 1 84467 576 0

THE POLITICAL DESCARTES
Reason, Ideology and the Bourgeois Project
ANTONIO NEGRI
ISBN-13: 978 1 84467 582 1

ON THE SHORES OF POLITICS
JACQUES RANCIÈRE
ISBN-13: 978 1 84467 577 7

STRATEGY OF DECEPTION
PAUL VIRILIO
ISBN-13: 978 1 84467 578 4

POLITICS OF MODERNISM
Against the New Conformists
RAYMOND WILLIAMS
ISBN-13: 978 1 84467 580 7

THE INDIVISIBLE REMAINDER
On Schelling and Related Matters
SLAVOJ ŽIŽEK
ISBN-13: 978 1 84467 581 4

GHOSTLY DEMARCATIONS

A SYMPOSIUM ON JACQUES DERRIDA'S
SPECTERS OF MARX

*Jacques Derrida, Terry Eagleton,
Fredric Jameson, Antonio Negri, et al.*

Edited by Michael Sprinker

VERSO

London • New York

First published by Verso 1999
This edition published by Verso 2008
Copyright © in the collection Verso 2008
Copyright © in the individual contributions the contributors 1999
Introduction © Michael Sprinker 1999
All rights reserved

The moral rights of the authors have been asserted

1 3 5 7 9 10 8 6 4 2

Verso
UK: 6 Meard Street, London W1F 0EG
USA: 180 Varick Street, New York, NY 10014-4606
www.versobooks.com

Verso is the imprint of New Left Books

ISBN-13: 978-1-84467-211-0

British Library Cataloguing in Publication Data
A catalogue record for this book is available from the British Library

Library of Congress Cataloging-in-Publication Data
A catalog record for this book is available from the Library of Congress

Printed and bound by ScandBook AB, Sweden

Contents

Acknowledgements

Pierre Macherey's 'Marx Dematerialized, or the Spirit of Derrida' first appeared in *Rethinking Marxism* vol. 8, no. 4.

Fredric Jameson's 'Marx's Purloined Letter' first appeared in *New Left Review* 209 (January/February 1995).

Terry Eagleton's 'Marxism without Marxism' first appeared in *Radical Philosophy* 73 (September/October 1995).

Aijaz Ahmad's 'Reconciling Derrida' first appeared in *New Left Review* 208 (November/December 1994).

A shorter version of Tom Lewis's 'The Politics of "Hauntology" in Derrida's *Specters of Marx*' first appeared in *Rethinking Marxism* vol. 9, no. 1.

Permission to reprint these texts is gratefully acknowledged.

Introduction

Michael Sprinker

The immediate occasion for Jacques Derrida's *Specters of Marx* – a symposium sponsored by the University of California at Riverside on the topic 'Whither Marxism?' – was perhaps not the most auspicious for producing the long-awaited direct encounter between Derrida and Marxism. The original lecture that later became a book was delivered at an academic conference held in a region, if arguably not a university, dominated politically by the Right. The conference title could not but evoke another, homonymic sense of Marxism's historical fate ('wither Marxism'), and it was mounted at a moment (April 1993) when the future of Marxism seemed bleaker than at any time since the defeat of the Second German Revolution in 1923. The environment for Derrida's lecture thus seemed an unlikely one for him to renew, if not precisely to redeem, an old pledge: to confront head-on the relationship of deconstruction to Marxism, to subject Marx's texts to the same kind of exegetical rigor that Derrida himself had already brought to bear on those of Plato, Rousseau, Heidegger and many, many others. *Specters of Marx* does partially satisfy that expectation, especially in its final two sections, which engage in close textual analyses of, respectively, *The Eighteenth Brumaire* and *The German Ideology*. But if one comes to the book in the hope that now, at long last, Derrida's (or deconstruction's, which is not quite the same thing) relationship to Marxism will be profoundly clarified or definitively resolved, one will almost certainly be disappointed.

The commentators in this volume differ about whether Derrida's mode of engaging Marx's texts, and Marxism more generally, is to be commended or condemned (or in some cases simply dismissed). That condemnation predominates was only to be expected, given the political positions occupied by the majority of the contributors, who, it will come as no surprise, tend to be on the Marxist side of the deconstruction/Marxism divide. Of course, it is among the several burdens of Derrida's argument to challenge this very binarism, as he makes plain in what to date must be the most frequently cited passage from *Specters*: 'Deconstruction has never had any sense or interest, in my view at least, except as a radicalization, which is to say also *in the tradition* of a certain Marxism, in a certain *spirit of Marxism* . . . But a radicalization is always indebted to the very thing it radicalizes' (*Specters of Marx*, p. 92; emphasis in the original). Yet it is this very gesture of affiliation – deconstruction as keeping faith with 'a certain spirit of Marxism' – that most provokes Derrida's critics, who respond in registers ranging from skepticism, to ire, to outright contempt. Readers can judge for themselves who gets the better of this debate. Suffice it to say here that whatever the limitations of *Specters* itself, in its account of contemporary capitalism, in its telegraphic rendering of the Marxist and communist traditions, and in its postulation of a 'new International' that remains determinately under-specified – despite what Derrida himself concedes are the large gaps requiring to be filled in before one can judge the value of his engagement with Marxism fairly – no Marxist today can afford to ignore the challenge he has laid down.

That challenge, put in its most brutally simplified form, is for Marxism to come to terms with its own past, politically and theoretically, to admit frankly and openly – as at least some of the contributors to this volume candidly do – the crimes committed in its name, the errors in which it indulged, the massively undemocratic forms of organization which it tolerated. Those ghosts have not even begun to be laid to rest; acknowledging their continuing existence remains among the most urgent tasks for any possible revival of the Marxist project.

That said, the challenge can be turned back equally on Derrida and deconstruction. In a lecture originally published in *New Left Review* 208 and included here, Aijaz Ahmad asserts unequivocally that the dominant political effect of deconstruction has been to give aid and comfort to the Right. (He refers primarily to the us, but one doubts the judgment would have been significantly different had his commination included Europe.) Whether or not deconstruction can finally be acquitted of this charge, Derrida and others must surely be called to the bar as witnesses and advocates in their own defense. By now deconstruction, too, has a history, one that Derrida has hitherto been reluctant to examine in any but the most schematic manner. The ghosts on both sides still walk.

One might characterize the areas of most direct engagement and disagreement as follows. First, there is a tangle of problems concerning the nature of capitalism as it has mutated since Marx's day. Eric

Hobsbawm, in his introduction to Verso's reissue of *The Communist Manifesto*, has asserted that Marx's vision of capitalism on the eve of the 1848 revolutions is even more perspicuous today than when it was written. In one sense, neither Derrida nor his critics would disagree. Whether, however, Marx's subsequent theorization of the capitalist mode of production, above all in *Capital*, still meets the criterion of scientific validity to which Marx aspired is a matter of some contention – and not only among the contributors to this volume!

Second, Marxist politics has always taken shape in and achieved its greatest political effects through mass organizations of the working class. From the later nineteenth century onwards, these have typically assumed the form of political parties, either clandestine (as with the Bolsheviks and many national Communist parties of the Third International) or above-ground and often with electoral pretensions (as eventually with the German SPD during the *Kaiserreich*, or with many Communist parties in and out of power to this day). One cannot emphasize too strongly this virtual *sine qua non* of Marxist politics. Derrida's insistent questioning of its value is surely the most pressing issue over which he and his critics contend. In the light of its checkered history, the pertinence of the party form to an emancipatory politics of the Left must, at a minimum, be subjected to serious, sustained scrutiny, if only to be reinvented anew.

Finally, there is the matter of ideology, its place in the corpus of Marxist concepts and its centrality to any account of society, historical or contemporary. Derrida steadfastly refuses to concede what Marx asserted (most directly in *The German Ideology*) and the majority of Marxists have continued to hold: that ideology can be banished by the science of historical materialism. This will not have been the first time that a French philosopher was vilified for hypothesizing that even a communist society would not be able to do without ideology. More than three decades have passed since Althusser first tabled his motion denouncing the humanist Marxism of the Khrushchev era. Derrida's stern rebuke of the familiar dogmatism frequently invoked to refute its premises constitutes the core of his challenge and provides unimpeachable testimony that he does indeed write '*in the tradition* of a certain Marxism, in a certain *spirit of Marxism*'.

It would be presumptuous to hazard any fuller characterization of the essays included below than the sketchy remarks offerered thus far. Again, readers can judge for themselves the merits of each, along with the justice of Derrida's treatment of them. If the texts don't exactly speak for themselves – but what text ever does? – they are nonetheless, on my reading of them at least, entirely lucid about their aims in relation to *Specters of Marx*. The contributors have paid Derrida the compliment of reading him closely, perhaps on occasion tendentiously, but for the most part not carelessly. Derrida himself has returned the favor by producing a text that scrupulously, if nearly always critically, examines their claims, in particular the criticisms of *Specters* that they level. He defends himself against the most virulent, while conceding that a great deal of further reflection on all the major motifs he and his interlocutors have introduced in this debate remains to be done. Although he cites the famous communist slogan, 'Encore un effort!', with some irony, it would seem that this injunction is of the most general pertinence, for Derrida and for all of us. Other readings of Derrida's book are possible – many have been written and published already – but none can escape entirely the probing questions and searching criticisms put in different ways by these essays. The history of deconstruction's engagement with Marxism is a long way from being at an end.

The Specter's Smile

Antonio Negri

... for though a mouse depends on God as much as an angel
does, and sadness as much as joy, a mouse cannot on that
account be a kind of angel, nor sadness a kind of joy.[1]

– Spinoza, Letter XXIII

It happens often that a great philosophy takes a step forward and
simultaneously takes a a step back, uninterruptedly circumscribing a
central nucleus of thought and a strong and coherent methodological
intuition. In *Specters of Marx*, Derrida gives a demonstration of his
philosophy's advancing, taking the method at the origins of deconstruction back to that specific historical entanglement which conditioned its
genesis: 'deconstruction, in the figure it initially took ... would have
been impossible and unthinkable in a pre-Marxist space. Deconstruction has never had any sense or interest ... except as a radicalization,
which is to say also *in the tradition* of a certain Marxism, in a certain
spirit of Marxism.'[2] It seems fairly clear that deconstruction is born and
unfolds in – while together fostering – that theoretical climate of the
rue d'Ulm where the work of Althusser, Foucault and Derrida, successively but to no lesser extent contemporaneously, takes place. More
specifically the genesis of deconstruction seems to go back to a mutual
exchange with Althusser's work, in his 'lecture symptomale' and in his
structural interpretation of the invasiveness of state ideological apparatuses, from *Reading 'Capital'*[3] to his study *Sur la reproduction.*[4] (It is
interesting to note that in his later writings, Althusser repeats his
conviction that Derrida is amongst the greatest philosophers of our
time.) Yet the deconstructionist[5] claim to a Marxist tradition and a
Marxist spirit is even more valuable if, beyond simple genealogy, we
take into consideration the rigorously critical direction that deconstruction embodies – a hermeneutic direction (in its own ontological

manner) which takes part in the dynamics of capitalism's historical and conceptual world only to oppose itself to it from the first through demystification – demystification of its language, in the first place, and then by way of and behind language, demystification of a 'metaphysics of the proper' and of state 'logocentrism' encapsulated in capitalism.

In this sense, what becomes increasingly important in the progressive constructing of deconstruction is the relation it engages in the transformation of its object, in other words the perception of that spectral redefinition of the real which it does not produce, but which it progressively registers as a paradigmatic mutation. Over a period of great acceleration in the transformation of the world, the hermeneutic, ontological, and critical aspects of deconstruction are, so to speak, constrained to contracting themselves together more closely, advancing as consorts. Here, the question 'whither Marxism?' is inextricable from the question 'whither deconstruction?', and both presuppose a 'whither capitalism?' As far as deconstruction is concerned, responding to the question 'whither Marxism?' in one way or another becomes the same as responding to the question 'whither capitalism?'. In one way or another – *in what way?* This is our focal interest in reading this book of Derrida's.

The 'specters of Marx' are therefore, in some way, the specters of capital. Those specters that appear in *Capital*, but above all, those specters that nowadays give shape to a society unanimously defined as 'capitalist' by political economy and public opinion. Marx has always played with specters, a 'whirling band of ghosts'[6] notes Derrida, perusing the pages of that founding work, *The German Ideology*. With good reason. Marx's preface states that the work's aim is to uncloak the 'innocent and childlike fancies' of that young Hegelian philosophy – 'these sheep, that take themselves and are taken for wolves' – and to show:

> how their bleating merely imitates in a philosophic form the conceptions of the German middle class; how the boasting of these philosophic commentators only mirrors the wretchedness of the real conditions in Germany. It is its aim to debunk and discredit the philosophic struggle with the shadows of reality which appeals to the dreamy and muddled German nation.[7]

Transferred onto the terrain of the critique of political economy, this project of a spectral reading of ideology is applied to the categories of society and capital, develops ontologically, and becomes definitively fixed in *Capital* (Derrida speaks of this in *Specters*, pp. 147–58). The specters narrated herein have a particular ontological pertinence: they reveal the complete functioning of the law of value. A specter is the movement of an abstraction that is materialized and becomes powerful: above all the abstraction of value which, in a bloodless movement, vampirizes all of the worker's labor and, transforming itself into surplus-value, becomes capital; money, secondly, which in a circular movement verticalizes itself and is consolidated into currency, i.e., in finance capital and in parasitic potentiality; technology, lastly – but also in principle – which, in accumulating itself, in constructing well integrated and firm lines of objective command, regulates and hierarchizes society and life. The phenomenology of capitalist production described by Marx in *Capital* demonstrates therefore how, by way of this spectral movement, a true and proper metaphysics of capital is produced, as well as the autonomy of its power. But because it unfolds itself in a spectral form and autonomizes capital, this phenomenology – Marx maintains – masks the real genesis of the process of capital's development. In order to dissipate capital's fictitious autonomy and its attendant interpretive categories, as well as to demystify the necessary order of the market's political economy, one must – according to Marx – take into account the method of production and exchange, analyze the powerful falsification of the centrality of the worker's labor that takes place therein, to break thereby the law of value's functioning and reconstruct the productive dynamics of society and of life on a free basis.

What's to be done, *today*, with this Marxist response, or better yet, with this specifically communist proposal? What's to be done with the Marxist specters, today?

With this in mind, we should take note of one of the first substantial contributions of deconstruction to updating the project of a critique of capitalism. Nowadays, we can actually do little or nothing with Marxian ghosts. What has changed isn't so much the spectral reality of the world produced by capital (the spectral mass has even become gigantic!) as much as it is the adequacy of the Marxian response. A century and a half ago, this response consisted in willing to speed away ghosts and, in so doing, in the revolt of the industrial working class, reappropriating those riches produced – in order to reform the productive praxis as well as the subjective, the human one . . . But what could this project mean, nowadays? With kindness, but with an equal force, Derrida opposes Marx in the same way Marx opposed Stirner: for the naïveté of taking a universalizing stance, in other words, for the inadequacy of the proposal for demystification. In reality, in Marx's work in both *The German Ideology* and *Capital*, the *non-spectrality* of the productive subject opposed the conditions for constructing capital's spectrality: the former was indicated through the activity of demystification and was expressed in the will of reappropriation, each and every time the movement of exchange-value clashed with the irreducible independence of 'use-value', therefore with a heterogeneity capable of generating an alternative. But where can this heterogeneity be found? Where can use-value and subjectivity be found at present? Today, the labor paradigm has greatly changed (in particular, the division between intellectual and manual labor and the alternatives linked to different projections of forms of value). Inasmuch as it concerns labor, the postmodern is certainly not just an ideological image, but the recording of a deep and irreversible transformation in which all traits of the Marxian critiques of value – more precisely, that theory of specters – stop short. 'These seismic events come from the future, they are given from out of the unstable, chaotic, and dis-located ground of the times. A dis-jointed or dis-adjusted time without which there would be neither history, nor event, nor promise of justice.'[8] Derrida's first conclusion is powerful. It introduces us to the new phase of relations in production, to the world of change in the labor paradigm. 'The time is out of joint' – but here deconstruction is 'in joint'.

Now if this mutation of labor is a given, if the law of value has been thrown 'out of joint' due to the fact that time is no longer a measuring gauge of value, nor use-value its real referent[9] – now then, why shouldn't deconstruction accept to move itself into this new critical perspective, there where these new dimensions of capital's political economy reveal themselves? Why does deconstruction accompany the efficacy of this critical move with a regressive pause (the immersion in the 'work of mourning')? Why does deconstruction want an aura of nostalgia which renders the ontological consistency of the new spectral dimension elusive and frankly ungraspable? In so doing, it works by effectively unhooking the hermeneutic of the present and of the future (which is also separated from the past and from the insertion into the new paradigm) from intense contact with the new spectral ontology. But why? Why, after having grasped the ontological element of this mutation, does deconstruction need to immerse itself anew in a transcendental continuum, relying on a phenomenological and noumenal time, both temporal and psychic, which has the effect of dramatizing and practically rendering the ontological discovery irrelevant, flattening it onto the obscure background?

We do not know how to respond to Derrida's sad sidestepping, nor do we know how to construct a straight line that would cut through his process's agonizing curves. Nevertheless, if we're unsatisfied with the lack of a cut-and-dried heuristic process, we know by contrast what the deconstructionist hermeneutic produces here. It produces a new theory of spectrality which corresponds with common experience: an experience of the everyday, and/or of the masses; the experience of a mobile, flexible, computerized, immaterialized and spectral labor. *A common experience of spectrality as clear as the sun.* The new spectrality is there – and we're entirely within this real illusion. We've nothing more than this real illusion before us and behind us. There's no longer an outside, neither a nostalgic one, nor a mythic one, nor any urgency for reason to disengage us from the spectrality of the real. There's neither place nor time – and this is the real. Only a radical 'Unheimlich' remains in which we're immersed. It's good that here deconstruction prevails in its agility in playing with the phenomenon, and that it hides itself by crouching in the set of relations that are on this side of the phenomenon, in the genesis of its appearing; but it would be just as good if, in taking this into account, operating in the world of political economy in this way, it described the phenomenology of a new productive reality, a social one – of a lifeworld that fully meshed with the new spectral reality. The subject is therefore unlocatable in a world that has lost all measure, because in this spectral reality no measure is perceived or perceptible. The 'specters of Marx' were so very different: here, they're no longer valid.

Nevertheless, 'one must *assume the inheritance* of Marxism, assume its most "living" part, which is to say, paradoxically, that which continues to put back on the drawing board the question of life, spirit, or the spectral, of life-death beyond the opposition between life and death. This inheritance must be reaffirmed by transforming it as radically as will be necessary.'[10] But how will it be possible to follow this task through, immersed as we are in the world of specters?

When the analysis passes from the hermeneutic and ontological viewpoint to the experience of the political, the picture given is terrible. The conspiracy against Marxism and the world evangelization of the free market, the construction of a global power 'without place' and 'without time', the structuring of the 'end of history', the media's colonization of consciousness and the impoverishment in the quality of work, the emptying out of meaning from the word 'democracy' – within individual countries and in international relations – these represent only a few of the hegemonic orders of capitalism in one phase of the spectral reconstruction of the real. How does one circulate within this new determination of being? At this crucial point, deconstruction refers back to a radical questioning of the problem of life and death, the opening of an experience of ethics and community. It's at this crucial point that a discourse on ethical resistance unravels, one that reflects on the experience of the gift and of friendship, that feels a certain affinity with the messianic spirit and reaffirms the undeconstructability of the idea of justice. The work of Derrida's that surrounds *Specters of Marx* serves to illustrate this approach: above all, *Force de loi*[11] and *Politiques de l'amitié*.[12] But how could one believe this protest or this ethical alternative to be effective in a world of forceful ghosts? How can ethical resistance become real – if indeed it can – before the overbearing ghostly dominion?

Derrida himself seems not to count on a useful result following an ethical insurrection. In *Specters of Marx*, he recognizes that 'barely deserving the name community, the new International belongs only to anonymity'.[13] In *Politics of Friendship*, when he introduces the notion of political friendship, he concludes by stating: 'it still deals with a fraternity, but a fraternity that leads infinitely beyond all the figures of the brother, a fraternity that no longer excludes anyone.'[14] There's something that's exhausted in these pages, like the shadow of that melancholic libertinism when, at the end of another revolutionary age, men who were still free testified in refusal of the Counter-Reformation and awaited the martyrdom of the Inquisition. We cannot content ourselves with this, perhaps because our Marxist heritage has already been proven in practice; more likely because – in dealing with specters – the eye, the other senses, and the mind begin to detect delineations of new realities. So is it possible then to proceed beyond the level of moral protest?

There's a word that rarely appears in Derrida's book: exploitation. This absence is understood accordingly: exploitation is in fact the category in which, more than any other, Marx would make 'a critical but pre-deconstructive ontology of presence as actual reality and as objectivity'.[15] We agree in deeming the Marxist ontology out of date, and *this* ontological description of exploitation, in particular. But is there any chance that this theoretical supersession has the consequence of really eliminating exploitation? No reasonable person could so affirm, in the same way that no reasonable person could insist on, exploitation's identical form then and now. The fact is that in speaking of exploitation, it's necessary to take into consideration not so much the categories that, *post festum*, denounce exploitation, but rather the mechanisms that produce it. Now, in the ghostly production of postindustrial capitalism, these mechanisms remain intact and become even more powerful.

Taking this situation into account means recognizing that if the law of value no longer works in describing the entire process of capital, the law of surplus-value and exploitation is, in any case, constitutive of the logic of production. The fact that some discursive sets occupy productive space and articulate its order (more so than do the masses of commodities) does not remove the other fact: that these discursive sets are themselves products of industrial capitalism, both cause and effect – circularly – of a general exploitative device.[16] Taking this situation into account therefore means recognizing that, aside from any objective (or any ontological, predeconstructive ...) measure, human labor, both mental and manual, is increasingly implicated in exploitation, prisoner of a world of ghosts producing wealth and power for some, misery and discipline for the masses. Together, in an indistinguishable manner, both exploitation and discursive universes travel the Internet, constructing themselves through communicative networks while fixing hierarchical and expropriative dividing lines therein. Accumulation nowadays consists in that kind of acquisition of knowledge and social activity taking place within these communicative horizons. At the same time, if those mechanisms of expropriation do not follow in the footsteps of the exploitative devices of industrial labor's old ontology, then they presuppose new ways – immaterial and ghostly ones.[17] On the one side, we have communication and the wealth that accumulates therein; on the other, we have the solitude, the misery, the sadness, the exodus and the new class wars that define this exploitation of labor in a world of immateriality and spectral production.

But allow me a brief parenthesis here. In the conclusion of his *Ethics, Definitio Affectuorum, Pars III*, Spinoza speaks of an emotion called a '*pathema* of the soul'[18] – which he defines as: 'a confused idea, by which the Mind affirms of its body, or some part of it, a greater or lesser force of existing than before, which, when it is given, determines the Mind to think of one thing rather than another.'[19] In the 'Explication' that follows, Spinoza speaks of 'a greater or lesser force of existing than before' born through the confrontation of experience that passes through the body and mind (or through active memory) with the body and mind's actual consistency. The *pathema* is therefore a dual state of mind, which is between passivity and activity and lives in the present though it is prefabricated in memory, enduring the past while turned towards action. Consequently, the *pathema* is also the perpetually uncertain but nevertheless open moment of an ontological passage which leads the mind to grasp the very nature of Desire, beyond the (past) determinations of existence or the (present) external dialectic of sadness and joy. I've always been struck by the spectral quality of this emotion, as well as by the constitutive dynamic that traverses it. Speaking elsewhere of this emotion, in relation to Y. Yovel's work on Marrano culture,[20] it seemed to me that one could recognize in it a sort of parable of the 'Marrano' or could transcribe the genealogical paradox that characterizes it as follows: condemned to choose between two religions that confound and torment him, the 'Marrano' refuses transcendence and chooses to live a worldly, laic and rational ascesis that will lead him towards a constitutive hermeneutics and an ethics of liberation. I now ask myself if this way – which leads from passivity to potential, in the twilight of the 'passion' and among the specters that haunt the 'Marrano's' life – isn't also a parable of the experience of change in the paradigm of productive labor – from materiality to immateriality – and a parable of change in the hope for communism here and now in the postmodern dimension.

Once this is said, the other face of exploitation must nevertheless be emphasized, i.e., the capitalist relations of production in the present age. No longer are capitalist relations of production exercised solely on a subject characterized through misery and a 'predeconstructive' referent to a generic human essence. On the contrary, the exploited subject appearing on this new scene, who must deal with ghosts, is presented rather as a flux, a mobile and flexible reality, a hybrid potential that traverses the spectral movement of production and, in so doing, continually reconstitutes itself anew. Today, exploitation, or, rather, capitalist relations of production, concern a laboring subject amassed in intellectuality and cooperative force. A new paradigm: most definitely exploited, yet new – a different power, a new consistency of laboring energy, an accumulation of cooperative energy. This is a new – post-deconstructive – ontology.

I believe that if we had the opportunity to lead deconstruction onto this new ontological terrain, we could exalt its hermeneutic capacity even further, for this hermeneutic capacity brings the spectral aspect of capitalist production to light. I also believe that, if this were the case, we could ultimately refer ourselves to several of deconstruction's suggestions related to the problem of resistance. It is in fact evident that when deconstruction comprehends that capitalist production is the production of ghosts, a dominion extending over and regulating linguistic universes, as well as the castration of desire, at this very moment it indicates lines of flight and sites of resistance: in being organized through an undecidable line firmly sustained through the decision to refute every logocentrism and to desert any form of senseless, disciplinary regime. So, is there still the possibility for rupture? And how so?

In order to answer this question, and in order to reincorporate important elements of deconstruction into this response, we must nevertheless refer ourselves back to fundamental qualities in deconstruction's way of proceeding – and now, in all likelihood, we must make distinctions among them. When it comes down to it, we've already said so: it seems that, in its approach, deconstruction remains prisoner of an ineffectual and exhausted definition of ontology. The reality principle in deconstruction is out of its element. When Derrida concludes his analysis of the Marxian ontology of value, ridding himself of its naïve ontology of presence – to the extent that it thinks of the possibility of dissipating spectrality from the starting-point of a consciousness representative of the subject – he does not produce an adequate ontological jump-start, aside from the correctness of his phenomenological approach. Derrida is a prisoner of the ontology he critiques. When phenomenology changes, he uses it to criticize the horizon of Marxian ontology, and rightly so – but he does so in an inconsequential manner, refusing to change the ontology itself or to reconstruct it according to the standard set by the phenomenological change. He doesn't want to see its occurrence beginning with the spectral and hybrid figures which today, in the age of postindustrial capitalism, produce wealth and reality (and which Derrida nevertheless defines with great care); he therefore does not want to see a movement of ontological constitution and/or the production of subjectivity. *Other* elements contributing to deconstruction's genesis, other than Marxism (principally elements tied to negative theology à la Blanchot or to the paradoxical Nietzscheanism of Bataille), take the upper hand here. Enlisted in this militia, the 'specters of Marx' become even more evanescent. Intellectual specters: where can their practice be found?

Here Derrida seems like a Hume who trespasses onto Schopenhauer's territory – as has happened elsewhere in the best moments of 'critical-critique' in the history of German ideology.

> What costs humanity very dearly is doubtless to believe that one can have done in history with a general essence of Man, on the pretext that it represents only a *Hauptgespenst*, arch-ghost, but also, what comes down to the same thing – *at bottom* – to still believe, no doubt, in this capital ghost. To believe in it as do the credulous or the dogmatic.[21]

No – here the discriminating factor is cut and dried, and it's neither credulity nor dogmatism, but the awareness – not only to come, but presently, alas, so present – that the ghostly reality which embraces and keeps us, not only in ideology but in the body, forms an ontology in which we're enveloped. But for this very reason, those old Marxian problems concerning exploitation and liberation are no longer signaled here as if, behind the ghostly reality, we should find something positive to rebuild on. On the contrary, those problems concern us to the extent that, *without an outside any longer possible*, without the precedent of a human universal, we fight against exploitation, an exploitation that is real and intolerable, and we can do this only in constituting a new reality, a new hybrid being, different each and every time, constructed and therefore snatched away from humanity's arch-ghosts with each instance.

If we want to deepen deconstruction's crisis over this issue, and explain why a correct phenomenology ends with an inadequate onto-logical opening, perhaps we should denounce the insufficiency of deconstruction's concept of practice. This is not to say that deconstruc-tion's practical application is a mere amalgamation of the decrypting and demystifying of linguistic disseminations: certainly not – and even if it were, it would somehow have an ontological connotation. *But this connotation guards itself from being constitutive.* Deconstruction has a tremendous stake in interpretation: but what would it tell us when the interpretation intersects with, or, better yet, is presented as, practice? Through various models of social and linguistic practices, performativ-ity maintains itself in a domain where the sense of belonging to being is left undecidable. And it's with the *idea of justice* that this knot is entangled, rather than unravels. And not by chance. In fact, when performativity comes to life in practice, when – in this concrete instance – it designates the overcoming of exploitation, exclusion, solitude and misery, it must find its direction in the constitution of being, thereby implicating the question of justice. *Specters of Marx* becomes one chapter in *Force of Law* . . . But it's precisely here that the knot does *not* untie, and in playing with the specters of being, rather than proposing an exit toward the future, or a new construction of justice that's mingled with new forms of spectral being, it turns back and loses itself in that which is 'inaccessible to man', in the 'infinitely other'. The game is played out in mysticism, in the recognition of an irresolvable founda-tion of the law, in the definition of responsibility as committing to an ungraspable ontological 'other'. Why? Why this regressive step back? Why does deconstruction get stuck in subordinating the new phenom-enology of the specter (which nevertheless has a productive and singular ontological base) to the oldest of reactionary ontologies: the theological one?

(But who should bear this work of mourning, and for what reason? Not the person working on a new theory of revolution. It's natural that theory be renovated, since it renovates itself according to a mutation of the real, the old theory being one of its fundamental agents, despite everything. Nor the person working for the construction of a new revolutionary organization. The person who fights or who has fought for communism is certainly not nostalgic for the old organizations, neither the Stalinist one, nor the folkloric one that survives on its fringes. The new communist experiment is born through the rupture with memory. A rupture distinct from any melancholy or resentment. And it's there that, in the present, amongst all and no specters, the only real continuity appears: that of the struggle, of the constituent spirit, of the ontological violence of transformation. The awaited event makes the past explode. A real coming-to-be.[22] In this same spirit, why should Walter Benjamin be considered a 'proto-Marxist'?)

'Whither deconstruction?' unhooks itself from 'whither capitalism?' and 'whither Marxism?'. Capitalism and communism continue to fight on terrain made up of new spectral figures, real nonetheless, and of new movements. Attached to the new social force of mass intellectuality, a radical form of Marxism can constructively respond to renewed forms of capital's regulation and to the exploitation of immaterial labor. At the other extreme, deconstruction insists on solitary transcendental horizons – without keeping in touch with practice and fleeing after having identified the possible determining factor of justice ... It's a shame, for *Specters of Marx* represents a remarkable introduction to a new practice.

A brief digression in closing. I don't feel that the critique of political economy developed in the register of deconstruction is enough to describe the complexity of spectral production that could be traced in Marx, in his work, in his actions and in his heritage. More specifically, it seems to me that if the specter of capitalism is substantially present in Derrida's book (and with that the more recent developments in the capitalist dominion), the 'specter of communism', on the other hand, is harder to identify, if not undetectable. If Derrida sharpens the 'arms of criticism' with great zeal and intelligence, the other spectrology nevertheless goes by the wayside, the one organized through a 'criticism of arms'. Communism's ghost is not only the product of a critique; it is also, and above all, a passion, destructive of the world of capital and constructive of freedom, 'the real movement that destroys the present state of things'. But permit me to give an example here. In Alexis de Tocqueville's *Recollections*,[23] we're told of a day in June 1848. We're in a lovely apartment on the left bank, seventh arrondissement, at dinnertime. The Tocqueville family is reunited. Nevertheless, in the calm of the evening, the cannonade fired by the bourgeoisie against the rebellion of rioting workers resounds suddenly – distant noises from the right bank. The diners shiver, their faces darken. But a smile escapes a young waitress who serves their table and has just arrived from the Faubourg Saint Antoine. She's immediately fired. Isn't the true specter of communism perhaps there in that smile? The one that frightened the Tsar, the pope ... and the Lord of Tocqueville? Isn't a glimmer of joy there, making for the specter of liberation?

Translated by Patricia Dailey and Costantino Costantini

Notes

1. Benedict de Spinoza, *The Collected Works of Spinoza*, ed. and trans. Edwin Curley (Princeton, NJ: Princeton University Press, 1985), p. 389. All future references cited as *CWS*.

2. Jacques Derrida, *Specters of Marx*, trans. Peggy Kamuf (New York and London: Routledge, 1994), p. 92. All future references cited as *SM*.

3. Louis Althusser and Etienne Balibar, *Reading 'Capital'*, trans. Ben Brewster (London: NLB, 1970).

4. Louis Althusser, *Sur la reproduction* (Paris: Presses universitaires de France, 1995).

5. ['Deconstructionist' rather than 'deconstructive', since the reference is to deconstruction 'as a whole' rather than to a critical move within it. – Translator's note.]

6. *SM*, p. 129.

7. Karl Marx and Frederick Engels, *The German Ideology*, trans. W. Lough (London: Lawrence and Wishart, 1965), p. 23.

8. *SM*, p. 170.

9. See Antonio Negri, *Marx Beyond Marx: Lessons on the Grundrisse*, trans. Harry Cleaver, Michael Ryan and Maurizio Viano, ed. Jim Fleming (South Hadley, MA: Bergin and Garvey Pub., 1984); second edition (New York: Columbia University Press, 1991).

10. *SM*, p. 54.

11. Jacques Derrida, *Force de loi; Le 'Fondement mystique de l'autorité'* (Paris: Galilée, 1994).

12. Jacques Derrida, *Politiques de l'amitié; suivi de l'oreille de Heidegger* (Paris: Galilée, 1994).

13. *SM*, p. 90

14. [My translation; Negri's citation without reference from the Italian edition. – Translator's note.]

15. *SM*, p. 170.

16. For a discussion of this point see chapters 6 and 7 of Michael Hardt and Antonio Negri, *The Labour of Dionysus* (Minneapolis, MN: University of Minnesota Press, 1994).

17. For a discussion of this see Robert Heilbronner and Lester Thurow's *Economics Explained: Everything You Need to Know about How the Economy Works and Where It Is Going* (New York: Simon and Schuster, 1994).

18. [Shirley translates (Indianapolis and Cambridge: Hackett Publishing Company, 1992) as 'passive experience' what Negri cites as the 'pathema del animo', and Elwes (New York: Dover Publications, 1955) translates as 'a passivity of the soul'. I have kept the Latin for 'pathema' throughout, as Negri does. – Translator's note.]

19. *CWS*, p. 542.

20. See *Studi Spinozana*, Hanover 1995, no. 10.

21. *SM*, p. 175.

22. [Negri uses 'a-venire', echoing Derrida's meditation on this term. – Translator's note.]

23. Alexis de Tocqueville, *Recollections*, trans. George Lawrence, ed. J.P. Payer and A.P. Kerr (Garden City, NY: Doubleday, 1970).

2

Marx Dematerialized,
or the Spirit of Derrida

Pierre Macherey

> How can he be there, again, when his time is no longer present?
>
> Jacques Derrida, *Specters of Marx*[1]

In 1993 a colloquium devoted to the future of Marxism was organized in the United States, one of the few places in the world where people still seem interested in this question.[2] Two lectures given on that occasion by Jacques Derrida have been collected in a work entitled *Specters of Marx*. This lumiunous and inspired book is, as are most productions of its author, a splendid work of art and is composed with an incredible virtuosity, without the latter in any way damaging the absolute clarity of its exposition. Derrida's book encourages a rereading of Marx's work which leads, on the levels of both theory and practice, to a free reappropriation of Marx's 'inheritance'. For it is indeed a question here of an inheritance, in the strict sense, that is, of that which can, in every sense of the word, 'return' from someone who is dead or, as one says, has disappeared [*disparu*]: the title of Derrida's book, *Specters of Marx*, obviously echoes *Marx Is Dead*, published in 1970 by J.-.M Benoist.[3] Father Marx[4] is dead: the time has come for him to return to his children, to us, in the form of his ghost or phantom, to whom we can address injunctions, conjurations and exorcisms, unless one does not return to him, like Hamlet in the shadow of his father – the reference to this long scene in Shakespeare's play returns as a leitmotif throughout Derrida's text – the famous remark by which Marx had himself contrived to establish his inheritance: 'Well said, old Mole.'

The formula 'specters of Marx' is written in the plural because it associates two uses, subjective and objective, of the genitive. It does not mean only the ghost Marx has become for us who are Marx's children or orphans; but it also evokes all the ghosts that already haunt Marx's work and confer on it, in that which its letter contains that is apparently most unalterable, a properly spectral air. Derrida proposes in his book – and this constitutes the essence of the latter's theoretical contribution – a rereading of Marx's texts in which reference to specters intervenes not only as a figure of rhetorical style but as a determination of those texts' content of thought. Derrida thus draws Marx's inheritance alongside what he calls a 'hauntology', in other words, a science of ghosts, a science of what returns. One could just as easily say a science of 'spirit', insofar as this is profoundly what returns in the manner of an inheritance.[5] These texts are essentially the following: the preface to the *Communist Manifesto*, with its famous appeal to the 'ghost of communism'; the passage from the *Eighteenth Brumaire* on the resurrection of the dead and history as repetition; the discussion with Stirner in *The German Ideology* on the phantasmatic character of the human essence; and finally, in the opening of *Capital*, the reflection the latter devotes to the enigma of the commodity and in particular the fetishism of political economy that makes relations among men 'return' fantastically in the form of relations among things.

Bringing out the 'spectral' passages in Marx's work presupposes that its 'spirit' should be interpreted according to an orientation which tends to 'filter' its inheritance,[6] so as to highlight the diversity of its components, which are not all spectral in the same way. For if the formula 'specters of Marx' is systematically put into the plural by Derrida, it is equally his intention to separate it, to distill its content.

> Not without Marx, no future without Marx, without the memory and the inheritance of Marx; in any case of a certain Marx, of his genius, of at least one of his spirits. For this will be our hypothesis or rather our bias: *there is more than one of them, there must be more than one of them.*[7]

There must be several spirits of Marx which are not necessarily homogeneous:

> What one must constantly come back to, here as elsewhere, concerning this text as well as any other (and we still assign here an unlimited scope to this value of text) is an irreducible heterogeneity, an internal untranslatability in some way. It does not necessarily signify theoretical weakness or inconsistency. The lack of a system is not a fault here. On the contrary, heterogeneity opens things up, it lets itself be opened up by the very effraction of that which unfurls, comes, and remains to come – singularly from the other. . . . And we do not have to suppose that Marx was in agreement with himself.[8]

Thus, rather than diverge from Marx, as those who reject his inheritance recommend, because they want to remain once and for all deaf to what the ghost's voice utters, one must above all pay attention to the internal divergences of his message, and not hold on to the artificial unity professionals of Marxism and anti-Marxism unanimously recognize in it.

With his histories of ghosts Derrida seems to play again with the formula Croce used to entitle the book he had devoted to Hegelian philosophy: 'What is living, what is dead.' A ghost is precisely an intermediary 'apparition' between life and death, between being and non-being, between matter and spirit, whose separation it dissolves. And an inheritance is also that which the dead return to the living, and that which reestablishes a kind of unity between life and death.

> ... one *must assume the inheritance* of Marxism, assume its most 'living' part, which is to say, paradoxically, that which continues to put back on the drawing board the question of life, spirit, or the spectral, of life–death beyond the opposition of life and death. This inheritance must be reaffirmed by transforming it as radically as will be necessary. Such a reaffirmation would be both faithful to something that resonates in Marx's appeal – let us say once again in the spirit of his injunction – and in conformity with the concept of inheritance in general.[9]

For an inheritance is not transmitted automatically but is reappropriated. To follow the spirit of Marx, to obey its injunctions, is not to repeat its formula mechanically, as if it were already finished; but it is actively to reaffirm its significance, for the latter must be produced or reproduced anew from the perspective of an interpretation which reveals what remains living in it. 'If the readability of a legacy were given, natural, transparent, univocal, if it did not call for and at the same time defy interpretation, we would never have anything to inherit from it.'[10] In fact, one does not inherit only from the past of the past, and it must even be said that, from that which is dead once and for all and cannot return, there can be no inheritance. Rather, one inherits from that which, in the past, remains yet to come, by taking part in a present which is not only present in the fleeting sense of actuality, but which undertakes to reestablish a dynamic connection between past and future: '... to ask oneself where Marxism is going, which is also to say, where Marxism is leading and where is it to be led: where to lead it by interpreting it, which cannot happen without transformation, and not where can it lead us such as it is or such as it will have been.'[11]

How does the interpretation Derrida proposes of the 'specters of Marx' transform the spirit of Marxism? Derrida establishes as a place in the present 'apparitions' of Marx the terrain where phantomachies unfold, and thus he reduces Marx's thought, from the moment when it was itself transformed into what returns to us – hence into an inheritance – to a history of ghosts. It is obvious, then, that Derrida, by using the hypercritique[12] he calls deconstruction, breaks with interpretations of Marx's thought which would proceed along the lines of a solidification or what could be called a 'de-derealization' of its content. This break occurs for the sake of a new interpretation of Marx's thought, which on the contrary allows its message to be de-ontologized, in relation to the figure of a Marx dematerialized as much as possible and thus closely identified with his specter or specters.

> When, for example, in evoking the history of ideas, the *Manifesto* declares that the 'ruling ideas [*die herrschenden Ideen*] of each age have ever been the ideas of its ruling class [*der herrschenden Klasse*]', it is not out of the question for a selective critique to filter the inheritance of this utterance so as to keep this rather than that. One may continue to speak of domination in a field of forces not only while suspending the reference to this ultimate support that would be the identity and the self-identity of a social class, but even while suspending the credit extended to what Marx calls the idea, the determination of the superstructure as idea, ideal or ideological representation, indeed even the discursive form of this representation. All the more so since the concept of idea implies this irreducible genesis of the spectral that we are planning to re-examine here.[13]

Thus is clearly invalidated the presupposition that, from a foundational perspective which is not without invoking a certain Platonism – we shall rediscover this reference later – establishes an insurmountable limit between an infrastructural materiality and a superstructural ideality, enclosed once and for all by a rigid topology in the difference of their respective 'places'.

The new science of spirit Derrida undertakes to promote, by opposing to the certainties of ontology the fictions of his 'hauntology', leads to the affirmation of a reciprocal communication of the material and ideal: there is a materiality of the idea, insofar as it is a ghost in which appearing is mixed together with disappearing;[14] and there is an ideality of matter, insofar as the latter is not only that which 'is' in the sense of a given whose simple presence would be fixed once and for all. The last chapter of the book, which is entitled 'Apparition of the Inapparent', particularly develops this theme by relying especially on the analysis of two canonical texts: the 'Saint Max' of *The German Ideology* and the analysis of the commodity at the beginning of *Capital*, texts from which Derrida undertakes to extract the elements of a theory of ideology insofar as the latter is established precisely in this gap between the material and the spiritual: a gap from the standpoint of which there is no longer anything purely material and/or purely spiritual, but only something invisible visible, insensible sensible, or incorporated, which, although the experience of ghosts testifies to it, is also dematerialized, as a matter which has spirit or spirit which has a matter.

It is in this way that, behind the vehement critique Marx opposes to Stirner, Derrida detects the most secret connivance that links them. If Marx harasses poor Saint Ma(r)x, identified with the pathetic figure of Szeliga, it is first because he bears a grudge against his own double, against that which is most Stirnerian in himself, revealed through this indelible attachment to ghosts which reveals the fact of wanting to exorcize all of them, and to do everything so that, once they were gone, it would be as if they had never been. This figure is that of the

> *paradoxical hunt* (whose figure, beginning before Plato, will have traversed the whole history of philosophy, more precisely of the ontological inquest or inquisition)....[15]
>
> Come so that I may chase you! You hear! I chase you. I pursue you. I run after you to chase you away from here. I will not leave you alone. And the ghost does not leave its prey, namely, its hunter. It has understood instantly that one is hunting it just to hunt it, chasing it away only so as to chase after it. Specular circle: one chases after in order to chase away, one pursues, sets off in pursuit of someone to make him flee, but one makes him flee, distances him, expulses him so as to go after him again and remain in pursuit.[16]

Here is diagnosed the profoundly denegative element of this speculative hunt which is authorized by the affirmation of the reality of the real, thus opposed to the specular, phantomatic, fantastic, or phantasmatic character of the ideal speculation that is supposed to give only a flimsy double of it. And what if, in this unstable relation whose terms do not cease to be inverted, the copy took the place of the model? If the prey, in the course of this speculative pursuit, took the place of the hunter? If the real in the name of which the apparition is exorcized, conjured, were itself only the double of its double? If it were impossible to escape the circle of speculation once and for all? It is this unease which secretly seems to eat away at the critique Marx opposes to Stirner and which begins anew the journey ahead of itself, as the trap of mimeticism and identification tightens on the one who is engaged always more blindly, always more lucidly. One is never freed so easily from ghosts, whose apparitions are all the fuller as one undertakes to reject or deny them, as if it were sufficient to say that they are nothing in order to make them disappear. And, one could add, Hegel was the first to have understood that a fundamental negativity 'haunts' this position of being as being, of the real as real, and nothing else. To oppose the speculative to the real would thus be to admit their

mysterious familiarity, which renders them inseparable from one
another, and which turns ontology into a hauntology, and vice versa.

Undoubtedly Marx is a party – and the whole question is to know if
he remained one – to this assimilation of ideology to a mystification, in
the strict sense of the production of myths or fables which transpose by
transcending, by making sacred, the profane play of real life. 'The
treatment of the phantomatic in *The German Ideology* announces or
confirms the absolute privilege that Marx always grants to religion, to
ideology as religion, mysticism, or theology, in his analysis of ideology
in general.'[17] Although Feuerbach had theorized it in his *Essence of
Christianity*, it is in the gap separating *Diesseits* and *Jenseits*, here and
there, earth and sky, that are formed the mysterious shadows, the
ghosts of speculation. To the very end Marx would have held on to this
presupposition which, according to Derrida, still underlies the entire
analysis of fetishism in *Capital* Part I, Chapter 1. By opposing the
mystical character of the commodity to that which constitutes its real,
actual body, 'in flesh and bone', to know its use-value, and by undertaking to explain the alchemical transmutation that converts one into the
other, Marx resumes the ambiguous journey situated between ontology
and hauntology, by discovering the horror, but also the derision, of a
reality full of specters, and which is perhaps only the specter of itself
and its own 'reality'. This economy, which is religious even before
being political, belongs closely to being and its images, like the sensible
and insensible, which is also a suprasensible, or the suprasensible of
the sensible.

> The Thing is neither dead nor alive, it is dead and alive at the same time. It
> survives. At once cunning, inventive, and machine-like, ingenious and unpre-
> dictable, this war machine is a theatrical machine, a *mekhane*. What one has
> just seen cross the stage is an apparition, a quasi-divinity – fallen from the
> sky or come out of the earth.[18]

In a world which has become to itself its own spectacle, the artificial
speculation of its natural order, things appear as other than they 'are';
and economic 'reality' holds together precisely in this double play
which makes relations among men pass for relations among things,
and vice versa. This is exactly what Marx says:

> The mysterious character of the commodity-form consists therefore simply
> in the fact that the commodity reflects the social characteristics of men's
> own labour as objective characteristics of the products of labour themselves,
> as the socio-natural properties of these things. Hence it also reflects the
> social relation of the producers to the sum total of labour as a social relation
> between objects, a relation which exists apart from and outside the produc-

ers. Through this substitution, the products of labour become commodities, sensuous things which are at the same time suprasensible or social.[19]

But, Derrida explains, at the very moment Marx recognizes the spectral character of reality, he denies it, by taking the same risk as Stirner of turning this reality back into the image of its image:

> To say that the same thing, the wooden table for example, *comes on stage* as commodity *after* having been but an ordinary thing in its use-value is to grant an origin to the ghostly moment. Its use-value, Marx seems to imply, was intact. It was what it was, use-value, identical to itself. The phantasmagoria, like capital, would begin with exchange-value and the commodity form. It is only then that the ghost 'comes on stage.' Before this, according to Marx, it was not there. Not even in order to haunt use-value. But whence comes the certainty concerning the previous phase, that of this supposed use-value, precisely, a use-value purified of everything that makes for exchange-value and the commodity form? What secures this distinction for us?[20]

To the ontological presupposition that affirms the primitive character of use-value, origin, or absolute model, prior to all its representations, derivations or distortions, hauntological deconstruction opposes the following suspicion:

> We are suggesting on the contrary that, before the *coup de théâtre* of this instant, before the 'as soon as it comes on stage as commodity, it changes into a sensuous supersensible thing,' the ghost had made its apparition, without appearing in person, of course and by definition, but having already hollowed out in use-value, in the hardheaded wood of the headstrong table, the repetition (therefore substitution, exchangeability, iterability, the loss of singularity as the experience of singularity itself, the possibility of capital) without which a use could never even be determined.[21]

And thus the great scene of exorcism with which *Capital* opens only proves the unavoidable presence/absence of these ghosts from which no one escapes, especially not one who undertakes to remove from them their weight of reality. For these images, in order to be images, are no less real, and are perhaps even more real.

The specters of Marx are thus sent back to the circle of their apparition; and if this movement shatters an illusion, it is the one commonly attached to the simple and primary character of being-real. The figure of Marx who emerges from such an analysis is indeed, as I said at the beginning, that of a dematerialized Marx. The book Étienne Balibar has just devoted to *La Philosophie de Marx*, to which Derrida refers several times, seems to him also to proceed along the lines of an integration of appearance to the real, which prevents establishing an elementary line of demarcation between the two:

Fetishism is not – as would be, for example, an optical illusion or a superstitious belief – a subjective phenomenon, a false perception of reality. Rather it constitutes the way in which reality (a certain social form or structure) cannot *not* appear. And this active 'appearing' (at the same time *Schein* and *Erscheinung,* that is, a lure and a phenomenon) constitutes a necessary mediation or function without which, in given historical conditions, the life of society would quite simply be impossible. To suppress the appearance is to suppress the social relation.[22]

In a sense Balibar is saying the same thing as Derrida, but he is saying it in an inverted way, from the perspective of a Marx one could call 'rematerialized', which restores to the 'appearances' of ideology their weight of reality, instead of denying every appearance of reality to reality, according to the profound inspiration that underlies the enterprise of a deconstruction. This enterprise of deconstruction, which draws Marx alongside his ghosts, succeeds perfectly on the condition of filtering his inheritance to the point of retaining from *Capital* only Part I, Chapter 1: Marx without social classes, without the exploitation of labor, without surplus-value, risks, in fact, no longer being anything but his own ghost.

On this point, we can admit that Derrida affirms his position with complete clarity:

... one is in opposition to two dominant tendencies: *on the one hand,* the most vigilant and most modern reinterpretations of Marxism by certain Marxists (notably French Marxists and those around Althusser) who believed that they must instead try to dissociate Marxism from any teleology or from any messianic eschatology (but my concern is precisely to distinguish the latter from the former); *on the other hand,* anti-Marxist interpretations that determine their own emancipatory eschatology by giving it a metaphysical or onto-theological content that is always deconstructible. A deconstructive thinking, the one that matters to me here, has always pointed out the irreducibility of affirmation and therefore of the promise, as well as the undeconstructibility of a certain idea of justice (dissociated here from law).[23]

But we cannot then avoid posing the following question: wouldn't this position of something undeconstructible – which recalls in its own way the Cartesian *cogito* – be itself a ghost, the ghost or the 'spirit' of Derrida?

Translated by Ted Stolze

Notes

1. Trans. Peggy Kamuf (New York and London: Routledge, 1994), henceforth cited as *SM.*

2. 'Whither Marxism?', an international colloquium organized in April 1993 by Berndt Magnus and Stephen Cullenberg at the University of California at Riverside.

3. *SM*, pp. 184–5 n. 9: 'the title of this present work may be read as a reply to that of J.-M. Benoist, however much time it may have taken or left to time, to the *contretemps* – that is to the *revenant* . . .'

4. 'The quasi-paternal figure of Marx', *SM*, p. 13.

5. On these questions Derrida had already explained himself in *De l'esprit* (1987).

6. *SM*, p. 34, Derrida speaks of a 'critical inheritance'.

7. *SM*, p. 13.

8. *SM*, pp. 33–4.

9. *SM*, p. 54.

10. *SM*, p. 16.

11. *SM*, p. 59.

12. One certainly thinks of the 'critical critique' of the young Hegelians with whom Marx was himself in debate.

13. *SM*, p. 55.

14. 'There is something disappeared, departed in the apparition itself as reapparition of the departed.' (*SM*, p. 6)

15. *SM*, p. 140. The reference to Plato is developed on p. 147.

16. Ibid.

17. *SM*, p. 148.

18. *SM*, p. 153.

19. Karl Marx, *Capital* Volume 1, trans. Ben Fowkes (New York: Vintage, 1977), pp. 164–5.

20. *SM*, p. 159.

21. *SM*, p. 161.

22. Étienne Balibar, *La Philosophie de Marx* (Paris: La Découverte, 1993), p. 60. All of chapter 3 of this book (pp. 42–77) is devoted to the question of ideology.

23. *SM*, pp. 89–90.

3

Marx's Purloined Letter

Fredric Jameson

Derrida's new book is more than an intervention; it wishes to be a provocation, first and foremost of what he calls a new Holy Alliance whose attempt definitively to bury Marx is here answered by a call for a New International.* Derrida reminds a younger generation of the complex and constitutive interrelationships between an emergent deconstruction and the Marx-defined debates of the 1950s and 60s in France (he has spoken elsewhere of his personal relationship to Althusser[1]): in this he is only one of a number of significant thinkers in so-called poststructuralism to register a concern with the way in which demarxification in France and elsewhere, having placed the reading of Marx and the themes of a properly Marxian problematic beyond the bounds of respectability and academic tolerance, now threatens to vitiate the activity of philosophizing itself, replacing it with a bland Anglo-American anti-speculative positivism, empiricism or pragmatism. The new book will also speak of the relationship of deconstruction to Marx (as well as of its reserves in the face of an implicit or explicit Marxist 'philosophy'). Derrida here takes the responsibility of speaking of the world situation, whose novel and catastrophic features he enumerates with all the authority of the world's most eminent living philosopher. He reads Marx's texts, in particular offering a remarkable new exegesis of passages from *The German Ideology*. He develops a new concept, that of 'spectrality', and does so in a way which also suggests modifications or inflections in the way in which deconstruction handles concepts in general. And he affirms a persistence of that 'weak messianic power' which Benjamin called upon us to preserve and sustain during dark eras. It is a wide-ranging performance, and a thrilling one,

* Some further philosophical issues, important but more technical, will be addressed in an expanded version of this essay to be published later by Verso.

particularly as it is punctuated by the great shouts and cries of alarm of the opening scenes of *Hamlet* on the battlements. I want to summarize the book more narrowly and then to comment in an unsystematic and preliminary way on points I find particular interesting.

The five chapters of *Specters of Marx* turn variously, as might be expected, around the issue of Marx's afterlife today. *Hamlet*, and the ghost of Hamlet's father, provide a first occasion for imagining what the apparition of Marx's own ghost might be like for us, who have not even heard the rumour of its reappearances. Some remarkable reflections of Blanchot on Marx,[2] the implied ontology of Hamlet's cry, 'The time is out of joint!', and the structure of the act of conjuring as such – calling forth, allaying, conspiring – now set the stage for what follows in the second chapter, namely, the conspiracy against Marxism, as well as Fukuyama and the ('apocalyptic') end of history, all of which reveals the international (but also US) political forces at work in the new world situation of late capitalism. This will now be the object of direct analysis by Derrida in chapter 3, 'Wears and Tears (tableau of an ageless world)', in which ten features of the new globalization are outlined, ranging from unemployment and homelessness to the mafia, drug wars and the problems of international law, and passing through the contradictions of the market, the various international forms of the Debt, the arms industry, and so-called ethnic conflict. These characteristics of Fukuyama's global triumph of democracy demand a new International and a transformed resurgence of the 'spirit of Marxism' (from which ontology has been expunged, along with Marx's own fear of ghosts). Two final chapters then offer rich readings of passages in Marx specifically related to spectrality. Chapter 4 returns to the *Communist Manifesto* and the *Eighteenth Brumaire*, not least in order to suggest Marx's own ambivalence with respect to spectrality as such; while the last chapter examines Marx's critique of Stirner and transforms the conventional view of commodity fetishism, whose dancing tables now strongly suggest poltergeists as much as they do items for sale on a shelf somewhere.

The narrative of theory

The question as to whether these are new themes for Derrida ought to involve a rethinking of the notion of the 'theme' in philosophical writing fully as much as a story about periodization. Indeed, changes within deconstruction in recent years have seemed to motivate a variety of descriptions. Modifications in the intellectual situation in which deconstruction has had to make its way have obviously played a fundamental role in its style as well as its strategies. As far as Marx is concerned, for example, the sympathies as well as the philosophical reservations with the Marxist problematic were as evident twenty years ago in the dialogues entitled *Positions*,[3] much of which are spent warding off the overenthusiastic embraces of his Leninist interviewers, as they are in the present work; in particular, the endorsement of materialism is a question to which we will want to return here.

Meanwhile, it can be supposed that the academic respectability a now multi-volumed deconstruction has begun to acquire in US philosophy departments (along with the consecration, in France, of the 'collège de philosophie' founded by Mitterrand's socialist government, with Derrida himself as its first head) has inevitably modified the appearance of a corpus long since given over to the care of merely literary intellectuals. On the other hand, you could just as plausibly argue that Derrida has grown more literary over the years, and has been ever more willing to experiment with language and with a variety of smaller discursive genres in ways that call the philosophical vocation of the earlier, more conventional works more strongly back into question, even where the vocation of those earlier works consisted in challenging academic philosophy itself.

Can a change in tone be detectable, since the waning of the older polemics and the gradual implantation of Derridean strictures on various forms of metaphysical thought (presence, identity, self-consciousness and the like) which from maddening gadfly stings have settled down into the status of doxa in their own right? Heidegger looms ever larger in this work, but is it fair to sense a new complacency in its dealings with this particular ghost, whose hauntings seem particularly inescapable? Is it not rather our own 'vulgar' reading of deconstruction as critique (implying that the sequel to the deconstruction of metaphysical concepts will be their replacement by something better, truer, etc.) which is responsible for this or that current astonishment that Heidegger's work continues to demand such respectful attention (even within the present book, as we shall see)? But as an intellectual operation, it was always a crucial necessity for deconstruction to move Heidegger, and in particular Heidegger's view of the history of metaphysics, centrally into the canon of philosophical reading, to impose Heidegger's problematic inescapably within contemporary philosophy: if only in order, in a second movement, to be able to draw back from Heidegger's own positions and to criticize the essentially metaphysical tendencies at work in them as well. It cannot really be a question of Derrida's 'development' or of the 'evolution' of deconstruction where the perpetually shifting emphases of this calculated ambivalence are concerned.

If that particular impression harboured the implied reproach that deconstruction has grown less political – less polemical, more mellow – in recent years, a complementary one could be expressed according to which it has grown more political, in the more conventional sense of the word. Indeed, a series of interventions on South Africa[4] (to which we must now add the dedication of the present book to the late Chris Hani) stand side by side with critiques of the new Europe and seem to prepare the 'committed writing' of the present text, whose subtitle significantly reads 'the state of the debt, the work of mourning, and the new International'; except that Derrida has always been a political figure, his specific public pronouncements going back at least as far as the controversy over the *loi Habib* in the 1970s (the Pompidou regime's attempt to 'exorcize' the spirit of May '68 by dropping the teaching of philosophy from the programme of the *lycées*).

Some of the confusion stems from the frame itself in which political interventions are necessarily evaluated and have their effectivity: the earlier occasion was a specifically French one, nor has Derrida often felt able to intervene in a US situation in which he has worked for so many years now. But on the new Europe he has found it important to express himself (see below), while virtually the first and more crucial thing he finds to say about Marx himself in the present work is as a thinker of the world market, the world political situation: 'No text in the tradition seems as lucid concerning the way in which the political is becoming worldwide' (p. 18).[5] It is thus globalization itself which sets the stage for a new kind of politics, along with a new kind of political intervention. Many of us will feel deep sympathy with his conception of a new International, as far as radical intellectuals are concerned: for the cybernetic possibilities that enable post-Fordism along with financial speculation, and generate the extraordinary new wealth that constitutes the power of the postmodern business establishment, are also available to intellectuals today on a world scale. It is not difficult to foresee networks analogous to those formed by exiles using print media in Marx's own time, but in a qualitatively as well as quantitatively modified framework (in both cases, the relationship of the working-class movements to which such intellectuals correspond is a rather different, more problematical development).

But now we must also observe that it is precisely this kind of periodization, this kind of storytelling – what has happened to deconstruction, how has it changed over the years, are these internal concerns consistent with the topics of the earlier writings? – that makes up the deeper subject (or one of the deeper subjects) of the present book on Marx, whose occasion certainly seems to be just such a story or periodizing effect: Marx, who seemed living, is now dead and buried again. What does it mean to affirm this?

In particular, notions of development, influence, conversion, include within themselves oversimplified narratives whose fundamental decisions turn on continuity and discontinuity, on whether to judge a given development as a 'break' with what preceded it, or to read this or that seemingly novel motif as standing in deeper continuity and consonance with earlier preoccupations and procedures. And the same question arises for Marxism, both within the works of Marx himself (do they really evolve, is there a 'break' as Althusser so famously insisted?) and in their uses over time (few thinkers, recalls Derrida, have so strenuously insisted on 'their own possible "ageing" and their intrinsically irreducible historicity . . . who has ever called for the *transformation* to come of his own theses?' [p. 13]). But the relation of Marx to narrative, and to the various possible narratives we might be tempted to invent about his work and the fortunes of his work is then, if not simplified, at least varied, by the fact that, not having been a philosopher exactly, Marx is to that degree ('not exactly') a part of the history of metaphysics: 'answers without questions', says Blanchot; which does not mean that Marx will not be reproached for certain ontological tendencies and temptations, but rather that these 'answers' somehow already escape ontology. Presumably one can at least tell about them the story of their 'temptations', which is what Derrida does (Marx's fear of ghosts).

It may also be worth suggesting that, along with the narrative, also goes argument. Does Derrida present arguments? Derrida's arguments are his readings, surely, and no one who has worked through some of the great philosophical *explications de texte* can doubt that he is saying something; but my feeling is that the very conception of argument here is not unrelated to that of narrative, in the sense of definitions and the clarification of proper names and characters, articulated terminology whose destinies we can then follow through the various conceptual peripeteias and even metamorphoses. Greimas thought one ought to be able to make a narrative analysis of the *Critique of Pure Reason*, and read its arguments as so many stories intertwining and reaching the appropriate narrative climaxes. In that sense, perhaps, Derrida is truly non-narrative; and readers who follow up his own careful indications (see for example his references on fetishism, p. 194, note 33: 'cf. in particular *Glas*, pp. 42, 130, 206 ff., 222 ff., 237 ff.') will surely be disappointed if they imagined they would find definitions in those places, and statements or propositions by Derrida as to the nature of fetishism and the plausibility of its various theorizations, that they could then take back in toto to the present context and introduce as the 'meanings' of the words they find there. Rather, it is as though these page numbers indicated so many themes, and documented the movement through Derrida's work of various image-clusters, as they used to be called in a now old-fashioned literary criticism: it would presumably be important to avoid the misleading overtones of words like 'image' or 'theme' (which are thought to be literary only on account of their philosophical uselessness) and to think these procedures in more rigorous ways.

Still, our examination of the new Marx book will not be particularly improved by neglecting the insistent question as to whether the new figurality, the figured concept of the ghost or spectre, is not of a somewhat different type than those that began to proliferate in Derrida's earlier work, beginning most famously with 'writing' itself and moving through a now familiar spectrum of marked terms like 'dissemination', 'hymen', along with the inversion of this practice, which consisted in modifying a letter in a word whose sound thereby remained the same (*différance*). Even beyond the issue of whether philosophy today can produce new concepts (and new terms or names for them), this goes to the whole issue of theoretical discourse today (or yesterday, if theory is really dead, as they tell us nowadays, or even if theory is only as dead as Marx, whose answers without questions played some role in its historical elaboration after all). This must first be addressed before we can examine the shape of the constellation mapped by *Specters of Marx*; the supplementary advantage of telling the story of the emergence of such discourse will lie in its analogies with problems of materialism to be considered later on.

At any rate, it seems safe enough to locate the situational origins of such theoretical discourse in the general crisis of philosophy after Hegel, and in particular in Nietzsche's guerrilla warfare against everything noxious concealed within the 'desire called philosophy' as well as in Heidegger's discovery that the philosophical system itself (or worse yet, the 'world-view') constitutes what he calls metaphysics (or what another tradition might describe as degraded or reified thought). As far as language is concerned, this means that any affirmation one makes is at least implicitly a philosophical proposition and thereby a component of just such a metaphysical system. The bad universalism of metaphysics has thereby infected language itself, which cannot but continue to emit and endlessly to regenerate the 'metaphysical' or the ontic, comically to affirm one proposition after another, which outlast their pragmatic uses and know an afterlife as what another tradition might call ideology.

But if all propositions are ideological, perhaps it is possible to limit the use of language to the denunciation of error, and to renounce its structural impulse to express truth in the first place. That this strategy turns language over to a certain terrorism, the practice of the

Althusserians and the *Tel quel* group can historically testify: Derridean-ism, which had its family relations with both, was not exempt either from the impression that when it was merely specifying someone else's position, this last was also in the process of being roundly denounced (none of Derrida's qualifications about the difference between decon-struction and critique ever really made much of a dent in this impression). For specifying the other position meant specifying it as ideology (Althusser) or as metaphysics (Heidegger, Derrida): identifi-cations which naturally enough led the unforewarned reader to suppose that truth was about to be put in its place, whereas Althusser taught us that we would never be out of ideology, and Derrida consistently demonstrated the impossibility of avoiding the metaphysi-cal. But both left their own 'ideology' or 'metaphysics' unidentified, unspecified: and I think it would be possible to show (and this for all so-called poststructuralism and not merely these two named bodies of theory) how into this void certain motifs emerged which were reified and turned into 'theories' and thenceforth into something like old-fashioned philosophies or 'world-views' in their own right. This is the point at which Althusser is supposed to be about overdetermination, and Derrida about writing: it is also the point at which their formal dilemmas seem closest to fundamental contradictions in modernism in general, and most notably to the one Barthes described in *Writing Degree Zero*, as that of avoiding the closure of a finished system of signs. The greatest modern literature, he said, tries to avoid thus becoming an official, public, recognized 'institutional' language in its own right; but if it succeeds, it fails, and the private languages of Proust or Joyce thereby enter the public sphere (the university, the canon) as just such 'styles'.[6] Others succeed by remaining fragments (Gramsci, Benjamin), something one cannot particularly decide to do in advance, however.

The constellation called spectrality

This is at any rate the situation in which it makes sense to talk about something like an 'aesthetic' of the Derridean text: a way of describing the philosophical dilemmas it renders as a kind of 'form-problem', whose resolution is sought in a certain set of procedures, or rather, in consonance with all of modern art, in a certain set of taboos. Here the taboos very directly govern the enunciation of new propositions, the formation of new concepts: the *Grammatology* seems to be the last text of Derrida in which the possibility for philosophy to produce new and Utopian concepts is raised, however it is there dealt with. Indeed, there is still a very strong Marxian flavour about the conviction that genuinely new concepts will not be possible until the concrete situation, the system itself, in which they are to be thought, has been radically modified. It is a conviction which only Tafuri has defended well down into the 1990s (and his own death);[7] the idea that intellectual innovation, not merely the invention of new solutions but, even more, the replacement of old problems with new ones, seems to wane after that failure which the French May '68 was perceived by intellectuals as being.

This failure will spell the end, not merely of sixties Utopianism in France (an analogous but far more thoroughgoing change in temperature can be registered in Foucault's works), but also the beginnings of demarxification and wholesale intellectual anti-communism, the beginning of the end of the hegemonic notion of the radical or left French intellectual. This has more than a merely formal importance for Derrida's own work: indeed we will later on want to see in *Specters of Marx* the overt expression of a persistent if generally subterranean Utopianism, which he himself (shunning that word) will prefer to call 'a weak messianic power', following Benjamin. But surely his own solution in the 1960s to the problem of conceptual innovation and philosophical Utopianism (so to speak) has its bearing on the capacity of this weak messianic power to weather the storm in his own work and not, as in so many others, to be desiccated and blown away for lack of deeper roots.

There is perhaps no corresponding disappointment and reversal in Derrida, since from the outset the form itself presupposed that philosophy as a system and as a vocation for conceptual innovation was at an end. But it presupposed this by means of a form-principle which navigated the problem of a tired acceptance of the traditional status quo by way of a simple solution: the avoidance of the affirmative sentence as such, of the philosophical proposition. Deconstruction thus 'neither affirmeth nor denieth': it does not emit propositions in that sense at all (save, as is inevitable in a work now so voluminous as this one, in the unavoidable moments of the lowered guard and the relaxation of tension, in which a few affirmations slip through or the openly affirmative sentence startles the unprepared reader – as most notably in the late-capitalism section of the present book [chapter 3], or the great essay in celebration of Nelson Mandela).

The question then necessarily arises how this taboo can actually be put into practice in the writing, and first and foremost where content can be generated in an exercise otherwise so seemingly *fruste* and barren as one thus vigilantly policed and patrolled by the intent to avoid saying something. Derrida's own personal aesthetic tastes – not merely the interest in Mallarmé, but above all, and well beyond the admiration for Ponge and Jabès, the fascination with Roger Laporte (of all contemporary writers the most intransigently formalist in the bad sense of writing about nothing but your own process of writing), documents a minimalism which is not quite put into practice in his own ultimately far richer philosophical texts.

This 'aesthetic' or solution to a historical form-problem is clearly enough a whole philosophical position in its own right: and to put it this way is also to understand why the issue of Derrida's literariness is poorly engaged or posed from the outset. For the deconstructive text is also 'postmodern' in the sense in which it flees the attempted originality of essayism. Not only does it not wish to generate a new philosophical system in the old sense (as in Ricoeur, or even more so in deliberately traditional/reactionary thinkers like J.-L. Marion, whose 'resistance to' or even reaction against theory can above all be measured by their return to and defence of the philosophical institution as such); it does not lay claim to a 'distinctive voice' or an 'original set of perceptions', as is the case with the tradition of the philosophical essay, in Cioran, for example, or Canetti, originality in that sense being suspect and as Brecht might put it 'culinary' or belletristic (something the canonized Blanchot seemed to overstep into theory, or, along with Klossowski, into the novel itself).

What saves the day here is the central formal role of the Heideggerian problematic, which assigns a minimal narrative to the entire project, and thus converts an otherwise random series of philosophical texts and fragments into an implicitly grand history: one of metaphysics within philosophy itself. This is the sense in which one might argue that Rorty's project, which effectively destroys philosophy itself as a history and as a discipline (and leaves its Samson-like destroyer in the self-trivialized role of an aesthete and a belletrist, when not a merely liberal political and cultural critic and commentator), is more radical than Derrida's, which manages to rescue the discipline secretly in this backdoor Heideggerian manner and thereby to invest its own texts with a certain dignity as moves and positions within a larger theoretical project: after which Heidegger himself, as we shall see again shortly, can be thrown to the winds and deconstructed as so much metaphysics in his own right.

This frame now enables the practice of deconstruction to find a consecrated form: that of the commentary or philosophical *explication de texte*, within which it can pursue its own augustly parasitical activity. It need no longer articulate its own presuppositions, nor even the results of its own textual critique of the various thinkers thereby glossed and architectonically undone or undermined: they themselves know it all in advance, these texts deconstruct themselves, as Paul de Man showed in his own indispensable supplement to nascent deconstruction as a 'methodology' (indeed, the crucial addition is to be found in his own essay on Derrida himself,[8] and on the latter's alleged critique of

Rousseau, which is shown to correspond to little more than Rousseau's text's critique of itself). With this, then, the aesthetic procedure of deconstruction is complete: it will be a form that posits some prior text of which it claims to be a commentary, appropriating portions – and in particular terminological subsections – from that text provisionally to say something which the text does not exactly say as such in its own voice or language, within a larger context which is the frame of the Heideggerian master-narrative, modified, enlarged or restricted as one will (later on very much by way of Lacanian-related additions which will come to look relatively feminist, as in *onto-logo-phallo*-centrism).

The resort to Heidegger reveals that no purely formalist strategy can ever succeed in any permanent way; and deconstruction is not the only example – but it is a particularly striking one – of the reification of a principle that wished to remain purely formal, its translation back against its own wishes into a philosophical world-view or conceptual thematics it set out to avoid being in the first place. Such are for example the esoteric readings of Derrida's texts as the expressions of a 'philosophy' of *écriture* or *différance*, and later on the transformation of 'deconstruction' into a full-fledged philosophical system and position in its own right.[9] These degradations and transformations confirm Derrida's emphasis on the *name* (or the *noun*, the substantive: the two words are the same in French). The question we have in the context of a reading of *Specters of Marx* is whether the new name of 'spectrality' represents yet another move in this interminable and ultimately necessarily unsuccessful effort to avoid names in the first place, or whether it can be seen as the modification of that strategy and as the attempt to strike away from the philosophical noun altogether in some new figural direction.

It seems at least plausible that the emergence of Benjaminian constellations in Derrida's work tends to displace the previous prominence of the Heideggerian narrative, and thereby to modify the exegetical strategies determined by this last (Marx however being in any case, as has already been observed, scarcely the prototype of the philosophical text or fragment you can deconstruct in this classical way in the first place). In order to verify this proposition, however, we must now look more closely at the nature of the present 'constellation', and at the same time return to a starting-point which is that of all contemporary theory and post-philosophical discourse, and not merely that of Derrida himself.

For from this perspective the central problem of the constellation called spectrality is that of matter itself, or better still, of materialism as such, that is to say, as a philosophy or a philosophical position in its own right. (This was incidentally the central issue Derrida discussed with 'the Marxists' in the 1972 interviews called *Positions.*) Or perhaps it might be better to say that it is the absence of the problem of materialism, its occultation or repression, the impossibility of posing it as a problem as such and in its own right, which generates the figure of the spectre. The latter is distinguished from the ideologeme 'spirit' and its traces in the philosophical project of phenomenology. In Derrida's reading of religion the messianic (political temporality properly conceived) is opposed to the metaphysical jargon of spirit, while the power of the latter in its sublimated public form is shown to be dependent on a primitive and quotidian metaphysics (the fetishism of commodities). This is the constellation which defines the relationship of spectrology to materialism.

A dubious materialism

As for materialism, it ought to be the place in which theory, deconstruction and Marxism meet: a privileged place for theory, insofar as the latter emerges from a conviction as to the 'materiality' of language; for deconstruction insofar as its vocation has something to do with the destruction of metaphysics; for Marxism ('historical materialism') insofar as the latter's critique of Hegel turned on the hypostasis of ideal qualities[10] and the need to replace such invisible abstractions by a concrete (that included production and economics). It is not an accident that these are all negative ways of evoking materialism.

Rather than conceiving of materialism as a systematic philosophy, it would seem possible and perhaps more desirable to think of it as a polemic stance, designed to organize various anti-idealist campaigns, a procedure of demystification and de-idealization; or else a permanent linguistic reflexivity. This is, among other things, why Marxism has never been a philosophy as such, but rather a 'unity-of-theory-and-practice' very much like psychoanalysis, and for many of the same reasons. This is not to say that a number of different Marxist philosophies have not been proposed: it has historically been felt to be compatible with Hegelianism, with positivism, with Catholicism, with various philosophical realisms, and most recently with analytic philosophy. For me, Lukács's *History and Class Consciousness* has always seemed the most ambitious attempt to argue a philosophical ground for Marxian and specifically for class epistemology; while Korsch makes the basic case for what has been called Marxism's 'absolute historicism', followed in this by what is for many of us the greatest American contribution to a specifically Marxist philosophy, Sidney Hook's early and self-repudiated *Towards an Understanding of Karl Marx,* which in addition boldly attempts a 'synthesis' of Marxism and American pragmatism.

What must be concluded from these remarkably discordant affiliations is clearly that Marxism is not a philosophy as such: 'answers without questions', we have heard Blanchot describe it, a characterization which allows for the optional coordination with and adjustment to this or that philosophy if we grasp the latter as a specific problematic or a system of questions. Is it plausible then to see in *Specters of Marx* the tentative offer to coordinate Marxism with deconstruction (something already argued in a well-known book by Michael Ryan)?[11] The question presupposes deconstruction to be a philosophy, something it has been clear I feel to be premature and misleading; if it is a matter of comparing procedures, and in particular positing analogies of situation (which might then account for the family likeness in the procedures), then this seems to me useful and the beginnings of a historical account (and indeed my remarks above are made in that spirit). If, however, it is a matter of constructing a new philosophical system, like the notorious Freudo-Marxisms of yesteryear, then the idea is perhaps rather to be deplored.

In any case Derrida's reserves about Marx, and even more strongly about the various Marxisms, all turn very specifically on this point, namely the illicit development of this or that Marxism, or even this or that argument, of Marx himself, in the direction of what he calls an ontology, that is to say, a form of the philosophical system (or of metaphysics) specifically oriented around the conviction that it is some basic identity of being which can serve as a grounding or foundational reassurance for thought. That this ontological temptation, although encouraged by the peculiar thematics of matter and 'materialism', is not limited to the physical or spatial areas but finds its exemplification above all in temporal dilemmas, we will see shortly. But for the moment we can suggest that under what Derrida stigmatizes as ontology are very much to be ranged all possible conceptions of a materialist philosophy as such.

A great number of Marxist traditions have themselves been alert to the dangers of such a philosophical ambition: over against the various purely philosophical projects listed above, therefore (which very specifically include any number of official materialisms, from Engels to Stalin and beyond), we also need to register those important moments in Marxian philosophizing in which materialism is specifically repudiated as a form of bourgeois thought, in particular in the guise of eighteenth-century mechanical materialism: this includes Marx himself, of course (particularly in *The German Ideology*); it also includes the first original attempt to rewrite Marxism in philosophical terms, that of Antonio

Labriola and a certain Italian historicism, which will clearly enough culminate in Gramsci's 'philosophy of praxis'. The euphemistic title, which in part we owe to the requirement to outsmart the Fascist censorship of his jailkeepers, nonetheless underscores the very different emphasis Gramsci placed on action, construction and production, as opposed to the relatively passive and epistemological emphases which have often been those of the 'materialisms'. Korsch has already been mentioned in this same lineage; but it would equally be important to mention Sartre and Breton as two Marx-related thinkers who both waged powerful polemics against materialism as a weird philosophical eccentricity; while it has often been observed that non-materialist currents – whether they be those of Platonism or of Maoism – are often more conducive to activism (when not indeed to outright voluntarism) than the various official materialisms have historically been. To go so far, however, is to raise the most appropriate anxieties about some new spiritualist agenda, anxieties which will also have to be dealt with in their 'proper' time and place.

The return of the repressed

Spectrality is not difficult to circumscribe, as what makes the present waver: like the vibrations of a heat wave through which the massiveness of the object world – indeed of matter itself – now shimmers like a mirage. We tend to think that these moments correspond to mere personal or physical weakness – a dizzy spell, for example, a drop in psychic 'niveau', a temporary weakness in our grip on things: on that reality which is supposed to rebuke us by its changelessness, the 'en-soi', being, the other of consciousness, nature, 'what is'. Ontology would presumably correspond to this last, to the right kind of weakening of consciousness in which it seems to fade away in the face of Being itself. This, which we trivialize by calling it a still relatively psychological name like 'experience', Heidegger insisted we think of as something other than humanist; here Being is the measure and not 'man'. Oddly, however, the belief in the stability of reality, being, and matter is, far from an exceptional philosophical achievement, little more than common sense itself. It is this that spectrality challenges and causes to waver visibly, yet also invisibly, as when we say 'barely perceptible', wanting to mean by that 'perceptible' and 'imperceptible' all at once. If this sense of tangible certainty and solidity corresponds to ontology, then, as something on which conceptuality can build, something 'foundational', how to describe what literally undermines it and shakes our belief? Derrida's mocking answer – hauntology – is a ghostly echo if there ever was one, and serves to underscore the very uncertainties of the spectral itself, which promises nothing tangible in return; on which you cannot build; which cannot even be counted on to materialize when you want it to. Spectrality does not involve the conviction that ghosts exist or that the past (and maybe even the future they offer to prophesy) is still very much alive and at work, within the living present: all it says, if it can be thought to speak, is that the living present is scarcely as self-sufficient as it claims to be; that we would do well not to count on its density and solidity, which might under exceptional circumstances betray us.

Derrida's ghosts are these moments in which the present – and above all our current present, the wealthy, sunny, gleaming world of the postmodern and the end of history, of the new world system of late capitalism – unexpectedly betrays us. His are not the truly malevolent ghosts of the modern tradition (perhaps in part because he is also willing to speak for them and to plead their cause). They do not remind us of the archetypal spectres of sheer class *ressentiment* in the servants of *The Turn of the Screw*, for example, who are out to subvert the lineage of the masters and bind their children to the land of the dead, of those not merely deprived of wealth and power (or of their own labour-power), but even of life itself. In that sense the classic ghost has been an expression of cold fury (most recently in the ghost who takes possession of Jack Nicholson in *The Shining*); ghosts, as we learned from Homer's land of the dead long ago, envy the living:

> Better, I say, to break sod as a farm hand
> For some poor country man, on iron rations,
> Than lord it over all the exhausted dead.[12]

Ressentiment is the primal class passion, and here begins to govern the relations between the living and the dead: for the step from envy to hatred is a short one, and if the truth were told, the ghosts we are able to see hate the living and wish them harm. Such would at least be the only materialist way of thinking about it, from which the most peculiar images begin to emerge, as in Sartre's *The Flies*, or in Brian Aldiss's *Helliconia Spring*, where the dead hang twittering like bats, ever poised and trembling for a raid on anything that moves with life and breath:

> they resembled mummies, their stomachs and eye sockets were hollow, their boney feet dangled; their skins were as coarse as old sacking, yet transparent, allowing a glimpse of luminescent organs beneath . . . All these old put-away things were without motion, yet the wandering soul could sense their fury – a fury more intense than any of them could have experienced before obsidian claimed them.[13]

Such ghosts express the fear of modern people that they have not really lived, not yet lived or fulfilled their lives, in a world organized to deprive them of that satisfaction; yet is this suspicion not itself a kind of spectre, haunting our lives with its enigmatic doubt that nothing can dispel or exorcize, as with the peculiar quotation with which Derrida's book begins: 'I would like to learn how to live finally': reminding us also to make a place for the ghost of Life itself, of vitalism as an ideology, of living and being alive as social and existential categories, in our anatomy of that spectrality to which it is yet another opposite.

So what we have to do with here is not only the past as such, but rather the repression of the past in full postmodernity or late capitalism: the extinction of Marx is part of that, part of that 'end' of something which will shortly, in distinction to the messianic, be identified as the apocalyptic (a world very much ending 'not with a bang/ but a whimper'). To say so is, however, to realize that there is a way not to grapple with this problem, and it is the equivalent here of the bad ontological or humanist solution, namely, the full-throated pathos with which the loss of the past and of tradition is deplored by philosophical and cultural conservatives (of whom Allan Bloom can stand as a distinguished exemplar): as though we could simply go back to some older form of historicity for which even Marx is part of the Western canon of great books and there already exists a coherent philosophical position with which we are free to identify if we choose to do so. But deconstruction repudiates the (ontological) idea that any such coherent philosophical positions ever existed in the first place; and the interesting problem Derrida will now confront is that of some tertium datur between the traditional-humanist and the trendiness of a certain poststructuralism and postmodernism with which it would be too hasty to identify his own thought (although the conservatives themselves inveterately make this identification, in their knee-jerk attacks on deconstruction in Derrida himself as well as in Paul de Man as 'nihilistic'). It is not a situation of binary oppositions in which you concoct some 'third way', golden mean, synthesis, or whatever: rather, I believe that the way out of this real if false dilemma, this actually existing contradiction whose very terms are nonetheless ideological through and through, lies in an analysis of its figuration. This is the sense in which I also believe, using an older language, that a certain formalism (albeit of an absolute nature, some kind of ultimate Gramscian or Lukácsian formalism) offers the opportunity to change the valencies on the problem, to adjust the lens of thought in such a way that suddenly we find ourselves focusing, not on the presumed content of the opposition, but rather on the wellnigh material grain of its arguments, an optical adjustment that leads us in new and wholly unexpected directions.

One of those directions, indeed, will be that of our very topic here, namely the nature of the conceptuality of the spectral, and in particular what that figuration is, and why we require something like it in the first place. Why does the spectral come as a kind of new solution to the false problem of the antithesis between humanism (respect for the past) and nihilism (end of history, disappearance of the past)?

A dislocated time

This is to retrace our steps and to ask ourselves once again why we need some new kind of concept/figure for the 'past', let alone for 'history': it is also to confront, not merely the ghost of Heidegger, but also the ghost of Hamlet's father himself: 'The time is out of joint!' How could the time, the present, be thought in such a way that it could then in a second but simultaneous moment be thought of as being 'out of joint', unequal to itself, unhinged, upside down, and so on: where the Heideggerian alternative – literally 'out of its hinges' – leads directly back to the great essay on Anaximander which is virtually the dead centre of all of Derrida's meditations on Heidegger and where it is precisely in these terms that Anaximander's own expression is analysed.[14]

For it is very precisely in this same essay on the 'proposition' in Anaximander that we find Heidegger's crucial statement as to the mode of experiencing Being and reality among the pre-Socratics, which is to say, his most direct formulation of everything lost in the 'modern' or Western, or metaphysical, repression of Being that followed on that opening. It is a passage in which, drawing on a seemingly unremarkable speech by Calchas the soothsayer in the *Iliad*, Heidegger articulates the difference between the early Greek experience of time and our own.

This essay, one of the rare places in which Heidegger is willing directly to evoke a spatio-temporal system radically different from our own, and even willing to make a stab at describing it for his (necessarily) modern readership, attempts to underscore the radical distinction of a pre-Socratic experience of the world from the one familiar to us and theorized from Aristotle to Hegel (and no doubt beyond), in which the present is simply an equivalent unit inserted between the homogeneous units of past and future.

The implication, and it is above all this which is 'idealistic' about such historicism, is that if we are able to imagine the temporality of such radical otherness, we ought to be able to bring it into being as a concrete social possibility and thereby to replace the current system altogether. In this way, an idealism which conceives of the mind as being free enough to range among the possibilities and sovereignly to choose to think a form radically excluded by the dominant system, leads on into a voluntarism that encourages us to attempt to impose that alternative system on the present one by fiat and violence. In Heidegger's case, this fantasy clearly found its fulfilment in the Nazi 'revolution', with its promise of radical social regeneration: Heidegger seems to have entertained the hope of becoming the primary theorist of such a revolution and to have withdrawn from active participation as soon as he understood that the new party apparatus was not particularly interested in his philosophical agenda, let alone in philosophy itself. But this idealist voluntarism is equally at work in other (extreme leftist) versions of radical social change, and even, in a different form, in liberal fantasies of the ways in which rational argument and public persuasion might be capable of bringing about systemic modifications in the logic of our social life.

It is clear at once that it must be this side of Heidegger's thought which is necessarily unacceptable to Derrida, or, if you prefer, inconsistent with the Derridean aesthetic I have described above, for which the positing of a realm of difference, the positive description of such a realm, is inadmissible. On the one hand, there is a logical contradiction involved in positing a phenomenon whose fundamental formal trait lies in its radical difference from everything we know, its resistance to all the categories by which we currently think our own world: something that raises the suspicion that it is little more than a subjective or ideological projection from out of our own present. Meanwhile, an even more serious ideological issue is raised by the essential historicism of such views, which posit a series of radically different forms throughout historical time, if not a more simplified binary opposition in which a modern state of things (either degraded or superior) is opposed to some pre-modern equivalent in which all the former's deficiencies are remedied or its advantages annulled. Heidegger's conception of a 'history' of metaphysics is there to document the feeling that late-nineteenth-century cultural and historical relativism of this historicist type is still very much with us: namely, the idealist notion that, within a general systemic determination by linear time, we can still somehow find it possible to imagine a radically different temporal experience.

It is significant that (at least on my reading) Derrida does not here specifically isolate historicism as a feature of conventional or traditional Marxism to be questioned and rethought (his principal targets in passing are class, of which more in a moment, and the notion of the Party, which is of course not yet present in Marx, whose comparable concept is rather that of the International itself). On the contrary, the emphasis of *Grammatology* would seem rather to reinforce this Heideggerian sense of a rigorous ('metaphysical') system within which we moderns are somehow caught and imprisoned. Structural or Althusserian Marxism, with its concept of an overlap and coexistence of various systems within a single social present (not to speak of Balibar's idea that in that sense all social formations are somehow already 'transitional' and that Marxism is the very theory of such transitionality[15]), offers a reply to this assimilation of Marx's 'philosophy of history' to conventional historicism. We will see shortly, however, that for Derrida teleological thought or 'philosophies of history' (what he will term apocalyptic thinking) lie essentially on the Right rather than on the Left; while the notion that Heidegger is himself somehow not so secretly historicist is not at all alien to Derrida and perfectly consistent with the various critiques he is willing to make of this particular, already 'ambiguous', figure.

What is also being implied here is perhaps the supplementary realization that the very force of the earlier Heideggerian/Derridean reversal (concepts of time up till now have been linear/all concepts of time are linear!) was a historical and a narrative one, even to the degree to which it overturned history and narrative. In that case, another defining feature of the current situation, another way of explaining the gradual loss of force of that particular reversal, would consist in positing this present as one in which the past and history, along with historiography and narrative itself (grand or not), have for whatever reason been eclipsed. In such a situation, it is not enough merely to reverse or even to cancel hegemonic or received narratives: the appearance of the ghost is a non-narrative event, we scarcely know whether it has really happened at all in the first place. It calls, to be sure, for a revision of the past, for the setting in place of a new narrative (in which the king was murdered and the present king was in fact his assassin); but it does so by way of a thoroughgoing reinvention of our sense of the past altogether, in a situation in which only mourning, and its peculiar failures and dissatisfactions – or perhaps one had better say, in which only melancholia as such – opens a vulnerable space and entry-point through which ghosts might make their appearance.

Undermining the unmixed

Supposing, however, that the need for some such strange 'concept' of spectrality had already been sensed, however obscurely and imperfectly, and a new kind of containment strategy invented whereby the untraditional mode of thinking were somehow made respectable in advance and pronounced to be consistent with the dignity of a (to be sure, altogether new) philosophical enterprise? There are indications here that for Derrida such an operation can in fact be identified, and that it is none other than phenomenology itself.

Spectrality can here be seen to open up wholly new and unexpected lines of rereading, which would seem to me susceptible of modifying current uses of Husserl's work. However that may be, such indications also suggest some further thoughts about the position and function of Husserl within Derrida's own, where the founder of phenomenology can be seen as both opposite and complementary to his Freiburger disciple and betrayer. For it is clearly the Heidegger operation which is the more visible and dramatic one, since it involves temporality and can be succinctly summed up by the (most recent) formula, 'The time is out of joint!' Heidegger is here used by Derrida as the name for all those temptations (which the German philosopher himself can be seen both as denouncing and as succumbing to all at once) to perpetuate some unmixed conception of time, some notion of a present that has won itself free of past and future and stands gleaming and self-contained, as a kind of mirage of parousia. Certainly the later Heideggerian emphasis on Being allows one to shift the gears of this critique somewhat in the direction of what it is certainly preferable not to call space, but perhaps (with an eye on Husserl) essences, rather than time, becoming and temporality.

But this very term of essence underscores the extraordinarily suggestive and useful role Husserl can be called upon to play in this same Derridean crusade: where Heidegger will offer the pretext for an onslaught on illusions of full temporal being, Husserl will provide a rather different set of occasions for tracking down and detecting such illusions when they manifest themselves under the guise of what Derrida's own language now identifies as the 'proper' or 'presence' (or any number of the other laboriously generated, technical Derridean words and terms). It would be much too loose and unphilosophical to identify these targets with what in Adorno is generally stigmatized as identity; and indeed any attempt (like the present one) to characterize the process generally, and not in the specifics of a given conceptual situation, falls back into culture critique, belles lettres, history of ideas and other degraded discourses. But I can have no other recourse in an essay like this, and can only try to characterize the object of this Derridean critique very impressionistically myself as what I will call the 'unmixed': what is somehow pure and self-sufficient or autonomous, what is able to be disengaged from the general mess of mixed, hybrid phenomena all around it and named with the satisfaction of a single conceptual proper name. This way of thinking about Derrida's work has two advantages, I believe: it can first provide a way for speculating as to the ways in which Derrida's own rigorous and local analyses strike a cognate tone with much else at work in current doxa and contemporary or postcontemporary intellectual life, which for whatever reason is also hostile to such pure or solid-colour unmixed concepts, which it (the *Zeitgeist*) identifies as old-fashioned and outworn, the boring conceptuality of yesteryear that is somehow unreflexive, unselfconscious (to use the vocabulary of yesteryear, however), and that we need to replace today with something infinitely more mixed and incestuous, miscegenated, multivalenced. Current intellectual politics, hybrid, or mestizo, such as those of queer theory, bring out into the open this particular prejudice in favour of the internally conflicted and the multiple (and suggest local reasons for such a philosophical need), but they are obviously far from being the earliest in this series which goes back at least to the crisis of the 'modern' with its Utopian dreams of unmixed languages and Utopian concepts. These came precisely to be seen as old-fashioned in the light of more complexly paradoxical intellectual operations; even the dialectic, for some of us the very prototype of a reflexive operation that secretly reversed all of the pre-existing stereotypes, was itself stigmatized as simply one more version of ontological thinking (in Derrida, for example, yet another instance of operations pursued within the closure of Western metaphysics). Philosophy, Derrida will say in his earlier written work, the thesis on Husserl, is 'the permanent recourse to the originary simplicity of an act or a being, of a conscious conviction [*évidence*] or a sense-perception [*intuition*]'.[16] In our present context that says it all, and the very vocation of Derrida's philiosopical life's work will now be discovered in the tracking down and identifying, denouncing, of just such resources, of just such nostalgias for some 'originary simplicity', for the unmixed in all its forms.

I have felt that it was important to describe this general vocation at this point, however, for yet another reason that now has to do with Marx himself and with Derrida's reservations about him. It can certainly be imagined that the attempt to do away with ghosts altogether, that the very fear of ghosts that 'haunts' the heart of such an attempt, offers a signal exemplification of just such a longing for primary realities, original simplicities, full presences and self-sufficient phenomena cleansed of the extraneous or the residual, the new itself, the origin, from which one can begin from scratch. We'll come back to this later on.

But there are two other features of the Marxian heritage which Derrida seems to assimilate to this more questionable side of the

Marxian enterprise, the Marxian tradition, and which it is appropriate
to deal with in the present ('phenomenological') context: these are
use-value and class. About use-value, surely one of the more slippery
concepts in Marx, it can be affirmed that it is 'always-already' if
anything ever was: the minute commodities begin to speak (*Capital*,
chapter 1; Derrida, p. 157), they have already become exchange-values.
Use-value is one of those lateral or marginal concepts which keeps
moving to the edge of your field of vision as you displace its centre
around the field, always a step ahead of you, never susceptible of being
fixed or held (like a leprechaun) by this or that determined, intent
and glittering eye. Use-value has always already vanished by the time
Marxism has begun: yet an uncertainty may well persist as to whether
even its residuality betrays a secret ontological longing at the heart of
Marxism, or at least at the centre of Marx's own writing. We will return
to it later on when we come to the 'fetishism of commodities' itself.

As for class, however, merely mentioned in passing as one of those
traditional features of Marxism that can be jettisoned en route by any
truly postcontemporary Marxism – 'this ultimate support that would be
the identity and the self-identity of a social class' (p. 55) – it seems to
me appropriate to take this opportunity to show how this very widespread conception of class is itself a kind of caricature. It is certain that
– even among Marxists – the denunciation of the concept of class has
become an obligatory gesture today, as though we all know that race,
gender and ethnicity were more satisfactory concepts or more fundamental, prior, concrete, existential experiences (these two reproaches
not being exactly the same): or else that social classes in the old
nineteenth-century sense no longer exist as such in the new multinational division of labour, or in the newly automated and cybernetic
industries of the postmodern (these two objections also not quite being
identical with each other). Finally and more empirically, the abandonment of the very category of class, even on the Left – perhaps one
should rather say, especially on the Left – corresponds to the evolution
of contemporary politics in which the old class parties are not around
any longer, so that intellectuals find themselves forced to identify with
groupings whose dynamics and rationale have quite different intellectual bases. I myself also think, as I want to show later on, that there
is a fundamental tendency and movement within Marxism itself to
be self-conflicted and at once to begin to distance features other
people assume to be intrinsically a part of this ideology, which thus
turns out to come into being at least in part by denouncing itself (as
so-called vulgar Marxism). To denounce class, and concepts of 'class
affiliation', is thus part of this primal self-definition within all the
Marxisms themselves, which have always wanted to make sure you did

not think they believed anything so simple-minded or orthodoxly reductive.

And this is of course exactly the gesture I will myself reproduce here, by reminding you that class itself is not at all this simple-minded and unmixed concept in the first place, not at all a primary building block of the most obvious and orthodox ontologies, but rather in its concrete moments something a good deal more complex, internally conflicted and reflexive than any of those stereotypes. Nor is it particularly surprising that the system should have a vested interest in distorting the categories whereby we think class and in foregrounding its current rival conceptualities of gender and race, which are far more adaptable to purely liberal ideal solutions (in other words, solutions that satisfy the demands of ideology, it being understood that in concrete social life the problems remain equally intractable).

It would be important, for example, to show how what is sometimes over-simply called 'class consciousness' is as internally conflicted as all the other categories in question: class consciousness turns first and foremost around subalternity, that is around the experience of inferiority. This means that the 'lower classes' carry about within their heads unconscious convictions as to the superiority of hegemonic or ruling-class expressions and values, which they equally transgress and repudiate in ritualistic (and socially and politically ineffective) ways. Few countries are as saturated with undisguised class content as the United States, owing to the absence here of any intermediary or residual aristocratic level (whose dynamics can thus, as in Europe, overlay the modern class oppositions and to a certain degree disguise and displace or even defuse those): all points in which the classes come into public contact, as in sports, for example, are the space of open and violent class antagonisms, and these equally saturate the other relations of gender, race and ethnicity, whose dynamics are symbolically reinvested in class dynamics and express themselves through a class formation, when they are not themselves the vehicle for the expression of class dynamics as such.

Yet it is very precisely just such internalized binary oppositions (for class relations are binary and tend to reorganize the other collective symbolic relationships in this form as well, race or ethnicity as binaries for example) which ought to render such phenomena privileged spaces for deconstruction as the method par excellence for detecting the operation of illicit binary oppositions at the same time that it also foregrounds the even more concealed ways in which – 'within the text', at it were – such oppositions deconstruct themselves (in the present instance, by way of Utopian fantasies). It should also be noted that everything that has been said here about subalternity holds for hegemonic or ruling-class consciousness itself, which bears within itself the fears and anxieties raised by the internalized presence of the underclasses and symbolically acts out what might be called an 'incorporation' of those dangers and class hostilities which are built into the very structure of ruling-class consciousness as a defensive response to them.

Finally, it should be stressed that class investments operate according to a formal rather than a content-oriented dynamic: it is according to a binary system that phenomena become assimilated to the fundamental play of class antagonisms. Thus to take a now classic example, the electoral struggle between Kennedy and Nixon in the early 1960s was strongly coded according to class: yet paradoxically, it was Kennedy, the liberal figure, whom the American masses consciously or unconsciously perceived as upper-class, owing to his wealth and his Harvard education, while Nixon, who clearly suffered the inferiorities and 'stigmas' of at least a petty-bourgeois class background, became at once translated into a representative of the lower (later, 'hard-hat') classes. Yet other oppositions, drawn from all the ranges of social experience, become recoded in much the same way: thus, in the modern period, the opposition between mass culture and high art acquires a very obvious class symbolism in the United States, despite the oppositional and anti-bourgeois stance of 'high art' in Europe; while with the arrival of theory and nascent postmodernity, it is theory which comes to be coded as foreign and thereby as upper-class, while 'true' creative literature – including both 'creative writing' and commercial television culture – is rewritten as a populist ethos.

Class is thus both an ongoing social reality and an active component of the social imaginary, where, with post-Cold War globalization, it can currently be seen to inform our various (mostly unconscious or implicit) maps of the world system. As a dichotomous phenomenon (there are only two fundamental classes in every mode of production), it is able to absorb and refract gender connotations and oppositions (along with racial ones); at the same time it is itself concealed and complexified by the survival of older residual class images and attitudes, aristocratic or (more rarely) peasant components intervening to distort and enrich the picture, so that Europe and Japan can be coded as aristocratic in the face of a plebeian US, while the Third World is joined by Eastern Europe as a generally subaltern area (in which the distinction between working class and peasant is blurred by notions like 'underdeveloped', which do not articulate the surplus-value transformed from Third to First Worlds over the course of history). As soon as the focus changes from a world system to a regional one – Europe or the Middle East, for example – suddenly the class map is rearticulated in new ways, just as it would be even further if the frame were that of a single nation state with its internal class oppositions. The point to be made, however, is not that all such class mappings are arbitrary and somehow subjective, but that they are inevitable allegorical grids through which we necessarily read the world, and also that they are structural systems in which all the elements or essential components determine each other and must be read off and defined against one another. This was of course most notably the case with the original dichotomous opposition itself, whose historical emergence in capitalism has been shown to involve a constant process whereby a working class becomes aware of itself in the face of business repression, while the ruling class is also forced into ever greater self-definition and organization by the demands and the threats of a labour movement. This means in effect that each of the opposing classes necessarily carries the other around in its head and is internally torn and conflicted by a foreign body it cannot exorcize (to return here to Derridean language).

Class categories are therefore not at all examples of the proper or of the autonomous and pure, the self-sufficient operations of origins defined by so-called class affiliation: nothing is more complexly allegorical than the play of class connotations across the whole width and breadth of the social field, particularly today; and it would be a great mistake for Marxism to abandon this extraordinarily rich and virtually untouched field of analysis on the grounds that class categories were somehow old-fashioned and Stalinist and needed to be renounced shamefacedly in advance, in order for Marxism to stage a respectable and streamlined reappearance in the field of intellectual debate in the new world system.

The respectable spirit

If phenomenology then identifies one pole of the experience of spectrality as that which has been officially contained and sublimated, transformed, into a respectable and indeed an institutional phenomenon (in this case one that can be reidentified with the academic discipline of philosophy itself), it remains to designate the other pole in which spectrality is appropriated by way of ideology as such and is translated into a powerful ideologeme whose structural possibilities can already be detected in the lexical field across which the ghostly apparition plays in all the modern languages.

For the ghost is very precisely a *spirit*, and the German *Geist* marks even more strongly the way in which a ghostly spirit or apparition and spirit as spirituality itself, including the loftier works of high culture, are deeply and virtually unconsciously identified with each other. You domesticate the ghost from the past by transforming it into an official representation of Spirit itself, or in other words, at least in American English, into what we call Culture, high art, the canon, in short the humanities in general.

Once again, however, the form of the polemics these phenomena have known in Europe is confusing when translated into American polemics and public debate; and therefore, particularly in the present instance, it is crucial to grasp the degree to which Derrida's own philosophical moves have to be grasped as ideological or rather anti-ideological tactics, and not merely as the abstract philosophical discussions as which these texts cross the ocean and become translated here. This will be the moment not only to return to the formal issue of 'idealism', as opposed to the various materialisms of Marxism, of deconstruction, and even of Paul de Man's version of deconstructive literary procedures; but also to insist on the very different resonance in Europe of such terms as *esprit* and *Geist* – and of their renewed ideological topicality in the new Europe of the end of the Cold War – as over against the more diffused rehearsals of such polemics here.

But in this respect one can see virtually all of Derrida's life work as an analysis and demystification of just such an ideology of the Spiritual and of idealism as continued to inform the European tradition: even the relations with postwar existentialism are informed by the sense that its phenomenological presuppositions remain profoundly idealistic. Americans are poorly placed to grasp the degree to which what Derrida follows Heidegger in calling the metaphysical tradition can also be seen very precisely as a kind of official public Idealism which, despite all the changes in philosophical fashion since the beginnings of the bourgeois era (where it can be seen to have been deliberately refashioned as a specific ideologeme), still holds public sway and is available for political manipulation. Indeed, the central critique of Heidegger himself, in an essay pointedly entitled *De l'esprit*,[17] and although crisscrossed by the (related) issues of sexuality and gender, very much turns on the suspicious and symptomatic return, in Heidegger's political writings of the early Nazi period (and most obviously in his inaugural lecture as Rector of the University of Freiburg), of a whole language of *Geist* and spirituality which his earlier more purely philosophical texts had explicitly stigmatized.

It is interesting to note that although Derrida fails to touch on the central figure in the Anglo-American reinvention of a politics of modernism *qua* spirituality – in the critical as well as the poetic work of T.S. Eliot – he does significantly single out Matthew Arnold.[18] Above all, however, he insistently returns to that French-language figure who was in so many ways the continental equivalent of T.S. Eliot (and whom the latter's cultural strategies, above all in his journal *The Criterion*, aimed at enveloping and as it were introjecting), namely Paul Valéry. Significantly a major portion of Derrida's polemic warning about the cultural politics of the new Europe – *L'Autre cap*[19] – is given over to Valéry's symptomatic thoughts about the menaced and vulnerable Europe of the period between the two Wars, for it is precisely this high-cultural European strategy, the Roman-Christian European tradition very precisely from Virgil to Valéry, that the current ideological operation of patching together a new pan-European cultural synthesis around figures like Milan Kundera (in the place of T.S. Eliot) has imitated and reproduced as in Marx's famous prediction (the second time as farce!). One is tempted to characterize these very openly high-cultural moves as a replay of '*Encounter* culture' (as the most successful attempt to play off a NATO high culture, now led by the US, against an anti-cultural Bolshevism[20]), but one today possibly available for intervention in a hegemonic struggle *against* the US competitor.

At any rate, these are the deeper political and class stakes involved in the anti-idealist theoretical and cultural struggles when those are grasped concretely in a European context; and it is very possible that some of these terminological polemics carry very different overtones here in the US. (Naomi Schor has for example suggestively argued, in a pathbreaking reconsideration of the significance of the work of George Sand,[21] that the latter's literary *idealism* was often more politically effective, energizing and enabling, than the 'realisms' or even 'materialisms' of her literary competitors.)

That question is then also at one with our starting-point, namely with the political and the class value of the slogans of 'materialism' as such. Paul de Man for example was always more open in his deployment of materialist positions than Derrida, at least in part because that particular philosophical strategy tended to undercut the high-spiritual apologia of his literary adversaries in the old New Critical establishment; it could also be argued that his own return to literature (which he defined as the kind of text that in effect was able to deconstruct itself and thereby virtually in advance to demystify the illusions of an idealist philosophy) stood somewhat in contradiction with this more explicitly anti-aesthetic *prise de position*. Meanwhile, it could also be argued, I believe, that the more open endorsement of materialism as such in de Man's writings tended rightly or wrongly to raise complicating issues of a materialist philosophy or ontology of the kind Derrida has always been careful to elude (both here, in *Specters*, and in the earlier interviews about Marxism in *Positions*).

The polemic foregrounding of 'spirit' and spirituality (high culture and tradition, *esprit* and *Geist*), however, now belatedly answers the earlier fears we acknowledged that are bound to be aroused by just this palpable reluctance to endorse materialism as a philosophical position. The distancing of philosophical (let alone Stalin's 'dialectical') materialism is not likely to lead to a recrudescence of spiritualism under the banner of the concept of spectrality very precisely because such a concept is designed to undermine the very ideology of spirit itself. Ghosts are thus in that sense material; ghosts very precisely resist the strategies of sublimation let alone those of idealization. This is also the sense in which 'Shakespeare' in this text is not the high-cultural signal it tends to be in the Anglo-American tradition: 'Shakespeare' on the continent, and in Marx's own personal taste, is not the mark of the high culture of European classicism, whether that of the French or of Schiller, but rather of a disturbing and volcanic 'barbarism'. Shakespeare plus Marx does not equal Schiller, let alone Bradley or T.S. Eliot's verse dramas, but rather Victor Hugo, whose *Misérables* indeed also make their brief appearance significantly and symptomatically within Derrida's pages, alongside the *Eighteenth Brumaire* itself.

The motif of 'spirit' as high culture represents the appropriation of spectrality as ideology, just as the project of phenomenology revealed a complementary appropriation as science. Now, however, it is time to see how Derrida deals with the issue of ideology as such, which his reading of the foundational Marxian texts on the subject specifically links with religion.

The inescapable phantom

We must therefore at once situate this discussion within the current European high-cultural revival of religion, a strategy which has its obvious relationship to the ideological operations of Spirit and of the European cultural tradition. The two in effect offer as it were distinct and alternate tacks, optional alternatives, for an endorsement of European late capitalism. This is not the place to paint the whole sorry picture of a simulacrum of religion as that has been set in place culturally everywhere from Godard's symptomatic *Je vous salue Marie* to Gorecki's Third Symphony: the picture would necessarily also include the current aesthetic revival, as that reproduces as it were a simulacrum of the older high-modernist 'religions of art'.

Postmodern aesthetic religion is then what looks like content when you are no longer able to acknowledge the content of social life itself: in a factitious simulacrum of content very much to be distinguished from modernist abstraction. When it comes to 'content' in the social sense – and in a certain way, since Marx, all content is social in this sense, or better still, the privilege of the Marxian discovery is to mark the moment in which all content is revealed to be social and secular – the triumph of market ideology and the immense movement of demarxification can also be seen as novel kinds of epistemological repression in which it is precisely the sociality of all content, its deeper link to political economy as such, which is occulted. The contemporary or postcontemporary problem of content can be approached in a different way, through the consensus in all the social sciences that the influence of Marx is so profound upon them all that it is no longer particularly relevant to isolate a 'Marxist' sociology, economics, political science, as such. In that case, however, demarxification in aesthetics faces a formidable task of well-nigh global dimensions: as it were to launder the content of contemporary experience and daily life in such a way that the multifarious traces of this deep and omnipresent 'Marxism' are tuned out or abstracted from the general spectrum by means of new kinds of representational technology, or at the least (since I will want to posit that none of these operations is particularly new), a newly specialized kind of aesthetic technology. At any rate, it will be my presupposition here that it is by way of a return to old-fashioned aesthetics – to beauty rather than to the sublime of modernism – and thence to the religion of art, following which it is only natural that the art of religion should then begin to rotate into view, that a certain aesthetic postmodern production finds itself able to produce works that give the illusion of substance (of 'having content').

But this aesthetic function of religion today, in the postmodern, is then also to be juxtaposed with another kind of resurgence of religion in the so-called contemporary fundamentalisms (and also in certain of the neo-ethnicities, likewise based on religious motifs): here we have to do, not with any survivals of traditional religious custom or ritual, or with pre-modern folkways of this or that type – all of which have been largely swept away by the prodigious movement of modernization at one with what we call modernism and modernity as such – but rather precisely with simulacra of what, in the postmodern present, are imagined to be those older folkways, with contemporary reinventions of tradition which affirm a neo-ethnic pluralism of free choice and the free reinvention of small group adherence (as opposed to the older constraints and indeed the doom or fate of racial or ethnic determinism in the pre-modern or early modern past).

For all these reasons, then, religion is once again very much on the agenda of any serious attempt to come to terms with the specificity of our own time; and it is in this sense that I read Derrida's insistence, at several points in the present text, on the way in which Marx's own theorization necessarily loops back into a reflection on religion as such.

This is to be sure also to be understood historically and exegetically, as the way in which any discussion of the problematic of the early Marx – or of the emergence of what might be thought of as 'mature Marxism' – necessarily posits a discussion of the specific intellectual debates in which Marxist thinking was formed, and from which the Marxian problematic ('answers rather than questions') itself emerged: namely the turn of Feuerbach, the moment of Feuerbach's intellectual 'revolution', in which the immense and crushing corpus of Hegel is simplified and reduced to a merely religious problematic (Marx will himself follow this line in his *Critique of Hegel's Philosophy of Right*). This last will then, in early Marx, be staged in a wholly new way by positing religion as the distorted projection of human productivity and human praxis. But that debate also drew its urgency from the institutional relationship – and not only in the German principalities of the early nineteenth century and the Holy Alliance – of state religion to state power: the attack on religion in that context will thereby be a scarcely veiled mode of outright political subversion (a far more openly political intervention, for example, than in the debate on Darwinism in the British context later on in the century). Derrida's reestablishment of a religious problematic as being henceforth inescapable in any truly renewed examination of Marx today is thus also to be thought in terms of this gap between the older (early Marxian) situation of established religion and our own world of religious 'revivals', which are effectively social simulacra. This gap might be reformulated as a problem in the following sense: if a certain Hegelianism is to be grasped as the after-image of the established religious institutions of his own time, where do we stand with respect to the *problem* of such a Hegelianism (Fukuyama) in our own time, with its very different recoding of religion?

But Derrida's methodological warning (about the fundamental role of religion in Marx's writing) also turns specifically on the twin phenomena – or perhaps one should say the dual conceptuality in Marx – of the theory of ideology and the theory of fetishism: and insofar as these are themes which emerge into full view only in the so-called 'mature' writing of *Capital* itself, they demand a somewhat different optic from the preceding one that holds for Marx's formative years: 'only the reference to the religious world allows one to explain the autonomy of the ideological [in Marx], and thus its proper efficacy, its incorporation in apparatuses [*dispositifs*] that are endowed not only with an apparent autonomy but a sort of automaticity that not fortuitously recalls the headstrongness of the wooden table' (p. 165). In another place, Derrida affirms 'the irreducibility of the religious model in the construction of the concept of ideology' (p. 148), thereby ambiguously warning us of the ambiguity of this last, which may be tainted as a concept by outworn conclusions from a fundamental analysis of religion as such, so that the latter might also permit us to detect religious and metaphysical remnants and survivals within the reality of contemporary secular ideology.

As for Derrida's dramatic rereading of the dancing table episode (which itself stresses the overtly dramatic or 'theatrical' mode of this particular presentation/representation [*Darstellung*] of value in an inert wooden thing), it seems rather to stress the ineluctability of the phantasmagoric in human and social experience, rather than the inseparable relationship of this particular phantasmagoria – the famous 'fetishism of commodities' – to one particular social form or mode of production. This was in another sense always the paradox of Marx's view of capitalism itself (and thus, as will be clear in a moment, of 'use-value'): for pre-capitalist societies and modes of production are by definition never transparent, since they must assure the extraction of surplus-value by extra-economic means. There is thus a sense in which only capitalism pursues economics by purely economic means (money and the market), and thereby also that in a larger acceptation all of the extra-economic determinations required by other or non-capitalist modes of production may be largely termed religious (tribal animisms and fetishisms, religion of the *polis*, religions of the god-emperor, or rationalizations of various aristocracies by birth). Capitalism therefore, as in the historical narrative we have inherited from the triumphant bourgeoisie and the great bourgeois revolutions, is the first social form to have eliminated religion as such and to have entered on the purely secular vocation of human life and human society. Yet according to Marx, religion knows an immediate 'return of the repressed' at the very moment of the coming into being of such a secular society, which, imagining that it has done away with the sacred, then at once unconsciously sets itself in pursuit of the 'fetishism of commodities'. The incoherence is resolved if we understand that a truly secular society is yet to come, lies in the future; and that the end of the fetishism of commodities may well be connected to some conquest of social transparencies (provided that we understand that such transparency has never yet existed anywhere): in which the collective labour stored in a given commodity is always and everywhere visible to its consumers and users. This is also to resolve the problem of 'use-value', which seems like a nostalgic survival only if we project it into what we imagine to be a simpler past, a past 'before the market', in which objects are somehow used and valued for themselves: but such a view can now be seen to overlook 'real' fetishism (as opposed to the symbolic kind that attaches to modern commodities), along with the various other symbolic ways in which use-value was projected onto objects in the societies of the past. Use-value lies thus also in the future, before us and not behind us: nor is it (and this is I think the real objection to the concept nowadays) distinct from and antagonistic to the phenomena which cluster around the function of information and communication, but must probably eventually come to include those in unimaginably complex ways.

This is in fact the other conclusion we will find Derrida drawing, at the end of this remarkable excursus in which the table dances again as it did for the first readers of Marx himself, and commodity fetishism becomes assimilated to the extraordinary agitation of poltergeists within our seemingly banal daily lives. For Derrida here wishes to assimilate the spectrality of these phenomena, which are more and other than what they seem as inert objects, to their sociality (Marx's collective production, stored labour-power), and thence to their 'automaticity' (what Sartre would have called the 'practico-inert'), their power to act and cause in ways more complex and undecipherable than the individual human mind or intention. We will not be able to identify this 'automaticity' plainly, however, until the final section, below.

Here we must on the contrary retrace our steps to the equally remarkable pages on Stirner, or rather on Marx's interminable settling of accounts with Stirner in *The German Ideology*.

In Stirner (and in Marx's laborious page-by-page commentary on his book), what interests Derrida is not the historical and social speculation but rather specifically the sections that deal with the dynamics of abstration as such.[22] In all these passages it is a question of how abstract ideas get replaced by real bodies: we are thus at an opposite pole to the problematic of Feuerbach and his speculations as to how images of the divinity are projected out of human potentialities, or that, even more linguistic, of Marx himself on the way in which Hegel hypostatizes properties and makes adjectives over into substantives. Here it is a matter of how the abstractions of the mind as it were illicitly become incorporated in their existential bodies: in other words, how we get back, in human and individual development, from the first mesmeriza-tion of the child and the adolescent by 'reified' ideas (in whose existence belief is invested) into the possession of a concrete individual body which is mine. As Stirner put it, 'in the period of spirits, thoughts outgrew me although they were the offspring of my brain ... by destroying their corporeality, I take them back into my own corporeality and *announce*: I alone am corporeal. And now I take the world as it is for me, as *my* world, as my property: I relate everything to myself.'[23] It is now a familiar existential therapy in which reified abstractions are reduced to concrete existential experience; but Stirner is even more complicated, insofar as the Hegelian paradigm – how humans recognize everything in the not-I and the non-human world ultimately as being their own productivity and as 'belonging' to them (so-called Absolute Spirit) – is also transferred onto an existential or individual framework: now Absolute Spirit gets an individual lived body and restores itself by reappropriating its own physical existence. Clearly, more than mere Hegelian ideologies are at work here, and much of the contemporary ideology of the body and of desire might also distantly recognize itself in Stirner's ancient spotted mirror. The passage is thus also a crucial one for any intersection between 'Marxism' and the various existentialisms and it is certainly wrong (or at least not enough) to say that Marx rejects this return to the body. He could not do so in the name of the abstractions Stirner himself seeks to dispel, for these are also his own target (they are the phantoms or spectres of the brain). Marx's dramatic insight lies in the identification of this allegedly concrete existential body as itself being a phantom, an imaginary body ('he makes his own body into a body of spectres').[24] The attempt to conquer and achieve concreteness via the expulsion of the spectres only leads to the construction of an even more imaginary entity, which I think of as my 'self': the existential path thereby leads, not into reality, but into an even more intricate unreality. Marx does not offer a counter-therapy, but the rest of *The German Ideology* (in particular the famous opening section on Feuerbach) is there to suggest that for him individual reality is to be found and achieved there where social reality is also to be found, namely in production itself, or in other words by going around before the invasion of the cerebral and reified conceptual phantoms, and beginning again from their point of production; by circumventing them rather than traversing them into what is vainly hoped and fantasized as being a truer reality after the reign of the phantoms themselves.

Derrida's interventions then take place at two points in this polemic: the first is that of Marx's own critique of Stirner's programme, which he restates as follows: 'In his abstract reconstruction of the various stages of life, Stirner gives us but a "spectral shade" that we ought to "confront" with its disappeared body, for what he has lost in this supposed destruction of specters is quite simply his body, "life" and "actual reality". He has lost his body out of love of his body' (p. 131). At which point Derrida adds: 'For this whole history remains under the control of the paradoxes of narcissism and the work of mourning.' It is a whole programme which we will not follow up on here but which as surely as anything else locks these discussions back into the principal concerns of Derrida's later work.

But then there is a second intervention, this one on Marx himself and on his very critique, haunted as one might well imagine by ontology as such. Marx wishes to exorcize Stirner's ghosts, the ghosts Stirner called down upon himself by his own awkward and misconceived exorcisms. It is however precisely this that will be Derrida's deepest reproach to Marx, if we may put it that way: it is this that he sees as underlying the temptation to ontology elsewhere in Marx (and even more omnipresent in so-called Marx-ism), the spectral project of a Marxist 'philosophy', for example, or the Marxist view of reality or of 'Man' (Althusser rejected the 'humanism' of the early Marx for what are surely much the same reasons). But all of the ontological temptations come from this deeper source, which lies precisely in Marx's own relationship to ghosts (and thereby to the past, to history, to death, and to life in the present): 'In short, and we will return to this repeatedly, Marx does not like ghosts any more than his adversaries do. He does not want to believe in them. But he thinks of nothing else. He believes rather in what is supposed to distinguish them from actual reality, living effectivity. He believes he can oppose them, like life to death, like vain appearance of the simulacrum to real presence' (pp. 46–7).

This is then Marx's fundamental mistake (if not 'error'): he wants to get rid of ghosts, he not only thinks he can do so, but that it is also desirable to do so. But a world cleansed of spectrality is precisely ontology itself, a world of pure presence, of immediate density, of things without a past: for Derrida, an impossible and noxious nostalgia, and the fundamental target of his whole life's work. But we can now go even further than this, and Derrida risks an analysis of this polemic with Stirner: 'My feeling, then, is that Marx scares himself, he *himself* pursues relentlessly someone who almost resembles him to the point that we could mistake one for the other: a brother, a double, thus a diabolical image. A kind of ghost of himself. Whom he would like to distance, distinguish: to *oppose*' (p. 139). But this fear now needs to be reconnected with the famous opening of the *Eighteenth Brumaire* in which the fear of bourgeois revolutionaries is evoked: their need for the ghosts of the past, for costumes and dead paradigms, to disguise this open freedom onto an uncharted future on which they are launching. One reply to Derrida's fundamental critique of Marx lies in this particular conjecture, namely that Marx may be more sensitive to the essential malevolence of the past and the dead than anything that can be found in the prototypical situation of mourning and melancholia as *Hamlet* archetypically configures it: mourning also wants to get rid of the past, to exorcize it, albeit under the guise of respectful commemoration. To forget the dead altogether is impious in ways that prepare their own retribution, but to remember the dead is neurotic and obsessive and merely feeds a sterile repetition. There is no 'proper' way of relating to the dead and the past. It is as though Derrida, in what some call postmodernity, is in the process of diagnosing and denouncing the opposite excess: that of a present that has already triumphantly exorcized all of its ghosts and believes itself to be without a past and without spectrality, late capitalism itself as ontology, the pure presence of the world-market system freed from all the errors of human history and of previous social formations, including the ghost of Marx himself.

The promise of a future

Now, however, we must ask what spectrality holds for the future: *Hamlet* was after all not a ghost story very specifically in this, that it did not merely tell about some grisly hold of the past on the present (as in *The Turn of the Screw*), but rather showed the apparition of the past in the act of provoking future action and calling for retribution by the living. The future is also spectral in that sense: it is not at one with a present (itself 'out of joint'), it has the distance from our own plenitude of the dead and of ghosts, its blurred lineaments also swim dimly into view and announce or foretell themselves. There can be *traces* of the future (to use a privileged Derridean word), and it is all of this that restores some immense temporality as tendency or Dao which has been flattened out by positivism and finally reduced to the present by the current social order.

From this perspective, for example, it might be argued that the earlier conception of textuality and *différance* allowed for a far more active deconstructive praxis, one energized by the impossible (Utopian) hope that something radically new might appear against all odds were it only possible to denounce these metaphysical survivals with enough force. Yet that is to neglect the other new themes that have accompanied 'mourning' and spectrality in the writing of the last decade as well: these include the resurgence of Lévinas's notion of the radical difference of the Other and the need to preserve that at all costs; the appearance of the very apparition of the other in the omnipresence of the address itself: '*Viens!*' (as compared to interpellation in Althusser, self-repression in the Foucauldian confession, or even Ricoeur's *kerygma*); and finally the repeated demonstrations of the impossible (as in the analysis of Mauss's *The Gift*),[25] which turn on the necessity and the urgency of keeping the impossible alive, keeping faith with it, making it continue to be somehow possible in its very impossibility. These motifs correspond to what I would myself be tempted to call the Utopian – and what Derrida himself assuredly terms the 'messianic' – in this recent thinking; they admonish us to seize the occasion of this

most recent and supreme text on Marx to realize that spectrality is here
the form of the most radical politicization and that, far from being
locked into the repetitions of neurosis and obsession, it is energetically
future-oriented and active. *Hamlet* also turned in its very narrative
structure on a call to praxis, whose contamination with the residual
survivals of the revenge-tragedy it needed to grapple with first and
foremost.

Such traces of the future, however, need their specific entry-point,
which is sometimes, when it is envisaged from a human perspective,
described as the prophetic, but which can also take another form which
has begun to occupy a significant position in modern theory and not
least in Derrida's own work, namely the messianic as such. The word
recalls Walter Benjamin, whose famous passages are indeed quoted and
carefully glossed by Derrida in the present text; it also suggests the
cognate messianism – the great millenarian movements – from which
Derrida is careful to distance the other verbal form.[26] Messianism, or
Utopianism, or all the active forms of millenarian movements and
politics, are obviously very much targets of political and hegemonic
doxa today: associated with all the imaginable varieties of political
movements you fear, paradigmatically Nazism and communism. Current liberal thought – it is of course conservative and not 'liberal' in
the loose American sense of the word – focuses fundamentally on such
projects which it identifies as the root cause of political evil in the
world: all are projects of systemic change as such, in other words,
of revolution. Yet it seems important to distinguish this traditional
'Marxian' concept, which we will find reappearing metamorphosed in
Derrida's thought later on as the 'messianic', from those other 'fundamental concepts of Marxism' which according to him 'rivet it to the
body of Marxist doctrine, to its supposed systemic, metaphysical, or
ontological totality (notably to its "dialectical method" or to "dialectical materialism"), to its fundamental concepts of labor, mode of
production, social class, and consequently to the whole history of its
apparatuses' (p. 88).

As materialism makes a fleeting reappearance in this passage, it is
worth remarking what has only been touched on in passing, namely a
curious feature of the history of these various Marxisms themselves,
that virtually all of them include within themselves a crucial denunciation of bad or 'vulgar materialist' Marxisms: that, as it were, it has
seemed impossible for any Marxism to define itself or to assert its
identity without this internal exorcism of the 'frère ennemi' or ghostly
double which would be this bad or vulgar Marxism, the reductive one,
what 'Marxism' is for everybody else, for the non-Marxists; and this
from Marx himself onward (whose 'I am not a Marxist' probably no

longer needs to be quoted). This surely has something to do with the contradictions within the materialist project itself, which we have already touched on, namely, the paradoxes of a 'materialist consciousness', which these various authentic or true Marxisms acknowledge by warning of the dangers of trying to bring that about by suppressing consciousness (or intelligence) altogether. No doubt also, however, the requirements of a doctrine and those of an organized party (here 'institution' or 'apparatus') which turn on the establishment of such a doctrine, play their role; and Derrida's 'International' 'without party, without country [*patrie*], without national community . . . without co-citizenship, without common belonging to a class' (p. 85) rejoins the allergy he shares with many others today to the older political formations.

Only a few of the wiser Marxisms have reintegrated this exorcism of a vulgar Marxism into their very structure as a way of thinking and a strategy all at once: here one thinks of various notions, like that of Korsch, of the oscillation back and forth from vulgar or determinist Marxism to a voluntaristic and theoreticist kind, depending on the situation in which it is called upon to act. Brecht vulgarized this notion in a pre-eminently usable way when he talked about that '*plumpes Denken*' or vulgar thought, reductive, materialist, vulgar analysis (including cynicism, debunking and the like) which any intellectualist and hyperintellectually dialectical (Frankfurt School-type) Marxism had to carry about within itself in order to remain authentic. The superstructure, for Brecht, needs in other words to stay reanchored to the base; the thought of the superstructure needs to carry the reminder of the base around within itself. It was then a duality or double-standard that Benjamin reversed and immortalized in his image of the chess player: the automaton on the outside, the revolutionary party that can be seen, with a little dialectical skill, to win every historical engagement and is carried forward by the 'inevitable' march of history, but whose moves are in reality made by a very different conception of history (and in the present context, of figuration), namely that represented by the dwarf of theology.

Nor was it clear either how Benjamin thought of revolution: except that as he was contemporaneous with one, in another part of space and time, namely the Soviet Union, he developed Proustian conceptions of simultaneity and coexistence to think that particular coevality. Yet alongside that other, revolutionary world, there existed this one, of the Paris of the 1930s and of Hitler next door, in which revolution was very far from happening, in which indeed it was unthinkable (and his guarded reactions to the Moscow purge trials suggest that this impossibility and inconceivability of revolution later on began to contaminate the other, minimally still Utopian sphere, and to extend to everything in the world). Benjamin thus offers the supreme example of the intellectual committed to revolutionary values in a world in which revolution cannot be expected to happen: it is this which makes up everything priceless in the experiment which was his life and work, and in particular gives its relevance and energy to the basic figure through which he was accustomed to think this impossibility, namely that very conception of the messianic to which Derrida appeals at the climax of his book on Marx.

But we must be very subtle in the way in which, particularly those of us who are not believing Jews and are very far from such kinds of beliefs, we understand the coming of the Messiah. The non-Jews imagine that Jews think of Messiah as a promise and a future certainty: nothing could be farther from the truth. Indeed, it was Benjamin's own close friend Gershom Sholem who wrote the definitive history of this illusion in his great biography of the apostate Messiah, Sabbatai Sevi,[27] who marks the moment in the history of the diaspora of a truly messianic moment that ran through the then Jewish world like wildfire. The apostasy of Sevi before the Grand Turk then profoundly marks the messianic idea, incises it with the pain of disappointment and the sharp experience of defeat. By the association of ideas at work in collective trauma a redemptive idea is soaked in the colours and dies of bitter disillusionment. The very idea of the messianic then brings the whole feeling of dashed hopes and impossibility along with it: and it is this that it means in Benjamin as well. You would not evoke the messianic in a genuinely revolutionary period, a period in which changes can be sensed at work all around you; the messianic does not mean immediate hope in that sense, perhaps not even hope against hope; it is a unique variety of the species hope that scarcely bears any of the latter's normal characteristics and that flourishes only in a time of absolute hopelessness, a period like the Second Empire, or the years between the Wars, or the 1980s and 90s, when radical change seems unthinkable, its very idea dispelled by visible wealth and power, along with palpable powerlessness. It is only in those trough years that it makes sense to speak of the messianic in the Benjaminian sense.[28]

As for the content of this redemptive idea itself, another peculiar feature of it must be foregrounded, namely that it does not deploy a linear idea of the future: nothing predictable, nothing to be read in the signs of the times, in the first few swallows or shoots, the freshening of the air. 'The Jews do not predict the future ... any moment is the strait gate through which Messiah may appear.'[29] This is the notion of the non-announced, the turning of a corner in which an altogether different present happens, which was not foreseen. It is also the sense in which, for Benjamin, the Social Democratic and then the Stalinist rhetoric of historical inevitability weigh down the historical present even more balefully: as in Proust, whatever is to happen, it will assuredly not be what we can imagine or predict. In this sense, Benjamin had a more historically vivid feeling for how revolutions actually happen, unexpected by anyone, even their organizers, a few people gathering in the streets, larger and larger crowds, suddenly the rumour spreads that the king has secretly left the city. It is this temporality which is the messianic kind, and about which the very peculiarity of the messianic idea testifies, which can thus not be 'hoped' for in any familiar way; nor is 'belief' in the Messiah comparable to any ordinary thinking about the future. Perry Anderson has some suggestive remarks about what constitutes the unexpectedness of revolution as such when he distinguishes between an unforeseen mutation or crisis in the base, in production, and the sudden spark generated by its contact with a specific mentality in the superstructure.[30] Both of those however can exist for long periods in unrelated states: neither is fruitful of eventness (as Heidegger might say) in and of itself; what is unpredictable is precisely the spark that flies between these two sealed and as it were unrelated areas. This helps us 'think' the messianic moment, the future event, in a somewhat more articulated way, it being understood that what the very concept of the messianic above all wishes to warn us against is that the event cannot be thought in the ordinary meaning of that word; and with this we rejoin Derrida's critique of conventional philosophical thought in general as a misguided attempt to think what demands a different preparation and approach.

Yet the messianic must be sharply distinguished from the apocalyptic in Derrida's usage, which is much more specifically the thinking of the 'end' and to which the charge of critical and negative doxa that nowadays attaches to revolution and the Utopian becomes attached: but with a fundamental difference. Fukuyama becomes the textbook example in the present work and the paradigm case of an apocalyptic pronouncement on the death of the past as such, the utter disappearance of that pre-history we still call History: in other words, the definitive exorcism of spectres and spectrality, the beginning of a market universe which is a perpetual present, as well as the instauration of truth: 'Whoever takes on the apocalyptic tone comes to signify to, if not tell, you something. What? The truth, of course, and to signify to you that it reveals the truth to you ... Truth is itself the end, the destination, and that truth unveils itself is the advent of the end'.[31] This is then the sense in which we ought to be able to distinguish an apocalyptic politics from a messianic one, and which might lead us on into some new way of sorting out the Left from the Right, the new

International in Marx's spirit from that in the world of business and state power. The messianic is spectral, it is the spectrality of the future, the other dimension, that answers to the haunting spectrality of the past which is historicity itself. The apocalyptic, however, announces the end of spectrality (and we remember that even in Marx it remained a temptation, and that Marx also sometimes imprudently talks about the end of history, but in the name of the beginning of a different one).

There is, however, finally another feature of the messianic that emerges in Derrida's discussion, and that unexpectedly opens this spectrality on another world of the real not normally deployed by these themes and images, these stolen and displaced words. This is the other face of modern or we might even say of postmodern virtuality, a daily spectrality that undermines the present and the real without any longer attracting any attention at all; it marks out the originality of our social situation, but no one has reidentified it as a very old thing in quite this dramatic way – it is the emergence, at the very end of Derrida's book, of spectrality, of the messianic, as 'the differantial deployment of *tekhnē*, of techno-science or tele-technology' (p. 169). As far back as *The Post Card* it had become clear to what degree Derrida's subversion of mainstream semiotics and communications theory fed into a vast 'dissemination' of his earlier concepts of writing and difference, which now emerged in the place in which a theory of communications technology would have existed were one possible.[32] But instead of becoming formalized in a new tele-technological 'theory' or turn, that constellation is here modulated in the direction of spectrality itself:

> [Spectral differentiation, the messianic] obliges us more than ever to think the virtualization of space and time, the possibility of virtual events whose movement and speed prohibit us more than ever (more and otherwise than ever, for this is not absolutely and thoroughly new) from opposing presence to its representation, 'real time' to 'deferred time', effectivity to its simulacrum, the living to the non-living, in short, the living to the living-dead of its ghosts. It obliges us to think, from there, another space for democracy. For democracy-to-come and thus for justice. We have suggested that the event we are prowling around here hesitates between the singular 'who' of the ghost and the general 'what' of the simulacrum. In the virtual space of all the tele-technosciences, in the general dis-location to which our time is destined – as are from now on the places of lovers, families, nations – the messianic trembles on the edge of this event itself. It is this hesitation, it has no other vibration, it does not 'live' otherwise, but it would no longer be messianic if it stopped hesitating ... (p. 169)

So it is that Marxism and its current spectrality, which not so unexpectedly intersected the weak messianic impulses of our own period, now both emerge in some post-semiotic universe of messages and into the virtualities of the new communications technologies: original forms of hesitation, a new kind of trembling or shimmering of the present in which new ghosts now seem on the point of walking. It will be remembered how Derrida opened up Lacan's still essentially semiotic and centred reading of Poe:[33] a letter never arrives at its destination . . . a letter always arrives at its destination . . . Perhaps we need something similar here: Marx's purloined letter: a whole new programme in itself surely, a wandering signifier capable of keeping any number of conspiratorial futures alive.

Notes

1. See M. Sprinker and E.A. Kaplan, eds, *The Althusserian Legacy* (London: Verso, 1993).

2. Maurice Blanchot, 'Les Trois paroles de Marx', in *L'Amitié* (Paris 1971), pp. 115–17.

3. J. Derrida, *Positions* (Paris 1972).

4. See 'Le Dernier mot du racisme' (1983), and 'Admiration de Nelson Mandela' (1986), in *Psyché* (Paris 1987).

5. All references within the text are to J. Derrida, *Specters of Marx*, trans. Peggy Kamuf (New York and London: Routledge, 1994).

6. Roland Barthes, *Writing Degree Zero* (New York 1968).

7. As, for example, in Manfredo Tafuri, *Theories and History of Architecture* (Cambridge, MA 1980).

8. Paul de Man, 'The Rhetoric of Blindness: Jacques Derrida's Reading of Rousseau', in *Blindness and Insight* (Oxford 1971).

9. As in Rodolphe Gasché's admirable *The Tain of the Mirror* (Cambridge, MA 1986).

10. Karl Marx, *Critique of Hegel's Philosophy of Right.*

11. *Marxism and Deconstruction: a Critical Articulation* (Baltimore 1982).

12. Homer, *The Odyssey*, trans. Robert Fitzgerald (New York 1961), p. 212 (Book 11, verses 462–4).

13. *Helliconia Spring* (New York 1987) p. 248.

14. 'The Anaximander Fragment', in M. Heidegger, *Early Greek Thinking* (New York 1984).

15. Étienne Balibar, *Cinq études du matérialisme historique* (Paris 1974).

16. *Le Problème de la genèse dans la philosophie de Husserl* (Paris 1990), p. 32. This splendid work from 1953–4 affirms a properly dialectical solution to Husserl's dilemmas (albeit in the form of a dialectic radically distinct either from Hegel or from the then influential Marxist dialectic of Tran-Duc-Thao). Derrida's endorsement of dialectical conceptuality here (p. 125: 'rien ne peut être désigné ou défini sans postuler immédiatement un discours absolument opposé') is significant not because it testifies to some hitherto unsuspected apostasy, but rather because it allows us to infer a subsequent moment in which deconstruction emerges as the result of intellectual dissatisfaction with dialectical categories as such. Derrida must subsequently have come to feel that, far from being thoughts or solutions in their own right, such terms and categories were to be read only as the signs or symptoms of unresolved problems. The further step, namely that such (genetic and temporal) problems and dilemmas, first in Husserl himself and then in the dialectic, were in fact unresolvable, offers a persuasive reason for deconstruction as such.

17. In *Heidegger et la question* (Paris 1990).

18. Ibid., pp. 90–1, note.

19. Paris 1991.

20. See Serge Guilbaut, *How New York Stole the Idea of Modern Art* (Chicago 1983).

21. Naomi Shor, *George Sand and Idealism* (New York 1993).

22. In Marx and Engels, *The German Ideology* (Moscow 1976), see the commentary on

Stirner, Part One, 'A Man's Life', pp. 136 ff.; Part Two, chapter 2, 'The Moderns', pp. 165 ff.; and on Stirner's 'dialectic', pp. 289 ff.

23. *The German Ideology*, quoted p. 137.

24. Ibid., p. 137.

25. See *Donner le temps. 1. La fausse monnaie* (Paris 1991), in which it is argued that the 'miracle' of the gift, that falls outside the Symbolic Order, is annulled whenever the gift is named and identified as such, the paradox being that gift always entails reimbursement (whence the reinsertion of the new institutionalized phenomenon in the exchange or market circuit of the symbolic).

26. '[W]e prefer to say *messianic* rather than *messianism*, so as to designate a structure of experience rather than a religion' (*Specters*, pp. 167–8).

27. G. Scholem, *Sabbatai Sevi: The Mystical Messiah* (Princeton 1973). For these and related insights I am greatly indebted to Craig Phillips.

28. I quote Derrida's own evocation in full:

> Ascesis strips the messianic hope of all biblical forms, and even all determinable figures of the wait or expectation; it thus denudes itself in view of responding to that which must be absolute hospitality, the 'yes' to the *arrivant(e)*, the 'come' to the future that cannot be anticipated – which must not be the 'anything whatsoever' that harbors behind it those too familiar ghosts, the very ones we must practice recognizing. Open, waiting for the event *as* justice, this hospitality is absolute only if it keeps watch over its own universality. The messianic, including its revolutionary forms (and the messianic is always revolutionary, it has to be), would be urgency, imminence but, irreducible paradox, a waiting without horizon of expectation. One may always take the quasi-atheistic dryness of the messianic to be the condition of the religions of the Book, a desert that was not even theirs (but the earth is always borrowed, on loan from God, it is never possessed by the occupier, says precisely [*justement*] the Old Testament whose injunction one would also have to hear); one may always recognize there the arid soil in which grew, and passed away, the living figures of all the messiahs, whether they were announced, recognized, or still awaited. One may also consider this compulsive growth, and the furtiveness of this passage, to be the only events on the basis of which we approach and first of all name the messianic in general, that other ghost which we cannot and ought not to do without. One may deem strange, strangely familiar and inhospitable at the same time (*unheimlich*, uncanny), this figure of absolute hospitality whose promise one would choose to entrust to an experience that is so impossible, so unsure in its indigence, to a quasi-'messianism' so anxious, fragile, and impoverished, to an always presupposed 'messianism', to a quasi-transcendental 'messianism' that also has such an obstinate interest in a materialism without substance: a materialism of the *khôra* for a despairing 'messianism'. But without this latter despair and if one could *count* on what is coming, hope would be but the calculation of a program. One would have the prospect but one would no longer wait for anything or anyone. Law without justice. One would no longer invite, either body or soul, no longer receive any visits, no longer even think to see. To see coming. Some, and I do not exclude myself, will find this despairing 'messianism' has a curious taste, a taste of death. It is true that this taste is above all a taste, a foretaste, and in essence it is curious. Curious of the very thing that it conjures – and that leaves something to be desired. (pp. 168–9)

29. Benjamin, *Illuminations* (New York 1969), p. 264.

30. Perry Anderson, *Arguments within English Marxism* (London: Verso, 1980), pp. 55–6:

> The most fundamental mechanisms of social change, according to historical materialism, are the systemic contradictions between *forces and relations of production*, not just social conflicts between classes generated by antagonistic relations of production alone. The former *overlap* with the latter, because one of the major forces of production is always labour, which simultaneously figures as a class specified by the relations of production. But they do not coincide. Crises within modes of production are not identical with confrontations between classes. The two may or may not fuse, according to the historical occasion. The onset of major economic crises, whether under feudalism or capitalism, has typically taken all social classes unawares, deriving from structural depths below those of direct conflict between them. The resolution of such crises, on the other hand, has no less typically been the outcome of prolonged war between classes.

31. 'On a Newly Arisen Apocalyptic Tone in Philosophy', in *Raising the Tone of Philisophy*, ed. Peter Fenves (Baltimore 1993), p. 151.

32. But now see Richard Dienst, *Still Life in Real Time: Theory after Television* (Durham, NC 1994), for a pathbreaking study of what the fact and existence of such technology does to the very possibilities of philosophizing (from Marx to Deleuze and Derrida).

33. 'Le Facteur de la vérité', in *La Carte postale* (Paris 1980).

4

Spirits Armed and Unarmed:
Derrida's *Specters of Marx*
Warren Montag

In memory of Ernest Mandel

This only will I add: we cannot know anyone except by his works.

– Spinoza, *Tractatus Theologico-Politicus*

One can only admire the gesture that constitutes *Specters of Marx*, a gesture whose very untimeliness marks it as a superbly timed intervention. Derrida has taken advantage of his institutional position, of his prestige, of the immense audience that he has acquired over the years as a result of his striking originality and productivity as a philosopher, to utter some words that are not only unexpected but, to so many for so many reasons, highly unwelcome. Foremost, of course, among these are the anti-Marxists (professional and otherwise) who hoped that, after so many false deaths (as Derrida reminds us Marx had already been declared dead in the fifties), Marxism had not only finally expired but was buried, never to be seen on this earth again. *Specters* must come as a particular embarrassment to a number of Derrida's self-styled disciples who believed that deconstruction was itself a declaration (if not a cause) of Marx's death, since Marxist theory (which was thus refused that heterogeneity which was otherwise said to be constitutive of any writing whatsoever) could be no more than a metaphysics or a metanarrative, both of which species were declared extinct some time ago. But the effects of *Specters of Marx* will be felt beyond the boundaries of professed anti-Marxism.

There are also the professional anti-deconstructionists (a cause that unites self-proclaimed Marxists with their most bitter adversaries in what would appear to be a quite unprincipled alliance), for whom any questioning of the concepts of 'history', 'reason' or 'truth', any examination of the way these concepts have actually functioned in different fields of inquiry over the past three centuries, can only lead, with a fatal necessity that no act of good will can circumvent, to skepticism ('there is nothing outside the text'[1] and therefore no reality to talk about or act on) and relativism (all discourses and practices are equivalent). Their accounts of Derrida's work bear so little resemblance to what he has actually written that they can be of little interest except, perhaps, as symptoms of an intellectual culture that cannot tolerate criticism (even in the Kantian sense) of its most cherished presuppositions. But if it is true that such attacks are only so much dust thrown up over Derrida's texts (among others: the anti-deconstructionists tend to define deconstruction very generously – Foucault was alternately chagrined and amused to find himself addressed quite frequently as a 'deconstructionist' on his visits to the US), they have nevertheless succeeded in obscuring certain works, in rendering them opaque to some who might have found them useful. One awaits their response to *Specters*.

Finally, there are those who think that Marx is dead without knowing that this is what they think, and Derrida's peculiar return to (the specters of) Marx, to the spirit as well as the letter of Marx's texts, namely to his critique of capitalism, not only as economy but as juridical theory and practice, as morality of exchange, discipline and punishment, can only prove disturbing. For too many Marxists today, especially in the Anglophone world, the capitalist market and the capitalist state have assumed the character of (human) nature. There was history but there no longer is any: all prior history was but an anticipation of that finally rational form of the distribution of goods, the market, which requires in turn only a state imbued with the proper morality to safeguard the interests of 'the weak' and 'the disadvantaged'. The spirit of Marx invoked by Derrida is quite different: it is the same spirit that overflowed the theoretical boundaries of *Capital*, spilling out at its margins and in its footnotes, speaking with dark irony of the discrepancy between the noble fictions that accompanied the rise of capitalism, its 'pompous catalogues of human rights', its celebrations of 'Locke, law and property', and the reality of dispossession, slavery and genocide. Derrida is heir to this difficult legacy at a time when the discrepancy between the triumphalist rhetoric of liberalism (economic and political) and the reality of the world it dominates has never been greater. *Specters* is thus an event, not simply a text, and no critique of deconstruction can alter or deny its real effects, effects for which all of us who continue to think and act in the spirit of Marx should be grateful.

It is not easy to speak as Derrida has done; indeed, it is not easy to speak at all when the old words often seem no longer to be heard or understood, when Marx appears, if not finally to have departed, then to be condemned to hover unseen and unheard over a world he cannot affect. But Derrida knows better: the narrative of the birth, life and death of Marxism, like the narrative of history's progress to its own fulfillment in the terminal forms of capitalism and liberal democracy (a narrative according to which Marxism plays the role of one of the ruses of reason, reason in an alienated state that it must overcome to be itself in its complex unity), is a narrative so faulty, so symptom-ridden, even delusional, that to fail to interrogate it could only itself be an act of bad faith or a form of denial. At the same time, while it may seem strange or even inappropriate that Derrida would choose this moment to write about Marxism, an area that he has, until now, approached obliquely at best, the network of theoretical presuppositions supporting the proposition that Marxism is dead (and history has ended) are precisely those to which Derrida has devoted some of his most notable inquiries. At work in all the anti-Marxist discourses of our time (rational or otherwise) is precisely the notion of presence, a notion that, some decades ago, Derrida argued was at the heart of Western onto-theology. In his early work Derrida used the term '*différance*' to capture the way that the production of meaning is never simply the re-presentation of what was already fully present, but is itself a movement of difference and deferral in which every origin is constituted retroactively, *nachträglich*, an origin never present except belatedly. The very question to which *Specters* offers a response (whither Marxism?) evokes a notion of the 'non-contemporaneity with itself of the living present' (*SM*, xix), a sense of the peculiar presence of that which is no longer or not yet present.

Indeed, as Derrida points out, Marxism itself, like Hamlet's father, first appeared upon the scene (of history) in the form of a specter (the first noun in the *Communist Manifesto*) performing the act of haunting (the first verb in the text) – strange words indeed to find in the first sentence of the inaugural program of an international communist movement. Can what has not yet been or what is only now coming into being *haunt* (a term usually reserved for the presence of the past even in its non-being, or its being-no-longer) the present or presence? The figure suggests that the invulnerability and inevitability of communism derive from its already being a specter, from the fact that its first coming is already a return, its first appearance already a repetition, its original presence already a representation of itself. It is thus irreducible to a present or presence which might become a past or absence: its very non-contemporaneity determines the possibility of its persistence. The 'spectrality', as Derrida calls it, of Marxism is its power, its being neither present nor absent, neither living nor dead.

To speak of specters, the lexicon of ontology is insufficient. Ontology speaks only of what is present or what is absent; it cannot conceive of what is neither. Thus it is replaced by a 'hauntology' adequate to the task of interrogating the spirit, that which is neither living nor dead. The linear time of birth, life and death, of the beginning and the end, has no place in the hauntic, which latter alone allows us to speak of what persists beyond the end, beyond death, of what was never alive enough to die, never present enough to become absent. What exists between presence and absence that prevents the non-present from simply disappearing? Using a different language, we might put the question another way: how does what is absent produce effects? 'What is the *effectivity* or the *presence* of a specter, that is of what seems to remain as ineffective, virtual, insubstantial as a simulacrum?' (*SM*, 10). To theorize 'the being-there of specters' or the ideality of the material and the materiality of the ideal, Derrida rehabilitates a concept that had long since been excluded from Marxist thought: spirit.

Such is Derrida's surprising defense of Marx (or at least his pro- legomenon to any possible defense of Marx), a defense of Marx against himself, against his intransigent critique of every apparition of spirit and of every spiritualism in philosophy. Thus, if it is the case that there is 'no future without Marx, without the memory and the inheritance of Marx' (*SM*, 13), Marx, or rather Marx's spirit, must not be understood to be the consciousness present to itself whose intention guarantees the unity and homogeneity of Marxist theory and practice. To be Marx's heir is difficult: there is no single spirit but a plurality of spirits. It is thus a question of 'a certain Marx . . . of at least one of his spirits. For this will be our hypothesis or rather our bias: *there is more than one of them, there must be more than one of them*' (*SM*, 13). Because of the 'radical and necesary *heterogeneity*' of Marx's legacy, because of the very plurality of spirits lingering, '*One must* filter, sift, criticize', one must '*reaffirm by choosing*' (*SM*, 16).

It might be tempting here to compare the Marx that Derrida has filtered from the multiplicity of spirits to Marx's texts themselves to ask whether there is or can be a spirit of Marx, or rather a Marxist spirit that Marx himself could only contemplate in externalized form as other or adversary (Stirner), to ask whether Marx against and despite himself produced the idea of spirit. But it might be at least as illuminating to determine the function of the concept of spirit in Derrida's text and thereby to identify the heterogeneity proper to it.

For Derrida, Marx's death or rather the death of Marxism is, at least in some important sense, incontestable: the collapse of the so-called Communist regimes and the quasi-disappearance of their affiliate parties around the world (as well as the mass organizations linked in however direct or indirect a manner to these parties) are signs that the body of official Marxism has given up the ghost. But if Marx is dead, his death does not remove him from the world; on the contrary, it insures his haunting presence *hic et ubique*. Marxism has been liberated from itself, from the externalized material form in which it was alienated from itself, the form of its own negation which has itself been negated, allowing the spirit of Marxism to recollect and recover itself, 'spirit knowing itself as spirit', to use Hegel's language. Thus in 'death' Marxism speaks with an authority that it could never possess in life; it sees even if we cannot see it seeing us and our world. Indeed, there is nothing any longer to be seen, only a voice to be heard, a tale that sounds and resounds after the teller is gone, an echo that leaps the temporal chasm that separates us from Marx. It tells of crimes and horrors and of the criminals who are the kings of our world. What remains to be understood is the ghost itself, the spirit of Marxism divested of its material, historical temporal forms, which in turn taken together comprised only one of the 'several different possibles that inhabit' (*SM*, 16) Marxism.

For (and this will surprise those who are familiar with Derrida's earlier work) underneath, behind or prior to the material manifestations of Marxism lies an undeconstructible 'idea of justice (dissociated here from law)' (*SM*, 90). Deconstruction which, according to Derrida, has always 'proceeded in a hyper-critical fashion' (*SM*, 90) and called for 'interminable self-critique' (*SM*, 89) is thus 'still to distinguish between everything and almost everything' (*SM*, 90). The remainder left when one subtracts almost everything from everything is what Derrida 'will never be ready to renounce' (*SM*, 90): 'a certain emancipatory and *messianic* affirmation' (*SM*, 89) as well as 'a certain idea of justice' (*SM*, 90). It is interesting to note that at this very point Derrida does not simply distinguish himself from 'anti-marxist interpretations' (*SM*, 90) of Marx with their onto-theological eschatologies, but also, and primarily, from the Marxism, described as 'the most vigilant' (*SM*, 89) (too vigilant?) reinterpretation of Marx, associated with 'those around Althusser' (*SM*, 89). The 'vigilance' of Althusser and Co. would appear to have been (the past tense is Derrida's) excessive, their hyper-hyper-critical procedure ignoring in its anti-teleological, anti-messianic zeal the crucial distinction between the critique of everything and the critique of almost everything (the latter precisely finds its meaning in and is supported by what it refuses to criticize or to renounce, an act that, in this passage at least, functions as a synonym of criticism.

But it appears that, in the guise of a critique of 'those around Althusser', Derrida has in fact reversed his own positions. After all, it was he who, nearly thirty years ago, wrote that deconstruction always 'falls prey to its own work' *(Grammatology,* 24). The notion of an undeconstructible spirit of Marx recalls the Cartesian *cogito,* as Pierre Macherey argued in his review of *Spectres de Marx,* insofar as it constitutes that which may not be doubted or 'renounced', an origin placed outside the field of play, *'un abri du hors-jeu',* a shelter whose 'destruction' according to Derrida was marked by the 'advent of writing' *(Grammatology,* 7) as the permanent subversion of a transcendental logos, or a superior instance above the field of struggle (as Althusser put it). The undeconstructible is the voice (or voices) of Marx's spirit, a voice that precedes and exceeds what is said (or done) at a given moment. How poor seems the actuality of Marxism, what has been said or done in Marx's name, in comparison with the spirit that lies beyond all criticism, a reservoir of 'possibles' waiting to be actualized. The death of all previously existing practical forms of Marxism, far from permitting those who would listen to the voice of Marx's spirit to remain 'spiritual' or 'abstract', enjoins us 'to produce events, new effective forms of action, practice, organization and so forth' *(SM,* 89) finally adequate to the hitherto unfulfilled 'promise' of Marxism.

It would thus appear that Derrida has arrived through, of all things, Marx, at a position directly counterposed to the letter and the 'spirit' of the key texts of the inaugural moments of deconstruction. It is difficult not to see an irony in the appeals to the wealth of spirit prior to and perhaps waiting for its material expressions or representations, a transcendental (we cannot avoid this word) spirit unaffected by the disappearance of the letter, an idea separate from its material forms which are always only secondary in relation to it. Have we not taken up a position of the primacy of voice over writing and the spirit over the letter, a position according to which, as Derrida expressed it in *Of Grammatology,* 'writing, sensible matter and artificial exteriority' constitute 'a "clothing"' (35) (or perhaps in the manner of Hamlet's father an armor)? Have we not arrived at what Derrida once denounced as logocentrism, but which might more accurately be called in this context 'pneumacentrism' *(Grammatology,* 17)? But *Specters* is in no way reducible to such a reading: the concept of spirit itself as it functions in *Specters* is haunted. There is a ghost of the ghost, the spirit divides into two.

Nowhere is the irreducible antagonism internal to *Specters* (as well as certain of Derrida's other works) exhibited more clearly than in the very opening of the text where he speaks of 'a trace of which life and death would themselves be but traces and traces of traces, a survival whose possibility in advance comes to disjoin or dis-adjust the identity to itself of the living present as well as of any effectivity' (*SM*, xx). From this Derrida concludes 'there is then *some spirit*' (*SM*, xx). The 'then' is a gesture of derivation: the possibility of spirit derives from the existence of what Derrida has called the trace, or 'that which does not let itself be summed up in the simplicity of a present' (*Grammatology*, 66). The trace does not derive 'from a presence or from an originary nontrace . . . one must indeed speak of an originary trace or arche-trace, yet we know that concept destroys its name and that, if all begins with the trace, there is above all no originary trace' (*Grammatology*, 61). It is the repository 'of a meaning which was never present, whose signified presence is always reconstituted by deferral, *nachträglich*, belatedly, *supplementarily*' ('Freud and the Scene of Writing', 211). Taken in this sense, the trace as concept would serve to mark the movements of difference and deferral that have characterized and continue to characterize Marxist theory and practice, which latter never could or will 'be summed up in the simplicity of the present'. Derrida has chosen to name this impossibility 'spirit'.

But this does not exhaust the meaning or function of the trace as a concept. In fact, if we take the case of two particular readers whose relation to Derrida's philosophical project is simultaneously privileged and, because of the very forms of this privilege, problematic, namely Althusser and Foucault, we find that the trace has produced two opposed interpretations. In an interview conducted by Fernanda Navarro in 1984, Althusser employed the idea of the trace in a discussion of materiality: 'materiality may be different from the matter of the physicist or the chemist or of the worker who transforms metal or earth. I will take it to the extreme: it could be a simple trace, the materiality of the gesture that leaves a trace, the indiscernibility of the trace that it leaves on the wall of a cave or on a sheet of paper. . . . Derrida has shown that the primacy of the trace (of writing) is found even in the phoneme emitted by the voice that speaks' ('Philosophie et marxisme', 43). Althusser of course refers to Derrida's critique of logocentrism, the privileging of voice over writing, the assumption of 'the essential and immediate proximity' (*Grammatology*, 11) of voice to mind and a corresponding 'debasing' of writing as 'mediation of mediation and as a fall into the exteriority of meaning' (*Grammatology*, 13) common to the European philosophical tradition even in its diversity.

According to such a conceptual order, the possibility of meaning depends upon an ideal origin that is necessarily transcendent in relation to the material forms of its representation or expession: 'the age of the sign is essentially theological' (*Grammatology*, 14). The relationship of writing and speech is like that of body and soul: 'Writing, the letter, the sensible inscription, has always been considered by Western tradition as the body and matter external to the spirit, to breath, to speech and to the logos' (*Grammatology*, 35). Derrida proposes to overturn this conceptual regime with a grammatology, 'a science of writing before speech and in speech' (*Grammatology*, 51), a science of the trace, the priority of writing not only over speech, but over spirit and thought.

According to Althusser's reading of Derrida, the trace allows us to grasp the idea of the irreducibility of writing to speech and speech to an immaterial thought, the notion that no matter how far back we search we never arrive at a moment of pure ideality, the moment of the idea prior to its materialization as voice (whose irreducibility to thought already confers upon it the status of a kind of writing): from the very beginning writing '*breached* living speech from within' (*Grammatology*, 57) and disrupted the presence of spirit to itself. At the origin then is the trace, a materialization behind which or before which there is nothing: the phrase 'always already' common to both Althusser and Derrida captures the sense of an ideal origin that is never present except belatedly, retroactively, paradoxically constituted by its material 'expression'.

Apart from his belated response to Derrida's critique of *L'Histoire de la folie à l'âge classique* (most of which concerned only Foucault's discussion of Descartes in the second paragraph of the second chapter), Foucault had only slightly more than Althusser to say about Derrida's early work: a few sentences in the *Archaeology of Knowledge* (1969), a brief passage in 'What is an Author?' (1969), and a few remarks in his responses to Derrida in 1972 ('My Body, This Paper, This Fire' and 'Réponse à Derrida'). To the extent that he offers an interpretation of the same works, however, his assessment is diametrially opposed to that of Althusser. While it may once have been possible to regard Foucault's brief remarks, which are admittedly fragmentary, undeveloped and unsystematic, as one of his typically overstated responses to his critics which often resembled satire more than argument, Derrida's 'turn' in *Specters* accords them a new interest. For as Althusser's reading of *Grammatology* (and some other early texts) makes it (with considerable justification) a materialist or at least anti-spiritualist work, Foucault insists that the notion of the trace (of writing), exactly as isolated by Althusser, represents transcendental-religious thought *en son ultime éclat*, a way of preserving the very hierarchy of thought-speech-writing (a hierarchy implicated in the category of the author) that Derrida would subvert. The idea of an originary writing, instead of calling into question every notion of an ideal origin, transposes it into 'an a priori transcendental' that replaces living voice with the living text, a ' "textualizing" of discursive practices' (*Archaeology*, 27). Foucault accuses Derrida of practicing 'a very determinate little pedagogy ... which teaches the student that there is nothing outside the text [*il n'y a rien hors du texte*], but that in it, in its interstices, in its lacunae and its silences, reigns the reserve of the origin; that it is in no way necessary to look elsewhere than here, not in the words certainly, but in the words under erasure' ('My Body', 27). Much of this, particularly the subtle transposition of '*il n'y a pas de hors-texte*' into 'there is nothing outside the text', appears to attribute to Derrida statements that are not to be found in his work and whose meaning seems to run counter to his philosophical objectives, both as they were stated and as they were realized. And yet Foucault's formulations found their way into a number of critiques of Derrida in the Anglophone world years before his response to Derrida was translated into English through, among others, Edward Said's counterposing of Derrida and Foucault in his essay 'The Problem of Textuality: Two Exemplary Positions' (1978). But in the light of *Specters*, certain of Foucault's critical remarks in 'What is an Author?' (1969) acquire a new interest. For Foucault denounces what he identifies as the spiritualist nature of the deconstructive enterprise in terms that are uncannily similar to those Derrida employs in *Specters of Marx*: 'to think writing as absence, is this not simply to repeat in transcendental terms the religious principle of a tradition at once unalterable and never complete, and the aesthetic principle of the survival [*survie*] of the work, of its living on [*maintien*] beyond death, and of its enigmatic excess in relation to the author?' ('Auteur', 795; 'Author', 120)

What reasons, beyond the biographical or the intellectual-biographical, can be adduced to explain the utterly opposed, even mutually exclusive, interpretations of the same texts and concepts? Either Althusser or Foucault or both produced interpretations that were purely arbitrary and subjective, interpretations that, by attempting to move beyond the letter of Derrida's text to its meaning, left the text behind altogether or, on the contrary, the contradictory readings are themselves already inscribed in the text in a manner that permits no resolution or harmonization. After all, what would authorize us to think that Derrida's texts would themselves escape the movement of difference-deferral that they describe, that they themselves would not possess the same irreducible heterogeneity as the texts they discuss? To recognize such a movement would exclude in advance any simple chronologization of the conflicts internal to Derrida's philosophical work, e.g., any notion that the materialist Derrida of the sixties was succeeded by the idealist Derrida of the nineties. Instead we would be compelled to explain the way in which, for example, Derrida's discussion of the trace is itself marked by a 'logic of the trace', in its very movement diverging from itself, its effects staggered, some waiting for a precise but unforeseeable combination of theoretico-practical elements to explode in a volcanic fashion, transforming the landscape around them. Does the conflict of which the opposing remarks of Althusser and Foucault are an indication then persist even into *Specters*? Is the concept of spirit as it functions in Derrida's text not itself subject to a 'logic of the spirit'?

It is precisely this conflict that would seem to be at play in the distinction between spirit and specter. A few pages into the work, Derrida announces: 'the spirit, the specter are not the same thing, and we will have to sharpen this difference' (*SM*, 6). The specter is much easier to define, to identify to the extent that spirit is that which escapes definition and identity. The specter 'is a paradoxical incorporation, the becoming-body, a certain phenomenal and carnal form of the spirit' (*SM*, 6). Why paradoxical? Because the spirit is seen only to the extent that it inhabits a visible, sensible body, it is heard only to the extent that its words are embodied in the materiality of voice. Paradoxical because the spirit produces effects only by taking on a material form. But as Derrida warns us, we must not confuse spirit and specter, spirit with its (material) appearances or incarnations: the spirit must exist 'before its first apparition', even if in the form of a promise or a hope. The promise must be detachable, separable from its material, historical forms, in order not to be exhausted by them, in them. Before and outside the flesh, the spirit. In this way, the spirit or a spirit of Marxism, that is, one of its promises, will survive the parties, unions and mass organizations, all the practical forms that Marxism has so far taken, one day, in the future, to be realized in new, perhaps better, forms. But the distinction between spirit and specter so crucial to Derrida is difficult to maintain; there is a constant danger (the inverse of the danger that, according to Derrida, faces Marx in *The German Ideology*) that spirit will disappear into its material manifestations and become confused with them that an otherwise unthinkable death of the spirit, the death of that which is beyond death, and therefore a death beyond the life after death takes place, the eruption of a dialectic without origin or end of the becoming real of the spirit, of a spirit always already materialized. We would then be confronted with a material world without anything (even a thing that takes the form of no-thing, beyond presence, beyond existence) prior to (a promise to be kept, a hope to be realized), before, behind or within the materiality of 'its' manifestations. Little wonder then that Derrida would attempt to halt the movement of deconstruction at precisely this point, to hold in reserve a beyond, beyond which it is not permitted (although clearly not impossible) to go: the 'undeconstructibility of a certain idea of justice' is grounded in that very idea of justice which cannot, must not be deconstructed. To deconstruct it would be to show the inseparability of this idea from a specific, singular material, historical existence, to dissociate Marxism from any 'messianic eschatology', that is, from the promise at its origin and waiting as the (possible) end of all the efforts expended on its behalf. A Marxism inseparable from its material forms, a Marxism without a transcendental promise or spirit, is dead, a body that has given up the ghost, or rather a body whose spirit has suffered that death beyond death, the death that survives life after death.

And yet the too solid flesh of Marxism will not melt, and every effort to resolve it into its spirit encounters an irreducible materiality, a materiality before which or outside of which there is nothing, no origin, no original spirit of Marxism of which its historical forms would be only expressions, secondary and inessential. The inescapable materiality of the spirit of Marxism, the fact that it always arrives 'clothed' in its material 'expressions', is captured in Derrida's discussion of the paradox attending the appearance of Hamlet's father: his spirit is covered with armor 'from head to foot', an armoring that 'no stage production will ever be able to leave out' (*SM*, 8), for the simple reason that if the spirit were not visible, if it did not inhabit a material form, it could have no effect on the world that it haunts. It can never reveal itself as spirit; it can only reveal itself by means of what might be merely a 'technical prosthesis' that both masks and protects it. We might say the spirit of Hamlet's father can only reveal itself by means of a material supplement that would appear to be foreign to it but without which it cannot be seen or heard.

But the spirit is not completely covered as Derrida first suggested. The visor of the helmet is up, revealing (and here is the paradox which in some measure escapes Derrida) not pure spirit but a face, the physiognomy and therefore the body, as opposed to the soul, of the murdered king. For us to maintain the distinction between the spirit and the specter, there must be some transcendental element, incorporeal and immaterial, which would nevertheless be present to the movement of corporealization or materialization which would itself always be derivative in relation to this ideal origin. But, as Derrida notes, 'for there to be a ghost, there must be a return to the body, but to a body that is more abstract than ever. The spectrogenic process corresponds therefore to a paradoxical *incorporation*' (*SM*, 126). In fact, if we read Derrida's description of the ghost in *Hamlet* to the letter, the spirit as spirit is never present, not even to or in its own objectification. The lifting of the veil reveals only another veil: inside the body of armor is only another body, the inside of the outside is only another outside. Even the spirit's voice is just that: not pure meaning or intelligibility but words, sounds, forces, movements, representations of an original intention that is notoriously absent, or rather, present only in its expressions. The helmet effect or visor effect thus, far from revealing the presence of spirit, marks instead its erasure, the trace of an origin which was never present.

But perhaps because it is precisely the meaning of Marx's work that is at stake in Derrida's text, we can no longer omit Marx from our discussion. For, as Derrida reminds us, Marx's materialism, for all its rigor, would appear to preserve a place for spirit. We might even go so far as to say that Marx's materialism (at least in *The German Ideology*) paradoxically produces a 'dematerialization' of a significant part of social reality whose ideality is affirmed in its very name: ideology. Thus Marx could write that ideology 'has no history' because it consists of 'phantoms' that are distillations of the 'material life-process' (*German Ideology*, 47). Ideology exists, but only outside the material world, even outside of reality. According to Althusser, Marx regarded ideology as 'a pure dream, empty and vain, constituted by the "day's residues" from the only full and positive reality' ('Ideology', 160), it consists of nothing more than 'ideas endowed by definition with a spiritual existence' ('Ideology', 167). The history and meaning of ideology are thus only to be found outside of it; it is nothing more than the ghost of the material world, a spirit to be chased away or exorcized. Indeed, ideology would seem to mark the process of a 'becoming immaterial' of the world.

As Althusser also shows, however, in 'Ideology and Ideological State Apparatuses', Marx's text is not reducible to the conception of ideology that admittedly dominates it. For when Marx writes of Stirner and Co. that 'it has not occurred to any of these philosophers to inquire into the connection of German philosophy with German reality, the relation of their criticism to their own material surroundings', he is, in a sense, noting what Derrida calls the helmet effect. For what the Young Hegelians regard as a spiritual enterprise, criticism in the name of Spirit, is spiritual 'only in their imagination' (*Holy Family*, 11). As Althusser explains it 'ideology always exists in an apparatus and its practice or practices' ('Ideology', 166) and 'the ideas of a human subject always exist in his actions' ('Ideology', 168). Is it significant that Derrida's sole reference to Althusser's famous essay is when he argues that the survival of a spirit of Marx after the disappearance of 'the "marxist" ideological apparatuses' (thus granting to the undeconstructible 'idea of justice' that is one of Marx's spirits a transcendence that Althusser explicitly refuses it) will deprive Derrida of any excuse for failing to heed the spirit of Marx? But does not the helmet effect, as Derrida employs it, compel us to recognize with Althusser the materiality in which spirit is always immanent? Can there be a spirit of Marxism that is not always already realized in practical forms, that can appear in the world in any other way than arm(or)ed from head to foot?

In 1841 Marx copied into a notebook the following passage from Spinoza's *Tractatus Theologico-Politicus*: '[the] right (*jus*) to command as they please belongs to sovereigns only as long as they really exercise the greatest power; if they lose this power, they lose at the same time the right to command' (*Cahiers*, 59–60). And perhaps no one had so rigorously developed what Derrida calls the helmet effect as Spinoza, for whom the social was a field of opposing forces and thus for whom there was no idea of justice not already immanent in power relations, no thought that was not immanent in action and no spirit without body. While Derrida ('Force of Law') seems to regard justice outside the law and the state (even a law and state to be realized) as beyond force (which, as Foucault has argued, is not the same thing as violence), and therefore endowed with an undeconstructible spiritual existence, Marx, in the spirit of Spinoza, spoke of a specter that could in no way be understood as 'what one imagines, what one thinks one sees and which one projects – on an imaginary screen when there is nothing to see' (*SM*, 100–01). On the contrary, the specter that confronted 'the powers of old Europe' certainly inhabited a bodily form which in fact it could not be said to pre-exist. Like the ghost of Hamlet's father, the spirit of Marxism, the idea of justice that it defines, the hopes and promises that it offers, all made their appearance in the world already armed: the strikes, disorders and riots of the working classes in Europe.[2] The movements of struggle and the diverse organizations that take shape within them, far from killing the spirit of Marxism, are the sole form in which it can, in its irreducible diversity, live. Subverting every pneumacentrism, Marx, very early on, rejected the Kantian notion of the 'weapon of criticism' in favor of a 'criticism of weapons', recognizing that theory became effective only to the extent that it was materialized in the form of mass movements: 'material force can only be overthrown by material force' ('Contribution').

Finally, it would seem that the importance of *Specters of Marx* lies rather in the questions and problems (rather than any answers or [re]solutions) that are produced by its movement, by the turbulence of its conflicts. How do we live the present, in its very non-contemporaneity with itself, without a spirit always walking before us, reassuring us with its non-presence, its negativity, as if to live would paradoxically be the ultimate death? How do we act in a historical present so immensely 'overdetermined' that it may be thought of, as Althusser suggested in his last writings, as a throw of the dice whose outcome is never what is expected or hoped for, or, if it is, not because we hoped or desired it? The non-contemporaneity of the present with itself is less a matter of spirits lingering than of untimely forces (the unity of which is never given in advance) that resist and discompose a domination which aspires to be total, that prevent the present from closing upon itself in the form of the totality of the world-spirit of economic and political liberalism. To combine these forces, to increase their power: such is the necessity and the imperative before us. For there is a chance, and nothing more than a chance, that the spirit armed may prevail. It is certain, however, that the unarmed spirit, no matter how just its cause, will come to ruin.

Notes

1. Unfortunately, the phrase '*il n'y a pas de hors-texte*', which stresses the materiality of texts, their irreducibility to something 'more real' than themselves, the need to seek another way of understanding their determination than through the concept of representation, was rendered 'there is nothing outside the text' – a phrase which, even with the French placed next to it in brackets, suggests an idealism foreign to *Of Grammatology*. Thus 'there is nothing outside the text' became the flash-point for a misunderstanding of Derrida's work that continues to proliferate today.

2. In the years preceding the *Communist Manifesto*, Marx and Engels studied the workers' movements, especially in England and Germany, very closely and described communism as the objective result of these struggles. See particularly Engels's comments on the revolt of the Silesian weavers in 1844 and his *Condition of the Working Class in England* (1845).

References

Louis Althusser, 'Ideology and Ideological State Apparatuses', in *Lenin and Philosophy*, trans. Ben Brewster (New York: Monthly Review Press, 1971).

——'Philosophie et marxisme', *Sur la philosophie* (Paris: Gallimard, 1994).

Jacques Derrida, 'Force of Law: the "Mystical Foundation of Authority"', in *Deconstruction and the Possibility of Justice* (New York: Routledge, 1992).

——*Of Grammatology*, trans. Gayatri Chakravorty Spivak (Baltimore: Johns Hopkins University Press, 1976).

——*Specters of Marx*, trans. Peggy Kamuf (New York and London: Routledge, 1994).

——'Freud and the Scene of Writing', in *Writing and Difference*, trans. Alan Bass (Chicago: University of Chicago Press, 1978).

Michel Foucault, *The Archaeology of Knowledge*, trans. A.M. Sheridan Smith (New York: Harper, 1976).

——'My Body, This Paper, This Fire', in *The Oxford Literary Review* 4.1 (1979), 11–27.

——'Réponse à Derrida', in *Dits et écrits* (4 vols, Paris: Gallimard, 1994), vol. 2.

——'What is an Author?', in *Language, Counter-Memory, Practice*, ed. Donald F. Bouchard, trans. Donald F. Bouchard and Sherry Simon (Ithaca: Cornell University Press, 1977).

——'Qu'est-ce qu'un auteur?', in *Dits et écrits* (4 vols, Paris: Gallimard, 1994), vol. 1.

G.W.F. Hegel, *The Phenomenology of Spirit*, trans. T.M. Knox (Oxford: Clarendon, 1977).

Pierre Macherey, 'Marx dématérialisé ou l'esprit de Derrida', in *Europe* 780 (avril 1994), 164–72.

Karl Marx, '*Le Traité Théologico-Politique* et la *Correspondance* de Spinoza: trois cahiers d'étude de l'année 1841', in *Cahiers Spinoza* 1 (1977), 29–157.

——'Toward a Contribution to the Critique of Hegel's Philosophy of Right', in *Collected Works*, vol. 3 (New York: International, 1975).

Karl Marx and Frederick Engels, *The German Ideology*, in *Collected Works*, vol. 5 (New York: International, 1975).

——*The Holy Family*, in *Collected Works*, vol. 4 (New York: International, 1975).

Edward W. Said, 'The Problem of Textuality: Two Exemplary Positions', in *Critical Inquiry* (Summer 1978), 673–714.

Benedict de Spinoza, *Tractatus Theologico-Politicus*, trans. Samuel Shirley (Leiden: Brill, 1989).

5

Marxism without Marxism

Terry Eagleton

There is no doubt that Derridean deconstruction was a political project from the outset, or that Jacques Derrida himself, in some suitably indeterminate sense, has always been a man of the Left. Nobody aware of the rigidly hierarchical nature of the French academic system could miss the political force of deconstruction's having originally germinated in its unwelcoming bosom, as the joker in the high-rationallist pack. In, but also out, since Derrida himself is a Sephardic-Jewish Algerian (post-) colonial, whose early encounters with a glacial Parisian high culture were, so one gathers, of an uncomfortably estranging kind. The Algerian connection, among other things, brought him close to Louis Althusser's celebrated circle in the rue d'Ulm, and so to a Marxism appealing in its anti-humanism while in other ways still too metaphysical for his taste. But Derrida has often been found insisting on the institutional rather than merely textual nature of deconstruction, so that it is not wholly surprising that the encounter with Marxism which, some decades back in *Positions*, he wryly announced as 'still to come' has finally, in some sense, arrived. He has, as the actress said to the bishop, been an unconscionably long time coming, and it is, as he is himself well aware, a mighty odd time to come; but the obvious point for a disgruntled Marxist to make – that Derrida has turned to Marxism just when it has become marginal, and so, in his poststructuralist reckoning, rather more alluring – is indeed too obvious to labour, if not to mention. If it is hard to resist asking, plaintively, where was Jacques Derrida when we needed him, in the long dark night of Reagan–Thatcher, it is also the case that Marxist fellow-travellers are thin enough on the ground these days to forbid one the privilege of looking a gift horse in the mouth, if not exactly of killing the fatted calf.

Even so, there is something pretty rich, as well as movingly sincere, about this sudden dramatic somersault onto a stalled bandwagon. For *Specters of Marx* doesn't just want to catch up with Marxism; it wants to outleft it by claiming that deconstruction was all along a radicalized version of the creed. 'Deconstruction,' Derrida remarks, 'has never had any sense or interest, in my view at least, except as a radicalization, which is to say also *in the tradition* of a certain Marxism, in a certain *spirit of Marxism*'. This would certainly come as unpleasant news to Geoffrey Hartman, J. Hillis Miller or the late Paul de Man, who would no doubt read it for what, in part, it is: a handy piece of retrospective revisionism which hardly tallies with the historical phenomenon known in Cornell or California as deconstruction, however much it may reflect the (current) intentions of its founder. Perhaps de Man and the Californians got it wrong, in which case it is strange that Derrida did not chide them for such an egregious blunder. Whatever Derrida himself may now like to think, deconstruction – he must surely know it – has in truth operated as nothing in the least like a radicalized Marxism, but rather as an ersatz form of textual politics in an era when, socialism being on the run, academic leftists were grateful for a displaced brand of dissent which seemed to offer the twin benefits of at once outflanking Marxism in its audacious avant-gardism, and generating a sceptical sensibility which pulled the rug out from under anything as drearily undeconstructed as solidarity, organization or calculated political action. It was thus something of a godsend to North American oppositionalists whose outlets for political action were dismally few, ratifying a historically imposed inertia in glamorously ultra-libertarian terms.

Deconstruction has always shown the world two faces, the one prudently reformist, the other ecstatically ultra-leftist. Its problem has been that the former style of thought is acceptable but unspectacular; the latter exhilarating, but implausible. If its stance towards orthodox Marxism is not much more than a kind of anti-dogmatic *caveat*, then there is little to distinguish it from a host of familiar anti-Stalinisms. Such is the trouble with a work like, say, the American deconstructionist Michael Ryan's *Marxism and Deconstruction*, which argues for dynamic, open-ended, unmetaphysical, anti-foundational, multi-levelled, non-mechanistic Marxism in a style that only a paid-up member of the Khmer Rouge might find mildly scandalous. How is a deconstructed Marxism different from, say, what the later Raymond Williams taught? If, on the other hand, deconstruction is to be more than some familiar *marxisant* revisionism or boring brand of left-liberalism, then it has to press its anti-metaphysical, anti-systemic, anti-rationalist claims to flamboyantly anarchic extremes, thus gaining a certain brio and panache at the risk of a drastic loss of intellectual credibility. The callower sort of epigones, who haven't all that much politically to lose, generally go in for the latter style of argument; the *maître* himself, who really *is* politically earnest and engaged, whose relevant contexts are Auschwitz and Algeria, Althusser, the ANC and Eastern Europe rather than Ithaca or Irvine, veers from one style to the other, rigorous philosophizing to portentous poeticizing, as it suits his purpose. The portentousness is ingrained in the very letter of this book, as one theatrically inflected rhetorical question tumbles hard on the heels of another in a tiresomely mannered syntax which lays itself wide open to parody. What is it, now, to chew carrots? Why this plural? Could there ever be more than one of them? Could this question even have meaning? Could one even speak of the 'chewing' of a carrot, and if so how, why, to whom, with what onto-teleo-theological animus?

The high humourlessness of Derrida's literary style – French 'playfulness' is a notoriously high-toned affair – reflects a residual debt to the academic world he has so courageously challenged. But there is no doubting the political passion at work in this book. If Marxism has become more attractive to Derrida on account of its marginality, it is also more appealing in the light of the unsavoury political alternatives to it. He is stirred to unwonted anger by the smug triumphalism of the New World Order, and relentlessly pursues the hapless Fukuyama through a series of admirably irate pages. If his critique is considerably less original than, say, Perry Anderson's essay on the subject, it is eloquent testimony to its author's enduring radicalism. Yet the truth is that Derrida – witness his embarrassingly disingenuous apologias for the collaborationist de Man – has never been at his most impressive when at his most politically explicit. His vague portmanteau talk here of 'tele-techno-medio-economic and scientifico-military forces', a kind of slipshod late-Frankfurt swearing, contrasts tellingly with the precision of his philosophical excursions elsewhere. Elsewhere rather than here – for what we have in this text, by and large, is a political discourse of an averagely-intelligent-layperson kind, and a philosophical rhetoric, of spectrality and the messianic, which is at once considerably more subtle and a good deal less convincing. The two registers subsist cheek-by-jowl without ever adequately interacting; the former committed yet rather crude, the latter exciting yet evanescent. They represent the two faces of Derrida, *émigré* and *éminence grise*, which have so far – but how could he wish it? – failed to merge into a persuasively coherent voice.

There is an exasperating kind of believer who holds what he does until he meets someone else who holds the same. At this point, confronted with the bugbear of an 'orthodoxy', he starts nervously to retract, or at least to qualify. There is more than a touch of this adolescent perversity in Derrida, who like many a postmodernist appears to feel (it is a matter of sensibility rather than reasoned conviction) that the dominant is *ipso facto* demonic and the marginal precious *per se*. One condition of the unthinking postmodern equation of the marginal with the creative, apart from a convenient obliviousness to such marginal groups as Fascists, is the rolling back of political movements which are at once mass and oppositional. The mark of a genuine radical is a hearty desire to stop having to be so obdurately oppositional, a sentiment one can hardly imagine as dear to the heart of a deconstructionist. If one takes the point of James Joyce's retort to an invitation to return to a newly independent Irish republic – 'So as to be its first critic?' – one also registers the self-indulgence.

Derrida has now taken Marxism on board, or at least dragged it halfway up the gangplank, because he is properly enraged by liberal-capitalist complacency; but there is also something unavoidably opportunist about his political pact, which wants to exploit Marxism as critique, dissent, conveniently belabouring instrument, but is far less willing to engage with its positivity. What he wants, in effect, is a Marxism without Marxism, which is to say a Marxism on his own coolly appropriative terms. 'We would be tempted to distinguish this *spirit* of the Marxist critique . . . at once from Marxism as ontology, philosophical or metaphysical system, as "dialectical materialism", from Marxism as historical materialism or method, and from Marxism incorporated in the apparatuses of party, State, or workers' International.' It would not be difficult to translate this into the tones of a (suitably caricatured) liberal Anglicanism: we must distinguish the *spirit* of Christianity from such metaphysical baggage as the existence of God, the divinity of Christ, organized religion, the doctrine of the resurrection, the superstition of the Eucharist and the rest. Or: one would wish to distinguish the *spirit of* deconstruction from the dreary intellectual paraphernalia of 'writing', 'difference', 'trace', organized journals and conventions, formal reading groups, movements to install the teaching of philosophy in French schools and so on. It is entirely possible to approve of the spirit of the Huns, with all its admirable robustness, while deploring what they actually got up to. If Derrida thinks, as he appears to do, that there can be any effective socialism without organization, apparatuses and reasonably well-formulated doctrines and programmes, then he is merely the victim of some academicist fantasy which he has somehow mistaken for an enlightened anti-Stalinism. (He has, in fact, no materialist or historical analysis of Stalinism whatsoever, as opposed to an ethical rejection of it, unlike many more orthodox currents of Marxism.) The truth is that he is hardly concerned with an *effective* socialism at all. Deconstruction, with its preoccupation with slippage, failure, aporia, incoherence, not-quiteness, its suspicion of the achieved, integral or controlling, is a kind of intellectual equivalent of a vaguely leftish commitment to the underdog, and like all such commitments is nonplussed when those it speaks up for come to power. Poststructuralism dislikes success, a stance which allows it some superbly illuminating insights into the pretensions of monolithic literary texts or ideological self-identities and leaves it a mite wrong-footed in the face of the African National Congress.

Derrida's indifference to almost all of the *actual* historical or theoretical manifestations of Marxism is a kind of empty transcendence – a typically deconstructive trumping of some alternative position which leaves one's own case invulnerable only in proportion to its contentlessness. Much the same can be said of his curiously empty, formalistic messianism, which voids this rich theological tradition of its content and retains its ghostly impulse only, somewhat akin to the Kafka who (as Walter Benjamin remarks) is left with nothing but the transmissible forms of a tradition which has dwindled to nothing. The critical, negative passion of his politics in this book is one which ought rightly to embarrass every academic radical for whom deconstruction is a sexy form of common-or-garden scepticism, or yet another way of keeping the literary canon alive by plodding through it yet again, this time with a scalpel in hand.

> Instead of singing the advent of the ideal of liberal democracy and of the capitalist market in the euphoria of the end of history, instead of celebrating the 'end of ideologies' and the end of the great emancipatory discourses, let us never neglect this obvious macroscopic fact, made up of innumerable singular sites of suffering: no degree of progress allows one to ignore that never before, in absolute figures, have so many men, women, and children been subjugated, starved, or exterminated on the earth.

This is not the kind of thing that is likely to go down well in Ithaca or Irvine, where they learnt long ago that ideology had ended and the great emancipatory discourses run thankfully aground.

And what does Derrida counterpose, in the very next paragraph, to the dire condition he so magnificently denounces? A 'New International', one 'without status, without title, and without name ... without party, without country, without national community ...' And, of course, as one gathers elsewhere in the book, without organization, without ontology, without method, without apparatus. It is the ultimate poststructuralist fantasy: an opposition without anything as distastefully systemic or drably 'orthodox' as an opposition, a dissent beyond all formulable discourse, a promise which would betray itself in the act of fulfilment, a perpetual excited openness to the Messiah who had better not let us down by doing anything as determinate as coming. Spectres of Marxism indeed.

6

Reconciling Derrida: 'Specters of Marx' and Deconstructive Politics

Aijaz Ahmad

> Hamlet has put on the crown, but is now wondering why he exists.
>
> – Régis Debray[1]

Institutum Studiorum Humanitatis has done me much honour in inviting me to deliver these lectures.[2] I am quite sure that my visit to Ljubljana at this juncture in your history will prove far more instructive for me than what little instruction I may be able to provide in the course of my lectures. Permit me, therefore, to start by offering my heartfelt thanks for this opportunity.

My hosts have proposed that since so much of my recent book, *In Theory*, refers to postmodernism on the one hand, nationalism on the other, I may, in these two lectures, reflect on those engagements and extend my critique in view of the current situation that you face in your part of the world, I and people like me face in ours. The engagement with contemporary nationalisms – under the working title of '*fin-de-siècle* nationalisms, East and West' – will come tomorrow. For the first lecture, I thought, I should now begin that engagement with postmodernism – or, more accurately, postmodern politics in the shape of poststructuralist theory – that I have been postponing for so long.

That was easier thought than done. For all the publicity that surrounds it, and for all the hyperbolic political claims it generates for itself, poststructuralism is, as you surely know, rather a technical subject, and in order to have a fruitful dialogue, one has to be sure that we are speaking of the same authors and texts – a very *elaborate* set of authors and texts – with more or less adequately shared familiarity. So, I prepared many notes but hesitated to actually write up the lecture, partly because I really did not know whether an occasion of this kind allowed a discussion of so technical a nature – and, indeed, to what purpose? This problem was resolved for me provisionally, in a more or less fortuitous manner, this last Friday when I visited the offices of the *New Left Review* in London and received from the editor a copy of the latest issue of the journal, which includes Jacques Derrida's 'A Lecture on Marx'. I read the 'Lecture' the next day, on my flight to Ljubljana. It struck me that Derrida himself had opened up the space for a dialogue – a *contentious* dialogue, maybe – between Marxism and poststructuralism, specifically deconstruction, as it now stands, after the dissolution of Communist states in the former Soviet Union and East–Central Europe. Derrida's text I read, as I said, on Saturday afternoon. Sunday I spent mostly in collecting my thoughts. The lecture itself, which is simply a reflection on the *kind* of opening that Derrida provides in his own lecture, I started writing this morning – which means that, for all the appearance of a confidently finished text, what you are going to hear is only an initial, provisional response.

A gesture of affiliation

I have chosen Derrida's text for my own reflections for the simple reason that it affords us an opportunity to assess the politics of deconstruction – in the hard sense of the word *politics* – as he now defines it. The section where Derrida offers a deconstructive reading of Fukuyama's much-publicized book[3] does not much interest me, I must confess, even though Derrida's characterization of that book – 'essentially, in the tradition of Leo Strauss relayed by Allan Bloom, the schoolish exercise of a young, industrious, but come-lately reader of Kojève (and a few others)' – is fairly on the mark. There have been very extended discussions of Fukuyama's work, especially in Britain and the United States, and Niethammer's *Posthistoire*,[4] which was published in German barely two months before Fukuyama published his original essay in English, had in any case already opened up a great many interesting ways of examining the lineages of what Fukuyama was to propose. Perry Anderson then extended Niethammer's leads with superb effect, acknowledging what strengths there were in Fukuyama's argument, in a fulsome essay on him and on the larger end-of-history tradition in European thought.[5] Coming so much later, Derrida's treatment of Fukuyama strikes me as conventional. The discussion would have been more fruitful had he offered reflections on the political and philosophical adjacencies between Fukuyama's end-of-history argument and the announcements of the end of all metanarratives that one finds routinely in the work of so many deconstructionists. But this substantial issue Derrida unfortunately does not take up. Had he taken up the challenge he might have come up against the fact that, between the two 'end' claims, Fukuyama's is, strictly on the philosophical terrain, much less naïve.

What interests me rather, is the *real* occasion of this text: Derrida's gesture of affiliation with the Marxist heritage, now that the moment of communism in Europe, East and West, seems definitively to have passed. But, then, Derrida also recounts a certain relationship between Marxism and deconstruction; seeks to displace our historic understanding of Marxism with a different kind of understanding, in a *messianic* tonal register; and, alongside a perceptive diagnosis of the main maladies of contemporary Europe, he nevertheless proposes what I can only call an anti-politics, even if one also hears in the many nuances of this word, 'anti-politics', that nuance of personal witness that Havel has sought to read into it.[6] This latter aspect offers me the opportunity, with reference to this *latest* and relatively more congenial text of deconstruction, to demarcate what it is that a Marxist of my kind would find unacceptable in deconstructionist ideas of politics, even when the ideas are at their very best, as they surely are in the text at hand.

Please note, first of all, the active sense in my title today: *Reconciling* Derrida. The title is not 'Reconciliation with Derrida', in the sense of an older conflict now resolved, or of an act already accomplished. Nor is it 'Derrida Reconciled', which would have had the nuance of a submission, a new-found passivity, on the part of Derrida, in relation to Marx – or for Marxism in relation to Derrida. In either case, we would then have a sense of a gratification too easily obtained. I mean, rather, the active sense of a process, and of a subject: a *mode* of reconciliation; Derrida in the process of reconciling; and we, therefore, in response to the process Derrida has initiated, participating in an *identification* – an identification also in the positive sense of identifying *with* the intent of this reconciling, as well as in the sense of identify*ing* that with which Derrida has here set out to reconcile himself. It is in this double movement of identification that the pleasures and problems of Derrida's text lie for us, the readers of the text.

The first question that arises, of course, is: what *kind* of text is it that Derrida has composed? Considering the plenitude of motifs and metaphors, and considering also the centrality of the *form* of rhetoric for the affects and effectivity of this text, one would be inclined to treat it primarily as a *literary* text. This literary quality is deeply embedded, then, in what I take to be its primary purpose, namely *performance*. We have, in other words, essentially a *performative* text in a distinctly literary mode. A text that offers not analysis but performance: a ritual performance of burial and recouping, hence the motifs of oath and spectrality and promise – a mourning for the dead, as well as the oath and the promise that the promises of the dead shall be kept; in short, a text of affiliation, and more than affiliation, a text of *filiation*, the invoking of the ancestral in a register of the spectral, the owning up to a Marxist descent and heritage, as the night of neo-liberal conservatism settles across Europe, and as Fascism – itself a resurrected spectre, in the guise now of new racisms and new patriotisms – stalks Europe: all the zones of Europe, Western and Eastern and Central.

The work of inheritance

Let us begin, then, where Derrida himself begins: his initial act of positioning himself within his own text by enclosing his text between two quotations from *Hamlet*, which foreground the Ghost of the dead father (obvious reference to Derrida's *title* – 'Specters of Marx' – as well as to the *theme* of the finality of the death of Marxism and to his assertion that *he* and his deconstruction, not communists and those who are generally known as Marxists, are the true heirs of Marx, the dead Father). Here is, then, the opening quotation, with its own repetition of a key phrase:

> The time is out of joint
> *– Hamlet*

Hamlet: . . . Sweare.
Ghost [beneath]: Sweare.
[They swear]
Hamlet: Rest, rest perturbed Spirit! So Gentlemen,
  With all my loue I doe commend me to you;
  And what so poore a man as *Hamlet* is
  May doe t'express his loue and friending to you,
  God willing, shall not lacke; Let us goe in together,
  And still your fingers on your lippes, I pray.
  The time is out of ioynt: O cursed spight,
  That ever I was borne to set it right.
  Nay, come, let's goe together.   *[Exeunt]*

There is thus the positioning: the Son alone with his Ghost, in a time 'out of joint'. (The quasi-religious tone will enter Derrida's own text somewhat later, but we already have the hint of the *Holy* Ghost and his famous Son – and the *loneliness* of the Son as he offers himself up as the unique sufferer for the sins of this Earth.) Then the theme of promise and oath; in this opening quotation, the Ghost speaks but one word only: 'Sweare,' whereupon 'They swear.' We have, in short, Hamlet in the act of bonding himself to the ghost of his murdered father, or rather to the *Spectre*, as Derrida would rather call it, recalling, somewhat later in his text, the famous phrase from the *Communist Manifesto*, according to which it is the spectre of communism itself that haunts the whole of 'old Europe'. The ghost, then, to whom our modern, metaphorical Hamlet binds himself is both, (a) that of the author of those words, Marx, but also, (b) the subject of those words, communism itself, the *thing* – that is to say, the history – that haunts 'old Europe', but which is said to be dead, as Hamlet's father was dead, so that Hamlet could bind himself not to the Father but to his haunting Spirit only. We begin, then, with the figure of the son in mourning ('Rest, rest perturbed Spirit'), caught in the act of bonding ('Let us goe in together'), with a promise on his lips so fateful that it has the force of a curse ('The time is out of ioynt: O cursed spight') but also of heroics in lone splendour ('That ever I was born to set it right'). The promise, then: what communism could not do, deconstruction shall. These themes of inheritance, of mourning, and of promise then haunt the whole of Derrida's own text, which he will bring to a near-close with the words of the Ghost himself – to which, too, we shall return in passing.

Let us attend, then, to the themes of 'inheritance' and of 'mourning', in Derrida's own words:

> Inheritance is never a *given*, it is always a task. It remains before us just as unquestionably as we are heirs of Marxism, even before wanting or refusing to be, and, like all inheritors, we are in mourning. (p. 40)[7]

But the dilemma of Derrida's text is that it remains entirely unclear as to what it is that he is mourning, and why *now*. Why has the collapse of the Soviet Union sent *him* into mourning? Why this identification, so beloved of the very free-marketeers whom he otherwise opposes in this text, between the collapse of European Communist states and the death of Marxism? When, in the past, has *he* identified the Soviet Union with Marxism itself, so that the demise of the one becomes the occasion for mourning the death of the other? In this one respect, at least, the motif of mourning that structures the meaning of this text appears to be based on something of a misrecognition of its moment.

In a broad sweep, Derrida identifies himself as one of those who have for roughly forty years 'opposed, to be sure, *de facto* "Marxism" or "communism" (the Soviet Union, the International of Communist Parties, and *everything* that resulted from them . . .)' (p. 33; emphasis added). That word, *everything*, is so definitive, so sure that actually existing socialisms – not even just the regimes but any party that ever became a part of the International – the regimes as well as the movements – never did anything good, that one does not know why the collapse of those socialisms should have sent him into mourning. Elsewhere (p. 54), he specifies that 'deconstructive thinking' ('the one that matters to me here') arose in opposition both to the ideologies of liberal capitalism and, in his own words, to 'the most vigilant and most modern reinterpretations of Marxism by certain Marxists (notably French Marxists and those around Althusser) who believed that they must instead try to dissociate Marxism from any teleology or from any messianic eschatology'. He is opposed, then, on the most general level, to *everything* that could be associated with the actual history of Communist parties and of the 'actually existing socialisms' of yesteryear; and, more specifically, he has always been opposed and is still opposed to the most 'vigilant' of Marxists in his own national tradition, i.e., Althusser and those around him. And what is it in this latter philosophical tradition that he so dislikes? That they tried 'to dissociate Marxism from any teleology or from any messianic eschatology' whereas, in his own words, 'my concern is precisely to distinguish the latter from the former'. In other words, his own deconstructive thinking seeks to 'dissociate' Marxism from 'teleology' but reconstruct it as 'messianic eschatology'. I shall soon return to this highly problematic issue of Derrida's view of Marxism as what he elsewhere calls '*messianic* affirmation' (emphasis in the original), but the question itself remains: if those whom deconstruction saw as its adversaries – the political adversary in the shape of Communist parties and actually existing socialisms; the philosophical adversary in the shape of the 'vigilant' philosophers of his own milieu and city – have both ended up in defeat, why should *Derrida* be in mourning? Why should he, instead, not be in a triumphant and jubilant mood?

I would suggest that this metaphor of mourning has a very precise and restricted application, to that side of Derrida's philosophizing imagination which *wants* to play Hamlet, *wants* to inherit the legacy of Marxism (now that Marxism is, on his view, as dead as a ghost), which *wants* to be the Prince – the Prince of Denmark; the Prince of Deconstruction – who would have the rectitude to set right a time that is out of joint. In short, he had hoped that the collapse of historical Marxism would coincide with at least the philosophical and academic triumph of deconstruction, not of the neo-liberalist right wing. He is in mourning, in other words, not so much because of the death of the Father per se, but because of the *kind* of death it has been, and for the fact that the kingdom has been inherited not by the Prince of Deconstruction but by the right-wing usurpers. (We may recall here a paradox that Derrida might well have considered but does not indicate in the text at hand: that in the actual play which Shakespeare wrote, the kingdom of the dead Father was inherited at length not by the Son, Hamlet, but by a bystander, Fortinbras. The Hamlets of this world are fated, it seems, to be besieged by usurpers and remain forever un-crowned.) This, then, is the actual object of mourning: not the death but the usurpation.

As regards the way Derrida formulates the issue of 'teleology' and 'messianic eschatology', he is right when he says that Althusser's philosophical project dissociates Marxism from both of these. Althusser surely sought to retain a concept of scientificity and to derive the project of socialism from the contradictions of capitalism itself, not from some voluntaristic or quasi-Hegelian notion of History whereby the working class is *ordained* to overthrow capitalism (i.e., a teleological but also primitive, cyclical notion of history in which the communist society of the future returns to the primitive communism of the remote past, only at a much higher stage, thus closing the circle in the form of a Second Coming in accordance with the messianic prediction of Sal-vation). Similarly, Althusser also insisted that what Marxism envisages as the communist society of the future will not be the end of history (no Hegelian longings here!) but *within* history, so that its development is itself subject to the contradictions that its own historical motion is bound to generate. This insistence was doubtless opposed, on the terrain of political polemics, to the Soviet pretence that what they had obtained was a harmonious state of the whole people that was free of primary contradictions. Equally, however, this insistence sought to free Marxism from a messianic salvation narrative whereby the alienated human beings of the present are given the *promise* of the Second Coming of communism in some distant future when human lives shall be free of all social contradictions, the self shall fully coincide with it-self, and being and consciousness shall be one and the same. We might also recall that what blinded legions of communists worldwide – count-less individuals who were by any standard both intelligent and heroic – to the crimes of Stalinism was precisely a 'messianic' view of the Soviet Union as the guarantor of the salvation of humankind. In capitalist eschatology, this 'messianic' image was stood on its own head: not the End-State of Good but, as Ronald Reagan forcefully put it, an Empire of Evil. These tableaux of Good and Evil, the 'messianic' and the Satanic, then effectively screened from view the actuality of the Soviet Union and the extreme complexity of its role in the world over some seventy years. In absolutizing the separation of the messianic from the teleological, what Derrida seems not to fully appreciate is that the 'messianic' tendency in certain kinds of Marxism has been deeply intertwined with teleological notions of history, so that it is philosophically not possible, for a politics aiming at full secularization, to struggle against teleology without waging a struggle against the messianic as well. Instead, Derrida seems to renounce the idea of socialism as a logical possibility arising out of the contradictions of capitalism itself and pushes it into the voluntaristic domain of acts of faith. Hence the quasi-religious quest of recouping the 'messianic'; hence also the motifs of 'oath' and 'promise' so preponderant that where one used to simply say 'socialism' one is called upon to only speak, in a remarkable circumlocution, of 'the promise of Marxism'. What, pray, *is* that promise?

One's reasons for being a socialist can be far simpler than 'awaiting' the 'event-ness' of the 'messianic promise'. Theoretically, the *possibility* of socialism arises from within the contradictions of capitalism. Morally, opposition to capitalism is its own justification since capitalism is poisoning human survival itself, let alone human happiness. In the present circumstances, the resolve to overturn this globally dominant system does indeed involve what Ernst Bloch once called 'utopian surplus'; but the Utopian aspect of the communist imagination need not translate itself into 'the messianic'.

Deconstruction and the Right

On the issue of usurpation (i.e., the pre-eminence of the ideologues of the extreme Right after the fall of European Communist states), Derrida is wonderfully eloquent and unremitting, as should be obvious from the following rather lengthy quotation:

> No one, it seems to me, can *contest* the fact that a dogmatics is attempting to install its worldwide hegemony in paradoxical and suspect conditions. There is today in the world a *dominant* discourse, or rather one that is on the way to becoming dominant, on the subject of Marx's work and thought, on the subject of Marxism (which is perhaps not the same thing), on the subject of the socialist International and the universal revolution, on the subject of the more or less slow destruction of the revolutionary model in its Marxist inspiration, on the subject of the rapid, precipitous, recent collapse of societies that attempted to put it into effect at least in what we call for the moment, citing once again the *Manifesto*, 'old Europe', and so forth. This dominant discourse often has the manic, jubilatory, and incantatory form that Freud assigned to the so-called triumphant phase of mourning work. The incantation repeats and ritualizes itself, it holds forth and holds to formulas, like any animistic magic. To the rhythm of a cadenced march, it proclaims: Marx is dead, communism is dead, very dead, and along with it its hopes, its discourse, its theories, and its practices. It says: long live capitalism, long live the market, here's to the survival of economic and political liberalism!
>
> If this hegemony is attempting to install its dogmatic orchestration in

> suspect and paradoxical condition, it is first of all because this triumphant
> conjuration is striving in truth to disavow, and therefore to hide from, the
> fact that never, never in history, has the horizon of the thing whose survival
> is being celebrated (namely all the old models of the capitalist and liberal
> world) been as dark, threatening, and threatened. (p. 38)

Derrida is surely right in pointing out the paradox that what he
accurately calls 'manic triumphalism' over the collapse of communism
coincides with a period of history in which capitalism is itself mired in
stagnation and riven by its own contradictions, becoming in the process
more threatened and threatening than ever before; a period not of
enhanced liberty but of far more brutal regimes of accumulation, and
of resurgent racisms and Fascisms. What, aside from the collapse of
communism, makes possible this global resurgence of the extreme
Right in the period of capitalism's own descent into stagnation (35
million unemployed in the advanced capitalist countries alone) and –
if the wanton destruction of Baghdad and the ongoing bullying of
numerous small states around the globe is any indication – increasing
violence? Derrida does not make the connection, but we might add
that it is precisely the collapse of the Communist regimes in the Soviet
Union, Eastern Europe and the former Yugoslavia[8] – combined with
the collapse of labour movements in Western Europe and the parallel
collapse of Third Worldist radicalisms in the backward zones of capital
– that has given licence to the ideologues of capital to move to the far
Right. Derrida's refusal of class politics even in this text of filiation with
Marxism (to which we shall come later) and his denunciation of
'everything' that the Communist parties ever did is so extreme as to
exclude the recognition that the *defeat* of communism and the global
triumph of the most brutal kind of capitalism, the *disorganization* of
labour movements and the *rise* of Fascisms across Europe, are parts of
a *single* process. The Cold War did not just fade away; it was *won* by one
side, *lost* by the other. This unity of a global process he would not
acknowledge but of the outcome he is properly aware and rightly
scornful as he points to the virtually global consensus that now encompasses 'the speech or the rhetoric of what in France is called the "*classe
politique*"' (p. 38), the culture of communication and the mass media,
and 'scholarly and academic culture, notably that of historians, sociol-
ogists and politologists, theoreticians of literature, anthropologists,
philosophers, in particular political philosophers, whose discourse is
itself relayed by the academic and commercial press' (p. 39).

As he himself summarizes this confluence:

> For no one will have failed to notice that the three places, forms, and powers
> of culture that I have just identified (the expressly political discourse of the

'political class', media discourse, and intellectual, scholarly, or academic discourse) are more than ever welded together by the same apparatuses or by ones that are indissociable from them. These apparatuses are doubtless complex, differential, conflictual, and overdetermined. But whatever may be the conflicts, inequalities, or overdeterminations among them, they communicate and cooperate at every moment toward producing the greatest force with which to assure the hegemony or the imperialism in question. They do so thanks to the mediation of what is called precisely the media in the broadest, most mobile, and considering the acceleration of technical advances, most technologically invasive sense of this term. (p. 39)

We can only register our agreement with Derrida that this triple structure of political, mediatic and academic discourses is held together, as he says, by a 'single apparatus' which is not only pervasive throughout Europe but also, as he superbly puts it, 'technologically *invasive*' in all the public and private domains. Elsewhere, he remarks that the rise to dominance of this interlocking structure of Western discourses coincided with and greatly contributed to the collapse of the existing socialist regimes. We may add that this global conjuncture, in which even social democracy, let alone communism, had entered a period of secular decline throughout northern and western zones of Europe, giving way to frankly right-wing regimes and pushing the remaining social-democratic regimes further to the right, contributed not only to the *collapse* of the Communist governments but also to the *triumph* of precisely those right-wing ideologies in those polities too that emerged out of the Communist collapse, in the former USSR as much as in Eastern Europe and the former Yugoslavia, to the extent that even the Left in these turbulent zones no longer offers any fundamental opposition to marketization as such. Had the labour movement been vigorous in Western Europe, with flourishing cultures of the Left in civil society and regimes of at least left-wing social democracy if not a real Left Front in place in the major West European countries, the regimes that ensued out of the collapse of communism would have been very different. Not for the first time in modern history, it was in the existing realities of Western Europe that the fate of the East European regimes, not to speak of the former USSR and Yugoslavia, was sealed.

Derrida does not address this issue. Nor does he consider what the anti-Marxisms of a whole host of post-'68 radicalisms in Western Europe might have contributed to the decline, at least in academic circles, of that very Marxism whose advertised demise has prompted him to make this eloquent intervention. The outcome – outright right-wing hegemony in consequence of the collapse of communism – produces in him, however, a very great disturbance, and logically so. In a particularly ambiguous historical conjuncture – which was marked by the lapsing of the Khrushchev reforms in the Soviet Union; the French 1968; the invasion of Czechoslovakia; the movements of national liberation in Vietnam and elsewhere in Africa and Asia; the emergence of a 'New Left' in diverse Western countries – in that conjuncture, poststructuralism generally, and Derrida's own deconstructionist project individually, had presented itself, in the sphere of intellectual productions, as an alternative *both* to Marxism and to conservatism. We shall not comment here on how much of a real political alternative it has been. Suffice it to say simply that the influence that deconstruction came to command in sections of the non-communist (often anti-communist) academic Left in American and European universities was certainly facilitated by the fact that it was *not* a discourse of the Right – even though many Marxists, including myself, have argued that in its unconditional war against political Marxism, in its antipathy toward working-class organizations and against *organized* politics of the Left, and in its advocacy of a global hermeneutics of suspicion, it unwittingly *contributed* to openings for resurgence of a fully fledged right-wing intelligentsia.

And I do mean it when I speak of 'unwitting contribution'. I say 'unwitting' because whatever other reservations I have about Derrida's work and influence (more about Derrideans, actually, than about himself), I have never thought of him as a man of the Right; and, surely, he hasn't actively *sought* the company of the right-wingers or the triumph of their 'dogmatics'; nor is this by any means the first time that he has declared affiliation with what he himself calls 'a certain spirit of Marxism'.[9] It is nevertheless symptomatic that even in this text – in this mode of 'reconciling' – Derrida takes no measure of how the great many attacks on political Marxism that have been launched by deconstructionists, especially in America, share a philosophical space with straightforward liberalist pragmatics and have been, in their political rhetoric, quite as shrill as that right-wing 'dogmatics' which he here deplores. Surely, he ought not to be held answerable for the deeds of those who invoke his name; and deconstruction has been too much an affair of narrow academic confines to have contributed greatly to the global triumph of capitalism, even if it so desired. Nevertheless, when he raises the issue of 'scholarly or academic culture', more specifically of 'theorists of literature . . . whose discourse is itself relayed by the academic and commercial press', then, surely, he might have considered the connections between deconstructionists and routine anti-communisms, especially in the United States where, by academic standards, his influence has been very large. Nor is it at all clear from the text at hand how – beyond his very salutary affiliation with what he calls 'a certain spirit of Marxism', and beyond the metaphorical language of 'inheritance' and 'promise of Marxism' – the politics he recommends is fundamentally different from the more sophisticated, less cruel kinds of liberalism.

Derrida is certainly not a man of the Right, as I just said. If I were to detail my own sense of his political location, I would have to take into account such legacies as that of romanticism, anarchism, surrealism, even some strands of political liberalism, but not of the conservative Right. So, it is useful to recognize that when Derrida uses the metaphors of 'inheritance', of 'mourning', and of 'promise' he does so from a genuine sense of loss, because the resurgence of the Right has been surely as agonizing for him as it would be, from a very different standpoint, for a Marxist. He has chosen the *tone* of his writing in this text very carefully. It is the tone of a dirge, a sermon to the vanquished, a language of healing the wounds so that new promises may be made that those promises of old shall be kept, even though in a new way. Listen, for example, to the following, so as to have some sense of this *tone*, part sermon, part dirge:

> We must pass by here, we too, we must pass over in silence, as low as possible to the earth, the return of an animal: not the figure of an old mole ('Well said, old Mole'), nor of a certain hedgehog, but more precisely of a 'fretfull Porpentine' that the spirit of the Father is then getting ready to conjure away by removing an 'eternal blazon' from 'ears of flesh and blood'. (p. 58)

It is in this *tone*, more than anything else, that one detects Derrida's will of reconciling himself to that which he has in the past largely opposed. But how does he translate this will to reconciling into analytic understanding of the past, political projection into the future, and an understanding of that very thing, namely Marxism, to which he is now reconciling?

His denunciation of the neo-liberal consensus is accompanied by an equally acute sense of the *kind* of Europe that is emerging: 'As at the time of the Manifesto,' he says, 'a European alliance is formed which is haunted by what it excludes, combats, or represses' (p. 44). Derrida's style here is as elusive as ever, but we can reasonably read – possibly over-read – him as referring to a great many things: states of Eastern Europe and the Balkan regions which this new Europe of the Union will assimilate only selectively, and largely as its peripheral pools of cheap labour; the non-European minorities who are stranded within this Europe so triumphantly *Western*; a whole range of non-European countries that North America and Western Europe treat only as objects of plunder, destruction, surveillance and policing. On this, we can agree with Derrida wholeheartedly. But his phrasing seems also to

suggest that this exclusionary thrust in European politics is a consequence of, or at least a marked feature in, the process that is bringing
about the Union. Strictly speaking, that is incorrect. Xenophobia is
much more acute among the Thatcherites, nationalists and Fascists
than among the die-hard European Unionists or in the Brussels
bureaucracy. What has happened, rather, is that the balance of social
forces in individual countries in Europe has moved so much to the
Right, and the Union is feeling such pressures from so many directions,
that it is in the process of writing a compact, in such areas as
immigration laws, which reflect those pressures.

Be that as it may. This line of Derrida's thought is at its clearest in
his critique of Fukuyama's conception of the world as an object of neo-
liberal globalization. Let me quote a significant passage:

> If one takes into account that elsewhere he [Fukuyama] treats as an almost
> negligible exception the fact that what he with equanimity calls 'the Islamic
> world' does not enter into the 'general consensus' that, he says, seems to be
> taking shape around 'liberal democracy' [p. 211], one can form at least a
> hypothesis about what angle Fukuyama chooses to privilege in the eschato-
> logical triangle. The model of the liberal state to which he explicitly lays
> claim is not only that of Hegel who privileges the 'Christian vision'. If 'the
> existence of the state is the coming of God into the world,' as one reads in
> *The Philosophy of Right* invoked by Fukuyama, this coming has the sense of a
> Christian event. The French Revolution would have been 'the event that
> took the Christian vision of a free and equal society, and implanted it here
> on earth' [p. 199 and *passim*]. This end of History is essentially a Christian
> eschatology. It is consistent with the current discourse of the Pope on the
> European Community: destined to become a Christian state or super-state,
> this community would still belong therefore to some Holy Alliance.
> (pp. 43–4)

Not the least refreshing aspect of this passage is Derrida's lucid
sense that a certain narrow-minded religious particularism – a conviction that what we have at hand today is a religio-cultural clash of
opposed civilizations – is a characteristic not only of some Islamicist
countries but also of the West itself, capitalist Europe itself, in its
moment of greatest triumph. One may even read into his formulation
a sense that, given its wealth and weaponry and 'technologically invasive' dogmatics, the recasting of the European Union in the image of a
Holy Alliance is likely to give it far greater aggressivity than what such
configurations as the fundamentalist–Islamicist one could muster. Derrida's warning here is well taken, even though a very plausible counter-
argument should also be kept in mind, to the effect that within the
existing conjuncture of the balance of class and other political forces
in Europe the Union appears both irreversible and in many ways a

progressive step; and that whether or not the impending Union is to become a Holy Alliance – a rejuvenated Christendom; a White Men's Club – will itself depend substantially on how well a Left position can be articulated and defended within Europe, and how much the Left itself can be made to commit itself to making Europe a truly open society, contrary to what the Thatchers and Le Pens of this world want.

Much of what Derrida says on this account one can accept readily, with a sense of comradeship, the past acrimonies between Marxism and deconstructionism notwithstanding. But what does he pose against the neo-liberal consensus and the particularist closures of Europe, as he speaks, in his own words, 'in the name of a new Enlightenment for the century to come' (p. 55)?[10] First, an affirmation of Deconstruction itself as a *radicalization* of Marxism:

> Deconstruction has never had any sense or interest, in my view at least, except as a radicalization, which is to say also *in the traditon* of a certain Marxism, in a certain *spirit of Marxism*. There has been, then, this attempted radicalization of Marxism called deconstruction . . . But a radicalization is always indebted to the very thing it radicalizes. (p. 56; emphasis in the original)

That deconstruction has been a radicalization of Marxism I shall not accept, but Derrida is welcome to his view; and what he means by radicalization will become clear in the next passage I am about to quote from his text. The point I wish to emphasize, however, is that Derrida is somewhat suppressing, somewhat rewriting the history of deconstruction when he claims that 'deconstruction has never had any sense or interest' in breaking with Marxism, or when he keeps insisting that deconstruction has always been a close relative of Marxism, only more radical. We shall not comment on the kind of parity that Derrida seeks to establish here (and elsewhere) between deconstruction, which has for over a quarter-century been essentially a textual hermeneutic in some limited academic circles, and Marxism, which has had, for better or worse (mostly for the better, I should say), a rather substantial role in the history of the world in the twentieth century, even if we ignore its origins in the nineteenth. That aside, it is certainly true that Derrida himself has generally kept his distance from the more egregious kinds of anti-Marxist radicalisms. However, a great many of his close collea-gues in North America, at Yale in particular, who were so instrumental in obtaining for Derrida his international status and from whom Derrida is not known to have distanced himself, had hardly any use for Marxism; some have been more hostile than others, but a hostility toward Marxism has been a common feature among them. More generally, it is a remarkable feature of Derrida's own account that all the error and evil seem to be on the side of a great many spirits of

Marxism, whereas the history of deconstruction comes out altogether unscathed.[11] For a philosopher so justly famous for deconstructing all rhetorics of innocence, this unproblematic account of deconstruction's own location in recent intellectual history is at least very surprising.

An ambiguous radicalization

With this clarification in hand, let us look at the *second* step Derrida then takes, repeating the charge that what even the most 'vigilant' of Marxist philosophers have understood as the thought of Karl Marx is simply a 'teleology' that 'cancels historicity'. Then, in a radicalization of Heidegger, he identifies true 'historicity' as an 'event-ness' which serves as a threshold for the 'messianic', as follows:

> Permit me to recall very briefly that a certain deconstructive procedure, at least the one in which I thought I had to engage, consisted from the outset in putting into question the onto-theo- but also archeo-teleological concept of history – in Hegel, Marx, or even in the epochal thinking of Heidegger. Not in order to oppose it with an end of history or an ahistoricity, but, on the contrary, in order to show that this onto-theo-archeo-teleology locks up, neutralizes, and finally cancels historicity. It was then a matter of thinking about historicity – not a new history or still less a 'new historicism', but another opening of event-ness as historicity that permitted one not to renounce, but on the contrary *to open up access to an affirmative thinking of the messianic and emancipatory promise as promise*. (p. 52; emphasis added)

I must confess that this identification of 'historicity' with opening up 'access' to 'the messianic' leaves me somewhat speechless. Even so, it is useful to note that on Derrida's view his going beyond Hegel, beyond Marx, and even beyond Heidegger, who comes in here for special praise, was *always* designed to recoup precisely 'the messianic'. In a related passage, a messianic kind of emancipation is identified with Marxism even more directly:

> Now, if there is a spirit of Marxism which I will never be ready to renounce, it is not only the critical idea or the questioning stance ... It is rather a certain emancipatory and *messianic* affirmation, a certain experience of the promise that one can try to liberate from any dogmatics and even from any metaphysico-religious determination, from any *messianism*. (p. 54)

Marxism is thus identified with the 'questioning stance', which is familiar enough from the self-definitions of Marxism itself, but it is then quickly identified, even more strongly, with '*messianic* affirmation' which is sought to be released not only from 'metaphysico-religious determination' but also from what he simply calls 'dogmatics'. This second use of the word 'dogmatics' is significant. Earlier in the text, specifically in the passage I have quoted already, Derrida had denounced the 'dogmatics' of the Right; now he is speaking of the 'dogmatics' of the Left, and even though he does not say so, he is clearly debunking, under the heading of this second 'dogmatics', all those organized forms of politics which have hitherto affiliated themselves with the name of Marx (including, notably, 'the Soviet Union, the International of Communist Parties, and *everything* that resulted from them', as he had earlier put it). We are thus on a very familiar territory: deconstruction as the Third Way, opposed certainly to the Right but also to 'everything', as he put it earlier, that the word 'International' has historically signified. We have detected a certain paradox already: neither the political nor the philosophical traditions usually associated with the name of Marx are allowed to be identified with what Derrida takes to be the 'spirit of Marx', and yet it is the defeat of *those* traditions that is identified as the moment of the death of Marx, which then becomes the occasion of this mourning. This paradox is now compounded further: in order to identify himself with this 'certain spirit of Marx', Derrida must not only strip Marxism of all its political practices and philosophical traditions, but he must also then recoup it only in the indeterminancy of a 'promise', in a 'messianic-eschatological' mode.

As words like 'messianism' and 'messianic' grow to haunt the latter part of Derrida's text so frequently, one is relieved to find that he is keeping his distance from metaphysics and religion. It would appear that Derrida is inspired here by Benjamin's virtually eschatological attempts to reconcile Marxism with Jewish mysticism. In a sense, what we have at hand is Derrida's rewriting of Benjamin's reflections on the Angel of History, but without Benjamin's actual location within Jewish mysticism (hence, perhaps, the proviso that he wishes to detach 'the messianic' from '*messianism*'); all that is left of that side of Benjamin's torment is the *language*, the rhetorical play of an emancipation at once secular and messianic: the image of the hopes of humankind once invested in religion, then invested in Marxism, now to be reinvested, as Derrida would have it, in deconstructionist 'radicalization'. It *is* a relief, as I said, that Derrida's messianism claims to be free of 'metaphysico-religious determination', but what is the crux of the *dogmatics* from which he seeks to liberate his messianic project:

> One may continue to speak of domination in a field of forces not only while suspending this ultimate support that would be the identity and self-identity of a social class, but even while suspending the credit extended to what Marx calls the idea, the determination of the superstructure as idea, ideal or ideological representation, indeed even the discursive form of this representation. (p. 41)

The condition of being free of 'dogmatics', then, is that we speak of 'domination' – a significant Nietzschean word, which Derrida uses here roughly as Foucault used to speak of 'power', as a virtually transcendent category – without ever referring to 'identity or self-identity of social class', or of 'superstructure' or even 'ideological representation, indeed even the discursive form of this representation'. It is on the ground of such renunciation – of social class, of ideology and its representations, of the idea of superstructure – that the coming of a *'new International'* is announced – now that the Second, the Third and even the Fourth are dead. And, what is this International?

> It [the 'new International'] is an untimely link, without status, without title, and without name, barely public even if it is not clandestine, without contract, 'out of joint', without coordination, without party, without country, without national community (International before, across, and beyond any national determination), without co-citizenship, without common belonging to a class. The name of new International is given here to what calls to the friendship of an alliance without institution among those who, even if they no longer believe or never believed in the socialist-Marxist International, in the dictatorship of the proletariat, in the messiano-eschatological role of the universal union of the proletarians of all lands, continue to be inspired by at least one of the spirits of Marx or of Marxism (they now know that there is *more than one*) and in order to ally themselves, in a new, concrete, and real way, even if this alliance no longer takes the form of a party or of a workers' international, but rather of a kind of counter-conjuration, in the (theoretical and practical) critique of the state of international law, the concepts of state and nation, and so forth: in order to renew this critique, and especially to radicalize it. (p. 53)

It is really quite remarkable how much this 'new International' is defined in terms of what it is not, how little in terms of what it is or might be. We had already renounced, in order to be free of 'dogmatics', a very large part of the Marxist conceptual apparatus: social class, ideology, superstructure. Now we are invited, in the process of reconciling Marxism with deconstruction, to locate ourselves squarely in an extreme form of anti-politics: 'barely public ... without coordination, without party, without country, ... without co-citizenship, without common belonging to a class ... alliance without institution ... a kind of counter-conjuration', and so on. Derrida does tell us that the task of the 'new International' is to produce 'critiques' (a very *writerly* 'International', it seems), and he also specifies the objects of 'critique' (nation, state, international law), but it remains unclear, beyond much explicit negativity (not this, not that) and beyond much voluntarism that is clearly implied, just *who*, other than some writers of critiques, are to be in this International. At least some phrases ('barely public', 'a kind of counter-conjuration') suggest something resembling a Masonic order.

Derrida does not specify what directions the critiques are to take, but the projected objects of the critiques of this 'new International' (nation, state, international law) are also remarkably unsurprising. A case could be made, I think, that, more than any other category (including the category of 'class'), both 'nation' and 'state' have been the very special objects of political thought over at least the past two decades, if not the past two centuries, from virtually every vantage point. Within contemporary France, this would notably include Étienne Balibar's scrupulous reconstructions of European political philosophy of the past two hundred years (via Kant, Fichte, Hegel and much besides) with specific reference to 'nation'. What new directions these projected critiques of nation and state are to take, Derrida does not say, so we are left to speculating about the directions of his own future work. The same applies to the reference to 'international law'. Is he announcing the intent to offer, in future texts, the workings of this 'law' on the international scale, much as Foucault assembled his narratives of the regimes of regulation and surveillance essentially in national frameworks? Or is he speaking, again in the language of metaphor, of what Marxists have usually called 'imperialism'? In Derrida's language of metaphoric indirection, the range of possibilities remains infinite.

But what *kind* of critique is this 'International' to produce?

> This critique belongs to the movement of an experience open to the absolute future of what is coming, that is to say, a necessarily indeterminate, abstract, desert-like experience that is codified, exposed, given up to its waiting for the other and for the event. In its pure formality, in the indetermination that it requires, one may find yet another affinity between it and a certain messianic spirit (p. 54) ... Barely deserving the name community, the new International belongs only to anonymity. (p. 55)

The remarkable feature of Derrida's 'new International' – another name for 'anonymity', it seems – is not only that it absolutizes the monadic individuals who constitute no 'community' but that it announces itself, quite aside from its Heideggerian echoes, in virtually religious cadences. For, if phrases like 'the absolute future of what is coming' invoke so many latent images of a Second Coming, in other phrases like 'desert-like experience' or 'waiting for the other and for the event', and in the invocation of an 'experience' that is at once indeterminate and already 'codified', we hear that powerful language of religious surrender and renunciation that is common to the mystical traditions in all three major monotheistic religions. No wonder, then, that the announced 'new International' has the quality, more or less, of a Masonic order.

The settling of accounts

Let us attend finally, before concluding our reflections, to the two main motifs in this text: spectrality and debt. Both are deployed in doubled registers: Hamlet's Ghost and the ghost of Marx,[12] our debt to Marx and the Third World's debt to the advanced capitalist countries. There is certainly textual pleasure in this play of doubleness, and far be it from Derrida to suggest literal parallels. Difficulties nevertheless abound. A central difficulty in Shakespeare's text, which supplies the main motif for Derrida's, is that the murder of the Father and the alleged incest, which set the play going, come to us not as verifiable 'facts of the case', enacted on the stage, but as rumour whispered in Hamlet's ear by a ghost, so that the spectrality of the ghost, who returns to tell the tale, is itself the main cause of our scepticism as to the 'facts of the case' even as we get absorbed in the action of the play. Hence the famous questions: Is the ghost itself a spectre of Hamlet's own imagination, even an incestuous inclination? Is the ghost truthful or merely malevolent? In short, the central issue of the *unreliability of account*.

In the quotation that opens Derrida's text, we detect an identification with Hamlet; in the one that appears toward the very end ('the foule crimes done in my dayes of Nature/ . . . that I am forbid/To tel the secrets of my Prison-House'), we detect a similar identification with the Ghost.[13] So we have another kind of doubling: the ambiguities of Derrida's own situating of himself between Hamlet and his ghost, but also alongside each, parallel but disjunct, in a play of identity and difference. And what happens, in this play of plays, to reliability of accounts? How *was* the Father murdered, and how are we to dispose of the matter of incest, as charge and as desire? (Dare we suggest something of an incestuous desire floating between its 'radicalization' and Marxism itself?) Shakespeare exercises a very deliberate, very authorial kind of authority in withholding from us the means to verify the truthfulness or lack of it in the account we get from the ghost. Could we ask, then, similar questions about Derrida's textual construction? What about *this* Marx – this 'certain spirit of Marx' – whom Derrida invokes, as the occasion of his mourning? Is this particular Marx, spectrality and all, a figment of Derrida's imagination, as *his* ghost might have been of Hamlet's? How *did* the death of Marxism come about? How reliable is *this* account which rests on the claim that the ultimate death was already foreknown, to the writer of this account,

since at least 'the beginning of the fifties', so that the final announcement of the death produces only 'the trouble of a "déjà vu", and even
of a certain "toujours déjà vu"'? Must all other 'spectres of Marx' be
dispensed with so that 'a certain spirit of Marx' may remain for Derrida
to effect an impossible but impassioned reconciliation? Whole histories
discarded as so much rubbish, so as to retrieve, well, not exactly a
corpse but spectrality? Before announcing the coming of the 'new
International', Derrida tells us pointedly that he never had any use for
the older ones. Might it be that there is in Derrida's text a misrecognition? We might at least entertain the possibility that the anti-politics he
advocates might well bring us not a 'new International' but a mere
Fortinbras – a 'new' order that is a variant of the very old one, a
systemic restoration that comes about through a process that neither
his ghost nor Hamlet could anticipate or survive.

About the doubleness of debt – ours to Marx, the Third World's to
imperialism – and about a possible disjunction, I shall be brief. Derrida
does not exactly say so, but there appears to me a rather large
difference between the two debts. The debt to Marx, I think, needs to
be *paid* and *settled*, whereas the Third World debt ought to be simply
cancelled. Where do we stand, then, in this play of disjunction, between
settlement and cancellation? If we are not to end up cancelling our
debt to Marx and start advocating the paying of the Third World debt,
it might be best to start thinking somewhat more accurately, less
metaphorically and performatively.

What, in the end, do we make of this act of reconciling Marxism
with deconstruction which presupposes the abandoning of all the
familiar categories of political Marxism, and which affects this reconciling on grounds that are not only messianic in self-declaration but also
replete with a powerful religious imagery, even though Derrida repeatedly affirms that for him 'the messianic' is *not* religious? There is in this
text, I think, a certain nobility of gesture: a refusal to identify with the
neo-liberal victors, a refusal to surrender one's own oppositional stance,
an affirmation of a will to endure beyond the triumphalism of the
Right, even the courage to identify with Marxism at a moment of
European history when it is more difficult to do so than it has been at
other moments in the past. For this, I think, one naturally feels a
certain affinity with Derrida. But Derrida still seems far too reluctant to
underake for deconstruction that autocritique which he recommends
to Marxism. No one needs the reminder that the whole Euro-American
edifice of deconstruction is deeply intertwined with Derrida's name;
and no one, I'm sure, needs to teach Derrida the crucial importance
of proper nouns in the many syntaxes of this world. Deconstruction
has always been primarily a textual hermeneutic; in its political

declarations it has always involved, to my understanding, not just extravagance but also too much methodological individualism, too voluntaristic a notion of social relations and of the politics that inevitably ensues from those relations. It is odd that in affirming his association with Marxism – or as he puts it, 'a certain spirit of Marxism' – Derrida yields none of these grounds, restates them in fact with great firmness, introducing now a tone of religious suffering at odds with deconstruction's own virtually euphoric self-affirmation of the past.

And what has been our own undertaking in the present text? Simply put: a deconstructive solidarity with 'a certain spirit of' Derrida – with his affirmative gesture in the face of all contrary winds. And the winds *are* strong! We are glad to say, as he himself says, that he is one of us. This new-found solidarity involves no acceptance of the principal categories of deconstruction on our part, beyond the application of certain deconstructive procedures of reading to his own text, just as his own gesture of affiliation with Marx includes the acceptance neither of the principal categories of political Marxism nor of the slightest responsibility for any part of its history. Ours is, as I said, a deconstructive solidarity.

Notes

1. Régis Debray, *Charles de Gaulle: Futurist of the Nation* (London: Verso, 1994), p. 99.

2. Delivered at *Institutum Studiorum Humanitatis* (European Institute for the Study of Humanities), Ljubljana, on 20 June 1994, the text of this lecture makes it quite clear that it was a *quick* response *strictly* to the text of Derrida's 'A Lecture on Marx' as published in NLR 205, May–June 1994. Subsequently a gracious friend made it possible for me to see the as yet unpublished translation of Derrida's book, *Specters of Marx: The State of the Debt, the Work of Mourning, and the New International,* trans. Peggy Kamuf (New York and London: Routledge, 1994). This gave me an ampler sense of the nature of his intervention, confirming a couple of my guesses, clarifying some issues, complicating some others. Thus, for instance, what Derrida means by 'international law' is spelled out in chapter 3; the theme of 'spectrality' now appears to envelop the book even more complexly than the extracts had suggested; and my sense that the spectre of Benjamin hovers behind the theme of 'the messianic' has been confirmed, though it is also clear that Derrida's deployment of this theme takes many very different directions. I have chosen, however, not to respond to the book at this time. I responded to those extracts *because* they had appeared in NLR, and that motivation remains. Derrida's book offers us a very closely structured text, and if I were to take up the whole of it I would be composing a response with a much broader scope of engagements. I greatly appreciate Derrida's gesture of solidarity with Marxism, so I am very glad to have read the book, but this reading does not significantly alter my view of the selection to which I was then responding and which still strikes me as representing quite fairly the fuller thrust of Derrida's thought. I have therefore amended the text of the original lecture as little as possible, for stylistic improvements only, and to accommodate just a few of the several questions raised by Rastko Močnik, Michael Sprinker, Robin Blackburn and Gopal Balakrishnan. I have also added a few footnotes, a couple of which refer to the book in passing. Lengthier comment on the book I have resisted.

3. Francis Fukuyama, *The End of History and the Last Man* (London: Macmillan, 1992).

4. Lutz Niethammer, *Posthistoire: Has History Come to an End?* (London: Verso, 1992); original German edition 1989.

5. Perry Anderson, 'The Ends of History', in *A Zone of Engagement* (London: Verso, 1992).

6. See *Václav Havel or Living in Truth*, ed. Jan Vladislav (London: Faber, 1986), for his particular deployment of the term 'anti-politics', even though my own usage of it here carries a very different and more obvious meaning.

7. Page numbers refer to Derrida's 'Lecture' as published in NLR 205.

8. It is somewhat curious that having said emphatically that he had been opposed to 'everything' that the Communist parties ever did, he now designates, in the passage we have just quoted, these very states as the ones 'that attempted to put into effect' what he clearly calls 'the revolutionary model in its Marxist inspiration'. There would appear to be a logical inconsistency between that total rejection and this description.

9. For an earlier expression of this affiliation, and especially for the very complex matter of Derrida's great personal regard for Althusser as well as disagreements between them, see 'Politics and Friendship: An Interview with Jacques Derrida', and Derrida's graveside oration after Althusser's death in E. Ann Kaplan and Michael Sprinker, eds, *The Althusserian Legacy* (London: Verso, 1993).

10. Derrida's use of the word 'Enlightenment' here appears deliberate and is in any case salutary, considering that in much writing that invokes his name, as it emanates especially from North America and the so-called Indian diaspora, 'Enlightenment' often appears as something of an evil empire, straddling a couple of centuries and constituting all modern colonialisms and imperialisms. Further along in the book, in the chapter entitled 'Wears and Tears', he puts the matter even more directly: 'It [Marxism] is heir to a spirit of the Enlightenment which must not be renounced.'

11. Derrida notes in his book, with some pleasure: 'Certain Soviet philosophers told me in Moscow a few years ago: the best translation of *perestroika* was still "deconstruction".' I would have liked to say to Derrida (provided that it was taken in the spirit of a joke): 'But look at what happened to *perestroika*!'

12. In his book, Derrida's deconstructive, detailed but very selective reading of several of Marx's texts relies heavily on the figure of the ghost and the image of 'haunting' in the rhetorical structure of many passages in those writings. I regret that I cannot now take up the matter of his protocols in that reading.

13. At the end of his book we also find a third, deliciously self-ironic identification – and ironic also about the actual occasion of his oration – with Horatio, again through a quotation: 'Thou art a scholar; speak to it, Horatio.'

7

After the Fall:
Through the Fogs of the 18th
Brumaire of the Eastern Springs

Rastko Močnik

> Marx n'aime pas . . . les phantômes . . . Il ne veut pas y croire.
> Mais il ne pense qu'a ça.[1]

Both the indisposition and the compulsion seem to result from what otherwise is the very motor of Marx's apparatus. If one of the central Marxian concepts is *overdetermination*,[2] then a theory of social structure (with a dominant) cannot be elaborated unless it comprises a theory of ideology.[3] Since historical conditions of possibility for the theory of ideology are such that they block its production *within their own horizon*, any theoretical enterprise dedicated, as Marx's is, reflexively to incorporate its own historical conditions of possibility, may have serious difficulties in providing such a theory. The same motive that propels Marx towards a theory of ideology also prevents him from producing it. Hence dismay and compulsion. Hence also the privilege of the spectral paradigm – suitable both to support polemical verve and to fill in theoretical blanks with stylistic bravura. We could start by regarding *spectrality* as a property of the utterance. At a first approximation, one would consider 'spectral' an utterance with a *dislocated* position of uttering. But since we could hardly claim that utterances normally possess comfortable and unequivocal localization, and since the burden to establish a link to its position of uttering – or even, at the limit, to *produce* such a position – rests upon the utterance itself, our provisional definition of spectrality has to be narrowed: is an utterance spectral with an inadequate, insufficient relation to its uttering position, an utterance somewhat incapacitated to establish such a relation; in other words, *an utterance unable to symbolize its position of uttering?*

Marx often insists upon the uniqueness of the capitalist mode. In what seems to be the most economical condensation of Marx's indications, i.e., in Althusser's reading, the uniqueness of capitalism resides in the structural feature that here the '(ideological) dominant' and the '(economic) determinant', differentiated in all other formations, *co-incide.* Two consequences follow:

1. In capitalist formations, ideological instances become 'autonomous', they have no direct structural impact, they have no grip upon the structure, for they are ('relatively') arbitrary; for our purpose, this means that they have difficulty symbolizing their 'positions', for there is nothing to symbolize – there being no 'positions' besides those produced within the economic sphere;

2. The economic sphere runs by itself, i.e., it must be capable of producing any of the ideological conditions eventually needed for its reproduction which, directly, takes care of the reproduction of the effect of 'social totality'.

Radical as they may seem, each of these theses can be supported further, the first one by an extrinsic, and the second by an intrinsic argument:

Ad 1. If a theory of ideology elaborates upon the relation between the discursive 'form' or 'economy' of an utterance and its (social) position of uttering, then the condition of its possibility resides in *historical processes* that make the distinction between the two 'visible', that *dissociate* utterances from their uttering positions. The condition is then the breakdown of *naturwüchsige* ties between utterances and uttering positions, the disappearance of 'natural' interdependence between the two orders.[4] The advent of conditions spelled out in (1) is therefore logically necessary for the project of a theory of ideology to be possible at all.

Ad 2. Unless we want to consider Marx's theory of commodity fetishism as a Hegelian or humanist residuum, the only way to give it some theoretical import is to interpret it as Marx's attempt to conceptualize *the symbolic efficacy of the economic sphere itself.*[5]

In the present paper, we will:

1. first, examine the aporetic conditions of possibility of the project of a theory of ideology;

2. next, examine the ways Marx formulates the aporia, what solution

he proposes, and how the insufficiencies of his account thrust the theory of ideology into the dead-end of the 'spectral' paradigm;

3. finally, present some elements of a theory of ideology that attempts theoretically to meet the paradoxes of 1 and 2; we will try to reflect upon the present ambiguous role of the ideology of 'human rights' and to show, at least in principle, how peripheral ethno-nationalist constructions of 'the social' follow as an effect of the global neo-liberal economic and socio-political offensive.

1. The aporia of the theory of ideology

In one of the texts where Marx achieves a positive theory of ideology otherwise absent from his corpus, he compares the bourgeois revolutions to the revolutions 'of the 19th century', and writes: 'Dort ging die Phrase über den Inhalt, hier geht der Inhalt über die Phrase hinaus.'[6] Although the passage contains all that is needed to start the construction of a theory of ideology, Marx does not proceed beyond a nice stylistic turn. The trope is symptomatic, though: Marx falls back on the chiastic construction so characteristic of his early writings. This seems an implicit recognition that the problem is detected, but not conceptualized: the mirror-like, 'imaginary' stylism indicates that symbolization has not been achieved.[7]

We can read Marx's counterposition on two levels. On the level of *sense*, Marx counterpoises 'historical content' to 'verbal formulation': he compares an *utterance* to its *effect*. On the level of the *formulation itself*, he poses *linguistic formalism* ('die Phrase') against the *effect of sense* ('der Inhalt') it produces. According to the latter reading, Marx suggests, but does not explicitly formulate, the problem of the relation between a *sentence* and an *utterance* (a historical occurrence of a formal linguistic structure, 'the sentence') – and thus indicates the problem of *intersubjectivity*. According to the former reading, Marx points to, but does not conceptualize, the relation between an *utterance* and the *communicational situation* an utterance both produces and acquires its sense from. The two readings can be reduced to the conceptual field of the dyad *uttering/utterance*, or, in more exact French, *énonciation/énoncé*: that is, to the problematic of ideology.

Why, having spread out the field, does Marx not proceed to elaborate its theory? The obstacle, it seems, resides in the paradox that the conditions of possibility of the very *idea* of ideology undermine the possibility of a *theory* of ideology.

This obstacle at least transpires from the Marxist tradition which, until Althusser, has conceived of ideology as of a certain regular relation between the utterance (*l'énoncé*) and the position of uttering (*position d'énonciation*). To arrive at such a conception, one has to have a notion of *the difference separating an utterance from the position wherefrom it has been uttered*; and one cannot have such a notion unless this difference has historically been produced or, at least, until the conditions to 'think' it have historically arisen. Historical and material conditions to set the agenda of a theory of ideology presuppose that there is no *naturwüchsig*, no regular link between the position an individual socially occupies, and the thoughts and utterances s/he produces; this also means the absence of any *naturwüchsig*, or regular, link that would tie an individual to her/his position, status, etc. in society. *The idea* of ideology thus presupposes a 'free' individual in the bourgeois sense, that is, a historical situation where there is no univocal or easily conceivable relation between the position an individual 'happens' to occupy, and the thoughts and utterances s/he 'happens' to think and to utter. *A theory* of ideology has to demonstrate precisely the opposite. The project of a theory of ideology – inasmuch as it conceptually presupposes a 'naturalness' of statuses, and of 'perspectives' that open therefrom upon the social 'whole'; and, on the other hand, inasmuch as it is not historically possible until the statuses and their respective 'perspectives' break down – is necessarily *belated.*

The position from where a theory of ideology can possibly be uttered undermines the very possibility of its utterance. Such a theory can elaborate upon the utterance/uttering-position relations *of any utterance but its own*. It is itself its own blind spot. It can take as its object any socio-historical situation but the one it depends upon for its possibility. Since socio-historical conditions of discursive formations are its object *par excellence*, such a theory is blind to its own object inasmuch as it carries it within itself. Consequently, not only do ideologies appear as 'spectral' to such a theory – it is its own spectre with respect to itself. In Hegelian terms, the idea of a theory of ideology is the concept of 'spectre'.

2. Commodity fetishism

In the light of these considerations, the theory of commodity fetishism is a *tour de force*.[8] What Marx sardonically calls 'the mystery of the commodity-form' is a quid pro quo;[9] its 'spectral' nature resides in the fact that there is no mystery: it is all out there, objectified in 'things', and it functions regardless of what its agents may eventually think about it – it actually functions regardless of whether they think about it or not.[10] The first effect of the introduction of the motive of fetishism is a rupture that radically redesigns the field of an eventual theory of ideology: ideology can no more be regarded as a matter of 'representations', it can no more be located in 'heads' – from now on, it is 'reified', it resides in 'things', regardless of what goes on in the 'heads'.[11]

The most that the Marxist tradition[12] has been able to make of commodity fetishism has been to consider it 'capitalism from the native's point of view'.[13] In Marxism, commodity fetishism is invested with the status of a 'constitutive illusion', produced by the specific mechanisms of capitalist economy. In Marx, though, the problem is more intricate:

1. On the one hand, he wants to develop the basic idea that in the capitalist mode, the economy is able to secure its own ideological conditions of possibility; accordingly, commodity fetishism is this 'ideology', immanent to the economic 'instance'.

2. On the other hand, Marx wants to deduce the 'ideological' or *the symbolic* capacity of the economic instance *from the structure of this instance itself*; his procedure definitely has an idealistic tinge, and results in the suspicious privilege he has, at least temporarily, to accord to the sphere of *exchange*: 'Whence, then arises the enigmatic character of the product of labour, as soon as it assumes the form of a commodity? Clearly, it arises from this form itself.'[14] There seem to be at least two motives for this strategy:

   a. Marx has to isolate the absolute condition of the capitalist mode – the structural constraint that makes of labour-power a commodity; he therefore needs to develop the concept of generalized commodity production first;

   b. Marx wants to analyse overdetermination within the economic instance itself; he does not develop the concept of overdetermination,[15] but organizes the dramaturgy of his texts by an implicit reference to this absent concept: the first formula he gives of the 'transformation of money into capital' is the exchangist formula 'M–C–M' ('money–commodity–money with a surplus added'), and in the sequel he plays with the 'Utopian' character of the *Mehrwert* – where does surplus-value come from? we see it as originating from exchange; but this cannot be! where from then? – and only then does he introduce the sphere of production.

The work-product fully functions as commodity in generalized commodity-exchange whose 'symbolic system' is dealt with by Marx in the preceding section on the 'value-form'. It is there that we must look for what makes for the merits and the eventual deficiencies of the commodity-fetishism hypothesis.

3. The impossible 'genesis' of the value-form

The decisive moment in Marx's attempt to conceptualize *the symbolic capacity* of the commodity-economy is the transition from 'the total or the developed value-form' to 'the general value-form'. This transition is both necessary (it is forced by the immanent 'deficiencies' of the 'total' form) and impossible to think, at least within the scheme of a 'development', especially if this development is conceived, as Marx tries to conceive it, as a development of a concept (of the concept 'value-form'). Marx spells out the 'deficiencies of the total value-form':[16] the bottom line is that this form cannot achieve totalization and overcome the contingency of the simple isolated equations that compose it in an infinite chain. Resuming the imperfect character of the two initial value-forms, the 'simple' and the 'developed or total', he uses a revealing metaphor: 'In both cases, it is, so to speak, a *private matter* of a particular commodity to give itself some form of value, and it performs this *by itself, without co-operation of other sorts of commodities.*'[17] Still, it is this very 'private', *autistic* perspective that Marx is forced to take as the support for the transition to the general form; worse, he has first to present this perspective, this point of view, as the attitude of *the agents of exchange*, and abandons the previous stylistic device, which consisted in presenting the 'development' as if it were the 'work' of commodities themselves:

> In fact: if *someone* exchanges his cloth for many sorts of other commodities and *expresses thus its value* in a whole series of other commodities, then *many other possessors of commodities* must necessarily also exchange their commodity for cloth and therefore [must] express the value of their different commodities *in the same third commodity*, in cloth. – If we therefore *invert* the series . . .[18]

The inversion Marx here targets is clearly not achieved in this development: the 'necessity' that other possessors 'express' the value of their goods in the same third commodity is bound to the contingency of the initial possessor's position; this 'necessity' only appears as such from a point of view that is itself contingent. What matters for our purpose, though, is that Marx is forced to introduce *intersubjectivity* in order to show that this intersubjectivity is *under constraint* of the value-form symbolism. We should therefore give this gesture of Marx's a strong interpretation: it is the structural constraint of the value-form symbolism that effectuates the specific type of intersubjectivity dubbed in the sequel 'commodity fetishism'.

The suspicious and unthematized interpolation of the mythical 'primal exchanger' comes more naturally if we abandon Marx's scheme of presenting the exchange. Given our present knowledge, we even should do that: for the minimal exchange circuit is not, as Marx presents it, dualistic:

'agent **A** exchanges a quantity z of commodity A against a quantity u of commodity B of agent **B**'

but is a ternary circuit, it is the minimal circuit that Mauss is led to present following a Maori native theory of exchange:[19]

'**A** gives A to **B** and **B** gives B to **C** <u>and</u> **C** gives C to **A**'

Freely using the aperture introduced by this model, we could rewrite Marx's total form in the following way:

'quantity z of commodity A = quantity u of commodity B = (z of A) = v of C = (z of A) = w of D = (z of A) = x of E . . .'

This is only another way of inscribing what Marx considers 'deficiencies' of the 'developed or total value-form': that it is only a potentially infinite chain of contingent singular expressions, unable to achieve any effect of generalization. But this notation makes explicit what is entailed in Marx's presentation: that equivalencies amongst specified quantities of items of the (not yet constituted) 'commodity-world' are, at every step, mediated by their equivalence to a specified quantity of the contingent 'initial' ('*the same third*') commodity.

In order to be able to invert the scheme, Marx resorts to two suspicious devices:

1. he frames the 'development of the value-form' in the manner of the Hegelian self-development of the concept: 'deficiencies' or contradictions of previous 'forms' teleologically propel this 'development' towards its accomplishment;

2. since this general framework only has the effect of condensing the problem on an unsurpassable threshold that separates the 'total' from the 'general' form, Marx feels forced to:

   a. *break down* the 'total' form back into a series of 'simple' equations, i.e., to abandon the progressive 'conceptual' achievement and thus to *disclaim the adequacy of the Hegelian procedure of 'development*';

   b. *invert* each of the 'simple' expressions thus obtained on the grounds of an implicit contention that an equation can be reversed without losing its 'truth-value'; by doing this, Marx renounces a distinction he has taken much trouble to establish, abandoning the dissymmetry between the 'relative value-form' on the right side of the equation and the 'equivalent form' on the left side; but since he will need this distinction again to establish the form 'general equivalent', since all of his development rests upon this distinction, we may say that the 'development of the value-form' cannot be accomplished without a move that is illegitimate according to its own conditions.[20]

Our solution to this problem would be: to maintain the heterogeneity of the two positions of the equation; to profit from the very deficiency of the 'total' form, from its openness or 'infinity'. The chain of equivalencies can thus freely be continued by adding specified quantities of new commodities: it would not be against its logic to add new items both on the right *and* on the left end of the series.

But this possibility to expand the chain *on both ends* changes everything: for having added an item at the left side, we will also put the 'initial' commodity into parentheses. In this way, we can solve the problem Marx cannot overcome; by rescuing the 'initial' commodity from its mythical position of the 'origin', we install it *in the function of the recurring 'same third' mediator* where Marx wants to see it: *we will have inverted the scheme.*

't of F = (quantity z of commodity A) = quantity u of commodity B = (z of A) = v of C = (z of A) = w of D = (z of A) = x of E = . . .'

Marx's problem is how to transfer the item which figures in the 'relative form' (on the left side) in the 'total form' onto the position of the 'equivalent form' on the right side of the scheme, and thus to obtain the form 'general equivalent'. In our elaboration, the 'initial' commodity is promoted to a status where it becomes indifferent to the constitutive oppositions of the chain ('use-value/value', 'concrete labour/abstract labour'), and functions as mediator to any equivalence, i.e., it acquires a monopoly upon the position of the 'equivalent form'. The function of the general equivalent is represented in our notation as the recurrence of the same commodity in the position of an obligatory mediating element of any equivalence.

This recurrence 'totalizes' the series of commodity-equivalencies into the 'commodity-world'. It also marks the compulsory nature of the structure of this world. It is the element under which any agent has to inscribe her/himself in order to become an exchanger. It is the *subjectivating element* of the chain. For by constituting a position of *indifference* to the opposition 'concrete labour/abstract labour', it designates the social character of the product, its 'commodifiability' – and, by that, it sets the conditions of 'socializability' of any agent who pretends to become an exchanger. The recurring function of the *degree-zero* of oppositions that constitute the chain marks *the condition of intersubjectivity* under the constraint of the generalized commodity-economy. By being indifferent to the distinction between 'concrete' and 'abstract' labour, it marks what is *expressed by* this distinction: *the separability of the possession from the possessor* (in the last instance: the separability of the product from the producer); it marks what is constitutive of a commodity – its *alienability*. By entering into the symbolic web of intersubjectivity as constituted by this recurring function of indifference, *a possessor 'subjectivates' him/herself into a proprietor*.[21]

4. The mystery of the notion of commodity fetishism

The metaphoricity Marx indulges in describing the symbolic efficacy of the generalized commodity-economy thus answers a double purpose:

1. it presents the 'commodity-world' as *symbolic system*;
2. it conveys *the specificity* of this symbolic system.

Elaborating the first point, Marx stresses the binding nature of commodity symbolism, its independence from the agents involved, the crushing constraint it imposes upon them: the 'humanist' *elocutio* serves mostly to accentuate this contrast, to convey the idea that the eventual 'human' nature of the agents is left out, is cut off, for, as agents in a commodity-economy, they are constituted by its autonomous logic, by its own symbolic register. On the side of the 'things', the same idea is presented by Marx's description of them as 'sensual-suprasensual' objects:[22] the surplus ('suprasensual') over their 'naturalness' comes from their belonging to the symbolic system and from their function according to its own constraints; it denotes the *material constraint* of the system.

The absence of a concept of 'the symbolic' has a further unfavourable consequence for Marx's elaboration: it *blends together* the nowadays trivial insistence on the material efficacy of a symbolic system, with an incipient analysis of the specific structuration of *this particular* system (our second point above). For if, as we know after Lacan, subjectivation always means alienation into a symbolic register, this particular 'commodity symbolization' entails a systemic alienation of its own: it is constituted by the alienability of the product from its possessor.

Marx is perfectly able to formulate this alienation *as it operates within the system*: not only does the commodity-economy entail *the capacity* of the commodity to be alienated, the capacity ideally inscribed in the commodity as its value (and expressed in its price) – it also entails *the necessity* that the commodity actually alienates itself into the general equivalent, that it 'realizes' itself on the market.[23] For the agent of exchange, this means the 'necessity' that her/his relation to the product-commodity has to be mediated by the symbolic system of the commodity-world. In the absence of a theory of 'the symbolic', 'subjectivation', etc., Marx is here forced to remain within the confines of his negative theory of the 'absence of *naturwüchsige* ties between the possessor and his/her possession', which only means that, in capitalism, this relation is no longer mediated by some system of personal ties; it is mediated by another system – the system of the commodity-world. Marx's negative theory takes a more concrete turn when specified upon the position of the possessor of labour-power: in capitalism, this position is determined by a double negative freedom – the freedom from the ties of personal dependence and the freedom from the means of production. By the effect of this double separation, the possessor of labour-power becomes *its proprietor*. This means that s/he *is constrained to* sell it on the market, and also that, in the circuit of exchanges, s/he figures *as any other agent of exchange*, as any other proprietor of commodities.

By projecting this well-known 'classical' Marxian development back upon the 'commodity-fetishism theory', a consequence appears that, on one side, is entailed by the commodity-fetishism hypothesis, but, on the other, undermines it, at least with respect to its *locus* within Marx's theory (where it is meant to demonstrate the capacity of the economic sphere to secure, by itself, the ideological conditions of its reproduction). The implication is that *the symbolic system of commodity fetishism cannot autonomously sustain itself.* It cannot be 'saturated' unless it is articulated to at least one supplementary symbolic system – which in our view is the juridical system of property regulations.

If the inscription of the agents of exchange into the system of value-symbolism *via* the signifier 'general equivalent' establishes their *reciprocity as exchangers*, their separation (or 'alienation') from their possessions *qua* commodities means their *emancipation as proprietors*. This already means that the completion, or the 'saturation', of the symbolic system of exchange presupposes that it be articulated upon another symbolic system, the system that regulates relations of property. The system of exchange creates *en creux* the necessity of another symbolic system. A system of *generalized* commodity-economy, together with the *universalistic* logic of the juridical system of which property regulations are a part, exert further pressure that this process of emancipation be completed by producing at its centre the figure, the juridical fiction, of the *abstract individual.* This logic had asserted itself already when it forced Marx to introduce the mythical figure of the 'primal exchanger' at a decisive moment of his (failed) development of the value-form; it also forces its non-theoretic entry through the 'humanistic' diction of the commodity-fetishism hypothesis: it is at work everywhere that Marx cannot but present the commodity system as a symbolic system of *intersubjectivity.*

Marx's failure on this point may have originated in his incapacity to redesign his early critique of human rights so as to articulate it to his critique of political economy. After the recent events in the East, we are again pressed to confront this problem: are human rights and capitalist exploitation part and parcel of the same bundle that can only be taken, or relinquished, *in toto*?[24]

5. Beyond commodity fetishism

But what does it mean, concretely, to assert that 'relations amongst humans take the appearance of relations amongst things'? In capitalism, this means that certain vital relations amongst social individuals 'take, in their eyes, the form' of *the relation between constant capital and variable capital*.[25]

For a fundamental 'relation amongst humans' to *appear* as a relation between two forms of capital, two conditions have to be satisfied: (1) the means of production on one side and the labour-power on the other have to assume the 'thingly' form of capital; (2) labour-power has to be separated from the other two production-factors, the means of labour and the object of labour, which together constitute the means of production. Satisfaction of the first condition can only be a consequence of the satisfaction of the second. Separation of labour-power from other production-factors is the determining structural feature of the capitalist mode. This separation, *Trennung, Scheidung*, is the structural cause of the capital-relation.[26] This separation is both *an effect of the class struggle and the demarcation line that separates the two classes confronted in this struggle*.

We have first endorsed Marx's thesis that commodity fetishism is an 'appearance' spontaneously produced by generalized commodity-exchange; we have then recognized a historically specific form of commodity fetishism in the relation 'constant capital/variable capital'; finally, we have recognized in this structural distinction between the two modes of existence of capital the separation which is 'the cause' of the structure to which this distinction pertains. We can now conclude that 'fetishistic' or 'reified' *appearance* plays a decisive role in the constitution and the reproduction of the structure 'of' which and 'in' which it is an 'appearance'. This 'appearance', by presenting *antagonistic* 'relations amongst humans' as *complementary* 'relations amongst things', cooperates in the constitution of distinct structural elements ('modes of existence' of capital) and *integrates* the constitutive line of (class) confrontation into an equilibrated relation between two 'reified' structural elements. The appearance is thus both an effect of the structure and the condition of its reproduction: it maintains the structure by contributing the illusionary, the *ideological*, moment needed by the structural division in order to produce both elements and the relation between them. Through this ideological illusion, the line of class struggle is effectively reified into elements-in-relation, into two modes of existence of capital.

Part of 'fetishism' (the blind spot, as we have tried to show, which both commands and undermines Marx's hypothesis) is the illusion of the self-sufficiency of capitalist economic relations: its corollary is that juridical institutions (regulations of property and contract) appear as autonomous, as distinct and independent of the economic 'sphere'. Under this perspective, commodity fetishism (including its very 'idea' in Marx) is an overdetermined appearance of the specific way in which ideological social 'registers', amongst them the juridical system in particular, *support* the capital-relation: they support it through relations of mutual independence and 'autonomy' – through specific 'non-relations'. The juridical construction of '*liberté-égalité*' operates through this constitutive non-relation to the economic sphere.

We could say that specific forms of 'commodity fetishism' constitute *the appearance* under which the capitalist mode and its corresponding social forms appear to the 'ideal participant' in this mode and in these forms. They are 'capitalism' as it appears to its 'ideal native', *regardless of his or her class position.* 'The ideal native' recognizes her/himself as an abstract individual, subject of contract and property (and subject of other ideological formations), and as 'emancipated' from relations amongst 'things'. Since it is the class struggle of the capitalist class that determines the class divide between the capitalist class and the proletariat as the distinction between two modes of existence of capital, 'the ideal native' is an individual for whom the field of the class struggle, *as organized by the class struggle of the dominating capitalist class*, appears as 'natural'.

The abstract individual is the point where the (bourgeois) juridical system saturates itself by separating (by 'ab-stracting') itself from the economic sphere. This separation also responds to a structural necessity of the economic system itself, for, as we have seen, it cannot be 'saturated' unless it is articulated through a specific relation of 'non-relation' to at least one other symbolic system. Under this description of the constraints imposed upon the production of the effect 'social totality' by the capitalist mode, we can give to the *structural fiction* of the 'abstract individual' a *positive* definition, contrasting with the negative definition it acquires within the bourgeois juridical system. The 'abstract individual' is the structural *locus* of the historical social individual situated at the intersection of (social) symbolic systems, articulated to each other by a relation of separation.

One can easily foresee that such an individual will have specific problems in subjectivation; or, conversely, that a theory of ideological interpellation, specified upon such a historical situation, will have to confront specific difficulties. One may surmise that the motif of the 'spectre' in Marx could be related to the latter; and that Marx's 'spectral' presence in our world could be linked to our embroilment with the former. Derrida is right to think the two together.

6. Human rights

Claude Lefort[27] has argued that the young Marx's critique of human rights[28] falls short of the historical rupture their institutionalization introduces by installing a new type of relation among individuals, that Marx's depreciation is blind to the revolution that the declaration of human rights produces in the symbolic networks of intersubjectivity. Lefort shows how Marx one-sidedly selects his quotations from the 'Declarations' in order to support the thesis that human rights are 'only' an abstract and illusionary political emancipation, and even in that are modelled upon the pattern of the right to property.[29]

In the light of the above, we would say that the institution of human rights performs its role of ideological articulation among different local 'systems' of capitalist relations of exploitation and domination *precisely because* it is 'abstract', precisely *as* 'political' (but also juridical, religious etc.) emancipation; we would further say that the 'right to property' only epitomizes the articulation-by-separation introduced by this new symbolism of intersubjectivity, for it is this right that allows a worker to enter into the wage-contract as a free contractor, and to 'realize' it as a mode of existence of capital. Lefort is right to remark that the young Marx may have underestimated the historical impact of the institution of human rights. They certainly introduce a new symbolic network of intersubjectivity, centred upon the juridical fiction[30] of the 'abstract individual': precisely by being separated, 'abstracted', from any and all particular social systems, the abstract individual functions as a 'relay' to, as the intersection of, any set of them.

Leaving out the 'property model', Lefort's thesis, at its strongest, can be formulated in the following way. The juridico-political system of human rights introduces a compulsory a priori recognition of a sovereign *position of uttering* (*position d'énonciation*) to every individual; it precludes all the obstacles – existent, potential or any that may still arise – to the unhampered exercise of this 'position' by the individual; this is *the symbolic network of the new intersubjectivity*. It is abstract not only because it is blind to any further determination of the individual occupying the uttering position other than her/his individuality, but also because it is abstracted from any concrete contents that may arise from an individual's exercising of this uttering position. It is due to this abstracted-ness of the uttering position that any utterance can be uttered and discussed: every and any utterance is under discussion, because no uttering position is in question. The same also applies to the utterances that constitute the catalogue of human rights: exercising the general privilege of a sovereign uttering position that falls to everyone, any proposal regarding the list can be made – and, after having passed through free public discussion, can eventually be institutionalized. The list of human rights is thus open, but this is a positive openness, for it is reflexively regulated by its own constitutive rule.[31]

This paraphrase of Lefort's thesis shows well the fundamental difficulty of the institution of human rights and its support, the 'abstract individual': they put too much stress upon the instance of the 'abstract individual'. The 'abstract individual' has to perform the function of 'totalization' of every symbolic system in particular, as well as to 'integrate' different systems by producing the effect of the 'social whole'.

(1) The first task, the totalization of particular symbolic systems, is achieved by the mechanism of *subjectivation*, i.e., by an individual's inscribing her/himself under the totalizing signifier of the system, the zero-signifier of systemic totalization.[32] The sovereign uttering position that the institution of human rights assigns to every individual is thus the abstraction of the formal mechanism that catapults the individual that assumes it to the 'point of view' of the 'native' of a particular symbolic system. That is, it situates the individual into the position 'from where' such a system appears as totalized. The 'abstract individual' is thus the figure of the predetermined dupe of any particular symbolic ('ideological') system.

(2) The second task of integration of different systems into a social 'whole' is achieved by *institutionalization* of the mechanism under (1). Different symbolic systems can only be 'integrated' with the help of some 'transversal' function, able to encroach upon any system in need of integration.[33] In individualistic societies, such a function seems to be absent. They solve the problem by relying upon a function that is present in all symbolic systems: the function of totalization, which, from another angle, is the function of subjectivation. Individualist societies achieve the effect of 'totality' by institutionalizing the function of subjectivation in the 'abstract individual'.[34]

7. Identity

The preceding developments only give an abstract framework for an eventual theoretical confrontation with the 'spectres' of our time,

Marx's in particular. To close our contribution, we will show how this apparatus may work in the analysis of a concrete case; its particular interest resides in its demonstrating how 'identitary politics', now held responsible for most, if not for all, massacres and miseries of the epoch, including those of this author's region, does not contradict the liberal individualistic construction of 'society': it may actually follow from it.

We have defined the individualistic situation as one of 'freedom of consciousness', i.e., as a situation where no simple relation can be established between an individual's 'uttering position' (however we may like to determine it) and his or her utterances; such a situation poses the particular problem of how to determine adequate belief-backgrounds upon which an utterance 'makes sense'. Generally speaking, an utterance acquires sense within the communicational situation it, at least partly, itself cooperates to establish. In order to escape the apparent vicious circle ('the utterance meaning comes from the communicational situation which is itself determined by the meaning of the utterance'), the interpreter looks for 'belief-backgrounds' against which the utterance makes sense; if there is a correlation between the speaker's expected belief-backgrounds and his/her 'uttering position', which is itself a part of the communicational situation, then the interpreter has some guidance in establishing appropriate belief-backgrounds. This guidance is, at least in principle, absent from an individualistic situation. In order to show how communication is possible in individualistic societies, which, at the limit, offers some insight into the question how individualistic social construction may be possible at all, we will first indulge in an intellectual experiment, and then offer a theory of the 'nation' as a historical solution to the aporias of individualism.

Lévi-Strauss, examining a thoroughly non-individualistic situation, developed the thesis that dualist social organizations somehow 'spontaneously' develop into ternary organizations. Without elaborating upon its possible relevance for this main idea, he suggested in the same article that in every society there exists an apparently non-functional *zero-institution*, whose only function is to make it possible for a society to exist. Although Lévi-Strauss's own demonstrative material is slim, it is possible to show that the introduction of a third component into a dualist construction is structurally necessary, and that this supplementary structural instance is the zero-institution.

Lévi-Strauss presents the example of the dualistically organized Winnebago village, and draws attention to the fact that informants from different moieties give drastically different accounts of the village-organization: although both representations are dualistic, one rests upon a diametric notion of dualism, and the other upon a concentric notion.

Winnebago village according to   Winnebago village according to
the informants of the upper moiety   the informants of the lower moiety

Figure 1.

From this presentation, we can deduce a *definition of the dualist social organization* that pinpoints the problem of 'totalization' in such a construction: *a dualist social organization is one which allows for two different dualistic conceptions of the social 'whole'.* Such an organization is then facing a structurally motivated communicational (and consequently social) breakdown that can only be avoided by the introduction of a *third* ideological conception, 'neutral' with respect to the other two representations of 'society'.

We can show this in a simplified model of the situation. Let the social world be composed of 'objects' (groups, households, individuals . . .) defined by three oppositions of distinctive features: 'cross-like vs. circular' (x/o), 'large vs. small' (X/x), 'bold vs. clear' (**x**/x). Let us assume that the 'members of the upper moiety' organize this world according to a diametric dualism, based upon the distinction 'clear vs. bold':

Figure 2.

$$
\begin{array}{cc}
X & O \\
x & o \\
\hline
\mathbf{x} & \mathbf{o} \\
\mathbf{X} & \mathbf{O}
\end{array}
$$

Let the 'members of the lower moiety' organize their representation of the social world according to a concentric dualism, based upon the distinction 'large vs. small':

Figure 3.

$$
\begin{array}{cc}
X & O \\
x & o \\
 & \\
\mathbf{x} & \mathbf{o} \\
\mathbf{X} & \mathbf{O}
\end{array}
$$

We could inversely suppose that members of the 'inner' group imagine the social space upon the concentric mode, and that the members of the 'outer' group do it according to the diametric scheme. The problem would remain the same: one scheme classifies together what the other one distinguishes, and separates what the other one keeps together. In other words: one's own representation of her/his position within the social space contradicts the representation of this position by the 'other', as defined by one's own scheme. The only exception are the pairs of the type 'x–o' ('cross-like–circular'), who are classified together in both schemes, although within different sets.

The two dualistic schemes can be integrated by *separating* what is held together in both of them, i.e., by the introduction of a third classification, based upon the distinctive feature that remains non-pertinent in both initial dualistic schemes. This 'third classification' then functions as the zero-institution:

Figure 4: The zero-institution

$$
\begin{array}{ccc}
X & \cdot & O \\
x & \cdot & o \\
\hline
x & \cdot & o \\
X & \cdot & O
\end{array}
$$

The achievement of the zero-institution is that the 'ego' sees her/himself at the same place where her/his 'other' sees him/her; or, that the other, as defined by my own scheme, sees me as I see myself, and sees him/herself in the position where I see her/him.

The supplementary separation introduced by the zero-institution also allows the 'initial' divisions to start functioning as 'cross-cutting' ties, i.e., it qualifies social divisions to function as means of 'social cohesion'.[35]

Under individualistic social construction, individuals entertain different 'conceptual schemes', but there is no other systemic relation to their uttering positions than the atomistic opposition 'self/other'. Under these conditions, the only 'structuration' possible is to determine the *outer border* of the communicational space where this opposition operates. This is the only 'third' or 'zero' institution that can be devised from the opposition 'self/other' atomistically dispersed all over the social field. This kind of zero-institution differs from the one we first developed on a non-individualist model in several ways:

(1) While the 'standard' non-individualist zero-institution *divides* a society from within, the individualist kind *unifies* the social field and defines its outer border. While the standard zero-institution *divides* a society into exclusive divisions, the individualist zero-institution *totalizes* a society into an inclusive whole.

(2) While the standard zero-institution defines itself in relation to *other institutions* of the *same* society, the individualist zero-institution defines itself in relation to the *same institution* of *other* societies.

We conceive *the nation as the zero-institution*, pertaining to *the individualist type of society*. It differs from the non-individualist zero-institution in that it is *inclusive in the heterogeneous dimension* (it includes other institutions of the same society), *and exclusive in the homogeneous dimension* (it excludes other institutions of the same kind, i.e., other nations); the standard non-individualist zero-institution, by contrast, is *exclusive in the heterogeneous dimension* and is *inclusive in the homogeneous dimension*.

The national zero-institution functions as a formal matrix within which any notional scheme can be effectuated. One of its 'realizations' can thus be the 'national language': it functions as the formal matrix of mutual translatability of all actual or possible notional schemes. Occupying the position from which the symbolic system of the national zero-institution appears to be a 'saturated whole' is thus, for every individual, a precondition to becoming a member of the national 'communicational community'. The identification with the subject for whom the zero-symbolic system appears as totalized is the *mechanism of (national) identity*.

In nationally constituted societies, the ideological struggle is about which ideology is going to overdetermine the zero-institution. The condition for achieving ideological hegemony is, for an ideology, to make its 'subject supposed to believe' (identification with whom may remain conditional: the beliefs ascribed to this subject may only be entertained by the interpreter as possible, and need not to be accepted as 'necessary') *coincide* with the 'subject supposed to know' of the zero-institution (identification with whom is a necessary precondition for interpretation under individualist construction). This coincidence may render compulsory for the interpreter the ideological beliefs entailed by the utterance under interpretation.

8. The new Orientalism

(1) 'This is a choice between Europe and the Balkans.'[36]

The imaginary geography[37] in the background of statement (1) is: (a) absurd; (b) dualistically organized. As (b), it allows for at least one more dualistic organization of the universe, and is therefore democratic; as (a), it does not make sense unless it is somehow 'normalized'. This normalization will automatically follow from the interpreter's attempt to 'understand' (1), since (s)he has to determine the distinction Europe/the Balkans', left unclear by (1). (S)he is promoted to a privileged position to define this division, for (1) actually conveys to its interpellee that it rests upon him/her to draw this demarcation line by her or his own choice: since it is up to the interpellee to choose whether 'Slovenia' will be in 'Europe' or in 'the Balkans', the demarcation between the two will, in any case, coincide with the outer border of the national zero-institution. In order to 'understand' (1), its addressee must always have identified already with the subject supposed to know of the national zero-institution; as the identitary subject, the interpellee of (1) can only realize that (s)he has always already made her/his choice. For (1) actually conveys this message: 'It is only as Slovenians that you can *know* what choice you have; and since you can only *have* a choice in Europe, you have, in the moment when you know you have a choice, already made it.' The soothing supplementary comfort provided by this logic is to promote the set of 'Slovenians' into a subset of 'Europe'. So why bother with unnecessary intellectual effort, after all?

(2) 'La France ne peut pas accueillir toute la misère du monde.'[38]

Jacques Rancière remarks that (2) makes a choice depend upon a discrimination which remains undetermined and which is marked by the non-transparent quantifier '*pas toute*, not all' (misery). The sense of (2) depends upon the distinction between 'good' and 'bad' misery, of which only the first is 'admissible' to France. Here too, the distinction magically becomes clearly defined, if made to coincide with the outer border which defines the national zero-institution. In (2), it is 'la France' that has always drawn this distinction already, relegating 'bad misery' beyond the confines of the set of 'les français et les françaises'. In this sense, (2) is somewhat tautological, but its point is to interpellate its addressees onto the position of the identitary subject of the zero-institution, from where not only does (2) make sense, but also the distinction it entails affirms itself as clear and done. What is more, the bad misery having been excluded, one can well open the debate over what could be possibly regarded as 'misery' in general, that is, one could start a social-democratic debate over the upper limit of 'misery'. In this way, (2) also entails an implicit surplus of pleasure, a discrete intimation of social welfare concern, of care for the poor.

Notes

1. 'Marx does not like ghosts ... He does not want to believe in them. But he thinks of nothing else.' Jacques Derrida, *Spectres de Marx* (Paris: Galilée, 1993), p. 83.

2. It is true, never explicitly spelled out as such, but *practised* as one of the pivotal concepts of Marx's theory. We take as read Althusser's reading and his interpellation of the concept of *la structure à dominante* into the inventory of historical materialism (cf. 'Structure à dominante: contradiction et surdétermination', ch. 5 of 'Sur la dialectique matérialiste', in *Pour Marx* (Paris: Maspero, 1969). The concept can certainly be further refined, but suffices in its Althusserian redaction for our present purpose. (For an elaboration with reference to the text of *Grundrisse der Kritik der Politischen Ökonomie [Rohentwurf], 1857–1858*, 'Einleitung' ([Berlin: Dietz Verlag, 1953]; cited from here on as

Grundrisse), see our 'Gliederung – rāzlenitev' [Gliederung – Articulation], *Problemi –*
Razprave, nos 147–9, Ljubljana, 1975.)

3. Since, historically and in 'pre-capitalist' formations, the dominant is some ideological instance (cf. 'catholicism, politics;' in footnote 33 to *Das Kapital* Volume 1, ch. 1 'The
Commodity', 4. The Fetishism of the Commodity and Its Secret': Karl Marx and Friedrich
Engels, *Werke*, vol. 23 [Berlin: Dietz Verlag, 1962], p. 96 [cited from here on as *MK*]); this
is the famous 'extra-economic constraint'.

4. Cf. Marx's remarks on the historical conditions of possibility of political economy
in the *Grundrisse*, pp. 25–7.

5. From Lukács's *Geschichte und Klassenbewusstsein* to the philosophy of praxis (in the
West, the best – the only? – known philosophically ambitious and theoretically relevant
Left critique of real socialism elaborated 'from within' and in permanent articulation to
contemporary political and social struggles under a Bolshevik-type regime), commodity
fetishism was regarded as a 'critique' of capitalism. It suffices to glance at the table of
contents of *Capital* to see how risky this interpretation is: the section on commodity
fetishism comes right after the 'genesis of the value-form', *before* the chapter on 'The
Process of Exchange' and long before division on 'The Transformation of Money into
Capital'. In our interpretation, the theory elaborates upon 'symbolic' implications of
generalized commodity-exchange, an abstraction from its historical context. Its eventual
shortcomings should, consequently, be linked to the insufficiencies of the preceding
'dialectical' (Engels *scripsit*) development of the value-form: the Hegelian flavour of the
latter derives, under our interpretation, from the absence of a concept of 'the symbolic'
in Marx; still, the very theoretical failure of the opening passage of *Capital* indicates,
according to our reading, a legitimate theoretical claim that Marx was unable to meet,
although perfectly able to put 'on the agenda' of revolutionary theory. To put the matter
schematically, the long-deferred defeat of the Bolshevik-type of revolutions in 1989 would
not have entailed, as it actually did, the global retreat of anti-capitalist struggles, had the
social and political movements, supported by relevant elaboration of theoretical insufficiencies of Marxian and Marxist problematics, active in the late seventies and during the
eighties, taken their theoretical background more seriously.

6. 'There the phrase went beyond the content, here the content goes beyond the
phrase.' 'Der achzehnte Brumaire des Louis Bonaparte', ch. 1, Marx and Engels, *Werke*,
vol. 8, p. 117; quoted by Derrida, *Spectres*, pp. 186 and 189.

7. In its 'form', the sentence actually mimics the 'contents' it conveys: for what else is
the double *rencontre manquée* between *die Phrase* and *der Inhalt*, if not a double figure of a
missed symbolization; on the other hand, the double squeeze of Marx's sentence
ominously forecasts the impasse of most currents of Marxism.

8. Accordingly, the 'spectral' vocabulary here takes on a parodic, or maybe even an
auto-parodic, tinge. One of the difficulties of Derrida's reading may be that, due to a lack
of attention to the logic of the *work* of theory in Marx, he *levels* different occurrences of
the spectral paradigm, and glosses over the theoretical background upon which they
acquire their 'depth', i.e., their textual relevance.

9. The commodity-form 'reflects to humans the social character of their own labour
as the objective character of the products of labour themselves . . ., [it reflects] the social
relation of producers to the common labour as the social relation among objects that
exist outside producers. . . . Only a certain social relation among humans themselves is
what here assumes for them the phantasmagorical form of a relation among things'; *MK*,
p. 86.

10. 'They do not know it, but still they *do* it'; *MK*, p. 88. The scandal of fetishism is
that it goes against Feuerbach's theory of religion: there is no imaginary complement to
earthly 'truth'; all the imaginary complement that there is is already materialized within
the earthly life of 'things'. Marx is led to conceive Feuerbachian 'vertical' alienation in
'horizontal' terms – but this necessity frustrates his project of the critique of Feuerbach:
as soon as he has laid down all the necessary apparatus to explain ideological alienation
in terms of praxis (cf. 5 and 9 of the 'Theses on Feuerbach'), in terms of the internal
contradiction of the worldly basis (Thesis 4) – it transpires that there is nothing left to
explain. This also blocks the project of *The German Ideology*. There is no other-worldly

complement to the misery of this world – the very development of the project of a theory of ideology undermines the possibility of such a project. This epistemic situation is a strict final corollary to the initial 'belatedness' of the project of a theory of ideology. ('Thesen über Feuerbach', Marx and Engels, *Werke*, vol. 3, pp. 533 ff.)

11. The situation is precarious, though; it can also be formulated in these terms: without (at least incipient) capitalism, no *theory* of ideology; with capitalism, no theory of *ideology*. It is worth noting that in the section on commodity fetishism, the *word* 'ideology' does not appear.

12. That is, those orientations which did not discard it as a Hegelian or humanist residuum: mostly theories in the Lukácsian style of *Geschichte und Klassenbewusstsein*; most importantly, the philosophy of praxis.

13. The term has been popularized by Clifford Geertz; cf. ' "From the Native's Point of View": On the Nature of Anthropological Understanding', in *Local Knowledge* (New York: Basic Books, 1983); the notion belongs to 'interpretation theory' in the humanities and social sciences, which contends that a description of social arrangements and practices cannot be complete unless it takes into account the meaning these arrangements and practices have for their ('native') agents, since this meaning is constitutive of them. The interpretive approach can claim its genealogy from Max Weber (the concept of *verstehen*) and generally from theories that make the distinction between 'explanation' (the task of the natural sciences) and 'understanding' (what the humanities do) (cf. Georg Henrik Von Wright, *Explanation and Understanding* (Ithaca, NY: Cornell University Press, 1971); also, Clifford Geertz, *The Interpretation of Cultures* (New York: Basic Books, 1971); Charles Taylor, 'Interpretation and the Sciences of Man', in *Philosophy and the Human Sciences: Philosophical Papers 2* (Cambridge: Cambridge University Press, 1985). If in this type of theory 'the native' functions as some sort of *petitio principii* that allows the theory to saturate social practices and systems, we propose to consider 'the native point of view' as the symbolic mechanism of saturation, pertaining to any 'symbolic system'. From the plurality of symbolic systems in any society it follows that there could be no unique 'native's point of view'; this leads to the question of *totalization* of (regional) symbolic systems into a social 'whole' (cf. Lévi-Strauss's 'order of orders'), and requires a stronger conceptual apparatus (like the concepts of hegemony or [ideological] domination).

14. *Capital* Volume 1 (Harmondsworth: Penguin, 1976), p. 164.

15. Although in the *Grundrisse*, p. 20, he does explicitly produce the formula of overdetermination: 'Production dominates [*greift über*] equally over itself in its counter-determination, as well as over other moments.' In its 'socialized' form, as an element of the overall structure, production 'dominates over' the concrete process of production, as well as dominating over 'other moments' – exchange, distribution, circulation. In the capitalist mode, production is 'socialized' by assuming the nature of generalized commodity production; hence the necessity to stress, at a certain stage of analysis, its 'lateral' determination by the concrete historical nature of exchange.

16. *MK* I, 1, 3, pp. 78–9.

17. *MK* I, 1, 3, p. 80; emphasis added.

18. *MK* I, 1, 3, p. 79; emphasis added, boldface indicates Marx's emphasis.

19. M. Mauss, 'L'Essai sur le don', in Mauss, *Sociologie et anthropologie* (Paris: PUF, 1985), pp. 157–61.

20. The treatment of the 'development of the value-form' in the second German edition of *Capital* (the edition of the 'last hand' of 1875, the one which, via Engels, became the basis for the canonical text of *Capital*) differs significantly from the presentation of the same concept in the first edition (Hamburg: Meissner, 1867). Marx incorporated the Appendix, 'The Value-Form', from the first edition into the text of the second edition. It is important for our discussion that, in the original version, Marx introduced the 'equivalent form' only at the third stage (on the level of Form III, defined as 'referring back to [*rückbezogen*] the second form of relative value'), where the commodity on the right side of the equation 'presents itself as the generic form [*Gattungsform*] of the equivalent for all other commodities' (Marx, *Das Kapital I*, Auflage 1867, in Marx and Engels, *Studienausgabe II: Politische Ökonomie*, ed. Irving Fetscher [Frankfurt am Main:

Fischer Verlag, 1966], p. 234). The sentence is followed by this fascinating formulation, which has been omitted in later editions: 'It is as if, besides the lions, tigers, rabbits, and all other real animals who, classified into groups, form diverse genera, species, sub-species, etc. of the animal kingdom, there existed also The Animal, the individual incarnation of all the animal kingdom.' It seems that Marx treated the problem we have diagnosed more successfully in the first version than in the second. The same may be true of commodity fetishism. It is worth noting that Engels displayed rather a reserved attitude towards the first chapter, 'The Commodity and Money', of the first version, and proposed to amend it in the Appendix along lines Marx did not follow; Marx himself first had a dismissive attitude towards the very idea of an appendix, originally suggested to him by Ludwig Kugelmann. See the following symptomatic passages from the Marx–Engels correspondence (in Marx and Engels, *Werke*, vol. 31); in particular, Marx to Engels, 3 June 1867: 'you have to let me know exactly your opinion about which points in the presentation of the value-form should specially be popularized in the appendix for the Philistine' (p. 301); Engels's reply of 16 June: 'what is here acquired dialectically should be presented at greater length historically' (p. 303); and Marx's rejoinder on 22 June: 'Regarding the development of the value-form, I have followed and not followed your advice, so as to behave dialectically also in this respect' (p. 306).

21. It is only in this way that we can demonstrate how 'the contingent relation between two individual possessors of commodities' becomes irrelevant (*MK*, I, ch. 1, 3, B, 1, p. 78 – 'The developed relative value-form', paragraph 2). This interpretation also answers the question why the (relative, transitional) privilege of the exchange: commodity production is production for the market, which means that the commodity character of the product is overdetermined by its exchangeability.

22. As a commodity, an object transforms itself into '*ein sinnlich übersinnliches Ding*': an allusion to Goethe's Mephistopheles, as S.S. Prawer reminds us in his unsurpassed *Karl Marx and World Literature* (Oxford: Clarendon, 1976), pp. 325 ff.

23. 'A price therefore entails both the commodity's capacity to be alienated for money *and the necessity* to be so alienated.' (*MK*, p. 118; our translation, emphasis added.)

24. The author of these lines has committed his political life to proving the contrary; so far, the enterprise seems to have failed practically; could it have better chances in theory?

25. 'Constant capital' is that 'mode of existence' of capital that does not increase in the process of production, i.e., the capital in the form of the 'means of production'; 'variable capital' is the 'mode of existence', *Existenzweise*, of capital that accrues in the process of production, i.e., capital in the form of labour-power. Cf. *Capital* Volume I, chapter 8, 'Constant Capital and Variable Capital'; in German *MK*, pp. 214 ff.

26. For the pioneering development of this problematic, see Étienne Balibar, 'Sur les concepts fondamentaux du matérialisme historique', in Louis Althusser et al., *Lire le Capital*, vol. II (Paris: Maspero, 1965; revised ed. Paris: Quadrige/PUF, 1996).

27. Claude Lefort, 'Droits de l'homme et politique', *Libre*, no. 7, 1980; reprinted in Cl. Lefort, *L'Invention démocratique: les limites de la domination totalitaire* (Paris: Fayard, 1981); in English, 'Politics and Human Rights', in Cl. Lefort, *The Political Forms of Modern Society. Bureaucracy, Democracy, Totalitarianism*, edited and introduced by John B. Thompson (Cambridge, MA: MIT Press, 1986).

28. Esp. in 'Zur Judenfrage'.

29. A re-examination of Lefort's writings is needed both for the impact they made on contemporary democratic and human-rights struggles in the 'real socialist' countries, and for their having genuinely articulated certain positions of theoretical and practical critique of leftist provenance. Some of us who have been involved in these struggles actually used to be wary of Marx's critique, not so much for its scepticism regarding the notion of human rights as for its ideological humanist background (the 'generic man' etc.). We now face the paradox that Lefort's seemingly sound theoretical construction has been proved sorely weak by historical processes, while Marx's ideological polemic has been validated. A possible explanation would be that Lefort's thesis is too narrow, for it only takes into account the construction of the state and its juridico-political system, and leaves aside the economic determinant. But this does not really damage Lefort's thesis,

since its narrowness can be used to its advantage. For it could further be argued that, in its bourgeois formulation, the notion of human rights is surely modelled upon the right to property (as the young Marx demonstrates), but that this pattern is not necessary for the notion itself. The argument could be strengthened by remarking that once the right to property has been introduced into the catalogue of human rights, all rights do indeed become structured upon its model, but that, conversely, once this 'right' is deleted from the list, the remaining components more genuinely articulate 'human rights' as a symbolic web of intersubjectivity, centred upon the sheer individuality, stripped of its predicates. To counter this line of reasoning, though, the argument can be twisted against itself, and then it weighs against Lefort's basic idea: for how could it have happened that capitalist economic relations were introduced by states and juridico-political systems which, precisely, took the form (to paraphrase Derrida) of human rights? In post-communist systems, it was precisely the notion of human rights that provided the ideological support for the restoration of capitalism, *imposed by force by the state and its juridico-political and ideological apparatuses.*

30. By naming it a 'juridical fiction', we want to stress its *material existence*, installed in and reproduced by various ideological apparatuses; at different intersections of these apparatuses, this fiction takes various local forms or figures: the figure of a free participant in public debate, of enlightened debater and reasonable arguer, the figure of the partisan of an enlightened self-interest at negotiations and in contracts, the subject of sincerity and authenticity of aesthetic ideologies (cf. Lionel Trilling, *Sincerity and Authenticity* [Cambridge, MA: Harvard University Press; London: Oxford University Press, 1972]), the identitary subject of different 'communities' (cf. Charles Taylor, 'The Politics of Recognition', in *Multiculturalism*, edited and introduced by Amy Gutmann [Princeton, NJ: Princeton University Press, 1992 and 1994]), the subject of rational choice, etc.

31. Although a smooth abolition of private property seems right at hand with this notion, the smoothness, curiously enough, seems to operate only in the inverse direction: restoration of capitalism has been freely voted in in all post-communist countries. True, there has been no alternative programme so far.

32. Cf. the function of the signifier *mana*, as isolated by Derrida in his reading of Lévi-Strauss's elaboration of Mauss's theories of magic and gift.

33. For Clifford Geertz, this 'transversal function' is assumed by 'common sense', assisted by the system of magic: 'common sense' articulates the expectations derived from existing 'regional systems' of practical wisdom, while magic as 'a kind of dummy variable', 'an all-purpose idea', fills in the gaps opened by the non-totalizability of the regional systems (see his 'Common Sense as Cultural System', in *Local Knowledge* [New York: Basic Books, 1983], p. 79); for Lévi-Strauss, this function is exemplarily performed by shamanism (cf. 'L'Introduction à l'oeuvre de Marcel Mauss', in Mauss, *Sociologie et anthropologie*).

34. One of the consequences is that dysfunctions, which necessarily arise because of the 'non-totalizability' of different social systems, directly articulate themselves as dysfunctions on the level of the individual subject. Becoming 'free and equal', the individual also becomes capable of mental 'illness'. Lévi-Strauss remarked on it in his introduction to Mauss, and Michel Foucault elaborated the theory of this paradox.

35. Max Gluckman defines the concept of the cross-cutting ties in the following way: 'men who are opposed to each other under one rule, are allied to each other under another rule' (*Politics, Law and Ritual in Tribal Society* [Oxford: Blackwell, 1965, 6th reprint 1984], p. 107; see also his *Custom and Conflict in Africa* [Oxford: Blackwell, and Glencoe, IL: Free Press, 1955, reprinted as paperback 1963]). The idea was already entertained by Marcel Mauss, and is most explicitly developed in his article of 1931, 'Cohésion sociale dans les sociétés polisegmentaires', now in *Oeuvres* 3 (Paris: Minuit, 1969). The concept not only entails the idea that social divisions are 'cohesive', and thus gives some anthropological background to the historico-materialist claim that the class struggle is both what tears a class society apart *and* what produces the effect of its 'totality' – but also opens possibilities to conceptualize the ways of producing this effect of totality.

36. Janez Drnovsek, Slovene Prime Minister, in an interview advocating the acceptance of conditions of 'joint partnership' imposed by the European Union upon Slovenia; *Dnevnik* [The Daily], Ljubljana, 3 June 1995.

37. It may be worth noting, as a curiosity, that the first instance of political use of a geographical map is attested in the Balkans: Herodotus (*History*, V, 49–54) recounts how Aristagoras, the tyrant of Miletus, came to the Lacedaemonian king Cleomenes and tried to persuade him to assist the Ionians, 'brothers in blood', in their rightful revolt against the shameful yoke of the Barbarian rule, with the help of a bronze tablet representing 'the whole world with all the seas and rivers', showing to the king the countries he would be able to subdue, and the road where he would then march upon the residence of the Great King. Cleomenes was not lured, for, instead of being charmed by the map, he asked Aristagoras how many days it took to march from the sea to the Great King; having been told that it took three months, Cleomenes kindly requested Aristagoras to leave Sparta before sunset and never to show up again.

38. 'France cannot accommodate all the misery of this world.' Michel Rocard, while Prime Minister of France, during the debate on immigration regulations; quoted by Jacques Rancière, 'L'Inadmissible', in *Les Bons sentiments*, no. 29 of *Le Genre humain*, Paris: Seuil, Spring–Summer 1995.

8

The Politics of 'Hauntology' in Derrida's *Specters of Marx*

Tom Lewis

> I felt that the concept of class struggle and even the identification of a social class were ruined by capitalist modernity. . . .
> Thus any sentence in which 'social class' appeared was a problematic sentence for me
>
> — Jacques Derrida, 'Politics and Friendship' (1993)

> The United States has become the most economically stratified of industrial nations. Even class societies like Britain, which inherited large differences in income and wealth over centuries going back to their feudal pasts, now have greater economic equality than the United States
>
> — *The New York Times*, 17 April 1995

For many intellectuals and scholar-activists, the publication of Jacques Derrida's *Specters of Marx* (*SM*) ended a long wait for Derrida's formal statement on the relation between deconstruction and Marxism.[1] With few exceptions, early theorists had portrayed deconstruction and Marxism as binary opposites, pitting the critique of 'presence' and 'totality' against a 'science' and 'praxis' that most no longer bothered to distinguish from Stalinism.[2] The desire to see Marxism reconciled with deconstruction, however, proved irrepressible throughout the late 1970s and 1980s. From special journal issues and conference sessions, to a wealth of individual essays and books, to Derrida's own 'fellow-traveling' comments in interviews and asides, few on the academic Left, or so it seemed, wanted to surrender their hopes that deconstruction might be politicized in a Marxist direction and that Marxism might be de-Stalinized thanks to a deconstructive turn. Now may be as good a time as any to abandon such hopes.

Among Marxists in the academy, responses to *Specters of Marx* have generally paralleled one of the two basic positions represented by Aijaz Ahmad's 'Reconciling Derrida: "Spectres of Marx" and Deconstructive Politics' and Fredric Jameson's 'Marx's Purloined Letter' (reprinted in this volume, chapters 6 and 3 respectively).[3] Ahmad salutes what he calls Derrida's 'gesture of affiliation', but in no way does Ahmad consider *SM* as having resolved basic conflicts between deconstruction and Marxism. While reciprocating Derrida's gesture by professing his own 'deconstructive solidarity with "a certain spirit of" Derrida (ch. 6, p. 108), Ahmad emphasizes that *SM* repudiates all of the core ideas and principles that distinguish Marxism as a theory of history and practice of politics. Jameson, by way of contrast, discerns a good deal to admire in Derrida's argument, although Jameson, too, shows no interest in constructing out of deconstruction and Marxism a new philosophical synthesis or system 'like the notorious Freudo-Marxisms of yesteryear' (ch. 3, p. 37). Jameson thus treats the 'specter' and 'spectrality' as figurations and argues that *SM* symptomatically registers, on the one hand, deconstruction's inability to break with philosophical idealism, and, on the other hand, Marxism's need to nurture its 'weak messianic' mode (à la Walter Benjamin) during 'the 1980s and 90s, when radical change seems unthinkable' (ch. 3, p. 61).

Opportunities will arise later in this essay to review some of the specific insights offered by Ahmad and Jameson. My concern will not be to try to decide which theorist has analyzed *SM* to better effect. I believe that Ahmad presents a sharper assessment of the political issues raised by *SM*, while Jameson provides a deeper explanation of the book's significance within Derrida's philosophical work. The points I shall seek to develop here fall somewhere between, or perhaps to the side of, Ahmad's and Jameson's essays. In brief, I shall argue the following:

1. Derrida is intervening not only in a scholarly context ('Marxology') but also in a political context (the end of the Cold War) where he hopes to fill a political vacuum among the broad Left.

2. *SM* presents a philosophical rationale for the abandonment of revolutionary socialism in favor of a new 'true' socialism.

3. Marxists should engage Derrida's 'politics of hauntology' in friendly but 'spirited' debates, for it is unlikely that this politics will succeed where European social democracy ('reform socialism') has failed.

Three premises inform my discussion. Whether one considers *SM* as providing a necessary perspective for the evaluation of Marxism's position in the world today depends on whether or not there already exists a *Marxist* theory that better explains, not only the collapse, but also the rise of Stalinism. Second, the attempt to establish the relationship between *SM* and its historical context must reckon, again, not only with the epochal events of 1989, but also with the bankruptcy of West European social democracy in the 1980s and 1990s. Finally, the current debates within the broad Left over the 'legacy of Marx' repeat in substance the main polemics Marx and Engels carried on with other nineteenth-century revolutionaries (Bauer, Stirner, Hess, Bakunin, etc.).

Death in the mourning

Early in *SM* Derrida takes pains to explain in autobiographical terms his reluctance to identify himself, in the past or the present, as a Marxist:

> For many of us the question has the same age we do. In particular for those who, and this was also my case, opposed, to be sure, *de facto* 'Marxism' or 'communism' (the Soviet Union, the International of Communist Parties, and everything that resulted from them, which is to say so very many things . . .), but intended at least never to do so out of conservative or reactionary motivations or even moderate right-wing or republican positions. For many of us, a certain (and I emphasize certain) end of communist Marxism did not await the recent collapse of the USSR and everything that depends on it throughout the world. All that started – all that was even *déjà vu*, indubitably – at the beginning of the '50s. Therefore, the question that brings us together this evening – 'whither Marxism?' – resonates, like an old repetition. (*SM* 14)

Yet reiterating 'whither Marxism?' in *SM* fails anew to lead Derrida to discover any satisfying answers. This should surprise no one, since at least one important continuity defines the political context of both Derrida's earlier and more recent utterances of the question: Derrida writes in a nation whose official Communist party arguably was, and may still be, the most Stalinized in Western Europe. Derrida thus manages only an ironic equivocation on the subject of his personal relation to Marxism. 'What is certain,' he writes, 'is that I am not a Marxist, as someone said a long time ago, let us recall, in a witticism reported by Engels. Must we still cite Marx as an authority to say "I am not a Marxist"? What is the distinguishing trait of a Marxist statement? And who can still say "I am a Marxist"?' (*SM* 88).[4]

Obviously, I should still like to say 'I am a Marxist.' The point to be made here, however, is that one's ability to affirm that statement depends on understanding Marxism as a living tradition. Now, if anything seems clear after reading *SM*, it is that Derrida views Marxism *not* as constituting a living tradition but rather as belonging, quite precisely, to the realm of the *undead*. Marxism today, in Derrida's terms, is at once 'spirit' and 'specter'; and, insofar as it is specter, 'one does not know if it is living or if it is dead' (*SM* 6). This fundamental lack of commitment to Marxism as an alive body of concepts – not to mention to Marxism as a repertory of activist strategies and tactics – gives rise to the main concerns of *SM*: (1) the repudiation of historical materialism, and (2) the renunciation of social revolution. To enforce these concerns Derrida sets in motion a textual process that rhetorically buries the body of Marxism (the dead) while simultaneously conjuring certain specters of Marx (the undead) which Derrida deems capable of still 'haunting' the crassest ideologies of capitalism after the fall of the Wall.

We first confront, then, the issue of *SM*'s occasional nature – literally, a wake for Marxism. Derrida delivered a prior version of this text orally over the course of two evening sessions at the multinational, multidisciplinary conference on 'Whither Marxism? Global Crises in International Perspective', held at the University of California-Riverside in April 1993. With regard to 'the ambiguous title "Whither Marxism?"', Derrida proposed that 'one may hear beneath the question "Where is Marxism going?" another question: "Is Marxism dying?"' (*SM* xiii). The dominant tone and setting of both the oral and written versions of *SM* thus resemble nothing so much as those of a vigil over a corpse or near-corpse.[5] Beyond the part of the book's subtitle (*the work of mourning*) which openly invites such a description, the text is strewn with doleful quotations from *Hamlet*, dwells obsessively on a particular set of religious motifs (messianism, eschatology), and uses an incantatory style to create a ritualized climate.

No comparison or contrast among concrete positions held by the various 'spirits' of Marxism, moreover, is allowed to disrupt this ceremonial space. One presumes that the shorthand designations for Marx's alleged 'spirits' might include such remarkably diverse names as Engels, Kautsky, Lenin, Luxemburg, Trotsky, Gramsci, Stalin, Mao, Castro, Guevara, Presidente Gonzalo, Carrillo, Mitterrand, González, Ochetto, Mandel, Cliff, the second-generation Western Marxist philosophers and aestheticians, etc. Derrida indeed promises in *SM* an evaluation of which 'Marxist' traditions should spiritually live on and which should truly die: 'We must never hide from the fact that the principle of selectivity which will have to guide and hierarchize among the "spirits" will fatally exclude in its turn' (*SM* 87). Derrida never openly delivers on that promise, however, and so *SM* remains comfortably limited to circumscribing a therapeutic space in which listeners or readers receive permission to incorporate and to forget 'Marxism' all at once.[6]

In 'Reconciling Derrida', Ahmad wonders what, after all, Derrida himself could possibly be mourning in *SM*:

> if those whom deconstruction saw as its adversaries – the political adversary in the shape of Communist parties and actually existing socialisms; the philosophical adversary in the shape of the 'vigilant' philosophers of his own milieu and city – have both ended up in defeat, why should *Derrida* be in mourning? Why should he, instead, not be in a triumphant and jubilant mood? (chapter 6, p. 93)

The answer, Ahmad suggests, is that Marxism has not died the death Derrida would have wished for it, insofar as '[Derrida] had hoped that the collapse of historical Marxism would coincide with at least the philosophical and academic triumph of deconstruction, not of the neoliberalist right wing' (chapter 6, p. 93). The spectacle of Francis Fukuyama and a host of even shriller free-marketeers crowing about history's end and capitalism's perfection thus forces Derrida into mourning Marxism's physical death and invoking the Marxist spirit of enlightened critique of capitalism.[7]

If, however, it is true that the display of right-wing triumphalism requires Derrida to mourn the death of Marxism in grand public fashion (where in other circumstances he might have mourned it privately or not at all), it is also true that Derrida's mourning of Marxism imposes on him in turn the necessity of rhetorically staging – now through the very pages of *SM* – the death he actually would have preferred Marxism to have died. Rarely does Derrida attempt to effect this 'friendlier' demise of Marxism by means of sustained argument. His running swipes against the concept of 'class', for example, are just that and no more.[8] Indeed, distinctively Marxist concepts and principles are most often dismissed out of hand in *SM* with little more than a nod to widely held poststructuralist positions in support of such moves. Derrida's gloss on Blanchot affords another such example:

> We are asked (enjoined, perhaps) to turn *ourselves* over to this singular *joining*, without concept or certainty of determination, without knowledge, without or before the synthetic junction of the conjunction and the disjunction. The alliance of a rejoining without conjoined mate, without organization, without party, without nation, without State, without property (the 'communism' that we will later nickname the new International). (*SM* 29)

Here, again, with one swath of the poststructuralist scythe, a good portion of at least one notable 'spirit' or tradition of Marxism is struck down without so much as a single deliberative word, say, on the role of the Bolshevik Party in 1917, Luxemburg on the mass strike, Lenin on the national question, Trotsky on 'permanent revolution', Marx on the nature of 'workers' power' ('the dictatorship of the proletariat'), etc.

SM does not so much embody an argument in favor of 'certain' Marxist 'spirits' over others, therefore, as it relentlessly drives verbal stakes through the heart of Marxism's claims to provide a viable knowledge of history capable of grounding an adequate practice of social transformation.

> To continue to take inspiration from a certain spirit of Marxism would be to keep faith with what has always made of Marxism in principle and first of all a *radical* critique, namely a procedure ready to undertake its self-critique. . . . We would distinguish this spirit from other spirits of Marxism, those that rivet it to the body of Marxist doctrine, to its supposed systemic, metaphysical, or ontological totality (notably to its 'dialectical method' or to 'dialectical materialism'), to its fundamental concepts of labor, mode of production, social class, and consequently to the whole history of its apparatuses (projected or real: the Internationals of the labor movement, the dictatorship of the proletariat, the single party, the State, and finally the totalitarian monstrosity). (*SM* 88)

Without anywhere demonstrating why such concepts as 'mode of production' or 'social class' no longer provide a critical purchase on reality, Derrida merely asserts his belief that every core concept of Marxist theory and practice deserves burial. The only spirit of Marxism he would allow to survive the apparent death of 'Marxism' in 1989 is its spirit of self-critique. Marxists, in other words, should now expend their energies in soul-searching, mourning and atonement, while leaving to others – especially deconstructionists – the task of interpreting the world in order to change it: 'Certain Soviet philosophers told me in Moscow a few years ago: the best translation of *perestroika* was still "deconstruction"' (*SM* 89).

Revolution ought to be 'spooky'

It would nevertheless be unfair to suggest that no argumentation takes place in *SM*, for the figure of the 'specter', especially as Derrida develops it in the context of Marx's critique of Stirner, precisely bears the burden of proof for Derrida's case concerning Marxism. Jameson defines the specter in this way:

> Spectrality is not difficult to circumscribe, as what makes the present waver: like the vibrations of a heat wave through which the massiveness of the object world – indeed of matter itself – now shimmers like a mirage. . . .

> Spectrality does not involve the conviction that ghosts exist or that the past (and maybe even the future they offer to prophesy) is still very much alive and at work, within the living present: all it says, if it can be thought to speak, is that the living present is scarcely as self-sufficient as it claims to be; that we would do well not to count on its density and solidity, which might under exceptional circumstances betray us. (chapter 3, pp. 38–9)

SM's specter figurally represents the inherent instability of reality. Granting only a fleeting modality to material being, it serves as the sign of an 'always-already' unrealized and unrealizable ontology, within both the social and the natural domains.

In this light, Derrida goes on to assert the need to replace 'ontology' with its near homonym (nearer in English than in French) 'hauntology': 'To haunt does not mean to be present, and it is necessary to introduce haunting into the very construction of a concept. Of every concept, beginning with the concepts of being and time. That is what we would be calling here a hauntology. Ontology opposes it only in a movement of exorcism' (*SM* 161). The specter thus may be said to represent more than the instability of the real; it also represents the ghostly embodiment of a fear and panic provoked by intimations of an impossible state of being. Recognition of the flawed or incomplete nature of being, Derrida suggests, can trigger emotional reactions aimed at denying or exorcizing such a recognition. These responses inevitably produce intractable libidinal investments in ontologies. 'Spectrality' surfaces in *SM*, therefore, as a kind of psycho-social dynamic arising out of the vicissitudes of ontology, and its workings will be the general 'truth' that Derrida detects through his own discussion, of Marx's discussion, of Stirner's discussion, of ghosts.

For those who are unfamiliar with Stirner's and Marx's texts first-hand, it may be helpful to recall that the entire tropology of spectrality as it appears in Marx's (and Engels's) *The German Ideology* [*GI*] – as well as most of this tropology as it appears in *SM* – is initially present in Stirner's *The Ego and His Own* [*EO*].[9]

> To know and acknowledge essences alone and nothing but essences, that is religion; its realm is a realm of essences, spooks, and ghosts.
>
> The longing to make spooks comprehensible, or to realize *non-sense*, has brought about a *corporeal ghost*, a ghost or spirit with a real body, an embodied ghost. How the strongest and most talented Christians have tortured themselves to get a conception of this ghostly apparition! But there always remains the contradiction of two natures, the divine and human, the ghostly and sensual; there remained the most wondrous spook, a thing that was not a thing. Never yet was a ghost more soul-torturing, and no shaman, who pricks himself to raving fury and nerve-lacerating cramps to conjure a

ghost, can endure such soul-torment as Christians suffered from that most incomprehensible ghost.

But through Christ the truth of the matter had at the same time come to light, that the veritable spirit or ghost is – man. The *corporeal* or embodied spirit is just man; he himself is the ghostly being and at the same time the being's appearance and existence. Henceforth man no longer, in typical cases, shudders at ghosts *outside* him, but at himself; he is terrified at himself. . . . The ghost has put on a body, God has become a man, but now man is himself the gruesome spook which he seeks to get behind, to exorcize, to fathom, to bring to reality and to speech; man is – *spirit.* (*EO* 56–7)

Why Derrida believes that Marx should be so captivated by Stirner's 'spectropoetics' is an issue to which we will soon return. For the moment I only want to speculate that much of Derrida's own fascination with Stirner stems from the fact that Stirner's dissatisfaction with religion parallels Derrida's dissatisfaction with ontology. The search for essences is unmasked by each author as an attempt to cover up the lack of presence at the center of concepts and identities. Both authors, moreover, locate the drive behind the search for essences in a fear which spawns the metaphysical systems that bear ultimate responsibility for violence in the world. The specter or embodied ghost eventually surfaces in both *EO* and *SM* as a figure of undecidability (divine/ human, ghostly/sensual) that must be exorcized as the Other if an (illusory) being and meaning (spirit) is to be acquired.

Regarding the historical debate between Marx and Stirner, Stirner denounces in *EO* the inherently repressive nature of a host of other institutions in addition to Christianity. Stirner in fact rejects all authority, arguing especially against the state and in favor of the primacy of the creative Ego (the 'principle of self-enjoyment'). Today Stirner is considered one of the main forerunners of fully developed anarchism; *EO*, for example, exercised a significant influence on the young Bakunin. In *GI*, however, Marx and Engels are less concerned to refute Stirner's blanket antistatism – 'there was not a single sentence clearly taking note of what we would now see as Stirner's anarchism' (Draper 1990, 114; see also Bottomore, ed., 1983, 310, 326) – than they are to rebut the idealism of Stirner's views on how society works and how social changes occurs. The following passages, while making for a lengthy quotation, fairly encapsulate Stirner's views on society and change:

Now nothing but *mind* rules in the world. An innumerable multitude of concepts buzz about in people's heads, and what are those doing who endeavor to get further? They are negating these concepts to put new ones in their place! They are saying, 'You form a false concept of right, of the

State, of man, of liberty, of truth, of marriage; the concept of right, etc., is rather the one which we now set up.' Thus the confusion of concepts moves forward. . . . (*EO* 88)

Society, from which we have everything, is a new master, a new spook, a new 'supreme being,' which 'takes us into its service and allegiance.' (*EO* 106)

I say: Liberate yourself as far as you can, and you have done your part; for it is not given to every one to break through all limits, or, more expressively: not to every one is that a limit which is a limit for the rest. Consequently, do not tire yourself with toiling at the limits of others; enough if you tear down yours. Who has ever succeeded in tearing down even one limit *for all men*? Are not countless persons today, as at all times, running about with all the 'limitations of humanity'? He who overturns one of his limits may have shown others the way and the means; the overturning of their limits remains their affair. (*EO* 106)

Revolution and insurrection must not be looked upon as synonymous. The former consists in an overturning of conditions, of the established conditions or *status*, the State or society, and is accordingly a *political* or *social* act; the latter has indeed for its unavoidable consequence a transformation of circumstances, yet does not start from it but from men's discontent with themselves, is not an armed rising, but a rising of individuals, a getting up, without regard to the arrangements that spring from it. The Revolution aimed at new *arrangements*; insurrection leads us no longer to *let* ourselves be arranged. . . . Now, as my object is not the overthrow of an established order but my elevation above it, my purpose and deed are not a political or social but (as directed toward myself and my owness alone) an *egoistic* purpose and deed.

The revolution commands one to make *arrangements*, the insurrection demands that he *rise or exalt himself*. (*EO* 219)

What Marx and Engels will find necessary to reply to Stirner, of course, can be abbreviated in this manner. (1) 'Mind' does not rule the world, nor is the 'confusion of concepts' the source of the individual's alienation and oppression in society. (2) Concepts such as the state, religion and property reflect real conditions whose determinations and effects cannot simply be thought away or ignored by the Ego. (3) The Ego is not the source of concrete experience but is rather itself another such abstraction as the state or religion. (4) To oppose 'the creative Ego to the dirty Masses' (Draper 112) in celebration of the Ego's achievement of a 'superior consciousness' does nothing to change the world, since, in terms of social structure, collectivities are the source of concrete experience.[10] (5) Egoism, understood as self-interest', ought to lead, not to Stirner's emphasis on unbridled individual human will, but to the socialist conclusion that only in a collectively won and democratically run society can the full conditions for the flowering of the individual personality be created and safeguarded (Draper 115). In short, for Marx and Engels, it is not in the realm of pure thought or consciousness alone but rather 'in *revolutionary activity* [that] the changing of oneself coincides with the changing of circumstances' (*GI* 29; my emphasis).

Now, in *SM*, Derrida does not exactly ignore these points of Marx's actual debate with Stirner, but he inflects them in a particular direction so as to establish 'spectrality' as an independent or autonomous 'problematic' (*problématique*):

> What Stirner and Marx seem to have in common is the critique of the ghostly. Both of them want to have done with the *revenant*, both of them hope to get there. . . . Marx seems to be warning Stirner: If you want to conjure away these ghosts, then believe me, I beg you [*je vous en conjure*], the egological conversion is not enough. . . . Marx is very firm: when one has destroyed a phantomatic body, the real body remains. (*SM* 129, 130, 131)

Derrida's manifest interest in this debate really does have very little to do with either its historical aspects or its specific variations in the present. Derrida explains that he devotes so much of his own text to Marx's critique of Stirner because he is impressed by the sheer intensity, even compulsiveness, of 'Marx's rage' at Stirner: 'Marx could go on forever launching his barbs and wounding to death. He could never leave his victim. He is bound to it in a troubling fashion' (*SM* 139).

Indeed, Derrida views Marx's relation to Stirner as one best defined by way of psychology.[11] It apparently does not matter that a number of writers other than Marx and Engels also consumed large quantities of paper and ink attacking Stirner when *EO* first appeared. Nor does it seem to count for much that the positions Stirner articulated in *EO* represented at the time and for the moment the maximum expression of the central rival philosophical tendency – the Young Hegelians – to which Marx had begun to oppose his new materialist conception of history. Instead, Derrida posits overwhelming emotions of identification and jealousy in order to explain why Marx should engage Stirner in protracted debate:

> My feeling, then, is that Marx scares himself [*se fait peur*], he *himself* pursues [*il s'acharne lui-même*] relentlessly someone who almost resembles him to the point that we could mistake one for the other: a brother, a double, thus a diabolical image. A kind of ghost himself. Whom he would like to distance, distinguish: to *oppose*. He has recognized someone who, like him, appears obsessed by ghosts and by the figure of the ghost. . . .. I am describing then this feeling: that of a Marx obsessed, haunted, possessed *like/as* Stirner, and perhaps more than him, which is even harder to take. Now, Stirner talked

about all this before he did, and at such great length, which is even more intolerable. In the sense given to this word in hunting, he *poached* the specters of Marx. (*SM* 139–40)

I would not ordinarily think it necessary to highlight this awkward bit of psychologizing on Derrida's part, except for the amazing fact that *SM* uses this same chunk of speculative fiction in order to explain the rise of Stalinism. Derrida has been discussing the various resonances of the first sentence of *The Communist Manifesto* ('A specter is haunting Europe – the specter of communism') when he introduces his reflection on the 'genesis of totalitarianisms', both Fascist and communist, in the twentieth century.

> To make fear, to make oneself fear. To cause fear in the enemies of the *Manifesto*, but perhaps also in Marx and the Marxists themselves. For one could be tempted to explain the whole totalitarian inheritance of Marx's thought, but also the other totalitarianisms that were not just by chance or mechanical juxtaposition its contemporaries, as a reaction of panic-ridden fear before the ghost in general. To the ghost that communism represented for the capitalist (monarchist, imperial, or republican) States of old Europe in general, came the response of a frightened and ruthless war and it was only in the course of this war that Leninism and then Stalinist totalitarianism were able to constitute themselves, harden themselves monstrously into their cadaverous rigor. But since Marxist ontology was *also* struggling against the ghost in general, in the name of living presence as material actuality, the whole 'Marxist' process of the totalitarian society was also responding to the same panic.... In a word, the whole history of European politics at least, and at least since Marx, would be that of a ruthless war between solidary camps that are equally terrorized by the ghost, the ghost of the other, and its own ghost as ghost of the other. (*SM* 104–5)

Jameson points out with reference to another passage in *SM* that Derrida's basic brief against Marx aims at deconstructing Marx's efforts 'to get rid of ghosts, he not only thinks he can do so, but that it is also desirable to do so. But a world cleansed of spectrality is precisely ontology itself, a world of pure presence, of immediate density, of things without a past: for Derrida, an impossible and noxious nostalgia, and the fundamental target of his whole life's work' (chapter 3, p. 58). In this last passage from *SM*, then, it becomes clear that Derrida views the political consequences of wanting and attempting to rid oneself of ghosts as nothing less than the gulag. Marxism's drive to establish an (its) ontology is held responsible for the rise of Stalinism, as well as for the emergence of every other copy-cat Stalinist regime in the present century.

One is tempted, of course, to pause in order to analyze the idealist character of the history proposed in this passage. One also wonders whatever happened to the poststructuralist ban on metanarratives: 'In a word, the whole history of European politics . . .,' etc. But the dimension of Derrida's argument that most needs to be brought to light and examined here stands out as its singular attempt to discredit *revolution* both as a political strategy for the present and as a social aspiration for the future.

According to Derrida's narrative of 'Marxism' in twentieth-century Europe (fleshed out with my details), first the Allied invasion (with armies from fourteen nations, including the US) of the new Soviet state at the close of World War One, and then the foreign-bankrolled civil war, caused a 'hardening' of Leninism; this 'hardened Leninism' eventually led to 'Stalinist totalitarianism'. Now, there are significant problems with Derrida's way of formulating the effects of foreign intervention on the October Revolution, but I am willing to concede his point in one respect: namely, that the Allied invasion of 1918 and the 'high-intensity' civil war which succeeded it exacted a tremendous toll upon Bolshevism in terms of the Bolshevik Party's traditional commitments to a multiparty state and internal party democracy. After that, however, I – and, I would imagine, most Marxists – would have to part company with Derrida.

The starting-point of Derrida's causal analysis of the fate of the Russian Revolution – the effects of a 'frightened and ruthless war' – would seem to recommend continuing with the elaboration of a *historical* explanation of the rise of Stalinism. This mode of explanation would involve the effort to view foreign intervention, along with a number of additional social and economic factors, as combining to produce Stalinism as a socially overdetermined result. Derrida, however, chooses a different mode of explanation – one that can only be described as *metaphysical*. Lenin inherited a Marxism, it is claimed, that fought not only against 'ontology' by haunting European capitalism but also against the 'ghost' by seeking to turn Marxism itself into an ontology. Lenin's emotional panic, at first over the real foreign threat to Soviet society, pushed him fully into 'ontological Marxism' and its fear of spectrality. Thus Lenin opened the door to Stalin's Terror once he began to exorcize his fear at the 'impossibility of Being'.

This is not the place to debate Derrida on the issue of whether Lenin led to Stalin,[12] but I do want to draw out the political implications of the idealist character of Derrida's assertion of a direct line from Marx to Lenin to Stalin. Consider this sentence again: 'But since Marxist ontology was *also* struggling against the ghost in general, *in the name of living presence as material actuality* [my emphasis], the whole "Marxist" process of the totalitarian society was also responding to the same panic.' What could this religious-sounding phrase – 'in the name of living presence as material actuality' – possibly mean in the context of Derrida's discussion of the first few years of the Russian Revolution? Moreover, what could such a phrase possibly mean in the context of any discussion of *socialist revolution* as a realistic and desirable alternative to capitalist society? From the perspective of deconstruction, the phrase can only mean that the very project envisioned under the name of revolutionary socialism ought to be abandoned as hopelessly 'ontological'. It can only mean that *revolutionary* socialist politics today should be considered as no more than terroristic rites of ideological exorcism. It can only mean that any and all future attempts to actualize the egalitarian ideals of socialism within material society remain doomed – a priori. Why a priori? Because of the 'impossibility of Being', of course.

Stirner, the great theorist of the Ego's supremacy, appears in *SM* as the figuration of Derrida's own metaphysical belief – or fear, if you will – that socialist revolution must inevitably suppress the individual: that not just Lenin, but also Marx, leads directly to Stalin.

A new 'true' socialism

Derrida's 'rehabilitation' of Stirner in light of Marx's critique aims to discredit the view that socialism can be won only by means of revolutionary class struggle. As such, it belongs to the same genre of 'post-Marxist' political philosophy as Ernesto Laclau and Chantal Mouffe's *Hegemony and Socialist Strategy* (1985). Stirner in Derrida's case, Eduard Bernstein in Laclau and Mouffe's – much of the rhetorical strategy of these books consists in resurrecting an oppositional 'ghost' to Marxism's revolutionary past, abstracting such a figure from the concrete circumstances of his or her debates with representatives of revolutionary currents within Marxism, and then claiming that the resurrected figure (or the analysis of the figure in Derrida's case) allows reformist insights better suited to our own 'new times'.[13]

Laclau and Mouffe used Bernstein's *Evolutionary Socialism* (1961 [1899]) in 1985 to support their argument that class-based politics – particularly the revolutionary politics of the classical Marxist tradition – are no longer relevant today under conditions of postmodernity. Yet, in his day, Bernstein eventually came to be faced with the undeniable reality of a resurgence of class struggle and class consciousness. Bernstein wrote during a period in which 'empirical reality seemed to bear out [his] optimistic picture of workers enjoying ever better lives within a more or less crisis free system. In 1895 there had not been a major crisis of German capitalism for nearly 20 years, real wages had been rising and the government had introduced the first rudiments of a welfare system' (Harman 1995, 23). The very next decade, however, saw workers' living standards begin to stagnate and wages start to fall.

The second decade of the century (1910–19) then produced an almost unimaginable upsurge in working-class militancy. In a similar fashion, whatever the reality of class struggle may have looked like to Laclau and Mouffe in the midst of Thatcher's and Reagan's glory days, their theories, too, are being challenged today by a renewed period of heightened class struggle around the globe.

Now, in Derrida's *SM*, the idea that these are 'new times' which call for strategies and tactics different from those of revolutionary Marxism makes its presence felt mainly through the thematic concern with the 'virtualization of space and time, the possibility of virtual events. . . . In the virtual space of all the tele-technosciences, in the general dis-location to which our time is destined – as are from now on the places of lovers, families, nations – the messianic trembles on the edge of the event itself' (*SM* 169). Jameson comments favorably on Derrida's presentation of this concern, primarily because he is able to relate Derrida's positive evaluation of the 'messianic' vocation of Marxism – 'keep hope alive!' – to Walter Benjamin's more familiar, and more Marxist, notion of the 'messianic (see chapter 3, pp. 61–5). As Jameson indicates, 'You would not invoke the messianic in a genuinely revolutionary period . . . It is only in those trough years that it makes sense to speak of the messianic in the Benjaminian sense' (ibid., p. 62). Thus the discussion of spectrality in its technological or virtual aspects in *SM* has as its premise the disappearance of the conditions that make for and enable organized class struggle in the 1980s and 1990s. The difference between Jameson and Derrida on this score is that Jameson thinks such conditions will some day return – probably in the far future – while Derrida thinks they are gone for good.[14]

The question of Derrida's perspective on class and class struggle thus becomes crucial here, for it informs the design of the New International Derrida proposes as the centerpiece of *SM*. The impulse toward creating Derrida's International stems from 'a profound trans-formation, projected over a long term, of international law, of its concepts, and its field of intervention' (*SM* 84). Human rights and distributive justice define the goals and interests of the new organiz-ation; the production of 'critiques' of various concepts (state, nation, etc.) as they appear within the discourse of international law defines the organization's principal activity. Yet the term 'organization' hardly fits Derrida's International, for, according to him, it will be more 'a link of affinity, suffering, and hope, a still discreet, almost secret link . . .' (*SM* 85). The New International will effectively be 'barely public . . . , without coordination, without party, without country, with-out national community . . . , without co-citizenship, *without common belonging to a class*' (*SM* 85; my emphasis).

To return for a moment to Ahmad's essay on *SM*, Ahmad rightly asserts that, given this description of the New International, Derrida has asked us 'to locate ourselves squarely in an extreme form of anti-politics' (chapter 6, p. 104). This impression is reinforced when Derrida goes on to portray the likely membership of his New International:

> Barely deserving the name community, the new International belongs only to anonymity. But this responsibility appears today, at least within the limits of an intellectual and academic field, to return more imperatively, and, let us say so as not to exclude anyone, by priority, in urgency to those who, during the last decades, managed to resist a certain hegemony of the Marxist dogma, indeed of its metaphysics, in its political or theoretical forms. And still more particularly to those who have insisted on conceiving and on practicing this resistance without showing any leniency toward reactionary, conservative or neoconservative, anti-scientific or obscurantist temptations, to those who, on the contrary, have ceaselessly proceeded in hypercritical fashion, I will dare to say in a deconstructive fashion, in the name of a new Enlightenment for the century to come. And without renouncing an ideal of democracy and émancipation, but rather by trying to think it and put it to work otherwise. (*SM* 90)

Ahmad hits home once again when he remarks that, with Derrida's New International, 'We are thus on a very familiar territory: deconstruction as the Third Way, opposed certainly to the Right but also to "everything", as [Derrida] put it earlier, that the word "International" has historically signified' (chapter 6, p. 103).

But the terrain is a more familiar one still, for it is none other than that of 'true' socialism as Marx critiqued it, not surprisingly, in *GI* itself. 'True socialists', according to Marx, do not consider the body of revolutionary socialist literature as 'the product of a real movement but as purely theoretical writings which have been evolved – in the same way as they imagine the German philosophical systems to have been evolved – by a process of 'pure thought.' . . . [They] are concerned with the 'most reasonable' social order instead of with the needs of a particular class and time' (*GI* 119). Starting from Marx's formulations, Ellen Meiksins Wood has convincingly analyzed the emergence in the late 1970s and 1980s of a new 'true' socialism, a term she uses in order to be able to state succinctly the political stakes and consequences involved in contemporary 'post-Marxist' theories such as Laclau's and Mouffe's.

Wood defines the new 'true' socialism as embodying several propositions in either explicit or implicit form, depending on the theorist(s) in question. According to new 'true' socialists, there is no longer – if there ever was – any privileged relation between the working class and the fight for full democratic rights and freedoms. Politics and ideology today float freely above economics, and socialism can and must be constructed independently of class. The tactics and goals required by this 'declassed' socialism are those of a 'plurality of democratic struggles' aimed at the achievement of 'universal' human rights. Cross-class alliances between dominant and subordinate classes are thus the preferred models for organizing. Intellectual elites, moreover, become the leadership of the movements for social change. This is because intellectuals are judged to be the people most sensitive and responsive to the kind of universalist, rationalist discourse that distinguishes the 'new true socialism' from a 'class-struggle socialism' allegedly tied to narrow, even 'sinister' interests of a material variety (see Wood 1986, 3–6).

On this definition, there can be no doubt that Derrida's New International possesses every feature of the new 'true' socialism. The New International declares itself 'without class', thus revoking the privilege given by classical Marxism to the relation between the working class and the struggle for socialism. The New International derives its existence from an abstract concern with human rights – a commitment that in its concrete forms is not antithetical to classical Marxism, but which revolutionary Marxists insist is unrealizable short of revoution, and which is properly 'undecidable' in the absence of class considerations.[15] Derrida's International further asserts the desirability of cross-class alliances (bosses alongside workers); its call to membership is addressed most of all to intellectuals – preferably, other deconstructionists. Finally, rather than the political need to build (or rebuild) genuinely revolutionary working-class organizations in the 1990s, it is the 'reasonableness' of the different social order suggested by Derrida in his critique of contemporary capitalism (*SM* 77–94) that sounds the keynote of Derrida's New International.

On class

One complex historical issue figures as the absent center of *SM*: social class. This is the same issue around which virtually every argument concerning 'postmodern politics' explicitly or implicitly turns. It may prove useful, therefore, by way of an extended conclusion, to present some of the reasons why 'class' should remain a privileged concept for Marxist theory – not only as an analytic instrument but also as a configuration of agency. This task can best be accomplished by: (1) dispelling some poststructuralist myths about the working class today; (2) counterposing a historical explanation to Derrida's hauntological account of the rise of Stalinism; and (3) indicating present and future prospects for class struggle.

The poststructuralist or generally postmodernist argument against the centrality of 'class' for contemporary constructions of political agency rests on two main assumptions. The first of these is the widely held notion that material production no longer constitutes the center of gravity of social formations. Technological change has instead brought about a new situation in which the circulation of information and media images exercises greater determinations within the social formation than do the production, exchange, distribution and consumption of commodities (see, for example, Lyotard 1984 [1979] and Baudrillard 1981). Proponents of this view recognize, of course, that information and images are themselves highly commodified in contemporary society. Yet they usually advance their arguments about shifts from commodities to information, Fordism to post-Fordism, production to reproduction, etc., as so many explanations of why the 'working class' is shrinking numerically and, hence, as so many justifications of their notion that the very foundation of 'class struggle' is disappearing from under our feet.

Many problems attend such formulations, but three replies seem most called for here. First, among the main enabling conditions for the informational work of the electronic stockbroker, the credit manager, the parts expediter, or the office clerk still remain the production, exchange, distribution and consumption of material commodities such as computer workstations, fiber-optic networks and programs. There exists, in other words, a means of production of information *machines* that is materially prior to the production of information. The same holds true for the production of visual and acoustic images throughout the mass media. In all the industries that deal in information and representations, moreover, the same processes of concentration and centralization of capital occur as in any old 'smokestack' industry. The recent wave of media/telecommunications/entertainment mergers in the US, as well as Microsoft's growing stranglehold over computer software, make this point bluntly.[16] Technological change and its effects thus still take place fully within capitalist relations of production.

Second, it is simply a mistake to claim that the working class is shrinking in terms of absolute numbers on a worldwide scale. Internationally, the number of industrial workers is greater than at any other time in history, and it is continuing to grow (Kellogg 1987). Nor should it be forgotten that a relative decrease in the number of industrial or 'blue collar' workers within technologically advanced societies is actually a development not ignored but clearly anticipated by Marx. As a matter of fact, the replacement of 'living labor' (workers) by 'dead labor' (machines) constitutes a cornerstone of Marx's all-important theory of the tendency of the rate of profit to fall. A political point about the structural capacities of contemporary blue collar workers follows here. Each individual blue collar worker who remains is now ten, twenty, or even a hundred times more powerful in terms of the ability to shut down production than each of the individual workers who were replaced by the machines operated by the remaining worker. 'Post-Fordist' techniques such as 'just-in-time' production, moreover, do not negate this power, they magnify it – as the victorious strike of members of United Auto Workers Local 599 at General Motors' Buick City plant in Flint, Michigan showed in 1994.

Third, the working class today is comprised of both 'blue collar' and 'white collar' workers. Displacement of workers from industrial to 'service sector' jobs does not entail a 'de-classing' of workers. Marx's conception of class, for example, stresses two criteria in defining the working class. Individuals form part of the working class if: (1) they must work for a living, as opposed to living off investments or inherited wealth; and (2) they have little or no control over the conditions in which they work and what happens to the products (or outcomes) of their work. On this definition, approximately 70 per cent of the population of an advanced capitalist society structurally belong to the working class (Callinicos and Harman 1987).[17] Not only auto, steel, textile and trucking workers, therefore, but also nurses, schoolteachers, bank tellers, janitors, many engineers, clerical workers, most retail sales floor workers, fast-food workers, a variety of information producers and handlers, and many others – this is the contemporary working class.

The contemporary working class is also a multiracial and multi-gendered collectivity. This fact is obscured by those postmodernists who habitually refer to workers as one group among many – women, African-Americans, Latinos, Native Americans, Asian-Americans, gays, lesbians, bisexuals, transgender people, workers, the homeless, the elderly, Québécois, Palestinians, Tutsi in Rwanda, Hutu in Burundi, etc. – to form a list of oppressions. Such a serial approach to oppression projects a false image of the working class – 'straight white men' – at the same time as it denies the common interests that provide a structural basis for unity in the working class. Indeed, the overwhelming number of lesbians, bisexuals and gays, Native Americans, Latinos, Asians and Blacks, as well as women with jobs, belong to the working class. At a time, therefore, when the limitations of identity politics have become painfully obvious (Smith 1994), the failure to recognize class as offering the most effective subject position through which to organize against racism and sexism is particularly regrettable.

This is not to say that every dimension of racial, sexual or national oppression can be reduced to a function of class exploitation, but it is to say, first of all, that you do not have to experience a certain oppression directly in order to prove a capable fighter against it. The organizing drive of the US Communist Party among Black sharecroppers in Alabama in the 1930s, or the relationship of active support that developed between gay activists and British miners during the Great Miners' Strike of 1984–5 and subsequent gay pride demonstrations – these are but two of a large number of examples that could be given of how Blacks and whites, and gays and straights, have worked together to fight oppression.[18] They are also good examples of how prejudices in society that normally serve to divide us can actually be broken down in the context of a common struggle.

Marxists are materialists when it comes to explaining behavior. It is not surprising that in times of low levels of struggle racist and sexist ideas exercise a strong hold on workers' consciousnesses. After all, workers do not control the means of dissemination of ideas – a fact which explains all the lies and crap seen on TV and taught in schools and universities. Nevertheless, when the success of a strike, or the ability to drive the Klan out of town, depends on solidarity between Blacks and whites; when the well-being of relatives or friends, or of oneself, depends on mass marches to end violence directed against homosexuals; when defending wages and benefits for male workers depends on winning equal pay and opportunities for women workers; when preserving jobs in one nation depends on actively supporting the building of unions in another nation – these are situations in which people's experiences begin to clash with the received ideas in their heads. And it is in such situations that racism and sexism can most effectively be challenged and large numbers of individuals be seen to change.

One last myth about the working class needs to be mentioned here. Derrida and other poststructuralists who show a concern with ethics presently emphasize – and sometimes glamorize – the homeless as a subject position for social change. Apparently, the view is that classical Marxism cannot account for the homeless as a group, excludes them, and ignores their revolutionary potential. At one level, this emphasis and criticism have some merit if they are meant as a reminder that Marxists should actively help to organize the homeless. No homeless persons, just as no unskilled workers, should be allowed to fall outside the political alliances necessary to win progressive reforms and, eventually, radical change. At another level, however, the emphasis and criticism recall one of the worst legacies of identity politics: namely, that the more oppressions you bear (lesbian, unemployed, physically challenged person of color, etc.), the more revolutionary credentials you automatically possess.

But the argument about the privileged relation between workers and socialism has never been – at least among non-Stalinists – a moral argument, nor has it been an exclusionary one vis-à-vis the oppressed. It is an argument about the necessity of workers leading a socialist revolution from below because of the structural positions they occupy in the economy. Women in the workforce, minority workers, students who work and heterosexual white male workers structurally possess the power to bring capitalist society to a screeching stop. They also possess the knowledge and skills necessary to run industry and services under socialism. Housewives, students, unemployed minorities and unemployed white men do not possess such a power or ability.

This is not to say that a revolutionary situation will not produce a vast and welcome range of movements for liberation of all kinds; as Lenin remarks somewhere, 'Whoever expects a "pure" revolution will never live to see it.' It is, however, to assert that the working class is central to the struggle for socialism. Entailed by this view is the fact that workers have an absolute interest in overcoming racial, gender and national divisions within the working class and in society at large. Black liberation, women's liberation, and gay and lesbian liberation are essential to socialist revolution – and impossible without it.

USSR, Inc.: bureaucratic state capitalism

Nevertheless, even if one is convinced that workers constitute the majority in society, and even if one is convinced that they possess the specific structural capacities required to bring about profound social transformation, one still needs to be convinced that a workers' revolution will actually institute and practice genuine democracy. After all, from Russia to Cuba, from China to Poland, from Algeria to Tanzania, the twentieth century is replete with examples of self-defined 'Marxist-Leninist' movements and parties that have installed totalitarian regimes and called them 'communist'. That is why it is indispensable to be able to put forward a Marxist explanation of the rise of Stalinism that successfully refutes claims such as Derrida's that Marxism leads inevitably to the gulag insofar as Marxism seeks to materialize its critical spirit in a real society.

In my view, such a Marxist alternative to Derrida's 'hauntological' account of Stalinism already exists: the Marxist theory of 'bureaucratic state capitalism'. Theories of state capitalism all have their roots to some extent in the classical Marxist tradition – in particular, Hilferding and Bukharin – and were designed, first, to explain the increasing integration of finance capital and the nation state in the early twentieth century and, later, as the implicit framework which justified attempts to build 'socialism in one country'.[19] The specific theory of 'bureaucratic state capitalism' to which I refer, however, was initially formulated in the late 1940s by the Palestinian Trotskyist Tony Cliff and subsequently developed by Cliff himself and revolutionary Marxists such as Chris Harman and Alex Callinicos (Cliff 1988 [1948]; Harman 1987 [1984]; Harman 1989; Harman 1990a; Callinicos 1981; Callinicos 1990; Callinicos 1991; and Howl 1990). Like Trotsky in *The Revolution Betrayed* (1972 [1937]), Cliff located 'the origins of the Stalin phenomenon in the conditions of material scarcity prevailing in the Civil War of 1918–1921, in which the bureaucracy of party officials began to develop' (Callinicos 1991, 19). Unlike Trotsky, however, who held until his assassination in 1940 that the USSR was a 'degenerated workers' state', Cliff argued that the 'USSR and its replicants in China and Eastern Europe were . . . bureaucratic state-capitalist societies, in which the bureaucracy collectively fulfilled the role performed under private capitalism by the bourgeoisie of extracting surplus-value and directing the accumulation process' (Callinicos, 1991, 19).

It is impossible to do justice to the richness of the theory of bureaucratic state capitalism in this space. Nor can criticisms of the theory be adequately answered here.[20] Yet it is worth providing a narrative sketch of what the theory of bureaucratic state capitalism has to offer as an account of the rise of Stalinism.[21] Those who are interested may then decide, should they wish, to pursue the topic through other readings. Supporting statistics and details are also available in many of the sources indicated above (especially Cliff 1988 [1948]; Harman 1989; and Callinicos 1991).

Marx and Engels emphasized two requirements for what they considered to be genuine socialist revolution. Socialist revolution would occur 'from below', that is, as the result of the *self-emancipation* of the working class; and the success of socialist revolution would depend on a context of substantial material abundance. The Russian Revolution, according to Cliff's analysis, fulfilled the criterion of socialist revolution from below, but it failed the criterion of material abundance. Already the most economically and socially backward country in the chain of European states, Russia suffered a devastating loss of population and means of production during World War One. The material scarcity which Russia experienced was further compounded between 1918 and 1921 by the outbreak of civil war and the Allied invasion of the Soviet Union, which aimed to crush the Bolshevik government.

These years – the years of 'War Communism' – fostered the development of a party bureaucracy in two principal ways. First, relations among party members, as well as relations between members and non-members, were militarized in a manner that encouraged loyalty and obedience as the defining party virtues. This development contrasted notably with the atmosphere of lively debate among comrades that had characterized the Bolshevik Party at the time of the October Revolution. Second, the Russian working class was destroyed in the civil war. Workers either died in action or were forced to flee the cities for the countryside to avoid starvation. Most of the experienced cadre of the Bolshevik Party – those who had provided leadership in the soviets before and immediately after the insurrection – were themselves killed off during the civil war, since they served in the best front-line military units. Thus, the Bolshevik Party found itself in 1921 as a working-class party with state power, but without an intact working class as its base. And it found itself in the position of having to replace seasoned cadre with new recruits whose main allegiance was to the bureaucracy that appointed them rather than to the revolution the Old Bolsheviks had helped to make.

But the internal crisis of the revolution – what Lenin referred to as Russia having become a 'workers' state with bureaucratic deformations' – was not the only factor that contributed to the eventual demise of the fledgling experiment in workers' power. Prior to 1923, every leading Bolshevik, including Lenin and Trotsky, had linked the fate of the Russian Revolution to successful socialist revolution in one or more of the economically advanced countries in Europe. Marx and Engels themselves had assumed that socialism needed to be won on an international basis. Once capitalism reached its imperialist stage, the conclusion that socialism required a transformation not just of the national but also (at least in significant areas) of the global economy became inescapable. Hence, between 1918 and 1923, the Bolsheviks looked to revolutionary and pre-revolutionary situations in a number of European countries – above all, Germany – for possible victories that could bring support to the Russian Revolution. With the failure of the second German Revolution, however, the revolutionary wave that began in 1917 came to a close in 1924. Many Bolsheviks began to take seriously the idea of developing 'socialism in one country'.[22]

Telegraphically stated, Stalinism *is* the doctrine of 'socialism in one country'. Although Bukharin actually authored the phrase, Stalin acted as its chief proponent and practitioner during the power struggle that followed Lenin's death in January 1924. This struggle, which lasted until 1929, pitted Bukharin's Right Opposition against Trotsky's Left Opposition and saw Stalin's Center first ally itself with the Right in order to defeat the Left, and then move independently to eliminate the Right. Generally speaking, the Right argued in these debates for permanently institutionalizing the New Economic Policy, which favored well-to-do peasants and the traders (Nepmen) who flourished after the return of the market in 1921. Trotsky and the Left, of course, attacked the Right's policy because they believed it undermined the basis of workers' power. The Left pushed instead for a more rapid growth of state industry – in part as a way of rebuilding the size and strength of the urban working class – and looked to increased Russian participation in the world market as a way of financing industrialization through loans and export earnings (Callinicos 1991, 28).

Because Trotsky and his supporters were convinced that a national solution to the contradictions of Russia's economy remained impossible, they vigorously opposed the doctrine of 'socialism in one country'.[23] Even so, Trotsky mistakenly viewed the Right and the interests of petty capitalism (Kulaks, Nepmen) as the main threat to workers' power. The doctrine of 'socialism in one country', however, precisely suited the interests of Stalin and the majority of party officials, who now despaired of world revolution. When the Center finally succeeded in using the doctrine of 'socialism in one country' to assert its own control over the means of production, Stalin and the bureaucracy began to wield a class power on the basis of a new form of property – state property.

> The political triumph of the Stalin faction, completed by the defeat of Bukharin and the Right in 1928–29, was . . . only the preliminary to a further transformation of Russian society, the forced collectivization and industrialization of the USSR. These dramatic changes, driven through during the period of the First Five-Year Plan (1928–1932), are sometimes described as a further installment of revolution, as 'Stalin's Revolution.' In fact, as Cliff argues, they mark the turning point at which the bureaucracy transformed itself into a ruling class collectively exploiting a vastly enlarged proletariat and systematically subjected to competitive pressures to accumulate capital. The 'Stalin revolution' was thus a *counter*-revolution, in which the remnants of the 'workers' state with bureaucratic distortions' surviving from October 1917 were destroyed and bureaucratic state capitalism was installed in their place. (Callinicos 1991, 29)

Material scarcity, the physical disintegration of the Russian working class, the defeat of the German Revolution, and the political triumph of the party bureaucracy with its commitment to developing 'socialism' in one country – these, then, are the main causes of the failure of the October Revolution. I am aware that a number of important questions and issues remain after the incomplete summary I have offered of how the theory of 'bureaucratic state capitalism' explains the rise of Stalinism. It is not possible on this occasion, however, to pursue other matters, such as how the theory analyzes the operation of the law of value in the Soviet economy so as to have predicted effectively the kind of crisis that led to the implosion of the USSR, or how the theory understands the process of 'Third-World' revolutions in the post-World

War Two era. But enough has been indicated to allow the core of the theory to emerge and to know that we stand here at a far remove from Derrida's metaphysical view of the Bolsheviks' eventual failure.

To recall, Derrida understands the rise of Stalinism in 'hauntological' terms: 'Since Marxist ontology was *also* struggling against the ghost in general, in the name of living presence as material actuality, the whole "Marxist" process of the totalitarian society was also responding to the same panic' (*SM* 105). If Ciff's analysis of the ex-Soviet Union in terms of 'bureaucratic state capitalism' proves more compelling, however, then Ahmad's earlier question concerning the whole project of *SM* – 'why is *Derrida* mourning?' – expresses a double irony. Not only may it surprise many Marxists that Derrida mourns what he considers to be the death of Marxism; it may also surprise many deconstructionists to learn that the death Derrida mourns is not Marxism's but rather that of a particular regime of state capitalism. For Marxists, there is nothing to mourn.

Contexts and conclusion

Pessimism about the willingness and the ability of the working class to fight for a better society accounts for a great deal of the kind of postmodern theorizing *SM* contains. Throughout Europe and in the US, intellectuals smugly declare that barricades and street demonstrations, along with the workers who were their protagonists, are relics of the industrial past – fit for prominent display in the museum, perhaps, but not viable for contemporary politics in an allegedly postindustrial age. New forms of struggle and especially new agents of social change, it is claimed, must either be found or theorized into existence. Hence, the perceived need arises for something on the order of Derrida's New International 'without common belonging to a class'.

I argued above that the contemporary working class includes both 'blue collar' and 'white collar' workers, and that the internationalization of capitalism has created a growing international working class. I thereby sought to contest the claim that the working class is increasingly smaller and irrelevant as a social force. I also indicated that divisions among the working class along lines of gender, race, nationality and sexual orientation have traditionally been the object of intense activity and theoretical discussion within Marxism. While recognizing the formidable obstacles encountered, I emphasized that it is possible to overcome such divisions through common struggle. Finally, I argued that only the working class – that is, individuals who may embody a number of specific identities but who act collectively on the basis of their shared interests as workers – possesses the structural capacity both to bring down capitalism and to create socialism. On this view, it is both theoretically and politically necessary to affirm the working class as the primary agent of social transformation.

Derrida's *SM* provides a stinging indictment of the contemporary world system, as well as a serious critique of recently published apologies for capitalism. As I have endeavored to show, however, *SM* also presents an elaborate case for reform socialism over and against revolutionary socialism. This case is based on what, in a friendly spirit, might be termed a 'misreading' of the Russian Revolution. Moreover, the main tenet of the case is the repudiation of the notion that the working class remains central to the project of winning socialism.

Among the more astounding dimensions of *SM*, therefore, surely must figure the social contexts in which the book appears. Derrida suggests a reformist road to socialism precisely at the end of a period in which the political and moral hollowness of traditional social democracy could not be in greater evidence. Socialist parties all over Western Europe, but particularly in France, Spain, Italy and Germany, have failed to preserve – much less extend – the gains for workers once embodied in the so-called 'welfare state' (Anderson and Camiller 1994; Ross and Jensen 1994; Camiller 1994; Abse 1994; and Padgett and Paterson 1994). These same Socialist parties have not just collaborated with but in numerous instances have actually initiated the attacks on workers, immigrants and the poor. As if all that were not enough, European social democracy has signally failed to organize an effective movement from below against the resurgence of Fascism and neo-Fascism.

Everything that can be said in criticism of Europe's Socialist parties equally applies to the Democratic Party in the US. An openly capitalist party, the US Democratic Party advertises itself as the friend of workers and minorities, relying on its image as a 'lesser evil' to secure electoral victories. Throughout the Reagan–Bush years, however, Democratic-controlled congresses signally failed to challenge the basic premises and policies of Reaganism. Even today, when faced with a cynically self-styled 'Republican Revolution', disagreements between Republicans and Democrats concern only how fast and how deep to cut social programs. If Republicans demand $270 billion in Medicare cuts, for example, Democrats respond by demanding $145 billion. The logic and necessity of slashing social programs are never questioned.[24]

Similarly, the Democrats collude with Republicans on issues of racism and immigration. Clinton, as much as any Republican, has contributed to the false stereotyping of the recipients of public assistance as African-American 'welfare queens'. And, while many Democrats are on record as deploring Proposition 187 as a legal measure, nearly all Democrats concede to Republicans that an immigration 'problem' exists. Thus, the Clinton administration has recently beefed up the number of border cops and ordered harsher treatment of undocumented workers.

No doubt Derrida's proposal for a New International represents in part a call to return to the values of 'authentic' reform socialism. In the US, Derrida's proposal represents a call to return to genuinely 'progressive' values. The bankruptcy of European social democracy, as well as the vicissitudes of the American Democratic Party, does indeed create political openings in which the socialist Left can and must seek to rebuild. Yet two points remain, each suggesting that attempts to revive reform socialism waste energies. First, the European Socialist parties which eventually found themselves authoring and imposing austerity measures on workers and minorities started out long ago with sterling anti-capitalist principles. Good intentions are not enough in this regard, however, since politics and the economy are separated in capitalist society, and the latter wields greater clout. Second, transformed by the discipline demanded by international capitalism, these nominally 'socialist' parties occupy several of the very governments against which workers are presently demonstrating in large numbers. Reform socialism has little to offer workers today.

Callinicos has cogently summarized the current crisis in Europe in this way: 'a major recession which has highlighted longer term weaknesses of European capitalism; a withdrawal of popular support from the mainstream political parties; and the resort to forms of political and social action which, consciously or unconsciously, tend to escape the limits of liberal bourgeois politics' (1994, 9). Soon after the publication of *SM* in France, for example, the country was rocked by militant strikes and demonstrations lasting almost nine months between fall 1993 and summer 1994: Air France workers; 1,000,000 French citizens marching against plans to privatize sectors of education; fishing workers; farmers; hundreds of thousands of French workers marching several times against unemployment and austerity decrees; tens of thousands of students marching, building barricades and burning fires in protest against tuition hikes and the uncertain, potentially dismal future they face.

Even as the recession seemed to be coming to an end in Europe, the anger of French workers and students exploded again in fall 1995 – this time with sufficient force to sustain a three-week strike in the public sector. Importantly, in the Air France strike, the anti-privatization campaign in education, the fight against changes in the universities and the recent public sector strike, real concessions were wrested from the state. None of this renewed workers' activity, nor the fact that victories can be claimed, provides strong support for *SM*'s assertions that barricades and working-class militancy are out of fashion.

In the US, too, polls show today that Americans are more skeptical about their government and its political parties than at any time in memory. A wave of militant demonstrations followed the 1994 congressional elections that gave Gingrich and the 'Contract With America' a majority in the Senate and House of Representatives. Massive marches on Washington in support of gay rights, women's rights and civil rights have also taken place since the 1994 elections. The number of strikes, moreover, as well as the number of production hours lost and workers participating in strikes, increased significantly in 1994. And no one who spent any time during the early 90s in Decatur, Illinois or Detroit, Michigan can have any doubts about the willingness of US workers to fight back. Both areas – which include the struggle of locked-out Staley Workers in Decatur and striking newspaper workers in Detroit – have been accurately referred to as 'war zones'. The violence routinely used by state and local cops has been fiercely answered by the militancy and stamina of workers and their families.

In every part of the globe political developments during recent years have been characterized by their speed and volatility. It is important, however, to emphasize the still uneven and ambiguous character of the emerging challenge to the existing order: 'It has begun to liberate forces – in the shape of renewed workers' resistance to capitalist attacks – which could unleash another upturn in the European [and US, *my insertion*] class struggle. But it has also given an opening to elements of barbarous reaction that had been confined to the political margins since 1945' (Callinicos 1994, 37). Nothing guarantees the growth of the Left as a result of the major struggles that look likely to occur over the next few years. The same political vacuum which creates opportunities for the Left is also creating, at least at this juncture, opportunities for the Right: 'As yet there is no clear cut direction to events that would mark a decisive shift either to the right or to the left. But the dynamic evolution of the crisis since 1989 gives no reason for thinking that the situation will remain so open' (Callinicos 1994, 36–7). In time, events will show whether their future directionality owes more to the subjective agency of the Left in this period – or to the Right.

That is why the question of socialist *organization* stands at the forefront of debate among the Left today. Derrida's *SM*, with its call for a New International, should be discussed as a serious contribution to this debate. Nevertheless, *SM*'s 'hauntological politics' must be firmly rejected as incapable of answering the demands of our time. 'The time is out of joint': Derrida repeatedly works this line from *Hamlet* in order to suggest that socialist revolution is impossible because of the metaphysical limitations of Marxism.[25] Our present time may indeed be 'out of joint', but it is not so because of bad metaphysics. Greater instabilities in an already crisis-prone system, deepening anger among the world's exploited and oppressed, and sharper divisions both within and among national and international ruling classes – these developments make our time one in which classical Marxism and its tradition of revolution from below have much more to offer than hauntology does in the international struggle for a democratic socialist society.

Notes

1. A shorter version of this essay was presented in the Marxist Literary Group's session on 'Derrida After Marx' held at the Thirty-Seventh Annual Convention of the Midwest Modern Language Association (St Louis, 1995). Portions of the essay also appear in Lewis (1996).

2. Norris (1982) sums up the early view that deconstruction and Marxism are irreconcilable. Norris (1990) subsequently asserts affinities between deconstruction and Marxism, once he starts to disassociate Derrida's own positions from the main tenets of postmodernism. Significant efforts to relate deconstruction and Marxism include Spivak (1988) and Ryan (1982). Of interest, too, is Jameson (1972, 183–5), as well as a special issue of *Diacritics* on 'Marx After Derrida' (Mohanty 1985). For a hostile discussion of Marxism from a deconstructive perspective, see Young (1990). In my opinion, Derrida's most extensive and accessible expression of his views on the relation between deconstruction and Marxism appears in Derrida (1993, 183–231).

3. Spivak (1995) and Laclau (1995) appeared after the main draft of this essay was completed. Spivak's essay covers a substantial range of theoretical and political issues and deserves a lengthy, detailed response which carefully attends to areas of agreement and disagreement. I cannot offer such a response here. Laclau's essay provides a mostly predictable poststructuralist/postmodernist account of *Specters of Marx* [*SM*]. The grounds of my many disagreements with it will become apparent in the course of this essay.

4. Derrida (1993) offers another, less equivocal statement about his personal relation to Marxism:

> If today it were possible to produce a new reading of Marx that would be necessary in order to 'understand and transform' [modern economics, geopolitics, literature and science], I would subscribe to it with open arms. If I could participate in such a project, I would do so with no reservations. Is it, moreover, certain that I am doing none of that now? . . . I state that I consider myself Marxist to the extent that I think that Marx's text is not an immobile given, and that we must continue to work, etc. (220, 221)

5. This is not the case with a number of the other presentations at the 'Whither Marxism?' conference, nor with all of the published proceedings in Magnus and Cullenberg, eds (1995), which is the companion volume to Derrida (1994).

6. Manuel Asensi worries from a deconstructionist's perspective that, on the question of discriminating among Marxisms, Derrida seems to want to offer us a principle of decidability in *SM* – something that Asensi finds shockingly 'undeconstructionist'. As I later show, Asensi is right to suspect that the 'specter', in itself a figure of undecidability, is nevertheless used in *SM* as a metaphysical criterion for discriminating between 'good' (i.e., reform socialist) Marxisms and 'bad' (i.e., revolutionary socialist) Marxisms. See Asensi (1994, 17).

7. 'We would be tempted to distinguish this *spirit* of the Marxist critique, which seems to be more indispensable than ever today, at once from Marxism as an ontology, philosophical or metaphysical system, as "dialectical materialism", from Marxism as historical materialism or method, and from Marxism incorporated in the apparatuses of party, State, or workers' International' (*SM* 68).

8. See Jameson's response (chapter 3, pp. 46–9) to Derrida's treatment of the notion of 'class': 'As for class, however, merely mentioned in passing as one of those traditional features of Marxism that can be jettisoned en route by any truly post-contemporary Marxism – "this ultimate support that would be the identity and the self-identity of a social class" [SM 55] – it seems to me appropriate to take this opportunity to show how this very widespread conception of class is itself a kind of caricature' (chapter 3, p. 46).

9. What forms part of the apparatus of spectrality in Derrida (1994), but which does not seem to appear in Stirner (1971 [1845]), is Derrida's 'visor effect'.

10. I am using the term 'concrete' here in Marx's sense: 'The concrete is the concrete because it is the concentration of many determinations, hence unity of the diverse. It appears in the process of thinking, therefore, as a process of concentration, not as a point of departure, even though it is the point of departure in reality and hence also the point of departure for observation [Anschauung] and conception'; cited from The Grundrisse, in Tucker, ed. (1978 [1972], 237).

11. Unlike Derrida, who stresses a shared problematic of 'spectrality' between Marx and Stirner, Callinicos (1996) discusses Marx's ambivalence toward Stirner in the context of their developing differences and eventually distinct problematics: 'The ferocity of Marx's critique of Stirner does not alter – indeed, by its obsessive length and detail, it tends to confirm – the impression that the two were both seeking to make their escape from Feuerbachian humanism, albeit in different directions' (39). Callinicos also observes that Auguste Cornu's Karl Marx et Friedrich Engels, IV (Paris: Presses Universitaires de France, 1970) supports the view that Marx had already made a radical break with Feuerbach before the appearance of Stirner's EO – even though this break became clear only in the Theses on Feuerbach, which were written in spring 1845 after the publication of EO (Cornu 1970, 133). See Callinicos's full discussion of Marx's relation to Stirner (1996, 38–40).

12. I share the view advanced by Rees (1991) on this matter. For criticisms of Rees's article, see Service (1992), Farber (1992), Finkel (1992) and Blackburn (1992). For Rees's response to his critics, see Rees (1992).

13. I do not mean to mechanically or sterilely juxtapose revolution and reform here. Rosa Luxemburg formulates the difference between reformers and revolutionaries quite well when she explains that, whereas both reformers and revolutionaries fight wholeheart-edly for reforms, reformers see the reforms as ends in themselves, while revolutionaries see them as necessary steps toward winning a society where such reforms can become permanent. Reformers and revolutionaries both fought for social change in the 1930s, 1960s and 1970s. Today, all these reforms are in danger of, or actually are, being rolled back. This is because they were institutionalized within the framework of capitalist society and therefore remain subject to the effects of capitalist crises. See Luxemburg (1989 [1898]).

14. For a cogent political perspective on the mass media that avoids the pessimism so widespread among academic Marxists today, see Nineham (1995).

15. The current debate in the US and Europe over confronting and shouting down Klansmen and neo-Nazis at public rallies is an example of a question of rights that is 'decidable' only from a class perspective. Should Fascists be denied 'free speech' because they would wrench away such a right from others if brought to power? From a working-class perspective, the answer, I believe, is 'yes'. From an abstract moral perspective, the answer would be 'no'. The general mistake made by those seeking to establish an abstract morality within a society still defined by class exploitation and oppression can also be illustrated by citing attitudes toward violence. Abstract moralists inevitably end up equating the violence of the oppressed with the violence of the oppressor. Is a slave who kills a slaveowner in the act of liberating him/herself, however, really to be judged by the same moral standard as the slaveowner? Or the woman who kills her would-be rapist in the act of defending herself from his attack? Or the colonial who takes up arms against imperialism?

Derrida's discussion of Lenin and the Russian Revolution implies a deficiency of morality in Marxism by equating Leninism and Fascist totalitarianism. But, as we have seen, Derrida's discussion lacks historical and explanatory substance. The following observation by Draper (1990) thus comes to mind:

> It is one thing if moralizing is presented *instead* of scientific analysis and proof. It is quite another if the moral appeal is simply a *symptom* of the perhaps inchoate feeling that social conditions are intolerable. From the standpoint of workers in present-day society, that is, from Marx's standpoint, the conditions *are* immoral and unjust in a definite sense; and when this condemnation appears as the summary of, not substitute for, a concrete socioeconomic analysis and program, it can be an invaluable energizer of social action and a driving force of political protest. (32)

Another observation, though not as charitable, also comes to mind:

> During an epoch of triumphant reaction, Mssrs. Democrats, Social Democrats, Anarchists and other representatives of the 'left' camp begin to exude double their usual amount of moral effluvia. . . . These moralists address themselves not so much to triumphant reaction as to those revolutionists suffering under its persecution, who with their 'excesses' and 'amoral' principles 'provoke' reaction and give it moral justification. Moreover, they prescribe a simple but certain means of avoiding reaction: It is necessary only to strive and morally to regenerate oneself. Free samples of moral perfection for those desirous are furnished by all the interested editorial offices.
>
> The class basis of this false and pompous sermon is the intellectual petty bourgeoisie. The political basis – their impotence and confusion in the face of approaching reaction. Psychological basis – their effort at overcoming the feeling of their own inferiority in the beard of a prophet.
>
> A moralizing philistine's favorite method is the lumping of reaction's conduct with that of revolution. He achieves success in this device through recourse to formal analogies. To him czarism and Bolshevism are twins. Twins are likewise discovered in fascism and communism. (Trotsky 1973 [1939])

This passage does not apply to Derrida's *Specters of Marx* in every respect, but it well describes the moralizing of much postmodern discourse on ethics. Here one need only recall Lyotard's original and prophetic call to arms against Marxism: 'Let us wage a war on totality; let us be witnesses to the unpresentable; let us activate the differences and save the honor of the name' (1984 [1979], 82).

16. I am grateful to Alex Callinicos for these examples.

17. Roughly 20 per cent would comprise the 'new middle class', and the upper 10 per cent would constitute the ruling class. In their analysis, Callinicos and Harman (1987) continue to employ Erik Olin Wright's (1978) fruitful theory of contradictory class locations. Wright (1985), however, repudiates this theory. See Callinicos's 'Appendix' in Callinicos and Harman (1987) for arguments against Wright's repudiation. See also subsequent criticisms of Wright (1985) in Wright et al. (1989).

18. See Kelley (1990) and Callinicos and Simons (1985).

19. See Resnick and Wolff (1993) for background on the term 'state capitalism' and its various uses and meanings. See Resnick and Wolff (1993 and 1994) for aspects of their own understanding of the nature of the Russian Revolution and Soviet state. Resnick and Wolff (1987) provides a description of what the authors mean by 'fundamental' and 'subsumed' class processes, and Resnick and Wolff (1988) sets forth their theoretical description of communist class processes. Because Resnick and Wolff have not yet completed their project of writing a detailed study of class processes in the ex-Soviet Union, however, I have chosen not to compare and contrast their theory with Cliff's in any detail at the present time.

Generally, some important areas of agreement between the two theories may exist. I perceive at least three major differences up to this point, however. (1) Resnick and Wolff characterize Cliff's theory as a 'power theory' of Soviet state capitalism. This is a mistake, for, in addition to considering issues of control over the means of production, Cliff (1988 [1948]) extensively discusses the process of appropriating surplus labor (see also Callinicos [1981], Harman [1987 (1984) and 1989] and Howl [1990]). From the outset, moreover, what distinguishes Cliff's theory of bureaucratic state capitalism from the power theories of state capitalism is precisely Cliff's refusal to conflate property relations and relations of production. (2) Resnick and Wolff apparently do not accord any integral role to international economic and political developments in determining the fate of the Russian Revolution; that is to say, their analysis (to date) remains focused on the national economy. (3) Resnick and Wolff do not draw the same sort of line between 'state capitalism' and 'workers' state' as is drawn by Cliff. Consequently, they have a different appreciation of workers' self-activity in the early years of the Russian Revolution (1994). As a further result, they balk at describing Stalin's assumption of power as a 'counterrevolution'.

20. Beginning in the late 1940s, the principal debate has taken place with Ernst Mandel and the United Secretariat of the Fourth International. See Mandel (1990; 1992) for contemporary restatements of his criticisms; and see Harman (1990b) and Callinicos (1992) for responses on behalf of the International Socialist Tendency. Callinicos (1990) provides a helpful 'genealogical' background to this debate, as does Harman (1990a). See also the appendices in Cliff (1988 [1948]) for a critique of other views on the nature of the ex-Soviet Union – in particular, Trotsky's definition of Russia as a 'degenerated workers' state', as well as Bruno R.'s and Schactman's theories of 'bureaucratic collectivism', which claim that the Soviet state was neither capitalist nor socialist but rather some new entity akin to a slave or serf society.

21. Elements of this narrative, of course, will be shared by other left anti-Stalinist accounts of the trajectory of the Russian Revolution.

22. Harman (1982) indicates just how vast the array of revolutionary possibilities actually was during the first few years of the Russian Revolution:

> The expectations of world revolution were to prove wrong. The years 1918–1924 saw empires fall – in Germany and Austro-Hungary as well as Russia. They saw workers' councils rule in Berlin and Vienna and Budapest as well as in Moscow and Petrograd. They saw some of the biggest strikes in British history, guerrilla war and civil war in Ireland, the first great national liberation movements in India and China, the occupation of the factories in Italy, bitter, bloody industrial struggles in Barcelona. But it was a period which ended with capitalist rule intact everywhere except Russia.
>
> This [outcome] was *not* inevitable. But it happened. And having happened, it undercut all the premises on which the Russian Revolution was based.
>
> 'Without the revolution in Germany, we are doomed,' Lenin declared in January 1918. . . . Stalinism, as much as Nazism, was a product of the lost German Revolution. (Harman 1982, 11, 12)

To Harman's list of social upheavals, of course, one could add the 'Red Summer of 1919' in the US.

23. Trotsky and the Left Opposition also made many costly mistakes in the course of their fight against the rising Stalinist bureaucracy. See Cliff (1991) and Deutscher (1959).

24. Yet it is easy enough to come up with a plan for deficit reduction that does not require slashing social programs. Corporate profits in 1994 were at a 45-year high. In the 1950s, corporations paid 39 per cent of total tax revenues. By 1990 they paid only 17 per cent. Today that figure is even less. What is to be done?

25. Laclau (1995) interprets Derrida's use of Shakespeare's line in this way:

> Time being 'out of joint,' the dislocation corrupting the identity with itself of any present, we have a constitutive anachronism that is at the root of any identity. . . . Marx . . . attempted the critique of the hauntological from the perspective of an ontology. If the specter inhabits the root of the social link in bourgeois society, the transcendence of the latter, the arrival at a time that is no longer 'out of joint,' the realization of a society fully reconciled with itself will open the way to the 'end of ideology' – that is, to a purely 'ontological' society which, after the consummation of the proletarian milennium, will look to hauntology as its past. . . . If, however, as the deconstructive reading shows, 'ontology' – full reconciliation – is not achievable, time is constitutively 'out of joint.' (88)

References

T. Abse, 1994. 'Italy: A New Agenda', in Anderson and Camiller, eds (1994).

P. Anderson and P. Camiller, 1994. *Mapping the West European Left*. London and New York: Verso.

M. Asensi, 1994. *Espectropoética. Derrida lector de Marx*. Eutopías Series, vol. 58. Valencia, Spain: Centro de Semiótica y Teoría del Espectáculo & Asociación Vasca de Semiótica.

J. Baudrillard, 1981. *Simulacres et simulations*. Paris: Éditions Galilée.

E. Bernstein, 1961 [1899]. *Evolutionary Socialism. A Criticism and Affirmation*. New York: Schocken Books.

R. Blackburn, 1992. 'Reply to John Rees'. *International Socialism* 2:55 (Summer): 107–12.

T. Bottomore, ed., 1983. *A Dictionary of Marxist Thought*. Cambridge, MA: Harvard University Press.

A. Callinicos, 1981. 'Wage Labour and State Capitalism. A Reply to Peter Binns and Mike Haynes'. *International Socialism* 2:12 (Spring): 97–118.

—— 1990. *Trotskyism*. Minneapolis and London: University of Minnesota Press.

—— 1991. *The Revenge of History. Marxism and the East European Revolutions*. University Park, PA: Pennsylvania State University Press.

—— 1992. 'Rhetoric Which Cannot Conceal a Bankrupt Theory. A Reply to Ernest Mandel'. *International Socialism* 2:57 (Winter): 147–60.

—— 1994. 'Crisis and Class Struggle in Europe Today'. *International Socialism* 2:63 (Summer): 3–47.

—— 1996. 'Messianic Ruminations: Derrida, Stirner and Marx'. *Radical Philosophy* 75 (Jan.–Feb.): 37–41.

A. Callinicos and C. Harman, 1987. *The Changing Working Class. Essays on Class Structure Today*. London, New York and Melbourne: Bookmarks.

A. Callinicos and M. Simons, 1985. *The Great Strike. The Miners' Strike of 1984–85 and Its Lessons*. London, Chicago and Melbourne: Bookmarks.

P. Camiller, 1994. 'Spain: the Survival of Socialism', in Anderson and Camiller, eds (1994).

T. Cliff, 1988 [1948]. *State Capitalism in Russia*, intro. and afterword Chris Harman. London, New York and Melbourne: Bookmarks.

—— 1991. *Trotsky, vol. 3. Fighting the Rising Stalinist Bureaucracy 1923–1927*. London, Chicago and Melbourne: Bookmarks.

J. Derrida, 1993. 'Politics and Friendship: An Interview with Jacques Derrida', in *The Althusserian Legacy*, ed. E. Ann Kaplan and Michael Sprinker. London and New York: Verso.

—— 1994 [1993]. *Specters of Marx. The State of the Debt, the Work of Mourning, & the New International* [*SM*], trans. P. Kamuf. London and New York: Routledge. Orig. *Spectres de Marx. L'État de la dette, le travail du deuil et la nouvelle International*. Paris: Éditions Galilée.

I. Deutscher, 1959. *The Prophet Unarmed. Trotsky, 1921–1929*. London and New York: Oxford University Press.

H. Draper, 1990. *Karl Marx's Theory of Revolution, vol. IV. Critique of Other Socialisms*. New York: Monthly Review Press.

S. Farber, 1992. 'In Defence of Democratic Revolutionary Socialism'. *International Socialism* 2:55 (Summer): 85–95.

D. Finkel, 1992. 'Defending "October" or Sectarian Dogmatism'. *International Socialism* 2:55 (Summer): 97–106.

C. Harman, 1982. *The Lost Revolution. Germany 1918–1923*. London, Chicago and Melbourne: Bookmarks.

—— 1987 [1984]. *Explaining the Crisis. A Marxist Reappraisal.* London, New York and Melbourne: Bookmarks.

—— 1989. 'The Storm Breaks'. *International Socialism* 2:46 (Winter): 3–93.

—— 1990a. 'From Trotsky to State Capitalism'. *International Socialism* 2:47 (Summer): 137–56.

—— 1990b. 'Criticism Which Does Not Withstand the Test of Logic'. *International Socialism* 2:49 (Winter): 65–88.

—— 1995. 'From Bernstein to Blair: One Hundred Years of Revisionism'. *International Socialism* 2:67 (Summer): 17–36.

D. Howl, 1990. 'The Law of Value and the USSR'. *International Socialism* 2:49 (Winter): 89–113.

F. Jameson, 1972. *The Prison-House of Language*. Princeton, NJ: Princeton University Press.

R.D.G. Kelley, 1990. *Hammer and Hoe. Alabama Communists During the Great Depression*. Chapel Hill: University of North Carolina Press.

P. Kellogg, 1987. 'Goodbye to the Working Class?' *International Socialism* 2:36 (Autumn): 105–12.

E. Laclau, 1995. '"The Time Is out of Joint"'. *Diacritics* 25, 2: 86–96.

E. Laclau and C. Mouffe, 1985. *Hegemony and Socialist Strategy. Towards a Radical Democratic Politics*. London and New York: Verso.

T. Lewis, 1996. *The Transformation of Theory*. Eutopías, Segunda Epoca, Documentos de Trabajo. Valencia, Spain: Centro de Semiótica y Teoría del Espectáculo & Asociación Vasca de Semiótica.

R. Luxemburg, 1989 [1898]. *Reform or Revolution*, intro. Donny Gluckstein. London, Chicago and Melbourne: Bookmarks.

J.-F. Lyotard, 1984 [1979]. *The Postmodern Condition. A Report on Knowledge*, trans. G. Bennington and B. Massumi. Minneapolis and London: University of Minnesota Press.

B. Magnus and S. Cullenberg, 1995. *Whither Marxism? Global Crises in International Perspectice*. London and New York: Routledge.

E. Mandel, 1990. 'A Theory Which Has Not Withstood the Test of Facts'. *International Socialism* 2:49 (Winter): 43–64.

—— 1992. 'The Impasse of Schematic Dogmatism'. *International Socialism* 2:56: 135–72.

K. Marx and F. Engels, 1970 [1845]. *The German Ideology* [*GI*], ed. with intro. C.J. Arthur. New York: International Publishers.

S. Mohanty, ed., 1985. *Diacritics* 15, 4 (Winter). Special issue on 'Marx After Derrida'.

C. Nineham, 1995. 'Is the Media All Powerful?' *International Socialism* 2:67 (Summer): 109–51.

C. Norris, 1982. *Deconstruction. Theory and Practice*. London and New York: Methuen.

—— 1990. *What's Wrong with Postmodernism? Critical Theory and the Ends of Philosophy*. Baltimore and London: Johns Hopkins University Press.

S. Padgett and W. Paterson, 1994. 'Germany: Stagnation of the Left', in Anderson and Camiller, eds (1994).

J. Rees, 1991. 'In Defence of October'. *International Socialism* 2:52 (Autumn): 3–79.

—— 1992. 'Dedicated Followers of Fashion'. *International Socialism* 2:55 (Summer): 113–26.

S. Resnick and R. Wolff, 1987. *Knowledge and Class. A Marxian Critique of Political Economy*. Chicago and London: University of Chicago Press.

—— 1988. 'Communism: Between Class and Classless'. *Rethinking Marxism* 1:1 (Spring): 14–42.

—— 1993. 'State Capitalism in the USSR? A High Stakes Debate'. *Rethinking Marxism* 6:2 (Summer): 46–68.

—— 1994. 'Between State and Private Capitalism: What Was Soviet Socialism?' *Rethinking Marxism* 7:1 (Spring): 9–30.

G. Ross and J. Jensen, 1994. 'France: Triumph and Tragedy', in Anderson and Camiller, eds (1994).

M. Ryan, 1982. *Marxism and Deconstruction. A Critical Discussion*. Baltimore and London: Johns Hopkins University Press.

R. Service, 1992. 'Did Lenin Lead to Stalin?' *Internationaal Socialism* 2:55 (Summer): 77–84.

S. Smith, 1994. 'Mistaken Identity – Or Can Identity Politics Liberate the Oppressed?' *International Socialism* 2:62 (Spring): 3–50.

G.C. Spivak, 1988. *In Other Worlds. Essays in Cultural Politics*. London and New York: Routledge.

—— 1995. 'Ghostwriting'. *Diacritics* 25, 2: 65–84.

M. Stirner, 1971 [1845]. *The Ego and His Own [EO]*, ed. with intro. John Carroll. New York and London: Harper & Row.

L. Trotsky, 1972 [1937]. *The Revolution Betrayed. What Is the Soviet Union and Where Is It Going?* New York, London and Sydney: Pathfinder Press.

—— 1973 [1939]. *Their Morals and Ours*. New York, London and Sydney: Pathfinder Press.

R. Tucker, ed., 1978 [1972]. *The Marx-Engels Reader*. New York and London: W.W. Norton & Co.

E.M. Wood, 1986. *The Retreat from Class. A New 'True' Socialism*. London and New York: Verso.

E.O. Wright, 1978. *Class, Crisis, and the State*. London: New Left Books.

—— 1985. *Classes*. London and New York: Verso.

E.O. Wright et al., 1989. *The Debate on Classes*. London and New York: Verso.

R. Young, 1990. *White Mythologies. Writing History and the West*. London and New York: Routledge.

9

Lingua Amissa:
The Messianism of
Commodity-Language and
Derrida's *Specters of Marx*

Werner Hamacher

—Cloth speaks. It is Marx who says that cloth speaks. And in saying that, he speaks the language of cloth, he speaks 'from its soul' as surely, in his assertion, as do the bourgeois economists he criticizes. Marx's language is the language of cloth when he says 'Cloth speaks.' But in the language of Marx, this language of the cloth is at the same time translated into the analytical – and ironic – language of the critique of the very same political economy which defines the categories of cloth-language. Marx then speaks, one must presume, two languages: the language in which the cloth expresses itself, weaves itself and joins with comparable fabrics, and another language which speaks *about* and *beyond* that cloth-language, loosens its weave, analyzes its relation to other, loosened weavings, entangling it in another categorial warp. But is it truly a question of two languages, two different linguistic structures, or merely of a doubling of one and the same? Does the critique of political economy speak *another* language, a *new* language, or merely a dialect of the cloth-language? Doesn't the doubling of a language perhaps belong to the structure of this language itself – doesn't the critique of political economy remain under the spell of this very economy? If Marx is indeed to speak a second, other language, then this new Marxian or Marxist language must fulfill at least one condition which cannot be filled by the language of cloth: it must disclose at least one category which as yet has no place in that political economy, a category which might betray itself in that language, might even bear witness to itself, but which cannot itself belong to the repertoire, to the matrix or patrix of that language. This other, this *allocategory* could – and even must – have an altogether peculiar form incommensurable with the categories of political economy, perhaps not even a form. It would not be the language 'of' the cloth, but instead, for example, a language in which a cloth and 'its' language first come into existence. Not, perhaps, a talking thing, perhaps a thing which does not – or does not simply – speak, something which, still unspeaking, *nonetheless* promises itself a language in advance of itself—

I am speaking – if I simply 'speak' – of cloth for two or three reasons: because, in the chapter which opens *Capital*, in the first volume 'The Production Process of Capital' under the title 'Commodities', in the section 'The Form of Value or Exchange Value', Marx speaks of it, claiming that the cloth itself speaks; because Jacques Derrida in *Specters of Marx* speaks of something like a cloth, an 'écran', as a projection surface for phantoms,[1] and because both references to the cloth sustain an uneasy relationship to one of the most powerful metaphors of the philosophical tradition: the metaphor of covering, veiling, mystification and fetish. And thus also of the fetish-table [*Fetisch-Tisch*] which in the chapter on 'The Fetishism of Commodities and the Secret Thereof' not only sets itself on its legs and on its head but also dances, and from whose 'whims' Derrida draws far-reaching consequences. These consequences concern the structure of the messianic as a dimension – an immeasurable dimension, to be sure – of the commodity and its language, be it table or cloth, screen or fantasy; they concern the commodity's messianic promise and consequently both the language of the commodity and the messianic of capital announcing itself in its commodities. The messianic that Derrida speaks of, the 'messianic without messianism', is for him – though he does with respect to Marx grant the religious a special status amongst ideological phenomena – not just a religious phenomenon, but one which arises from the structure of phenomenality itself – from its spectrality – and which therefore must betray itself in the dominating archi-phenomenon of the economic world: the commodity. Developed commodity-analysis – thus one could delineate one of the guiding ideas of Derrida's reading of Marx – must be an analysis of its spectrality – and this means both of the phenomenality of the commodity and of the excess beyond this phenomenality, its paraphenomenal spirituality and spectrality. This means as well – and indeed beyond traditional phenomenologies and Marxisms – that this expanded commodity and capital analysis must contain an analysis of its messianic power or (and here I am thinking of Benjamin's famous formulation) of its messianic *weakness*, and in no

way as an appendix, not as an 'ideological' or 'propagandistic' orna-
ment, not as a proclamation or as good tidings to be presented beyond
this analysis of the commodity-world, but as an integral and indeed
'grounding' element of this analysis itself. The commodity cloth not
only speaks, it promises (itself) something else, and it *is* its promise of
something else: as a phenomenon it is, like every phenomenon and
every possible and real world, spectrally and henceforth messianically
constituted.

Cloth, then speaks. This is what Marx writes. 'We see, then,' the
section dedicated to 'The Relative Form of Value' reads,

> everything our analysis of the value of commodities previously told us is
> repeated to us by the cloth itself, as soon as it enters into association with
> another commodity, the coat. Only it betrays its thoughts in a language with
> which alone it is familiar, the commodity-language. In order to tell us that
> labor creates its own value in its abstract quality of being human labor, it
> says that the coat, in so far as it is worth as much as the cloth, and therefore
> is value, consists of the same labor as it does itself.[2]

The commodity-language translated – cited – by the language of Marx's
analysis, this commodity-language 'betrays' something and indeed
'betrays' what one would not commonly expect of commodities, would
not expect, for example, of cloth: 'thoughts'. The cloth not only speaks,
it also thinks. But it speaks and thinks exclusively in the exchange with
other commodities, with its own kind, with regard to them and to the
possibility of finding in them its echo or its reflex. The cloth is *pragma*
or even *zoon logon echon* only insofar as it is also a *zoon politikon*. But its
politics, commodity politics, is subordinate to the strict injunction of
equality amongst abstract concepts. Commodity-exchange-language is
accordingly restricted to a grammatical-syntactic minimum in which
only propositions of equality can be formed. Such propositions regularly purport that a particular quantum of one thing is equal to a
particular quantum of another thing, regardless of whether this thing
presently exists or not. Hence the statements of commodity-language
are not propositions of existence but arithmetical propositions of
relation which can claim validity even if the existence of one of their
members is not assured. They can thus at any time contain a suggestion
never made good by a reality or which can never be made good. Yet
the claim of universal validity of this arithmetical communication
amongst equals means that commodity-language is structured as a
functional suggestion of equality, and that its propositions of equivalence – and it knows no propositions which cannot be reduced to
propositions of equivalence – only speak, in principle, by feigning the
equivalence of their elements. In speaking with one another, commod-

ities *promise* one another their exchangeability: the sole medium in which they can exchange with and change into one another. In speaking, commodities thus promise one another commodity-language as the language of their universal communication. Their propositions, however arithmetical and reduced they might sound, are thus not constative without being at the same time simulations, projections, announcements or claims. They seem to have, to take up a popular and suggestive word, a performative character.

If the grammar of propositions in commodity-language is restricted by the horizon of equivalence, if the pragmatics of these propositions is essentially that of a fiction, i.e., of the performance of a logical claim or a historical announcement, then their semantics is also circumscribed by an economically narrow horizon: they are all propositions about value. In Marx's example, the cloth comes to an understanding with the coat not about its lovelife or the weather, but solely about the relation which the cloth maintains to it and, by way of it, to itself as exchange-value. In its semantics, as in its grammar and its pragmatics, commodity-language is an abstract and speculative language: it disregards all 'natural' determinations and relies exclusively upon those formal determinants pertinent to its abstract relation of symmetry. And for this reason it is not only a language of exchange but also a language of turning, of reversal, of specular inversion. In it, every single commodity is abstracted from its individuality and presents itself as a representative, an expression or equation, as the quid pro quo or metaphor of a general substance, of labor. 'In order to tell us, ' Marx says,

> that labor creates its own value in its abstract quality of being human labour, it [the cloth] says that the coat, in so far as it is worth as much as the cloth, and therefore is value, consists of the same labor as it does itself. In order to inform us that its sublime objectivity as value differs from its stiff and starchy existence as a body, it says that value has the appearance of a coat, and therefore in so far as the cloth is itself an object of value, it and the coat are as like as two peas.[3]

In order to state the difference – the very difference of its value from its body – the commodity states its equality with something else. It makes itself, it produces itself as value and transforms itself into a value-thing only by disregarding itself as a thing, positing itself as value through its abstract and speculative equation with another. When a thing – the cloth, for example – socializes with another thing in the form of equality, equivalence, symmetry and reversability, it – this cloth – gives itself what it formerly lacked, it gives itself a value and thus appears for the first time in the world of commodity-society, appears for the first time in the world and *appears* for the first time. Its turn into the other of itself is thus the very bringing forth of the cloth, rendering it an object of exchange and, by means of that exchange, also one of use. In turning itself, as the logic of its language commands, in standing itself, as Marx says, 'on its head', it sets itself first of all on itself, on its 'own' feet: it becomes an object only by disappearing as an object and submitting itself to the abstract, the speculative, the 'super-sensual', 'the sublime objectivity as value'. Use-value is hereafter 'the material through which its own value is expressed';[4] it is indeed a material only by the grace of exchange-value and this means, as commodity-language decrees, it *is* only *as* value. And this value, as it presents itself in the 'simple value-form', in the original figure of commodity-language, for its part never exists otherwise than as such, as its 'embodiment' in the material of use-value. The coat, Marx writes, is the '"carrier of value," although this property never shows through, even when the coat is at its most threadbare. . . . Despite its buttoned-up appearance, the cloth recognizes in it a splendid kindred commodity-soul.'[5] What can be recognized of one commodity in another only in a non-sensuous way, since it never shows through as a 'natural' aspect, this 'commodity-soul' is nevertheless incarnated: even the cloth which 'as value' is the same as the coat and thus 'has the appearance of a coat'[6] such that they are 'as like as two peas'.[7]

The actuality of general and abstract value – an actuality conferred upon it by what Marx calls the language and soul of the commodity – is from its very inception reversed, inverted into what Marx calls its natural form: the exchange language of commodities is a language of the inversion [*Vertauschung*] of language and the reality of commodities – an inversion which seems that much more unavoidable as there seems to be no other language and no other reality than that of commodities.

The cloth, the commodity, speaks in man as well. According to the logic of commodity-language, 'As he neither enters into the world in possession of a mirror, nor as a Fichtean philosopher who can say "I am I,"' Peter must 'see and recognize' himself as a human being in Paul and win his 'form of appearance' as Peter only by identifying himself as the incarnation of his generalizing reflection.[8] Only in the speculative medium of commodity-language, only in commodity-language as a mirror-language do Peter and Paul come to themselves, come to be selves as specimens of the 'genus homo' and come to this genus at all. Commodity-language is thus the pattern of humanization which raises everyone who avails himself of it to the apostles Peter and Paul of general humanity and equality. Hence 'man', though Marx explicitly disputes it, does come into the world with a mirror, for before there is a specular other and the I appears as its incarnation or reincarnation, he does not exist as 'man'. The mirror-I creates the I just as the value-mirror creates the commodity. The speculative dialectic of self-constitution thus follows the speculative pattern of commodity and capital production. And similarly, self-constitution is only possible as the turn [*Verkehrung*] of the pre-human shape of the 'I' into the representative of its non-human, absolutely formal abstraction. I, man, thing and commodity appear only by appearing as elements of the value-form and as formed by the value-form. Their language is solely a form-positing, value-positing, equalizing one – a commodity-language in which they are constituted and conserved as commodities.

Their language forms them – the 'humans' as well as the 'things' – into commodities. Commodity-language, then, does not mean that there are commodities which, in addition, are endowed with a particular language; it means that they are commodities only by virtue of this language and that this language alone qualifies them as commodities, identifies and forms them. Commodity-language appoints them commodities, syntagmatizing them as commodities and performing them as commodities. Both in *Capital* and in his earlier writings, Marx constantly stresses that the universal commodification prevalent with the development of capitalism presents the result of a complex history of technological, economic and political developments, and indicates an irreversible progress in the freeing up of the forces of production as well as in the liberation from slavery, servitude, inequality and poverty. Commodity-language is not only a historical – that is, finite – language, it is also, as his footnote on the speculative genesis of the 'genus homo' shows, a language of equalization, socialization and autonomization and hence of the promise of further liberations from the burdens, on the one hand, of isolation and on the other, of hierarchical organization – even of the liberation from concepts of freedom determined by commodity-language. This involves above all the messianic promise of liberation made by Judeo-Christianity. Religion does this, Marx insists in all of his writings, within the boundaries of the speculative proposition of commodity-language. The '*Wertsein*', the 'being worth', of the cloth, he writes (in the same section about the relative form of value), 'is manifested in its equality with the coat, just as the sheep-like nature of the Christian is shown in his resemblance to the Lamb of God.'[9] Christianity celebrates the 'cult of abstract man'[10] just as commodity-language celebrates the cult of abstract human labor. The sheep's nature and the abstraction of God are reconciled in the lamb as the incarnation of formal equivalence: they appear as equal because equality itself appears in them. Commodity-language is thus not only a language of the bourgeois economy, it is not merely the language of the constitution of the abstract bourgeois subject and hence the language of the ontology of subjectivity, it is at the same time the language of theology, of ontotheology and especially, Marx adds, 'in its bourgeois development, in Protestantism, Deism, etc.'[11] The messianism of Christianity is, in a word, the messianism of commodity-language, its promise of redemption the promise of commodities: they embody a general, constant and transhistorical value. It is in this sense that the following comment from Marx is to be understood:

> Let us remark, incidentally, that the language of commodities also has, apart from Hebrew, plenty of other more or less correct dialects. The German 'Wertsein,' 'to be worth,' 'to be valuable,' for instance, brings out less strikingly than the Romance verbs 'valere,' 'valer,' 'valoir,' that the equating of commodity B with commodity A is the expression of value proper to commodity A. Paris vaut bien une messe![12]

Marx sees languages, including Hebrew, the holy language and language of the tradesman, as dialects of the universal commodity-language. The Romance verb 'valere' articulates its political and theo-economic message most precisely in Henri IV's utterance uniting the conversion to Catholicism with the convertibility of value which is to reside in French capital and its political functions. *Paris vaut bien une messe.* This is the formula of theo-economic transubstantiation, the formula of the messianism of the commodity-language.

The cloth, then, the commodity, speaks. It speaks a historical language which claims to be universal and transhistorical. It speaks an abstract language limited to a single statement, value, and a single grammatical structure, equation, yet claims nonetheless to be valid for an unrestricted variety of singularities. It is a language of exchange [*Verkehr*], but only as a process of turning [*Verkehrung*]. Marx accomplishes three massive transformations in the following sentences: Use-value becomes the form of appearance of its opposite, value.[13] 'Concrete labor becomes the form of appearance of its opposite, abstract human labor.' And, thirdly: 'Private labor takes the form of its opposite, namely, its directly social form.'[14] These exchanges and transformations can nonetheless only be effected in the medium of commodity-language because its individual elements all refer to a common substratum, to a commodity which belongs to the series of all other commodities and simultaneously, in order to guarantee the consistency of this series, as the only one which must remain excluded from it, its general equivalent, the money-commodity. Money is the transcendental of commodity-language, that form which vouchsafes all other forms their commensurablity, appearing as a copula in all the statements and postulates of commodity-language. This copula, which only apparently has a completely formal character, does indeed refer to a historical referent and is itself both historical and historicizing: it refers, namely, to the 'common substance'[15] at work in all elements of commodity-language, refers to what is common and – by virtue of its formalization – equal to all: it refers to human labor. Commodity-language is thus – and this would be its more complete if still insufficient characterization – a transcendental schematizing language of the social substance 'labor' in a particular historical epoch; it is the transcendental ergologic and ergo-onto-theo-logic of capitalism.[16]

This characterization of commodity-language is not yet complete; amongst the missing determinants, I name at this point only the most important and apparently most perverse: that it is a language at all. When confronted by the curious double term 'commodity-language', every rhetorician or semiotician worth his salt would be immediately tempted to speak of a metaphor or personification or, more precisely, of a prosopopoeia. That would not be wrong, but still less would it be right. Not wrong because commodities 'normally' and 'naturally' do not speak. Yet commodities are not natural; rather, as Marx correctly says, they are things with a 'supernatural quality', their value 'something purely social'.[17] Only – and this follows from the analysis of the simple value-form – this 'supernatural quality', this being a value-thing (*Wertding*), is of such a kind that it does not remain supernatural but becomes an objective quality, quickly dons a 'natural skin',[18] becomes 'sensuously supra-sensuous',[19] that is, supra-sensuous in a sensuous way, and begins to speak as a relatively independent thing. Marx thus does not use a metaphor or a prosopopoeia, but the commodity of which he speaks is itself structured as a prosopopoeia. The cloth does not speak figuratively but, because it is a commodity and hence a figure, it actually speaks. A language devolves to it – and indeed the only language dominant in the commodity-world – because language is both abstract and material, i.e., the incarnated form of man's expression and the form of organization of his labor. That commodities – and moreover everything affected by them – speak a language, and perhaps *the* language, is what Marx calls their fetish character. Commodity fetish – that means commodity-language. What is the secret thereof?

What is it that the cloth veils when it veils itself and speaks? What can't the cloth say? What alone can it *not* say? What, when speaking, does it keep secret? 'Whence,' Marx asks in the chapter 'The Fetishism of Commodities and the Secret Thereof', 'whence, then, arises the enigmatic character of the product of labor, as soon as it assumes the form of a commodity?' And his answer is: 'Clearly, it arises from this form itself.'[20] It is this value-form, he explains – that is, commodity-language as *objective* form – which imprints human labor with the objective character of products, imprints the time of that labor with the character of value, and imprints the relations amongst producers with the character of relations between products. Production becomes a product, time an object, man a thing. The 'enigmatic character', the 'phantasmagoric form', the 'mystical character' of the commodity as a 'twisted thing, abounding in metaphysical subtleties and theological whims', this 'deranged form', its fetish character, is not something detachable from the product in order to unveil its real, authentic, true character and, as an object, thereby to clear up the self-misunderstanding of worker, labor and time. Derangement, twistedness, and enigma belong for Marx to the irreducible, constitutive 'categories' of bourgeois – that is, to date the most advanced – economy: 'They are thought-forms which are socially valid, and therefore objective, for the relations of production belonging to this historically determined mode of social production, i.e. commodity production.'[21] And he continues: 'The belated scientific discovery [of this fetish character of commodity-form as an objective thought-form] by no means banishes the semblance of objectivity possessed by the social character of labor.'[22] If Marx thus notes that '[p]eople are not aware of this, nevertheless they do it,'[23] he adds just as quickly that they also must do it *when* they are aware of it. Forms of knowledge, insofar as they are forms and insofar as they are those of knowledge, can for their part be none other than those of commodity-language and thus must a priori be 'deranged', 'phantasmagoric', 'mystical' and 'fetishistic'. Commodity-language itself 'objectively veils' social relations 'instead of revealing them plainly'.[24] 'Objectively veil' means: objects themselves are the veil which commodity-language spreads over their substance, the social conditions of production; the objectivity of objects is the fetish; the objectivity of materials, of representations and forms, is the covering which presents itself in commodity-language as irreducible. The cloth veils the cloth. The object 'cloth' must be the veil over the actual *cloth* which is woven by historical social life. But precisely this weaving of social life results – in deed as in knowledge – in commodity-exchange as in the forms of its recognition in an object – in the object 'cloth', and thus is a process of a self-veiling, a self-mystification, self-fetishization. The object named by commodity-language is the fetish by which the conditions of production are not so much veiled as transformed. When the cloth speaks, the cloth, alas, speaks no more. Cloth now speaks only and exclusively in this way: the cloth 'itself' no longer speaks, it already speaks in the categories, the words and the grammar of commodity-language. Only the deranged cloth 'abounding in metaphysical subtleties and theological niceties' can speak. Commodity-language itself speaks only as the commodity 'language', exchanging itself for equivalent commodities or languages and serving the profiteering of capital. And that is its capital secret: that it can conceal none. It does not veil something behind or underneath it, it does not conceal some *thing* at all; as mere categorical form it veils this very form, itself, and with it its formation: the generative structure preceding its transcendental fetishistic frame. What it says, it is, here and now, in objective, material form.

Although he calls it a 'derangement', Marx makes no secret of the fact that commodity-language is correct and that this is what produces its dominating authority. It does not speak a language other than historical reality; it is this reality in the forms of language – in 'objective thought-forms', in 'categories'. He writes, once again in the chapter on the fetish character of the commodity: 'If I say the coat, the boots, etc., relate to the cloth as the general embodiment of abstract human labor, the derangement of this expression is obvious. But if the producers of the coat, the boots, etc., relate these commodities to the cloth – or to gold or silver, it makes no difference – as a general equivalent, the relation of their private labor to social collective labor appears to them precisely in this deranged form.' The derangement of the commodity-language-form lies then in the transcendental function appended to the general equivalent – to the cloth, to gold or social collective labor – for as a transcendental, it has the structure of a universal measure which simultaneously and *despite* its universality is to be incarnated in a particular, either material or abstract form. The cloth as a *general* equivalent veils or inverts the cloth, a historically determined *single* product. As transcendental form, the cloth must efface the singularity of everything it encompasses and paralyze that history into objects: commodity-language is therefore mystifying and fetishistic, a ghost because it cannot express the producedness of products but only their stable form, not the historicity of products but only their perpetual objectivity, not the singularity of labors but only their abstract function. Commodity-language is the language of static categories denying past and future. The task falls to historical analysis to prove them historical and historicizing categories, and to disclose for them another future. Marx writes:

> The categories of bourgeois economics consist precisely of forms of this kind [the deranged forms of the general equivalent, of gold, of cloth]. They are thought-forms which are socially valid, and therefore objective [thought-forms which have sedimented in objects], for the relations of production belonging to this historically determined mode of social production, i.e. commodity production. The whole mystery of commodities, all the magic and necromancy that surrounds the products of labor on the basis of commodity production, vanishes therefore as soon as we escape to other forms of production.[25]

The escape into other forms of production is an escape from a prison of immobile 'objective thought-forms' of the categories of commodity and capital, the escape to a freedom which only historicizing, singularizing, non-transcendentalizing language can achieve. (And achieve, perhaps, only at the cost of being persecuted on this flight by the ghost of commodity-language.)

The cloth – and through it capital – thus speaks not only in the transcendental forms of ergontology, it speaks not only in the pure forms of measure and equivalence or of controlled surplus and regulated asymmetry, it also exhibits these forms in an objective form, as objective reality, as material cloth. It is a language not only of abstract formalism but also of the deranged material incarnation of this formalism, that is, a deranged transcendental-historical concretism, a *formaterialism*. Abstract value, labor and time have woven themselves into the warp of cloth and now speak – how else might they speak? – only through it and as it.

—The cloth, the web, speaks, that is: the specter speaks. It speaks – it haunts. Commodity-language, the fetish, is a specter: the material incorporation of universal abstractions, neither flesh nor blood, but materially appearing form, a morphantom.—

The 'critique of political economy' is understood as the critique of this spectral incarnationism. It bids the table, which, 'in relation to all other commodities, stands on its head' and has thereby become a fetish,[26] to stand again on its four legs, just as it tries to invert the Hegelian dialectic in order to discover 'the rational kernel in the mystical shell'. For, as Marx says in the afterword to the second edition of *Capital*: 'With him it is standing on its head.'[27] Marx here presupposes that those legs exist without a head, that there is a rational kernel without a covering and that there could be a social form of production unaffected by the value-form. Marx does believe in a language other than the transcendental one of formaterialism. He believes in a true language [*eine wahre Sprache*] which remains undisguised by commodity-language [*Warensprache*], but at the same time offers numerous arguments for the view that this other language, too, is caught in the net of commodity and value categories. He insists that historical-individual labor, with its specific time, is the true, actual substance and the secret of social appearance; but at the same time he leaves no doubt that this substance has until now never appeared other than in the mystifying and theologizing veil of the value-form. He propagates an ontology of production but objects that it has heretofore been possible only as an ontology of products and hence only as a pseudology or spectrology: 'The belated scientific discovery that the products of labor, in so far as they are values, are merely the material expressions of the human labor expended in them, marks an epoch in the history of mankind's development, but by no means banishes the semblance of objectivity possessed by the social character of labor.'[28]

In chapter 48 in the third volume of *Capital*, 'The Trinitarian Formula', an often-cited passage opens the prospect of a form of production which is no longer capitalistic. The end of labor, more precisely, of forced and commodity-producing labor, is pledged. Marx writes:

> In fact the realm of freedom actually begins only where labor which is determined by necessity and mundane considerations ceases; thus, in the very nature of things, it lies beyond the sphere of actual material production.... Beyond it [the realm of necessity] begins that development of human energy which is an end in itself, the true realm of freedom, which, however, can blossom forth only with the realm of necessity as its basis. The shortening of the work day is its basic prerequisite.[29]

What Marx promises here – and he *promises* it even if he states it under the form of a scientifically-grounded announcement – and what he hears as the promise of capitalism's production and circulation processes is not so much the liberation *from* labor as the liberation *to* it. That is, to labor itself, to labor as 'an end in itself', to labor as the true self of man realized solely in itself and no longer in objective forms, thus no longer incarnating itself, no longer hiding a secret – not even the secret that it has no secret – and no longer cultivating theological whims. Only performance, auto-performance (the promise says), speaks in the substantial labor-language of a future society and defines the 'realm of freedom' as a realm of completed ergocracy. But doesn't this promise necessarily remain the promise of capital, of self-capitalizing and abstract labor, the promise that labor itself is capital, a self-producing and self-reproducing substance? The 'realm of freedom', Marx states expressly, can 'blossom forth only with the realm of necessity as its basis'. The future would then be only a prolonged present of capital, there would be, as in every substantialism, no future at all, but only, once again, a present, only an eternal return of the specter which already claims to be the so-called present now. Communism, then, would only be the ideology of capitalism declaring that its further development would culminate in the true unveiling of its theo-economic secrets – of the sacrament of labor. I leave it at this question, for labor or the development of human capacity as its own end could in its innermost structure, even if Marx takes care not to speak of it in programmatic concepts, also indicate something else: a severing of labor from production, from the generation of the means of subsistence, finally from itself as a substance which shows itself in objects and embodies itself in man; this structure could, in short, indicate an internal disjunction of labor and its autoteleology and thereby its liberation not only from need but from itself as unquestioned necessity. In this sense *The German Ideology* explains that 'in all revolutions up till now the mode of activity always remained unscathed and it was only a question of . . . a new distribution of labor to other persons, whereas the communist revolution is directed against the preceding *mode* of activity, does away with *labor* . . .'[30] The 'automatic system' of 'big industry', he writes in the same connection, 'makes for the worker not only the relation to the capitalist, but labor itself, unbearable'.[31] With respect to ideology and the practical terror of labor which reigns in all totalitarian regimes (including those which have called on the legacy of Marx), and also under the 'liberal' welfare capitalism of Western democracies, it is not the last question which one should direct towards Marx. It is the first. The liberation from labor is the object of the Marxist promise, the aim of the world-historical development of the capitalistic form of production, the vanishing-point of the communist revolution.

There will be no more labor: this is the promise of commodity-language. And this promise no longer simply belongs to the 'categories' or 'objective thought-forms' of a transcendental commodity-language and the ergontology articulated therein; it no longer simply belongs to its syntax of equivalents and quid pro quos, it does not belong to the de-historicizing rhetoric of statements of what is and what is incarnated in commodity relations; this promise says that a language other than commodity-language is possible, and insofar as it is possible it is necessary; it says that categories other than those of commodity-language and that something other than a categorial language will be invented. This promise is itself already no longer a category; it indicates something structurally different; it is, one could say, an allocategory which speaks beyond – but also in – all 'objective thought-forms' of commodity-language, opening up its syntactic arrangement and its meaning to something else beyond any conceivable form.

It is, once again, a question of the language of the commodity-world and what it promises. A question of commodity-language and its promise. It is this promise, deciphered by Marx in the framing of the commodity-world, which Jacques Derrida makes one of the centers of his book on Marx. I have developed the question of commodity-language, which plays no role there, in some detail in order to gain easier access to the questions this book has prompted for me. They concern the formalism of the messianic promise, the structure of the performative, the status of labor and the conjunction which Derrida's book establishes between these and the appearance of the spectral. My

remarks – even if it is not 'written on their face' – have the character
of questions in progress; they are not entirely tied to the hope of
passing into effective questions or determinations; they do not mean to
be immediately productive, nor aim at achieving predetermined theoretical or practical aims. All of these terms are very much implicitly or
explicitly up for discussion and, if at times in another way, are already
under discussion in the texts by Derrida and Marx to which I refer
here.

Cloth speaks. Derrida translates: the specter – or perhaps the spirit
– speaks. And he immediately begins to differentiate, to specify, to
classify: there is not only one specter but several, always more than one
and this 'more than one' or 'no more one' already makes out the
constitutive structure, the structure of destitution, of the spectral. The
specters are irreducibly plural – for Marx in the texts he cites by way of
exorcism or conjuration, for Marxists and anti-Marxists, the persecutors
and doomsdayers of Marxism and also for those who never believed
that Marxist-inspired states existed – Derrida enumerates them, analyzes them and writes their spectrology. And this spectrology, in turn,
is haunted by the specters of Marx, Freud and Nicolas Abraham,
Husserl and Valéry, Benjamin, Heidegger and Blanchot. One might
enumerate a few more, but their number is in principle not to be
fixed; they are transnumeral. Specters, parting from the departed and
on the brink of becoming independent, consist of splits, live in fissures
and joints, in intermundia, as Marx, a familiar of Democritus' and
Epicurus' systems, says of Epicurus' gods:[32] they are monsters of difference. The spectral exists, despite this irreducible disparity, if only in
the disquieting or self-complacent question of whether it *actually* exists.
In the spectral, something past, itself provoked by something to come,
something outstanding and as of yet still in arrears, demands its rights
here and now. The spectral is, one might therefore say, that which is
most present amongst the things which can be experienced because it
appears precisely in the open joint between future and past – or more
exactly, where its apparently tight connection is out of joint. What
appears as spectral is always the future and the future of the past as
well, that which is not yet and will never be present. If one can speak
of a temporalization of time, as Heidegger and after him Derrida do,
then time is temporalized by the future. 'The truly temporal in time is
the future' – so Schelling claimed in his 'Aphorisms on Natural
Philosophy' and added, by way of explanation: 'It is the clear product
of sheer imagination.'[33] But productive imagination, from which time
and its various dimensions arise, is neither for Heidegger nor for
Derrida the decisive originating instance, the *exstance* of temporalization. It is not the productive *Einbildung* and unifying imagination (*In-*

Eins-Bildungskraft), it is much more the *dé*imagination or image-*weakness*, the abstinence from images and their retreat which releases time from itself and temporalizes. Marx, who was never far from placing a ban on images of the future and preferred – but surely any preference can be nothing but paradoxical – reading the future only in the strains and asynchronicities of the 'present', speaks of the future only in the mode of proclamations, conjurations and announcements. Why, then, is the representation of a specter tied to the future?

For Derrida, the specter answers the question of the future. 'What of the future?' he asks, and his answer is: 'The future can only be for the ghosts' (37; Fr. 69). The phantom is also the answer to the question of the 'messianic extremity' which Derrida – in one of the most important terminological decisions of his book – gives the name 'eschaton'. 'Is there not a messianic extremity, an *eskhaton* whose ultimate event (immediate rupture, unheard-of interruption, untimeliness of the infinite surprise, heterogeneity without accomplishment) can exceed, *at each moment*, the final term of a *phusis*, such as work, the production, and the *telos* of any history?' (37; Fr. 68). This messianic extremity, which goes beyond every telos and every labor; this extremity without which no future can be thought because thinking itself is indebted only to it; this extremity, unthinkable in advance, which can be neither an object of knowledge nor of perception, and only precisely because it evades the controls of both perception and knowledge, keeps the possibility of the future open – this *openness* of the future could only attest to itself in the sheerest abstraction beyond form or, if related to forms, only in their irreparable disintegration. Derrida's repeated challenge to distinguish between eschatology and teleology (37; Fr. 68) seems to insist on precisely this difference between a form determined by telos as its border and the extremity which in the border, or at it, traverses the border and, being external and *exformal*, can no longer fall under the category of form, of categorial thought-form or perception-form. But if the future is an allocategory of the transformative and exformative, if it 'a priori' diverges from the categorial framework of forms of thought, perception and intuition, then it must be without appearance, aphenomenal, and can only attest to itself in the disappearance of all phenomenal figures, in the continued dissociation of its phantasmagorias. The future 'is', if it is at all, that which shows itself insofar as it effaces the signs it permits. It presents itself only in the retraction of its signs. It is aphanisis[34] antecedent and subsequent to every possible phenomenon. How, then, can it belong to phantoms? What can the sentence mean: 'At bottom, the specter is the future, it is always to come, it presents itself only as that which could come or come back ... [*Au fond, le spectre, c'est l'avenir, il est toujours à venir, il ne se présente que comme ce qui pourrait venir ou revenir . . .*]' (39; Fr. 71).

The questions sketched in the background of Derrida's Marx book – at least *some* of its questions – can presumably be paraphrased as follows. How can the future bear witness to itself? And how, *as* the future, can it attest to its futurity? How is it possible that the sheer possibility (under whose aspect alone actuality exists at all) does not appear as a void of the actual but rather as the way of its arrival – as a path of actualization remaining open to other arrivals? The figure which comes closest to answering these questions, the figure of figuration, is the specter in all its disparity – as phantom, spirit, ghost, appearance and spectrum. It is that 'figure' which massively and under the most disparate names haunts Marx's texts – whether as phantasmagoria or enigma, as fetish or ideology, as theological whim or objective veil – and which is the phenomenon, or phenomenon of phenomenality, for which the walls and cloths between fields as various as literature and philosophy, psychoanalysis, economics, theology and politics are permeable. The most disparate types of discourse are haunted by the specter because the specter is what differs from all of them – and from itself. In it transpires something between material and spirit, apparition and disappearance, foreclosing both from the outset. But as complex as this figure of figuration and defiguration, this archi-figure of difference, might be, it still remains a figure. Derrida's concern is not to conjure it but to analyze the visitations and persecutions, to analyze the rites and formulas of exorcism in which it keeps recurring: a large part of his book on Marx is dedicated to the reduction of the dominant spectral figures to what is irreducibly spectral in them. I will name only three or four of those figures of the figure.

There is first of all the specter of the father, whose '*patrimonial* logic' (107; Fr. 173) unfolds, as it also does for Hamlet and the ghost of his father, between Marx and his father-in-law Ludwig von Westphalen and, more massively, in the metaphorical scenarios of *The Eighteenth Brumaire of Louis Bonaparte*. Derrida introduces the relevant remarks with the ambiguous formulation, used here for the first time, of the *persécution de Marx*: the ghost is what *persecutes Marx* – what he was persecuted by and what he himself persecuted. Derrida, who in *Glas* speaks of a *mère sécutrice*,[35] would not have set the word into this scene of confrontation with the father without deliberation. The *persécution de Marx*, wherever it threatens, is experienced as a *pèresécution*. Testifying to this are the myriad sarcastic remarks aimed at the Pope, the 'father of the people', God the Father, at all religious and political authorities and institutions which Derrida, in a cadenced rhythm, does not fail to call by name. Even today the history of Marxism is inseparable from

the history of this *pèresécution*: it is a history of the persecution of
Marxism by presumptive paternal authorities and a history of the
persecution which Marxism itself as such an authority must meet with.
It is a history of the rivalry for paternity and thus of a doubling of the
father, of being a double, of the duplicity of origin and future, of the
double gait, of the *double pas*, of the *pas-pas*. In his early texts – most
elaborately in 'Pas' in 1976 – Derrida developed this peculiar structure
of the unavoidable and simultaneously deconstitutive doubling of
originary instances, the structure of deorigination and disorientation, a
bi- and destructure, in all its complexities; for our purposes here it
should be recalled that this duplication first of all splits and de-posits –
that it exposes this authority to a movement which, prior to authority,
is more powerful than every authority and therefore can no longer be
measured against the standard of authority; this duplication of the
father and of *pèresécution* also entails a bifurcation of succession, of the
persecution, sequence and logic of sequentiality; it thus tears apart the
logic of both consequence and genealogy, of both temporal linearity
and familial homogeneity; and this duplication also opens the logic of
performance – if this is understood as the logic of an originary,
inaugurative speech act and therefore as paternalistic, as the logic of
pèreformance – onto that field in which one father turns against another,
a *pas* turns against a *pas* – against its 'self': in which it becomes a logic
of pas-pas-formance, and consequently no longer of an originary positing, but of a disoriginary one, an ex-positing. Derrida does not make
explicit this turn from the logic of performance to the allologic of its
internal antagonism and hence to the aporia of performance, but it
can be read in his text.

There is, secondly, and not at all far removed from the father in
Derrida's text, the mother in the form of the 'mother tongue'. She is
an indispensable prerequisite for the assumption of the paternal inheritance, but it is equally indispensable that she be forgotten. Derrida
writes: 'This revolutionary inheritance supposes, to be sure, the one
that ends up forgetting the specter, that of the primitive or the mother
tongue. In order to forget not what one inherits but to forget the pre-
inheritance on the basis of which one inherits' (110; Fr. 180–81). This
'forgetting of the maternal' (*l'oubli du maternel*) is necessary 'to bring
the spirit in itself to life', but it makes life itself into a 'life of forgetting',
into 'life as forgetting' of the maternal specter (109; Fr. 180). The life
of the Marxist spirit – or of its specter – consequently remains as
infinitely bound to the specter of the mother as to this forgetting. The
figure of the mother survives solely in its limitless disappearance.

Derrida dedicates his most detailed analysis to the third specter in
this familial phantom story, to that of the brother: it is the specter of

Stirner and his gallery of ghosts. According to Derrida, Stirner for Marx is the 'bad brother' (122; Fr. 198) because he is the 'bad son of Hegel' (ibid.). After Derrida has spoken of his own feelings ('*mon sentiment*': 139: Fr. 221–2), he continues, in the only passage which strikes an explicitly autobiographical tone: 'My feeling, then, is that Marx scares himself, he himself pursues relentlessly someone who almost resembles him to the point that we could mistake one for the other: a brother, a double, thus a diabolical image. A kind of ghost of himself. [*Une sorte de fantôme de lui-même.*]' (139; Fr. 222).[36] Marx has no end of this brother, the double and specter of himself, because he recognizes in him his own jealous identification with Hegel, the father, and sees that he is himself not this father, that he is thus not himself, that he is his own, that is, not his *own* reflection. For him as for Stirner, the proposition of the indubitable ascertainment of self and existence must assume the dubious form 'Ego=ghost' (133; Fr. 212)[37] or 'I = my bad brother.' The I has a priori given itself over to another, to its specter. Its haunting, Derrida says, is 'an operation without action, without a real subject or real object' – whereby (which he does not say) the indispensable premise of every speech act theory to date disappears: that performatives are *acts* of real *subjects.* Every political action consequently threatens to become an automatic farce in a spectropolitical theater. Since Marx least of all can tolerate that, he must separate himself from his Stirnerian specter, from his self and his property, in an endless chain of distancing maneuvers – but precisely for this reason he must incessantly conjure it up, let it return and keep it close at hand. He must promise both himself and the subject of political action a future different from Stirner's specter-future – yet must let this very promise be repeatedly haunted by the threat of its merely phantasmatic character. The *persécution de Marx* does not cease to be his *frèresécution* and his *mèresécution,* for the very reason that it was, from the very beginning, a *pèresécution.* 'For the singular ghost, the ghost that generated this incalculable multiplicity, the arch-specter, is a father or else it is capital' (137; Fr. 221).

It is not difficult to find in Derrida's remarks the assumption that Marx, precisely because he took up a permanent hunt for father and capital, wanted to attain and maintain this capital in order to attain and maintain himself in it. Regardless of whether under the sign of a world-historical law or under the sign of self-preservation, whoever ventures on the persecution of another always intends in this other himself, his own prerogative or his claim on a power equal in principle and, just for that reason, under dispute. He must persecute in another the likeness of himself – but since he pursues only an alienated and estranged figure of himself, his persecution occurs from the very beginning under a doubled and doubly contradictory sign: he cannot be himself without having seized the other, but as this other he can no longer be himself, being merely his alienated, unfamiliar and false figure, a phantom of himself. From this aporia of self-persecution it perforce follows that a self is only possible as a persecuted and phantasmatic self; that the chance for self-preservation now lies in keeping itself apart from itself; and that the structure of the subject – of the egological, world-historical subject in class struggle – is ultimately determined as an irrecoverable but permanently persecuted head-start: as project and projection, as a persecuted project and as the project of the persecution of projection. I, as the formula of the Marxist, agonistic, class subject is rendered by Derrida, I is not only an other, I is the irrecoverable other which the I persecutes, the phantom of a future I and an I still virtualizing its past figures out of its futurity, of a phantasmal father and of virtual capital. I can only be a future I, and must therefore be an unattainable I – I must be phantom-I. The I *is* only as a promise, and this promise in which the I speaks beyond every given language in advance of itself and can, from this 'advance', first speak to itself at all – this promise must always also be an announcement and a threat, always the threat and what is threatened, the virtual subject and *sujet*, the project of the persecution in the temporal cleft between an irrecoverable 'in advance' and an unrepeatable 'beforehand'.

—The I does not speak, it is always the cloth that speaks: the projection onto the cloth and the cloth as projection. What speaks is the project which the I holds and withholds, veils and presents for the I. What speaks – and promises and threatens – is the fetish: of the I, of the father, of capital. Language exists only as the language of the capital fetish, labor fetish, substance fetish – not, however, as this substance, essence, labor, not as language it*self*: unless its *self* be its absolute advance, its pre-language, its promise.

—Cloth speaks. But cloth only speaks in order to *attain* the cloth – in order to obtain it, to appropriate it to itself, to pull it to itself and don it, hold it fast and dissolve into its ideal. That the cloth speaks means that a promise alone speaks. And it means that a double threat also always speaks in this promise: it might fulfill its promise – and thereby make an end of language – and it might never fulfill its promise – and thereby degenerate into the infinite simulation of simulations.

—The cloth – promise, project, ideal, capital and fetish of the I – is always also a religious linen, Veronica's veil, with the impression of abstract man announcing his return, his resurrection and reincarnation; the linen in which capital speaks and this capital, *Monsieur le capital* as Marx called it, promises only itself, promises only a specter, promises only, once again, the cloth. Capital is an infinite project – a project of its advent, its return, its revenues and its revolution.—

Derrida reconstructs the individual shapes and dramas of this family history of specters, and conjectures 'that the figure of the ghost is not just one figure among others. It is perhaps,' he offers for consideration, 'the hidden figure of all figures.' I quote:

> And the fantastic panoply, while it furnishes the rhetoric or the polemic with images or phantasms, perhaps gives one to think that the figure of the ghost is not just one figure among others. It is perhaps the hidden figure of all figures. For this reason, it would perhaps no longer figure as one tropological weapon among others. There would be no metarhetoric of the ghost. (119–20; Fr. 194)

But the original figure, the archi-specter – as the preceding commentary has shown and as the following will – is the specter of the father and thus the promise that he will be the father, that he will rise again as the son and lead abstract man to real man and to salvation. *La figure cachée de toutes les figures* is certainly not a figure amongst others, but it is always and above all a figure. It is the figure of figuration itself, the transcendental or quasi-transcendental figure of generation – that which is also figured as a transcendental in the Marxist value-formula and in the commodity-language he deciphers, that which he figured as historical and historicizing, quasi-transcendental, that is: as money (or, in the function of the general equivalent, as cloth) and further as capital. However invisible and hidden amongst other figures it might be, this figure is not anonymous, nor particularly uncanny or unfamiliar; it bears a name and a familial one; it is called for Marx, as Derrida reads him, the phantom of the father. The archi-figure of this ghost bears the name of one of the figures which conceals it. In it, in the name of the father, the meta-figure – one is strangely enough to assume it is maternal, a mater-figure – becomes a phenomenal figure of generative, paternal phenomenality. The transcendental becomes empirical; phenomenality becomes phenomenal and nominal. The promise of the specter in its paternity, in its spectrality, dictates the drama of the *pèresécution de Marx*, because the promise of the father, the promise which the father makes to himself, precedes his reality and remains after his disappearance, and thus there remains as well the promise of universal capitalization, of the presence of the father, of *pèresense*. In the promise, he is ahead of himself, he is his own grandfather and his own grandson, is himself, both momentarily and invisibly, his own ghost, the promise of the father is his *own* messianic, promessianic operation and *aupèreation*.

And at the same time, not his own, never his own. For in the promise of the father, ahead of himself, he must at the same time asynchronically and anachronically fall behind himself; he can only promise, not realize, his own paternity, and hence can never promise himself *as* father. The *promise* of the father – this belongs to its aporetic structure, to its irremovable covering – will have never been the promise of the *father*. The father is only promised – and always by something other than the father. The promise does not promise. Its privileged figure, identifiable with what is *called* father, with what is *promised* under the name of father, is entrusted to something other than the father; it is a liminal figure, hidden amongst all figures, a figure without figure – and consequently a figure which does not satisfy the determinations of figurality and can only by virtue of this insufficiency permit what is called 'figure'. One could thus say of the 'figure hidden beneath all figures' what Derrida does not say, or does not say this way: a finite figure, a figure without figure, it is the disclosure and opening of all figures, it is what *in* all figures is irreducible to a single figure and thus the event of an *adfiguration*, an a-figuration, an *affiguration*.

—The cloth speaks and in it, capital. But the cloth, capital, speaks neither in propositional statements nor in categories or objective thought-forms; rather, the cloth speaks in promising itself capital. Thus they do not speak, neither capital nor the cloth, nor commodity-language; instead, they disclose the possibility of speaking which cannot be reduced to their 'real abstractions', that is, to the politico-economic grammar and rhetoric of the categories of commodity-language – whose figures, in turn, exist solely in the mode of the promise. Neither capital nor labor is the agent of its project; both are only the historical protagonists of a structure which does not resolve into any grammatical, rhetorical or pragmatic figure – and therefore also not in the figure of the performative as it is traditionally determined. The promise is not a figure but the promise of a figure. An infinite and always deficient promise, it is the pre-figure (Husserl would perhaps say archi-figure) of all possible figures which is never fulfilled and closed off in a figure, the unpromissable affiguration of labor, capital and cloth. Arising from this infinitely generous and generative promise which always keeps coming, but precisely therefore keeps not arriving and not coming, arising from this ungenerous and ungenerative promise, capital, labor and cloth never exist *as such*. Always promised and withheld in the promise, neither language nor the promise speaks. Or: language is nothing but this unfulfillable, unrealizable promise of language. (And since it is unfulfillable and unrealizable, it is impossible to ascertain whether it will ever have been a *promise* of language or a promise of *language*. 'It' can always also have been something other than a 'promise', and always something other than 'language'.)—

The promise, once again, cannot be a statement, a description or an assertion. It must play itself out in a mode of saying which corresponds to nothing given, nothing present, nothing extant and therefore can in no way be placed under the logic of representation, imitation or mimesis. It is neither some kind of conventional sign – for the future is no future if it corresponds to conventions and can be indicated by means of a conventional code – nor is it the promise of a sign at all – for at least a representable or ideal signified would have to correspond to it: but this is, for its part, only a promised correspondence. Every promise, foremost, only *promises* to be a promise and to correspond to its concept and, moreover, to its content. The correspondence is therefore not the horizon of the promise; the promise is the horizon of the correspondence. Since this horizon can only be infinite, all adequation and consensus concepts of truth fail to offer a sufficient determination of the promise and of all other future-oriented and future-disclosing speech forms. But not of these alone. For if language and the cognition possible in it is always an imparting, then its statements must without exception have the character of assurances or truth claims whose verification can in principle only be expected from future correspondences. Language is only language at all in view of a future language. Even if they are not solely and explicitly offered in the form of the promise, all statements, including those usually termed thetic or constative, are structurally asseverations or announcements whose conditions of verification remain, in principle, unfulfilled.[38]

In order to account for non-constative speech forms, and furthermore for the prospective structure of language in general, a discourse of action developed with Hobbes in late rationalism, in skeptical empiricism with Hume, in Kant's transcendental philosophy, and then, with Fichte, culminated in a discourse of an originary act (*Thathandlung*), understood either as a contractual promise, as the leading imperative of all linguistic utterances or as the autothesis of the transcendental I. Language was thus no longer thought of as the correspondence of a statement of a pre-existing object but as the autonomous or autonomizing act of a social or individual subject positing itself. It is this theory of the speech act of an empirical, transcendental and ultimately absolute subject which, by way of labyrinthine detours and transformations, has since then led to what is known as 'speech act theory'. Here the promise is one amongst the possible so-called performative speech acts which must be conducted within certain conventions to be 'successful'. Indeed the very choice of the concept 'performative' resonates with the assumption of a pre-existing rule, of a law or an agreement: the pre-established formal rule is 'realized', 'executed', or 'fulfilled' by a particular performative. Classical speech act theory does not inquire after the conditions under which conventions can be linguistically prepared and established – and precisely for this reason, it cannot account for the performativity of its performatives. Since it does not inquire after the constitution of conventions and their subjects, it typically proceeds from self-governed, intentional subjects who merely reproduce themselves in their linguistic conventions, thereby deviating from its only productive methodological principle of not recurring to instances independent of language to explain linguistic events.

Since 'Signature Événement Contexte', Derrida has repeatedly, critically and productively concerned himself with the limits of Austin's and Searle's theories, particularly with their conventionalist and presentistic premises, using – as he does again in *Specters of Marx* – the concept of the performative. In the figure of conjuration and conjurement – that is, the figure of exorcism and sworn assurance, like the conspiratorial association of persecutors, which is itself exposed to persecution – he emphasizes the significance of an 'act', 'that consists in swearing, taking an oath, therefore promising, deciding, taking a *responsibility*, in short, committing oneself in a performative fashion' (50; Fr. 89); and Derrida speaks of a 'performative interpretation . . . that transforms what it interprets'. He continues: 'An interpretation that transforms what it interprets is a definition of the performative as unorthodox with regard to speech act theory as it is with regard to the 11th Thesis on Feuerbach ("The philosophers have only *interpreted* the world in various ways; the point, however, is to *change* it")' (51; Fr. 89). He writes about the future discussed in *The Communist Manifesto* as 'the real presence of the specter' of communism: 'This future is not described, it is not foreseen in the constantive mode; it is announced, promised, called for in a performative mode' (103; Fr. 186). In, as he continues, the 'performative form of the call' (ibid.), this future tries to establish itself in the Communist Party. In the *Manifesto*, as this 'manifesto' itself proclaims, the party manifests itself and thereby the future. Its promise, its performative act, is thus staged in Marx's text as the instantaneous positing of what is not yet – and perhaps never will be – present. Derrida diagnoses: 'Parousia of the manifestation of the manifest' (103; Fr. 169). This 'absolute manifestation of self' (104; Fr. 170) can only take place by asserting the actuality of a real, incontestable institution for its future; it can only take place on the double terrain of the not-yet-real and actualization and must therefore be both: unreal and real, *spectreal*. Derrida therefore speaks of 'the singular spectrality of this performative utterance' (104; Fr. 170). He thus emphasizes in performatives the character of parousia, of manifestation, of absolute self-positing; but he does not do so without binding this self-positing to an auto-phantomization. Every speech act which inaugurates something new, calling to life a subject, a contract or the Communist Party, posits something under the conditions of reality which has heretofore not existed: it therefore calls to life a thaumaton, a monster or a specter. Performatives, one could translate Derrida's thoughts, spectrealize – and are themselves, if like *The Communist Manifesto* they institute a novelty, *spectrealities*.

Events, and principally the event of the promise, perform, and to be sure they spectralize in performing; they are phantom-parousias first and foremost because they move in the medium of language and thus of the appresentation of what is never immediately present. The border between the 'immediate present' and the future, between the familiar and unfamiliar, is a priori and without exception porous because it, along with the terrain separated by it, is defined only by language, by both discursive and non-discursive language, as their common medium. 'And if this important frontier is being displaced,' Derrida writes, 'it is because the medium in which it is instituted, namely, the medium of the media themselves (news, the press, tele-communications, techno-tele-discursivity, techno-tele-iconicity, that which in general assures and determines the *spacing* of public space, the very possibility of the *res publica* and the phenomenality of the political), this element itself is neither living nor dead, present nor absent: it spectralizes' (50–51; Fr. 89). It spectralizes, in other words, because it speaks. And because it promises. All language, whether explicitly oriented toward the future or not, whether explicitly acting or appearing under the screen of neutral statements, promises to communicate something, promises itself the conditions for the preservation and fulfillment of its promise, and promises itself an addressee in whom its statements can achieve their aim. When speaking and promising occur, indissoluble combinations of actuality and suggestion form, combinations of the living and dead, of the present and absent, because in this language, this 'medium of media', no oppositions but only co-implications exist. For this reason whatever appears – and it is only in this medium that something can appear at all – necessarily escapes the opposition being and non-being, life and death, and the ontological categories of presence and absence. 'It requires, then, what we call . . . *hauntology*,' Derrida writes. 'We will take this category to be irreducible, and first of all to everything it makes possible: ontology, theology, positive or negative onto-theology' (51; Fr. 89).

Every logic of capital and labor, every logic of commodity-language, of the form of equivalence, of exchange, and therefore every logic of controlled planning, technological development and politico-economic prognosis must accordingly be founded in this hauntology of a (as Derrida has it) fundamentally irreducible spectrality of medial language, of the language of the promise, of the futurial and performative, the futuro-formative language of an unsecurable project. Labor is no more a given fact than capital; it is not a transcendental form of value determination or essence of anthropo-technological systems without first being a project, a credit, an advance *on* and a head start *into* a future which can in no way be determined as fact, transcendental or substance. What follows from the idea of 'hauntology' is, first of all, that language does not belong to the system of capital, nor to that of labor, that language does not define itself as commodity-language; that it only assumes the character of productive or reproductive labor when the equivalence form is generalized and has repressed the credit-character of capital as well as the project-character of labor; that language does not have under all conditions (and hence not essentially) the character of a communicative exchange operation, of a propositional adequation or a positional act; and that, even if it can still be characterized as 'performative', the concept of performativity must submit to drastic transformations – transformations which detach it both from the instances of conventionality and positivity, from communicability and continuity with its tradition.

Derrida does think here of language, the medium of media, as a performative engagement, but as one which first of all, essentially and irreducibly, is an engagement *with* others, *against* other others and *for* a future, which has never been actualized in this performative engagement but possesses, instead, the amphibious virtuality or 'spectreality' which alone is adequate to the medial character of language. Language is the medium of futurity. Whatever enters into it, or simply comes into contact with it, is already pulled into a space where the characters of reality are founded precisely upon the not-yet of this reality – and are unfounded in that conventions are, and remain, only in anticipation, positings exist only in process and are hence exposed, continuities are suspended, communications and their rules are not fulfilled but announced, attempted and promised. If, as Derrida does here – like Benjamin (who seems to have left an impression on *Specters of Marx* hardly to be overestimated) – one thinks of the mediality of language from its relationship to the future; if one thinks of it from its promise – much like Heidegger (whose traces are equally unmistakable and numerous in *Specters of Marx*) – then the futurity of language, its inherent promising capacity, is the ground – but a ground with no solidity whatever – for all present and past experiences, meanings and figures which could communicate themselves in it. Language is a medium insofar as it opens the place of arrival, opens the gate to what is to come, the entrance of an unpredictable and topographically indeterminate other: the topos of the U-topic. Neither what is to come 'itself' nor the purely present and yet both 'at once', language is, in the form of the promise and the announcement, the field of interference where what is to come transforms the meaning of every present figure, rendering it legible *sub specie futurae*. If language did not open itself to future possibilities, if it did not promise itself as something else whose verification is still pending and can only be awaited from the position of another, then it would have no possible meaning, it would be nothing but the superfluous replica of what is already known and could never, in its singularity, impart itself to another. Communication – and therewith every being-with-another, every being – is a promise. Since the other which is to come, which is announced or promised, can never be the object of a theoretical determination within the categorial frame of assured epistemological means, but can only be the project of a practical execution which itself must be determined by this project – and therewith by what is fundamentally indeterminate – this praxis can no longer merely be thought of as the 'act' of a constitutive and self-constitutive subject, no longer as a 'performance' within a framework of conventions, but only as an event which with every occurrence discloses other rules, discloses other conventions, other subject forms and other performances, alterformances, alterjects, allopraxes. If language is a promise, it is always the other who speaks. And this other cannot be an alter ego, but only the alteration – and *alteralteration* – of every possible ego. What imparts itself in the promise must therefore go beyond all forms of transcendental subjectivity and their politico-economic institutions, it must go beyond capital and the labor which it determines, and from this *exceedence* it must transform all its figures in advance, transform them by promising them and shifting them into the 'trans' of every form. From its very inception, it must be beyond everything posited in any way, a monster at the limit of appearance, of visibility and representability. It must be, however so gently, an ex-positing.

If I understand it correctly – and as understanding is also always a 'performative' enterprise and therefore an alteration, here too the 'correct' understanding does not move along without displacements, transformations and perhaps distortions – this is nothing other than what Derrida means with the expression 'the singular spectrality of this

performative utterance' (of *The Communist Manifesto*). It is the spectrality and more precisely the spectreality of a project which, prepared
from far off, announced for the first time in the history of European
societies, in philosophical and scientific form, universal unlimited
freedom. 'The form of this promise or of this project,' Derrida emphasizes, 'remains absolutely unique. Its event is at once singular, total,
and uneffaceable – uneffaceable differently than by a denegation and
in the course of a work of mourning that can only displace, without
effacing, the effect of a trauma.' And Derrida continues:

> There is no precedent whatsoever for such an event. In the whole history of
> humanity, in the whole history of the world and of the earth, in all that to
> which one can give the name history in general, such an event (let us repeat,
> the event of a discourse in the philosophico-scientific form claiming to break
> with myth, religion, and the nationalist 'mystique') has been bound, for the
> first time and inseparably, to worldwide forms of social organization (a party
> with a universal vocation, a labor movement, a confederation of states, and
> so forth). All of this while proposing a new concept of the human, of society,
> economy, nation, several concepts of the State and of its disappearance (91;
> Fr. 149–50)

The event of the Marxist promise – whose singularity, once again, lies
in its boundless and yet organized universality – precisely because it is
an absolute novelty in this determined, universal, organizational form
and cannot be reduced to any social, religious or philosophical conventions which might have anticipated it, is therefore a *trauma*: a traumatiz-
ing injury of the politico-economic and social-psychological corpus, of
the religious, linguistic, technical and scientific corpus of all traditions,
a traumatic promise which tears apart a techno- and eco-onto-logical
topology and its mechanisms of displacement and which cannot be
healed by any traditional form of social, psychic or scientific labor, by
any 'labor of mourning'. The Marxist promise which pledges the
abolition of labor cannot be recovered by any labor. It marks an
absolute limit of ergontology.[39]

—Cloth speaks – but with Marx it speaks for the first time in the form
of a universal and infinite promise. No longer as a promise already
indicated in the cloth's 'indigenous' woven structure and finally, in the
mid-nineteenth century, grasped in clear words with teleological resolution, but instead as a promise which unprogrammatically tears its
previous weave and its tendencies and, in this traumatization, promises
for the first time the cloth in its absolute, universal actuality: beyond
every labor, beyond every handiwork and every fabrication, pure mesh.
A peculiar mesh, one which is a tear; universal because singular;
singular because redeemable in repetitions; in need of repetition

because unrepeatable, infinite and therefore irrecoverably and unrealizably finite.—

The promise in question here must consequently first of all be thought of as the 'medium of all media' and as the projection into a future which is not the teleologically predetermined goal of a past history, and thirdly – and therefore – as a traumatic experience in which the form of experience itself suffers a tear and is put to a halt. The medium of all possible media is a tear and an opening, a *rendering possible* of all media, opening the empty place which alone gives room to a spectral actuality, to an actuality only as a specter and which itself can only appear as a space of spectrality. The promise, the traumatic opening of another time – or, indeed, of something other than time – of another future – or something other than the future perhaps; the promise, which does not continue conventions and does not fulfill the rules of its performance but breaks through conventions and inaugurates other rules – and perhaps something other than rules – the promise does not perpetuate history, it starts and makes history possible; this unique promise of something itself unique and new will, according to Derrida, as 'a messianic promise . . . have imprinted an inaugural and unique mark on history' (91; Fr. 150). This marking of history, which in actuality is its opening and nothing less than the *historizing* of history, is regularly and explicitly characterized by Derrida as its spectralization. He writes of the democratic and the communist promise, of those 'infinite promises' which do not govern their own conditions of fulfillment: '*just* opening . . . messianic opening to what is coming, that is, to the event that cannot be awaited *as such*, or recognized in advance therefore, to the event as the foreigner itself, to her or to him for whom one must leave an empty place [*laisser une place vide*] – and this is the very place of spectrality' (65; Fr. 111). And: 'At bottom, the specter is the future, it is always to come, it presents itself only as that which could come or come again' (39; Fr. 71). And:

> In this regard [that is, with regard to its untimeliness and the untimeliness of the future], communism has always been and will remain spectral: it is always still to come and is distinguished, like democracy itself, from every living present understood as plenitude of a presence-to-itself, as totality of presence effectively identical to itself. Capitalist societies can always heave a sigh of relief and say to themselves: communism is finished since the collapse of the totalitarianisms of the twentieth century and not only is it finished, but it did not take place, it was only a ghost. They do no more than disavow the undeniable itself: a ghost never dies, it remains always to come and to come-back [*il reste toujours à venir et à revenir*]. (99; Fr. 163)

The specter haunting Europe and beyond is a promise of democracy and communism which traumatically opens up a new world history, a history for the first time neither mythical nor limited, a world history of liberation, justice and equality. It must announce the most general and most formal form of a future society and at the same time must promise the unpromissable: its absolute singularity and incommensurability with every generalization. The democratic and furthermore communist promise thus announces, in absolute formality and absolute singularity, performatively – *biformatively* – two futures irreducible and irreconcilable to one another: an unlimited universal rule and a singularity free of every imaginable rule. It is the promise of a coming democracy only by being this double and aporetic promise; a performative only by being this *biformative*. But this singular universal promise is aporetic in yet another respect. As the promise of a future which is universal, it must be the promise of a just future of all pasts; but it cannot be the promise of the future of *all* pasts without also being a restrictive promise from a particular generation of *limited* pasts and hence without being itself merely a past promise, a wraith and an echo, the revenant of promise, broken over and over or betrayed or fatal. Pluriformative and reformative, the revolutionary performative of the absolute messianic promise is also a *perverformative* that turns against itself and in each of its traits tends to erase itself – and not for any empirical or contingent reason which might have been avoided or eliminated, but from a structural necessity which not a single promise can escape, in particular not the promise of singularity.[40]

—The language of the cloth is always also an echolalia. Things said resound in it once more, every shred and tatter of word and phrase pursue the speaker into a future of semblance and echo, into an echo chamber, a tomb: a specter monologue in diverse voices. But this necrophilic language of the nymph Echo is still a language of *philía*, keeping the dead alive and preserving it for other times – or something other than time.—

Specters of Marx is not about this multiplication in the performative structure of the promise, but indeed about the multiplication, the dissociations and the antagonisms of specters, spirits, phantoms, ghosts and fetishes – and since it is the promise and the future disclosed in it which Derrida characterizes as the phantom par excellence, his text is, in a mediated way, also about the dissociation and original perversion of the performative. It is about the difference *within* the performative and how this difference can haunt in no other 'figure' than that of the monstrous figure of a specter. I cite here three passages which address precisely this problem. 'There are several times of the specter. It is a proper characteristic of the specter, if there is any, that no one can be sure if by returning it testifies to a living past or to a living future, for the *revenant* may already mark the promised return of the specter of living being. Once again, untimeliness and disadjustment of the contemporary' (99; Fr. 162). The specter can come from the past as well as from the future; its spectral quality is its double allegiance, which can in no way be decided upon by means of theoretical cognition, since every cognition of that kind must already be related to the spectral and, in turn, can do nothing but 'performatively' send out its own specters. There is a time fissure through the spectral which distributes it across two times that are heterogeneous to one another, distributes it into a double chronicity and an asynchronicity, an achrony which lets the past appear in what is to come and what is to come in what is past. But no matter how even the distribution of times may be, Derrida's formulation suggests with sufficient precision that there is no symmetry between what is past and what is to come: specters of the past can only appear when conjured by the promise of another future. In the final footnote of the book, this theme of an asymmetrical, future-inclined asynchronicity is taken up once again when Derrida writes: 'Given that a revenant is always called upon to come and to come back, the thinking of the specter, contrary to what good sense leads us to believe, signals toward the future. It is a thinking of the past, a legacy that can come only from that which has not yet arrived – from the arrivant itself' (196; Fr. 276). The future delivers specters and even in the specters of the past, however lethal they might be, launches the promise of another future for this same past. The promise of an absolutely other future testifies to hope in even the bloodiest pasts. To make other futures possible, they must undergo the risk of their pairing with dangerous futures and confront their own effacement. The performative of the promise, directed toward other possibilities of the past and future, is thus unavoidably linked to a threat to this promise itself and thereby to the effacement of this performative. There is no rendering possible of possibilities which might not also make this rendering itself impossible. No promise in which the possibility of its breach was not also voiced, no act into which its annulment does not intervene.

—No cloth which could not be taken apart thread by thread; no weave which would not end in an open seam, would not consist of such seams, were not woven from its unraveling, from its runs. The cloth, a Penelope of itself.—

In principle every performative is an aporetic agonistic biformative – or, to write the word for French ears and eyes, a *bifformative*: What it

inaugurates includes the possibility of its erasure (its *biffure*), and only
with the inclusion of this possibility does it have the chance to begin.
The performative does not perform – unless it still 'performs' the
possibility of the 'not' of its performing and is in-formed by this 'not';
it is, in French once again, a *pas-formative*. It is the start of a speech act
in which an egologically structured subject should constitute itself, a
start which is close to being this act itself, hence an *adformative*; but
since it can be nothing but the start and *opening* of this practical and
therein self-sufficient act, an opening in which its possibility is knitted
into the possibility of the impossibility of succeeding, it can itself never
assume the definitive form of the performative, will never finally be
accomplished and remains, the event of the threshold before every act,
parapractical, an act without act before every possible act, *aformative*.
The structure of language is *afformative* – both adformative and aformative – and it is only its onto-ego-logical speech-activist interpretation
which is recorded in the concept of performatives, therein main-
taining the suggestion that logos has incarnated itself, that it is
'accomplished'.[41]

The promise, and in particular the Marxist promise, the first and
only to announce and prepare the universal actualization of freedom
and individuality, opens possibilities; but it opens them with all the
dangers and threats linked to this disclosure. These dangers include
the repetition of the familial, national and religious myths which it
claims to rid itself of. Here belongs as well the danger – of activating
the performative of the promise according to the schema of the jealous
persecution of the father. Performatives of *pèresécution* must always be
able to also be *pèreformatives* and thus formatives of the father – and of
the kind in which, in the first and last instance, the father and his son
and his holy spirit promises and forms itself. And if not a father, then
nearby to him a mother in a *mèreformative* of the mother tongue or,
perhaps even closer to the father, a rivalrous brother in a *frèreformative*.
What else could promise, manifest and form itself here but the least
uncanny and the most familiar specter: the Holy Family beneath its
head, capital? Or – as the past eighty years have demonstrated; it
amounts to the same thing – the Communist Party, this other Holy
Family beneath its head, the capital of labor?

What, once again, would be the difference between specter and
spirit, between the phantom of all failed or missed pasts and that spirit
of the future in which they would be redeemed from their silence,
their distortion and falseness? Derrida expressly poses this question in
connection to a passage from *The German Ideology* in which Marx
sneeringly states as Stirner's ventriloquist, 'that you yourself are a ghost
which "awaits salvation, that is, a spirit"' (136; Fr. 217). The difference

between specter and spirit, in Derrida's commentary on Marx's citation
of Stirner, is *différance*.

> The specter is not only the carnal apparition of the spirit, its phenomenal
> body, its fallen and guilty body, it is also the impatient and nostalgic waiting
> for a redemption, namely, once again, for a spirit. The ghost would be the
> deferred spirit [*l'esprit différé*], the promise or calculation of an expiation.
> What is this differance? All or nothing. One must reckon with it but it upsets
> all calculations, interests, and capital. (136; Fr. 217)

If the specter is the holding back and avoidance [*Hinhaltung und
Hintanhaltung*] of the spirit, it is the unending longing for the spirit as
well. The messianic promise haunts in the shattered and criminal forms
of social and linguistic life as a specter and links even its most mythical
forms, its terroristic performatives, its familial obsessions, to the expectation of their redemption. A life ruined retains the longing for the
just one – and thus, and *only* thus, in a kind of minimal-ontodicy, is
itself 'justified'. For what would redemption be if all pasts were not
redeemed along with all their disappointments, tortures and disgrace?
What would freedom be if the dead were not also liberated, at least
those who live on in us – and are there others? Even the conditions of
capital and labor are subjected to *other* conditions: those of their
change, those of their possible other future. Nor would the ontologization of the afformative to the performative, and furthermore into the
pèreformative, be possible without the afformative, the future-oriented
structure of the promise, which vows the transformation of that structure into a predictably and programmatically untamable other
language – and perhaps something other than language – into another
form of action – perhaps even something other than form and than
action. And, perhaps, something other than the future.

For what would the future be if it could not be something other
than the future?

The point is not to conjecture it, design plans, formulate intentions
or suggest precautions for it. Nor is it to speculate about the future or
speculate with it. It is a matter of unfolding all the implications of
futurity and the only way of access to it, speculation, and thereby to
make more audible the language of this futurity and its spectreality,
the language of the promise. For the sake of futurity, it must first of all
concern its formal structure alone and therefore practice a suspension
of all contents which might combine with it. What is offered and what
Derrida repeatedly shows in *Specters of Marx* is an ultra-transcendental
epokhè, almost without comparison in political theory up to now, of the
objects and contents of a future politics and their rigorous reduction
to the sheer form of futurity. Accordingly he distinguishes between the

'Marxist ontology grounding the project of Marxist science or critique' and a 'messianic eschatology' which as the unrealized promise of justice and democracy goes beyond every critical ontology of what is present at hand and of what is predictably or programmatically graspable. The contents of the future's determinations aside, the *essential* difference between the Marxist critique and the religions, ideologies and theologemes it criticizes (and which criticize it) dissolves. Their solidarity, notoriously dismissed by both, consists in what neither can think as the content of its doctrines or object of its concepts, but what both are caught up in as the implication of those concepts and doctrines. Derrida writes:

> While it is common to both of them, with the exception of the content (but none of them can accept, of course, this *epokhè* of the content, whereas we hold it here to be essential to the messianic in general, as thinking of the other and of the event to come), it is also the case that its formal structure of promise exceeds them or precedes them. Well, what remains irreducible to any deconstruction, what remains as indeconstructible as the possibility itself of deconstruction is, perhaps, a certain experience of the emancipatory promise; it is perhaps even the formality of a structural messianism, a messianism without religion, even a messianic without messianism, an idea of justice.... (59; Fr. 102)

This suspension of contents with which the messianic structure of the promise – one could say: the structure of the *promessianic* – is exposed must not be misunderstood as indifference toward future or present institutions: it is the only form under which such institutions first become possible. 'This indifference to the content here is not an indifference,' Derrida emphasizes, 'it is not an *attitude* of indifference, on the contrary. Marking any opening to the event and to the future as such, it therefore conditions the interest in and not the indifference to anything whatsoever, to all content in general. Without it, there would be neither intention, nor need, nor desire, and so on' (73; Fr. 123–4). What Derrida calls 'the messianic without messianism' is thus what in every promise, in every imperative and every wish – and altogether in language – reveals 'the necessarily pure and purely necessary form of the future as such' (ibid.). It is, one could say, the necessary possibility which precedes everything actual, everything necessarily actual and everything possible. It is the historicity of history itself: a futurity always open and thus open to something else. Marxism – and, since there are several competing Marxisms, amongst them nationalistic, totalitarian, and terrorist, one must specify: that Marxism which pursues a politics of emancipatory universalism – is the instance of the articulation of this messianic promise; it is the instance of this articulation even when, and perhaps only when, the messianic does not assume the organizational form of one party but of several, even if, and perhaps only if, it is not bound to the sufferings and hopes of a single class and thus not to the traditional conception of the proletariat, and only if the messianic and its Marxism is not corrupted by a program, if it is corrupted neither by its alliance with labor nor by a temporal and historical schema of succession, a development or linear sequence.

The spirit of Marxism – or the one inheritable specter haunting for one hundred and fifty years – is thus first and foremost the absolutely abstract formality of the promise: the opening of a future which would not be the continuation of pasts but for the first time exposes the claim of these pasts, the opening of another time – a time other than the time of labor and capital – the opening of a history which in fact gives all previous history its room for maneuver [*Spielraum*]. The spirit of Marxism is, in short, the promise, the absolute 'in advance' of speaking; it is the pre-structure, the structure of possibility of every experience – and is thus essentially temporalization and historization. But as such it commands an eschatological movement which cannot be halted by any representational content or foreseeable purposes. The messianic eschatology underlying every fundamentally critical thought, every longing and every one of the simplest statements, and underlying in particular the Marxist project urging justice beyond internationalism, democracy and all positive legal forms, must, for the sake of the historicity and futurity of these absolutely formal and universal imperatives, be distinguished from classical teleology. Derrida insists upon 'distinguishing ... any teleology from any messianic eschatology' (90; Fr. 147).[42] There is no pre-established telos for 'the messianic without messianism' which could be recognizable now, programmatically striven for and ultimately achieved in some particular organization of social life. As the universal structure of experience, it cannot be presided over by any guiding figures whose design was not already obliged to that structure and therefore was not already surpassed, in every one of their positions, by it. Messianic hope is thus divested of all determined and all determinable religious, metaphysical or technical figures of expectation; this continued divestment itself opens every past history to a new future one, and can therefore be nothing other than an 'expectation without a horizon of expectation' (65, 192; Fr. 111, 267). From this decisive determination of the messianic which is repeatedly marked in Derrida's text – that it must remain indeterminate, that it is messianic without a horizon – it follows for the promise, and the structure of its performativity when the messianic tendency first arises, that this promise too must *stricto sensu* be open and that it must be a performative without a horizon. Only with this characterization is the ground cleared for the

messianic movement, for the Marxist project and a politics of emancipation: it is *performing without a performative horizon*, the *perforation* of
every horizon, transcendental – and, more exactly, atranscendental –
kenosis of all linguistic and non-discursive forms of action. But what
does that mean?

Derrida does not pursue the structure of a horizonless performativity
further in *Specters of Marx*. For him, this structure is marked by its
mediality – as the 'medium of all media' – by its openness and hence
by its illimitable futurity. The way in which these three traits join
together in the spectrality or spectreality of the Marxist project and
affect the structure of the performative is given no closer investigation.
There is, however, a hint, repeated several times, and commented upon
in two of Derrida's more recent texts, 'Foi et savoir' and 'Avances'. In
his Marx book Derrida concedes – and it is important that it occurs in
the form of a concession – that the unconditional hospitality which the
horizonless promise accords to the other, the future, justice and
freedom, could be 'the impossible itself', and he adds: 'Nothing and
no one would arrive otherwise, a hypothesis that one can never exclude,
of course' (65; Fr. 111–12). One can thus not exclude, but rather must
concede and admit that the promise of an arrival *also* promises *no*
arrival, that it promises something not arriving and thus promises
precisely what can in no way be promised. But it is clear that this non-
advent does not overtake the promise – every promise – like an accident
from the outside (perhaps from that other who was promised but who,
due to his volition, power or impotence, does not come); rather, this
non-arriving belongs to the very structure of the elementary promise:
insofar as it is a promise, it must be open to something which denies
itself knowledge, evidence, consciousness and the calculability of a
program, and thus always and in every single case cannot arrive. The
promise would not be a promise if it were a statement of fact or the
prognosis for a causal chain of development. It lacks the egologically
anchored certainty which should belong to epistemic calculability.
Regardless of what is promised, the promise as such already concedes
that it may not be kept, that it may be broken and can only be given in
consideration of its possible breach. A promise is given only under the
premises of the possible retraction of its offering. Since the promise is
altogether the initiating act of language (and hence is language
'itself'), the opening of both selfhood and relation to the other, of
sociability, history and politics, its structural unrealizability cannot help
but suspend them all and, in them, their constitutive relation to the
future. Insofar as the future exists, the promise offers it only under the
proviso of the future's possible non-advent. And this reserve, this
absolute discretion of a possibly impossible future, is inscribed into the

promise and with it into the opening of the future; it is inscribed into the very futurity of the future.

The tie between the performativity of attestation (*performativité testimoniale*) and the techno-scientific performance discussed in 'Foi et savoir' is linked by a 'performative of the promise', which Derrida emphasizes is at work even in lies and perjuries, and without which an address, a turn to the other would be impossible. He writes: 'Without the performative experience [*expérience performative*] of this elementary act of faith, there would be neither a "social relation" nor an address to the other, nor any kind of performativity of productive performance joining, from the very beginning, the knowledge of the scientific community to practice, science to technology.'[43] Since this elementary promise – and that also means: the promise as the medium of all discursive and non-discursive institutions – is for its part bound to the iterability of markings, it follows that there can be:

> [n]o future without inheritance and without the possibility of *repeating*. No future without *iterability*, at least in the form of a relation to itself and of the *confirmation* of an originary Yes. No future without messianic memory and the messianic promise, without a messianicity older than all religions, more original than all messianisms. No speech, no address to the other without the possibility of an elementary promise. Perjury and a broken promise lay claim to the *same* possibility.[44]

Everything, in short, begins with the possibility – with the possibility of projecting possibilities in the promise and of confirming these possibilities, repeating and transferring them. The possibility of the promise is already the possibility of its repetition. But were this repetition merely to result from the automatism of the perpetually selfsame, the promise would become program and evidence, prophecy and providence. If the opening of the future ushered in by the iterability of the promise – one could say: if *futuration* were the act of a knowing consciousness – then the future itself would be something entirely knowable and technically executable and would thus be, instead of the future, its annulment. The iterability coextensive with the promise thus has two sides: it opens the future as a field of possible confirmations and even fulfillments, and it discloses it as a future which can block every future. The possibilities of the future always include the possibility that there is no future. The possibilities of iteration always include the possibility that it is not a transformation but rigid fixation; the possibilities of the promise always include the possibility that it is not only unfulfillable but also unperformable: every promise, in principle, necessarily can be interrupted by accident or coincidence. These two possibilities, irreducible because equally original, turn every futuration into *affuturation*: into the opening of a future which, because it must always be able to be a future without future, an annulment of the future, can irrevocably disavow this very opening. Not *the* future is opened, instead – iteration is immediate pluralization – multiple futures are opened; but to these futures always belongs at least one which no longer permits talk *of* a future or *in* one. At least this one, this annulled and null-future, necessitates the experience of future possibilities always at the foundation of their possible impossibility, futures at the foundation of their future non-advent. There is no relation to the future not undone by the irrelation to its inherently possible absence at every point – thus a relation to irrelation – an irrelation itself – and hence not a relation to the future at all. *A-futurizing*, we speak and act at the future, on the *threshold* to it, not *in* it, not in the open but in the opening – and in an opening which (otherwise it were none) can always be the opening to an end, to a conclusion or obstruction.

The possibilities disclosed in the messianic opening of the promise relate to this promise not as external addenda following a logic other than that of the promise. They are possibilities only insofar as they are possibilities disclosed by the promise. If for Derrida the promise is messianic, this does not mean that it is the promise of a messianic lying outside it, still less the promise of a messiah, but simply this: that the grounding structure of the promise itself is the announcement and expectation of another, a just life and another, a true language. Consequently – and therefore alone – the irreducible possibilities imparted in the structure of every promise also necessarily include the possibility that it is the promise of a god or a messiah. The messiah of a promise, he is nothing but this promise that the promise is real and in truth a promise; he is nothing but the promise to say the truth about the promise and to keep this promise as it was made. God himself would be the promise that the promise *is* a promise: the one who testifies to its truth as its highest guarantor. In order to be able to promise something, the promise itself must first of all secure its own status and to this end project an absolute – and therefore ungeneratable – instance of its attestation. To be a promise at all, every promise, even the most profane, must produce a god. 'Without god, no absolute witness. No absolute witness who could bear witness to the attestation itself.'[45] What the promise takes as the witness to its truth must be absolute, must be a god and *one* god – but must also *not* be god, not an absolute and not a witness, for if the promise were certified by an absolute witness then it would no longer be a promise, no longer directed toward the future and no longer the precarious opening of a possibility; it would be the statement of an absolutely certain actuality.

The one absolute witness must be able to be none – no god – he can be a god only in that he can also not be one, he must remain able to let his potency go, beyond all capacities – and can only attest to the promise as this one and none. 'Without god, no absolute witness [*point de témoin absolu*]. No absolute witness who could bear witness to the attestation itself.' The necessary possibility of a god, posited by the structure of the promise itself, is by the same necessity ex-posited to the necessary impossibility of god. If the messiah is heralded, summoned and called into life by the messianic structure of finite language, then he must be held back by the same structure, withheld, always overdue and longed for. No god, no messiah, who would not be missing. None who was not still absent in his presence. None who was not promised and promised away by language: spoken away and removed, removed and re-moved. None who would speak. The messiah cannot be promised – but can *only* be promised, and thus only promised as the unpromissable which breaks every promise.

What makes the messianic structure of language and experience not into a theological, but an anatheological and atheological structure is precisely what the titles 'messianic' and 'the messianic' still mask. As the messianic, like the title 'god' for a theology (whether positive or negative), is only valid as the name for an absolute entity if an element from the structure of the promise is isolated, semanticized and ontologized, so the carefully chosen, purely formal title 'the messianic without messianism' could still arouse the misunderstanding that it indicates a stable transcendental structure of projective actions directly aimed at an open future, disclosing the future. That would not only lead to a messianization and theologization of the future (Derrida cites Lévinas' 'Dieu est l'avenir'[46]), it would not only mean the ontologization of an isolated element from the structure of the promise, but it would also be contrary to precisely those aspects which Derrida stresses in his analyses of the promise and to his question of what could be a more consistent inheritance than an 'atheological inheritance of the messianic' (191; Fr. 266). The messianic is always what longs for, discloses and promises an unanticipatable, unprefigurable other; but exactly because it is not prefigurable, because it is an other, the messianic must by necessity refuse to promise it, must thwart its promise to retain its promissability and instead of pledging a future, appresents, in its exposition, futurity. Only the *ammessianic* is messianic: that which opens the messianic tendency and concedes at the 'same' time the possibility of its discontinuance, *hic et nunc*. As there must be a possibility of no future so that there can be a future, so must the messianic always be open to its lapse, if it is to be messianic at all. It – every it – must also possibly not exist so that it might exist: the law of that law issued by the promise, the law of the exposing of the law 'itself,' an atranscendental movement which precedes every transcendentality of hope, belief, wish, and every ontologization or semanticization. This movement precedes every being as something in which every 'pre' is given up. 'Messianic promise' – that means the anasemiosis even of the 'pre' of every *promise* in a possibility potent to the extent that it is impotent; a possibility which can only mean by pre-ceding non-meaningfully every meaning and every bidding. 'The messianic', like 'the future', is a misnomer; its gap cannot be filled by the misnomer 'ammessianic' but only made more precise and commented upon.

'Advances', Derrida's preface to *Le Tombeau du dieu artisan* by Serge Margel, is a study on the aporetic structure of every promise. It argues the connection between doing [*Machen*] and lack [*Mangel*], performance and finitude. Promises are only possible under the conditions of their possible breach. They are the most exposed forms of linguistic and consequently existential fragility. 'In order to be a promise,' Derrida writes, 'a promise *must be capable* of being broken and therefore capable of *not* being a promise (for a breakable promise is no promise).'[47] Though Derrida does not pursue it in this way, the consequence for the structure of performativity is clear: since this structure cannot grant the certainty that it is really the structure of *performativity*, since it *must not* grant this certainty if the structure is to have a chance to correspond to it, the *form* of the performative in its performance must itself be suspended. The performative is what exposes its form, the horizon of its determination, *ex-poses* itself as an act – a doing not lacking something else but lacking this doing 'itself' – a completion from which both the plenitude and the carrying through 'itself' immediately slips away – and whose 'self' can lie in nothing other than permitting this exposing and slipping away. An *actus ex-actus*. A performative which must be structured, distructured as *afformative* in order to be able to operate, open or posit: as open *toward* the form of an act, but for this reason *divested* of the form of this act; an amorphic or anamorphic event over which no figure rules and from which no final figure results because it is essentially *affigurative*; moreover it is, each time, a singular, non-iterable – and therefore *errable* – occurrence because the conditions of its repetition must also always be the conditions of its unrepeatability. Therefore Derrida's reference to the 'perversion' of the promise into a threat[48] can only be misleading: every promissive, every promessianic performance, without changing its character, is by necessity itself already the threat not only of not being kept, but of *not being one* at all.

If, once again, a future can be, it can only be so as one which can also *not* be. This possibility is not an alternative articulable in the disjunction 'either a future or none', for only insofar as there is a future, is there none; only insofar as there are open possibilities, is there also the possibility that none will be preserved *as a possibility*. But if what is called presence or actuality is always determined by the opening towards the future and *as* this opening, then presence *appresentating* (in a sense other than a Husserlian one) is always that in which every future is pending. This opening which is the present, must, *hic et nunc*, be something other than future, more than *a* future: pluralities of futures, but also more than futures, a pluperfect-future; not only another time and other times, but what would no longer be time. The promise would be the place where this other time and this other than time occur. It is the place – the atopic place – where possibilities are indeed opened, but only those constitutively lacking the conditions of their verification and actualization. Whatever might *become* a promise without ever indeed being so, belongs to at least two 'times': a time of a future which can come and of a future which cannot come; a time which renders possible and one which renders impossible this very rendering. The promise is thus the place of the aporia of temporalization; hence the place of an *attemporalization* which must precede every possible time, every possible future, every possible possibility and with which, here and now – for this too is a promise – not only other times occur but also an other than time.

—A cloth before time and before temporally determined speech – a cloth of promises, a pre-discursive material which promises 'itself': the cloth is originally twofold, the cloth of the promise, and another (which is not there) of the confirmation that it is a promise. They do not exchange with one another, do not communicate with each other under a common discursive ideal and yet, in their absolute disjunction, they are a community – a possible–impossible community before every equivalence, before capital and before the labor and its time measured by capital. And because before labor, also beyond it: atranscendental material. Now.—

As a promise exposed to the uncertain possibilities of the future, every act risks not being one. Each act, however closely determined it might otherwise be, must a priori *leave open* at least one extreme possibility – and leaving open means risking and risking failure – the possibility of no longer falling under the regime of an intentional subject and thereby no longer qualifying as an act. The open place of this extreme possibility which (in)determines the field of any and every action is no longer a place of doing but of *letting*. Every performative must contain the structural concession that its horizon is not its own, that it is not altogether the horizon of performativity – of positing, of

productive imagination, of labor – that it is instead open to other
horizons and, at the limit, ahorizontal, open to possibilities not given
by it but given *to* it, ceded, imparted or left. Performatives, speech acts
positing facts or opening possibilities, exist only when they are conceded room for maneuver and when they give themselves over to this
maneuvering: when, even before they can be performatives, they are
admitted into a field which one can provisionally call that of *admissives*
or *amissives*. These ad- or amissives cannot be thought of as fundamental speech acts, for they involve neither acting nor executing; they are,
rather, admitted and conceded, granted and left, and in such a
manner, a manner unregulatable and unique each time, that an
admission or cession can at the same time be a letting go and
discarding, an abandonment and a loss.[49] To say 'I promise' I must also
say 'I admit my promise' and 'I admit it in view of its admission by the
other to whom it is addressed.' But to *admit* a promise means unavoidably to concede its potential failure, its potential breach and even its
potential inadmissibility; hence, to treat its admission not as an assured
fact but as a rendering possible which does not exclude its rendering
impossible as well – the possibility of the impossibility of this rendering
possible. 'I promise' therefore always also means: 'This promise is
admitted on the condition of its unreliability and its possible inadmissibility.' All performatives are therefore (even if, in programming,
semanticizing, ontologizing the field of their projects, they deny it)
structured as admissives, all admissives structured as amissives: they
admit, concede and leave themselves to a field over whose determination they have so little defining power that they cannot even grant it
being, not even an unlimited, secure, solid possible being, an actual or
necessary being. They admit and leave themselves to what is not
projected with them: they are amissives insofar as they risk their own
loss, their impossibility. Admissive, amissive: the Marxist promise is the
opening of a world, of a society, of a language, which – *lingua missa,
lingua amissa* – aims at a just life in every trait, and for this very reason,
in every trait, must be open to another and still another – and also to
none. But if the opening onto another life and another language still
follows the temporality of a rendering possible, then this never exclud-
able – and, for the sake of the opening itself, indispensable – opening
onto another life which would be none, and onto a language which
would be no language, this opening onto the occlusion of the opening
follows at the same time the temporality of the rendering impossible;
and the promise of language knits itself – for the sake of this promise
– into the promise of the prohibition not only of a particular language
but of every language. A promise, above all the most relinquished, the

most admitted of promises, exists not in a language, but in the cleft of language.

The promise, the messianic, ammessianic promise, opens itself as a time cleft. And indeed as the time cleft of a world, as a world cleft. Marxism is historically the first promise which made a claim on unlimited universality in freedom and justice, the first and only not biased by racisms, nationalisms, cultisms or class ideologies, but promising instead a world common to all and to each his own.[50] This world must be promised, demanded, desired and made possible before it can exist. But if it is ever to exist, it will be a world under the conditions of this promise, of this longing and this rendering possible; it will therefore be an aporetic world whose idea lies in infinite conflict with its every singular actualization and in conflict with its always possible annulment. This conflict is as unavoidable as the promise from which it arises. What can never be conclusively avoided but, to be sure, can be opposed – what *must* be opposed – is the possibility contained within the tendency of the promise of not being a promise but instead a totalitarian program, an immutable prescription, plan or, quite simply, of not being at all. What must be opposed is the organization of the future; and what fights against it is the longing that the future might be otherwise, other than other, not merely *a* future and not merely *future*. This is the rift in the world which the world has opened up with the Marxist promise of a *world*. It has become no longer necessarily a cleft between different classes – but it is still this class antagonism as well; it is first of all a rift between a future which opens other futures and not merely futures, and a future which would be the end of all futures, the end of history in the automatized terror of private interests, in the tortures of exploitation and self-exploitation, in the vacuous self-sufficiency and ritualized mutilation of others and of the other possibilities of history. What must be opposed is the mutilation of past history – but how past? – and future history – but future beyond every arrival – and thus the destruction of that present which opens itself to the entrance of history. What *must* be opposed is the death of the promise in theoretical certainty and practical complacency – of the promise which precedes both, declaring that neither is sufficient, that both must let themselves be opposed, and that this 'must' and this 'let' must be able to exist beyond certainty and complacency, beyond this death.

The promise, *afformatively*, Derrida makes clear, is a desert, formal, *afformal*, in its infinite abstraction and limitless expanse, an insurrection against the suggestions of fulfillment and of successful culturation, a landscape of fury and longing for all that is absent. This insurrection and this fury and this longing of the promise could be the beginning, the perhaps unconscious and unpractical, surely inconsolate beginning both of language – of another language – and of politics – of another politics and of something other than politics. They speak, askew and 'deranged', spectreal and compromised, in commodity-language as well. The point is to articulate it more clearly, and not merely to articulate it.

— Cloth of sand. 'Language, too, is desert, this voice that the desert needs . . . ,' Blanchot writes.[51]

> The desert, not yet time and not yet space, but space without site and time without generation. . . . When everything is impossible, when the future, given over to fire, burns . . . then the prophetic word announcing the impossible future still says the 'nevertheless' which breaks the impossible and restores time. 'Truly, I will give this city and this land into the hands of the Chaldeans; they will invade it, burn and raze it, and *nevertheless* I will lead back the inhabitants of this city and this land from every region whither I have cast them away. They will be my people, and I will be their god. Nevertheless! *Laken!*'[52]

Translated by Kelly Barry

Notes

1. Jacques Derrida, *Spectres de Marx* (Paris: Galilée, 1993), p. 165. The corresponding passages cited here are from the English translation, occasionally modified (*Specters of Marx*, trans. Peggy Kamuf [New York and London: Routledge, 1994], pp. 100–1 [*SM*]). 'The specter is also, among other things, what one imagines, what one thinks one sees and which one projects – on an imaginary screen [*écran*] where there is nothing to see. Not even the screen sometimes, and a screen always has, at bottom [*au fond qu'il est*] a structure of disappearing apparition [*de l'apparition disparaissant*].' Two pages earlier is written: 'All phantasms are projected onto the screen [*écran*] of this ghost (that is, on something absent, for the screen itself is phantomatic, as in the television of the fugure . . .)' (99; Fr. 163). The screen, the cloth is the ground-figure which appears only in disappearing and in which disappearing appears, thus the abyss as ground and the figure as none. (*SM* page numbers are indicated in the text from here on. The second number refers to the French text. My citations refer generally to the available translation but deviate from it where required by the French text.)

2. Karl Marx, *Capital: A Critique of Political Economy*, Volume 1, trans. Ben Fowkes (New York: Vintage, 1977), p. 143. The translation has been slightly modified where necessary. Hereafter indicated as *Capital* with the page number.

3. *Capital*, pp. 143–4.

4. *Capital*, p. 144.

5. *Capital*, p. 143.

6. *Capital*, p. 144.

7. Ibid.

8. In a footnote to the observation that the body of a commodity is the value-mirror of the other commodity, its body being the reflection of something disembodied and thus the incarnation of something general in an impossible simulacrum, Marx explains: 'In a certain sense, a man is in the same situation as a commodity. As he neither enters the world in possession of a mirror, nor as a Fichtean philosopher who can say "I am I,"

a man first sees and recognizes himself in another man. Peter relates to himself as a man through his relation to another man, Paul, in whom he recognizes his likeness. With this, however, Paul also becomes from head to toe, in his physical form as Paul, the form of appearance of the genus homo for Peter' (p. 144).

9. *Capital*, p. 143.

10. *Capital*, p. 172.

11. Ibid.

12. *Capital*, p. 144.

13. *Capital*, p. 148.

14. *Capital*, pp. 150–1.

15. *Capital*, p. 151.

16. Marx makes the historicity of this ergontology clear in a note on the failure of the 'great investigator' Aristotle in the face of the value-form: he was not yet able to recognize 'human labor' as the 'common substance' of different commodities because the 'concept of human equality' did not yet have the 'permanence of a fixed popular opinion' (*Capital*, pp. 151–2). This also means that human labor in its function as a standard and value-substance has since then become not the truth of political economy, but that this function has become a 'popular opinion' supporting the historical truth of capitalist economy.

17. *Capital*, p. 149.

18. *Capital*, p. 148.

19. *Capital*, p. 165.

20. *Capital*, p. 164.

21. *Capital*, p. 169.

22. *Capital*, p. 167.

23. *Capital*, pp. 166–7.

24. *Capital*, p. 169.

25. Ibid.

26. *Capital*, p. 163. [The pun, in Marx and Hamacher, on 'Tisch' and 'Fetisch' is lost in translation. – Translator's note.]

27. *Capital*, p. 103.

28. *Capital*, p. 167.

29. Karl Marx, *Capital* Volume 3, quoted from *The Marx–Engels Reader*, ed. Robert Tucker (New York: Norton, 1972), pp. 319–20.

30. *The German Ideology*, in ibid., p. 157. Hereafter indicated as *GI* with the page number.

31. Ibid., pp. 149–50.

32. *Capital*, p. 172.

33. Aphorism CCXIV in Schelling's *Sämmtliche Werke*, part 1, vol. 7 (Stuttgart and Augsburg: Cotta, 1860), p. 238.

34. ['Aphanisis' refers to withdrawal from phenomenality; its provenance ultimately derives from Ernest Jones and was taken up by Lacan in relation to castration. – Editor's note.]

35. *Glas* (Paris: Éditions Galilée, 1974), p. 134b.

36. And again a little later: 'a kind of double or brother [*une sorte de double ou de frère*]' (141; Fr. 224). Here Derrida takes up again a theme of great importance in his reading of Lacan ('Le Facteur de la verité' in *La Carte postale* [Paris: Aubier-Flammarion, 1980]).

37. 'I am,' Derrida continues, 'would then mean "I am haunted": I am haunted by myself who am (haunted by myself who am haunted by myself who am . . . and so forth). Wherever there is Ego, *es spukt*, "it spooks" . . . The essential mode of self-presence of the *cogito* would be the haunting obsession of this "es spukt" ' (133; Fr. 212).

38. In various attempts since 1983, I have developed in more detail what is sketched here and in what follows, first in 'Das Versprechen der Auslegung' (in the *Festschrift* for Jacob Taubes, *Spiegel und Gleichnis*, ed. N. Bolz/W. Hübener [Würzburg: Könighausen & Neumann, 1983]; now in *Premises – Essays on Philosophy and Literature from Kant to Celan* [Cambridge, MA: Harvard, 1996], then in 'Lectio' and in 'Afformative, Strike' (in *Walter Benjamin's Philosophy*, ed. A. Benjamin/P. Osborne [London: Routledge, 1994]), etc. It always remains astonishing to me that the theme of the promise which I – prompted by

Heidegger's analyses of the pre-structure of being there – first observed in Kant and Nietzsche has become one of the points of convergence between Derrida's work and my own.

39. On the concept of 'ergontology' used here several times already, I refer to my 'Working Through Working', in *Modernism/Modernity*, 3:1 (Jan. 1996), pp. 23–55.

40. Derrida uses the word 'perverformative' in *La Carte postale*.

41. In inventing the word – or pre-word – 'afformative' (for the first time in 'Afformative, Strike') or 'biformative' I allow myself the same license which Austin used in introducing the concept 'performative'. (See W. Hamacher, 'Afformative, Strike', trans. Dana Hollander, *Cardozo Law Review* 13, 4 [December 1997].) I recall, not to soften the peculiarity of these concepts but to emphasize the peculiarity of concepts codified and conventionalized since then, that Austin did not leave it at 'performatives' but also speaks of 'illocutives' and 'perlocutives', of 'verdictives', 'exercitives', 'commissives', 'behabitives' and 'expositives' (see *How to Do Things with Words* [Cambridge, MA: Harvard University Press, 1962], pp. 153–64).

42. As far as I can see, the only author besides Ernst Bloch in the tradition of 'messianic' Marxism who prepared this important difference was Walter Benjamin in his 'Theological-Political Fragment'. The first sentences read: 'Only the Messiah himself completes each historical event, and indeed in the sense that he himself first redeems, completes, creates its relation to the messianic. That is why the Kingdom of God is not the telos of historical *dynamis*; it cannot be made an objective. Seen historically, it is not an objective but an end' (*Gesammelte Schriften*, vol. II/1 [Frankfurt: Suhrkamp, 1977], p. 203 [my translation – K.B.]). 'The messianic' for Benjamin is end and not aim, eschaton and not telos – and is in fact even 'a messianic' without a messiah, for he alone could complete and create the very reference to the messianic. Derrida's proximity to Benjamin is unmistakable at this point. The – minimal – distance is marked by the fact that for Benjamin there can be only the absolute paradox of a '*messianic without the messianic*', for the messianic cannot be a category of history. But, conversely, he also writes: 'The profane [the historical] is thus not a category of the Kingdom, but a category, and indeed one of the most decisive, of his gentlest approach' (p. 204). It is only in this sense that Benjamin can write: 'The relation of this order [of the profane] to the messianic is one of the most essential lessons of historical philosophy' (p. 203).

43. 'Foi et savoir – Les deux sources de la "religion" aux limites de la simple raison' in *La Religion*, ed. Jacques Derrida and Gianni Vattimo (Paris: Seuil, 1996), p. 59 [my translation – K.B.].

44. Ibid., p. 63.

45. Ibid., p. 40.

46. Ibid., p. 73.

47. Paris: Minuit, 1995, p. 26. [The translation is mine – K.B.]

48. Ibid., pp. 42–3.

49. Both words are modifications of *mittere* – throw, fling, send, dispatch, release – and both mean 'let go, permit, give up, admit', *admittere* with an additional accent on 'permit and let happen' and *amittere* with the accent on 'give up, discard, lose, forfeit'. Hence *fidem amittere* means 'to break one's word' and *amissio* 'loss (by death)'. In the phrase *res publica amissa*, the meaning of admission has also been completely eclipsed by that of the loss of the republic.

50. 'It [big industry],' Marx writes, 'produced world history for the first time, insofar as it made all civilized nations and every individual member of them dependent for the satisfaction of their wants on the whole world, thus destroying the former natural exclusiveness of separate nations' (*GI*, p. 149). This industrially produced 'whole world' is still torn into classes under capitalist conditions of production; only the communist revolution could make of it a 'world'. Therefore we do not *know* what a world is.

51. Maurice Blanchot, 'La Parole prophétique', in *Le Livre à venir* (Paris: Gallimard, 1959) pp. 118–20 [trans. Kelly Barry].

52. [The Hebrew 'Laken' would be the paraphone of the German 'Laken', which also means 'cloth'. – Translator's note.]

10

Marx & Sons

Jacques Derrida

I have to admit it, without delay: these reflections will not merely be inadequate. That much was to be expected. The reader will also quickly recognize in them the form of inadequacy known as anachronism. The awaited answers will be at one and the same time – one more time – premature and belated.

Premature: they will, alas, often take the incomplete form of an experimental foreword, and display its rhetoric as well. This will remain the embarrassed preface to a 'response' I would like to adjust, some day far in the future, to the impressive, generous provocation of the texts preceding mine in this volume. These texts – most of them, at any rate – will continue to accompany me, each in a different way. They will sustain my reflections, and thus also my political commitments and evaluations.

At the same time – if one dare speak of a *same* time – I could be accused of being inexcusably late, and of yielding to the allure of another rhetorical fiction, another literary genre, the afterword or postscript – to, not *Specters of Marx*, but, rather, the 'response' that I have been preparing for too long, and in vain. And that I have also been planning to write for too long, from even before *Specters of Marx*. For, if I may recall this here, *Specters of Marx* was already meant to be, after its fashion, a kind of 'response', and only a response – as much to a direct invitation as to an urgent injunction, but also to a longstanding demand. To be sure, the 'yes' of a responsibility, however originary that *yes* may be, is still a response. It echoes, always, like the response to a spectral injunction: the order comes down from a place that can be identified neither as a *living present* nor as the pure and simple *absence of someone dead.*

This amounts to saying that the responsibility for this response has already quit the terrain of *philosophy as ontology*, or of ontology as a discourse about the effectivity of a *present-being* (*on*), something we shall have to consider again at length. For, as will already have been noticed, all the debates initiated in this book intersect, at one moment or another, in and around a question that, although it takes apparently abstract and speculative form, is still a question there is 'no getting around', as they used to say in France a few decades ago, one that remains 'in the commanding position'. It runs as follows: what is to be said about *philosophy as ontology* in the inheritance left us by Marx? Is what has come down to us from Marx, or will yet come down to us, a *political philosophy? A political philosophy qua ontology?* And what are we to make of this apparently abstract question? Is it legitimate? Urgent? Why does everything seem to bring us back round to it, by way of the texts just read in this volume or the problematic realms known, for example, as 'politics', 'the political', 'ideology', the future-to-come [*l'à-venir*] as 'messianic' 'revolution' or 'Utopia', the 'Party' or 'classes', and so on?

Whether my responses are belated or premature, I will not, in any event, have succeeded in properly adjusting the timing of them [*à en ajuster le temps*]. One would be justified in saying, then, that I might have anticipated this failure – might have seen this anachronism coming. Indeed, is a certain untimeliness not at once the temporality and the theme of *Specters of Marx?* Yes, I doubtless did dimly foresee what is happening [*ce qui arrive*] here. From the outset, I must doubtless have deemed it inevitable. But I did not dare dodge it, preferring, as the phrase goes, to *rush headlong into defeat* [*courir à l'échec*], as one says in French. I preferred facing up to a rout rather than disappearing the moment I expressed my thanks to the authors of this book – for that, above all, is what I wish to do here. I prefer to come before them disarmed and 'speak to' them that way at the moment they do me the honor of addressing me, even if they do so in a critical vein, and even if what I am getting ready to tell them, in a way that is not merely inadequate, but also oblique and occasionally impersonal, can only be a disappointment – and, at times, cause still greater annoyance to those who already feel duty-bound to be annoyed.

In short, the matter is clear enough by now: I have not managed to 'respond' *here*; I will not succeed in responding, and there is, perhaps, no need to do so *here.* This for a number of reasons I would now like briefly to lay out.

In the first place, it would have been too difficult a task. It would have been presumptuous of me, arriving after everyone else, in a position at once panoramic and central, to claim the right to the last word in the form of a precise reply to the measure of everyone, and every one of these texts. That would have been an unplayable scene. Which is all for the better, because it is not a scene I like. The reader will judge for himself – the reader of *Specters of Marx* and, now, of this book as well, and of all the discussions it engenders. There is a good deal of *work* in view, and that is the first thing I look forward to, gratefully. For, in my opinion, these texts are, from first to last, each in its own way and almost without exception, texts that *work*. And, as such, they call for something other than a 'reply'. Other work, another work, however modest and inadequate, should go out to meet them – so as to cross paths with them, rather than merely respond to them. That almost all these texts are sites where original work is in progress is something I think no one who reads them can doubt. They are, almost all of them, and almost from first to last, remarkable for their concern to *read* rather than simply to turn the page and move on. Nearly all seek to analyze, understand, argue – to elucidate, not to obfuscate. Nearly all seek to discuss rather than insult (as one so often does today, to avoid asking oneself painful questions), to object rather than belittle or, in cowardly fashion, wound.

But it will also have been noticed that each does so, each time, setting out from a different axiomatics, a different perspective and a different discursive strategy. I would even say, raising the ante, that each sets out from a different *political* philosophy and *politics*. Let me emphasize those two words, so as to put the accent on what I called, a moment ago, the busiest point of intersection, the most common passageway for all the questions raised again here: how are the words 'philosophy' and 'political' to be understood and *thought* from now on? And, first of all, Marx's *thought*, the one we are heirs to (or which, on a perhaps bold, albeit apparently commonplace hypothesis, we *would* or *should* be heirs to, as if we were 'Marx's sons')? *Is* Marx's thought *essentially* a philosophy? *Is* this philosophy *essentially* a metaphysics *qua* ontology?[1] Does it hold a more or less legible ontology in reserve? Should it? What fate ought we ourselves to deal out, today, in an active (and therefore also political) act of interpretation, to what it '*essentially is*'? Is that a given, or a promise we should make come about? Or displace? Or make again, or reinterpret differently, sometimes even going so far as to abandon the very value of *essentiality*, which runs the risk of being too closely bound up with a certain ontology? Voluminous works ought to be devoted to this flurry of questions alone ('what, in sum, is to be said of philosophy in Marx or since Marx?'). It would be hard for *all* those who have collaborated on this book to reach agreement on that subject, for it seems to me that no one agrees with anyone else *on that subject* here. For example, to mention some of the most compelling essays in this book, where does Negri, who would like to see the chance for a new ontology in Marx's thought, agree with Jameson, who seems, in contrast, in a gesture I shall come back to as well, to take it for an established and fortunate fact that 'Marxism has never been a philosophy as such'? I will try to show why I am not prepared to subscribe to either of these two conclusions. Yet another – at least one more – of these numerous books would be required to clarify the debate launched in the final lines of the section of Jameson's essay entitled 'The narrative of theory' (about the matter – inevitable, insuperable, permanently on the agenda – that Althusser called 'ideology' and that 'Heidegger and Derrida', according to Jameson, call 'metaphysical' in discourses whose 'motifs' have in some cases been 'reified' and thus become 'theory'). The same goes, I think, for the concept of the political, but also for that of political philosophy, and, especially, between 'philosophy and politics', for the concept which is undoubtedly the hardest to situate throughout all these texts, the concept of ideology.

Yet there is something more, something other than this difference in philosophies and political philosophies. If we raise the ante a little higher – a move that makes things more interesting, but, I think, that much more difficult as well – the texts brought together here in a polylogue by Michael Sprinker (to whom I would like to express, at the outset, my deep and cordial appreciation for the opportunity he has thus provided us, provided me) put divergent 'styles', practices, ethics and politics of 'discussion' to work, along with different rhetorics and diverse ways of writing theory. It would be absurd, and, indeed, insulting, to attempt to level out those singularities by pretending to address all the contributors in one and the same voice, one and the same mode, so as to respond to each and every one equitably – and, consequently, to respond to none.

I have, then, just raised the ante. I have effectively suggested that the difference in 'political philosophies or politics', the differences – which others would also label 'ideological' – as to *political position*, and, accordingly, the differences between the various *theses* are not the most serious, however difficult they may sometimes be to overcome or even discuss. In my estimation, that is not where the distances or contradictions separating us ultimately lie, even assuming that they exist. For these differences and points of contention, if they existed and could be regarded as such, would presuppose, at a minimum, a basic agreement, a common axiomatics concerning the thing or *things* under discussion: philosophy, politics, political philosophy, the philosophical, the political, the politico-philosophical, the ideological and so on. It would be taken for granted, or presupposed, that there was common accord about the fact that the stakes of these discussions, assessments and interpretations bear legitimate names [*noms*], common or proper nouns [*noms*] – 'philosophy', 'politics' or 'the political', 'political philosophy' or the 'philosophy of the political', 'Marx' – so many words and things about which, today, 'heirs' ('Marxist' or not, 'Marxists' of this or that 'family', belonging to this or that generation, this or that national tradition, with this or that academic background, etc.) would proceed to conduct debates bearing on the proper name 'Marx' (that is, on Marx's heritage, spectral or not, and his 'filiation') – but in the *same* language, and setting out from a *common* axiomatics.

As one can imagine, such is not the case in this book. A circumstance which may make it that much more interesting for some, necessary or tragic for others, a babel of tongues verging on meaninglessness for still others. Whence, in any event, the difficulty of the task of whoever comes along last, claiming, not that he should have the last word, but that he has read all these texts before writing his own. How can one undertake to formalize all these idiomatic, untranslatable differences, even while pretending to speak to one and all from, as it were, a metalinguistic position, the position at once the most advantageous and the hardest to find, the most absurd and the least tenable, and, at any rate, the most unjust? Whence the defeat I am *rushing headlong into, the defeat* to which, as another French expression has it, my discourse *is doomed* [*est promis*].

I may perhaps be permitted to mention here, at the very outset, even before beginning, the most troubled interrogation of *Specters of Marx*, and the most anguished, bearing as it did on the legitimacy and, simultaneously, the timeliness of a book that was initially a lecture delivered at a specific moment, a lecture which 'took a position' in response to a significant invitation in a highly determinate context. This question was, to be sure, left suspended in a place from which the strategy of this discourse and its address were organized; but, today, it seems to me that *virtually none* of the texts in this volume have taken it seriously or directly into account as a question. It is, precisely, a threefold question: (1) the question of the 'political' (of the essence, tradition and demarcation of the 'political', especially in 'Marx'); (2) the question of the '*philosophical*' as well (of philosophy *qua* ontology, particularly in 'Marx'); and therefore (3) the question of the topoi all of us believe we can recognize in common beneath these names – particularly the name '*Marx*' – if only to indicate disagreement about them. These three questions ('the political', 'philosophy', 'Marx') are indissociable. If there were a 'thesis' in *Specters of Marx*, or a hypothesis, it would, today, presuppose this indissociability. The three themes of this thesis (or hypothesis) are, today, one. They are in search of the common topos which they already have, which is theirs even if we do not perceive it, the locus of their historical articulation.

The thesis (or hypothesis) of *Specters of Marx* expressly links these three themes in presenting *itself*. But this self-presentation is not a manifesto. It is not the auto-manifestation of any Manifesto, in the tradition of the political Manifesto as analyzed by *Specters of Marx*, in connection with, precisely, the *Manifesto of the Communist Party*. Although I have resolved to quote myself as rarely as possible here, I would nevertheless like to cite a passage drawn from the analysis of the 'Manifesto' form [*la forme 'Manifeste'*] of the text that opens: '*Ein Gespenst geht um in Europa – das Gespenst des Kommunismus.*' The attempt to explain Marx's title made it necessary to discern in it, intertwined in one and the same performative event of a signature (the 'proper name' of Marx or anyone else associating himself with it or allowing himself to be represented by it), the political (in the guise of the Party or International) and the ontological (the philosopheme of present-being, of the present of a living reality, etc.). Here the spectral is regarded, by Marx, as being nothing more than an ideologeme, a phantasm to be expelled:

> When, in 1847–48, Marx names the specter of communism, he inscribes it in a historical perspective that is exactly the reverse of the one I was initially thinking of in proposing a title such as '*The Specters of Marx*.' Where I was tempted to name thereby the persistence of a present past, the return of the dead which the worldwide work of mourning cannot get rid of, whose return it runs away from, which it *chases* (excludes, banishes, and at the same time pursues), Marx, for his part, announces and calls for a presence to come. He seems to predict and prescribe: What for the moment figures only as a specter in the ideological representation of old Europe must become, in the future, a present reality, that is, a living reality. The *Manifesto* calls, it calls for this presentation of the living reality: we must see to it that in the future this specter – and first of all an association of workers forced to remain secret until about 1848 – becomes a *reality*, and a *living* reality. This real life must show itself and manifest itself, it must *present itself* beyond Europe, old or new Europe, in the universal dimension of an International.
>
> But it must also manifest itself in the form of a manifesto that will be the *Manifesto* of a party. For Marx already gives the party form to the properly political structure of the force that will have to be, according to the *Manifesto*, the motor of the revolution, the transformation, the appropriation then finally the destruction of the State, and the end of the political as such. (Since this singular end of the political would correspond to the presentation of an absolutely living reality, this is one more reason to think that the essence of the political will always have the inessential figure, the very anessence of a ghost.)[2]

In *Specters of Marx*, the presentation of the hypothesis does not present *itself*, in the proper sense. The hypothesis or thesis is *not posed* [*ne se pose pas*, literally, does not pose *itself*]. Even if it did present itself or 'pose itself', it would do so without manifesto [*sans manifeste*] or auto-manifestation. Without presenting itself in the present, it neverthe-less takes a position, as one says – its 'position' or rather 'supposition', that is, the 'responsibility' thus assumed – *as* a *transformation*, and therefore as a *heterodox* or *paradoxical trans*position of the 11th of the *Theses on Feuerbach*.

Therefore, *as* a faithful–unfaithful heritage of 'Marx', unfaithful *for being* faithful ('unfaithful for being faithful': *with a view to* being faithful and, at the same time, *because* it is or would be faithful).

Therefore, *as* a hypothesis or postulate: about what an inheritance in general can and must be, namely, necessarily faithful *and* unfaithful, unfaithful *out of* faithfulness. This book is a book about inheritance, though it should not be confined to the 'sons of Marx'. It is, more precisely, a book about what 'inherit' can, not *mean* [*vouloir-dire*] in an *unequivocal* way, but, perhaps, enjoin, in a way that is contradictory and contradictorily binding. How to respond to, how to feel responsible for a heritage that hands you down contradictory orders?

Though I do not pretend to reconstitute this movement here, I would nonetheless like to recall what, at a particular moment, tied together, *on the one hand*, 'the very possibility . . . and the phenomenality of the political', or, again, 'that which makes it possible to identify the political'; and, *on the other hand*, the possibility of a 'hauntology', in which a discourse on (I do not say a science of) spectrality remains 'irreducible . . . to all that it [a "hauntology"] makes possible: ontology, theology, positive or negative onto-theology', which also means, even before one begins to speak of 'Marxist philosophy', the 'philosophy' whose limit Marx was, in my opinion, never able to thematize.

For one of the 'red threads' running through *Specters of Marx* is nothing less than the question of the 'philosophical' in Marx.[3] The three questions are intertwined. How are we to delimit: (1) the 'phen-omenality of the political' as such? (2) 'philosophy' as onto-theology? and (3) a heritage as a heritage of 'Marx', by the name and in the name of 'Marx'? Now it is at the moment when these three questions are tied together that I attempt to define the act which, carrying one beyond the question-form of the question, consists in 'taking a *responsi-bility*, in short, committing oneself in a performative fashion'.[4] In *Specters of Marx*, I added:

> This dimension of performative interpretation, that is, of an interpretation that transforms the very thing it interprets, will play an indispensable role in what I would like to say this evening. 'An interpretation that transforms what it interprets' is a definition of the performative as unorthodox with regard to speech act theory as it is with regard to the 11th Thesis on Feuerbach. ('The philosophers have only interpreted the world in various ways; the

point, however, is to change it' [*Die Philosophen haben die Welt nur verschieden interpretiert; es kommt aber darauf an, sie zu verändern*].)[5]

The gesture that I thus hazard is, of course, one that others will always be entitled to *judge*. It can be deemed productive or not, efficacious or imaginary, real or fictive, lucid or blind, and so on. I myself, *by definition*, have no 'theoretical' or 'practical' certainty on this score. Indeed, I would even claim that one neither can nor should have such certainty at the moment one assumes responsibility for doing or saying something that is something other than the necessary consequence of a program. However, the form of my gesture would seem to include, at a minimum, the demand that one *read*, a demand which remains, for its part, at once theoretical and practical: it asks that people take into account the nature and form – I would go so far as to say the avowed intention – of this gesture, if only to criticize its utility, possibility, authenticity, or even sincerity.

Three types of consequences necessarily follow. Before essaying a more precise response to the texts assembled in this volume, I will simply situate these typical consequences. I cannot engage in the necessary discussion of them here, but this reminder of basic principles should be taken to apply to all that follows.

(1) *The question of the question* or the putting into question of the question. Although I have just pointed to a cluster of questions, and although *Specters of Marx* multiplies interrogations and constantly recalls the critical urgency of all sorts of problems that must never be cast aside, it is also marked, like all the texts I have published in the past ten years (since, at least, *Of Spirit: Heidegger and the Question*), by a heavy insistence on the dependent character, or even a certain secondariness, of the *question-form*. Whence a certain divisibility, whence the fold [*pli*], or, as others would say, the duplicity assumed by a discourse which attempts to do two things that are, initially, difficult to reconcile: *on the one hand*, to reawaken questions mesmerized or repressed by the answer itself; but, simultaneously and *on the other hand*, to assume the (necessarily revolutionary) affirmation as well, the injunction, the promise – in short, the quasi-performativity of a *yes* that watches over [*veille sur*] the question, preceding it as an eve precedes the following day [*comme sa veille même*]. One example of this ambiguous respect for the question (critical or hypercritical; dare I say 'deconstructive'?) is, perhaps, provided by those moments when, in propounding a new question, I promptly – almost simultaneously – cast doubt upon a rhetoric of the question (which must not be reduced to that of a 'rhetorical question'): 'One question is *not yet* posed. Not as such. It is hidden rather by the

philosophical, we will say more precisely *ontological response* of Marx himself.'[6] This question is precisely that of the specter or spirit. Without pausing, almost in the same breath, I explain why I thought I had to beware of these words, especially the alternative 'question/response'. And it is at this point, doubtless not fortuitously, that the word 'perhaps' surges up, one of those 'perhaps*es*' which have for decades explicitly marked the privileged modality, *messianic* in this instance, of the statements that matter the most to me (it so happens that I elucidated, at length, the meaning and even, if the word may be hazarded, necessity or ineluctability of this 'perhaps' the year after *Specters of Marx,* in *Politics of Friendship*):[7] 'But all these words are treacherous: *perhaps* it is no longer at all a matter of question and we are aiming instead at another structure of "presentation", in a gesture of thinking or writing . . .'[8]

(2) *Depoliticization, repoliticization.* What should come after this decon-struction of Marxist 'ontology', in my view, is exactly the opposite of a depoliticization, or a withering away of political effectivity. Rather, the point, as I see it, of radically re-examining the premises subtending the relationship between 'Marx', theory, science and philosophy is to provide the beginnings of an account of *disastrous historical failures* on both the theoretical and political plane, as well as to effect a different kind of *repoliticization* of a certain inheritance from Marx. First, by shifting that inheritance toward a dimension of the political divested of everything which – for better but especially for worse, in our modernity – has welded the political to the ontological (in the first place, to a certain conception of the effectivity or present-being of the universal cast in terms of [*selon*] the state, and of cosmopolitical citizenship or the International cast in terms of the Party).[9]

As for the disasters I have just very elliptically named, which are, I repeat, *theoretical-and-political* disasters, they should trouble us, should they not? Should they not give ideas – a few, at any rate – to all the patented Marxists still prepared to dispense lessons from on high? To the statutory Marxists, and those of whom we have the statues [*statu-taires et statufiés*], to all those who still consider themselves entitled to indulge their penchant for irony at the expense of those difficult allies who have not joined them from the beginning in the orthodoxy of their dogmatic sleep? To the official Marxists who act like difficult children with the difficult allies, when the latter do their best not to give in, after the disaster has taken place, to the worse sort of resig-nation – theoretical and political, once again? To be sure, in the present book, at any event (this is the reason I am pleased and grateful to take part in it), Terry Eagleton is, fortunately, the only (and nearly the last) 'Marxist' of this stripe. He is the only one (virtually the only one and virtually the last) to maintain that imperturbably triumphal tone. One can only rub one's eyes in disbelief and wonder where he finds the inspiration, the haughtiness, the right. Has he learned nothing at all? What proprietary right must still be protected? Which borders must still be patrolled? To whom is 'Marxism' supposed to belong? Is it still the private preserve or personal property of those who claim or proclaim that they are 'Marxists'? As for Gayatri Chakravorty Spivak, she will at least have had the merit of manifesting uneasiness or remorse in a recent text. She reports the thoughts of 'a friend' there. What was this friend friendly enough to tell her? That if she had always had some 'trouble with Derrida about Marx', 'maybe that's because,' she confesses, transcribing, 'I feel proprietorial about Marx.'[10]

'Proprietorial' is a very good word. I would suggest making it still more precise: prioprietorial. For, spelling it that way, one lays claim not only to property, but also to priority, which is even more likely to provoke a smile. A friendly suggestion, indeed, which it is not enough to repeat on every page to show that one has understood it. For, a bit later on the same page, we read: 'Is it just my proprietorial reaction . . . ?' Four pages further on, the remorse is growing increasingly compulsive, while remaining just as ineffectual: 'Is this my proprietoriality about Marx? Am I a closet clarity-fetishist when it comes to Marx? Who knows?'[11]

Who knows? I, for my part, do not, but I must confess that, like the friend whose warning Spivak reports, I fear she is. What will never cease to amaze me about the jealous possessiveness of so many Marxists, and what amazes me even more in *this* instance, is not only what is *always* a bit comic about a property claim, and comic in a way that is even more theatrical when what is involved is an inheritance, a textual inheritance, and, still more pathetic, the appropriation of an inheritance named 'Marx'! No, what I always wonder, and even more in *this* instance, is where the author thinks the presumptive property deeds are. In the name of what, on the basis of what claim, exactly, does one even dare *confess* a 'proprietorial reaction'? Merely making such a confession presupposes that a title deed has been duly authenticated, so that one can adamantly continue to invoke it in defending one's property. But who ever authenticated this property right, especially in the present case? On the preceding page (p. 71) of an essay that is unbelievable from first to last, Spivak had already written the following, in a final gleam of lucidity that nothing could reflect better than this statement does: 'Now comes a list of "mistakes" that betrays me at my most proprietorial about Marx, perhaps. The reader will judge.' True: this reader, among others, will have judged: the list in question is, first and foremost, a list of the misreadings to be chalked up to Gayatri Spivak herself – who is well advised to put the word 'mistakes' in inverted commas in advance. Some of her errors stem from an outright inability to read, exacerbated here by the wounded resentment of her 'proprietoriality about Marx'. Others are due to her unbridled manipulation of a rhetoric I shall, for lack of time and space, illustrate with only one example.[12] I single it out because it bears directly on the 'depoliticization-repoliticization' which concerns me here, in this second point. Defining the requisite conditions for the repoliticization that I would like to see come about, I wrote: 'There will be no repoliticization, there will be no politics *otherwise*.'[13] In other words, I was insisting on the fact that, in the absence of the conditions I define in this context, we will not succeed in repoliticizing, something I obviously desire and which it plainly seems to me desirable to do. Now, the individual who suspects herself, on solid grounds, of feeling a bit 'proprietary' about Marx, here drops the 'otherwise', cuts off the sentence, and ascribes to me – erroneously, without putting the words in inverted commas, but giving the page reference in *Specters of Marx* (that is, p. 87) – the following statement (in addition to a series of 'we wills' that are not mine): 'We won't repoliticize [*SM* 87]'! – as if she were entitled to attribute these words to me in a straightforward, innocent paraphrase, as if I had advised against repoliticizing, *precisely at the point where I emphatically call for the exact opposite!*[14] When I first read so massive a falsification, I could hardly believe my eyes, and was, above all, hard put to decide whether it was deliberate or involuntary. But whether deliberate and/or involuntary, this is a serious matter. To put it coldly and categorically, everything would seem to suggest that it is not possible to raise questions and express concern about *a* determinate politics or *a* determination *of* the political without promptly being accused of depoliticization in general. But, of course, a repoliticization always involves a relative depoliticization, an awareness that an old conception of the political has, in itself, been depoliticized or is depoliticizing.

Nothing touching on 'politicization' or 'repoliticization' has escaped the lucidity of Jameson, whose powerful, scrupulous analysis the reader will already have read. Jameson notes that 'spectrality is here the form of the most radical politicization and that, far from being locked into the repetitions of neurosis and obsession, it is energetically future-oriented and active.'[15] Yes, confidence; Spivak is in any case right to say 'the reader will judge.'

I am not in the process of saying that, if Marxism is faring so poorly, especially in the academy, the blame lies with the 'Marxists', or a few academic 'Marxists', let alone with some of those I have just mentioned

(Spivak, Eagleton, or Ahmad). That, as one can imagine, would assuredly be saying too much. The problem, alas, has very different dimensions. Let us only say that now that the harm has been done, and the causes and effects being what they are, the symptomatic modes of behavior I have just described do not help matters any, as one says, or contribute to setting things right.

(3) *The perverformative.* The allusion I have just made to 'quasi-performativity' would seem to signify at least two things, two in a single word. These two things stand in an essential relation to the need for repoliticization, at the juncture where it seems to me that, under certain conditions, efforts to repoliticize should be pursued.

(A) In *Specters of Marx*, as in all of my texts of at least the past twenty-five years, all my argumentation has been everywhere determined and *overdetermined* by a concern to take into account the performative dimension (not only of language in the narrow sense, but also of what I call the trace and writing).

(B) *Overdetermined*, because, at the same time, the aim has been other than to apply an Austinian notion as it stood (here too, I hope that I have been faithful–unfaithful, unfaithful out of faithfulness, to a heritage, to 'Austin', to what is one of the major bodies of thought or main theoretical events – undoubtedly one of the most fertile – of our time). I have for a long time been attempting to transform the theory of the performative from within, to deconstruct it, which is to say, to overdetermine the theory itself, to put it to work in a different way, within a different 'logic'—by challenging, here again, a certain 'ontology', a value of full presence that conditions (*phenomenologico modo*) the intentionalist motifs of seriousness, 'felicity', the simple opposition between felicity and infelicity, and so on. This effort will have begun with, at the latest, 'Signature Event Context', and been pursued everywhere else, especially in 'Limited Inc.' and *The Post Card*. I am pleased to see that Fredric Jameson has so clearly perceived certain relations of continuity and coherence between *The Post Card* ... and *Specters of Marx*. As to what Hamacher here says about and does with what – in, precisely, *The Post Card* – I callèd, in 1979, the 'perverformative',[16] which he ties in with more recent texts like 'Avances', it is, in my view, one of the many luminous, powerful gestures of his interpretation, in a text that is impressive, admirable and original. Because I find myself in close agreement with Hamacher, and am prepared to follow him down all the paths he thus opens up, I can do no more here than pay him simple, grateful homage. (Thus there is, despite appearances, nothing paradoxical about the fact that I say very little about his essay here, contenting myself with inviting the reader to read and reread it while weighing its every word.)

After these preliminary remarks, I must rather summarily announce the choice I felt I had to make in attempting to 'respond', in an unfortunately limited space, to the essays in this book. So as not to neglect the themes which are, in my view, the most urgent, the most general, and also the ones the most frequently addressed by all the various essays, I shall graft a conceptual order onto a more 'personal' one. While responding to everyone in turn (except, occasional remarks aside, Eagleton and Hamacher, for the counterposed reasons I have just mentioned), I shall sometimes overstep the logic of this order so as to refer, now and again, to the recurrence of the same theme or objection in several different essays. This is the least unworkable solution, one I have had to adopt, in an economy that was not of my choosing, to respond in the least unjust manner possible, in a limited space, to nine different texts, nine different strategies, or, it might even be said, nine different 'logics'.

To begin with, a reminder. As those who do me the honor of taking an interest in my work can testify, I have never gone to battle against Marxism or the Marxists. Why, then, should I have come to hope for a *reconciliation*? (I here underscore the word that appears in Aijaz Ahmad's title, and repeatedly in his text; it is, in sum, its leitmotif.) What might be the interest of such a reconciliation? Had my major concern been 'reconciliation', even as Ahmad understands the word,[17] I would have written a very different book. If one carefully rereads the paragraph in which Ahmad expatiates at length upon all the subtlety of his title, 'Reconciling Derrida', it becomes clear that what is at issue is neither a 'reconciliation with Derrida' nor 'Derrida reconciled' ... 'on the part of Derrida, in relation to Marx – or of Marxism in relation to Derrida'.

A shift from Marx to Marxism, then: why? *Who* is Marxism? Ahmad? All those he comes forward to represent? But already, in *this* book alone, there is no possibility of agreement or homogeneity among all the 'Marxists', all those who call themselves or are called 'Marxists'. Even if it were possible to identify all of them as 'Marxists', it would still be impossible to identify them all with one another. There is nothing wrong with this, in my view, but it should make the identifying label 'Marxist' more uncertain than ever (I discuss this more than once in *Specters of Marx*).

Ahmad goes on to say: 'In either case, we would then have a sense of gratification too easily obtained.' In question here, then, is something more like a reconciliation of myself with myself ('Derrida in the process of reconciling') in the course of a process of 'identification'. I shall have to insist on this point, while avoiding, precisely, narcissistic identification (although I have elsewhere hazarded statements about narcissism that are hardly in keeping with the consensus). It is necessary to insist for at least two reasons:

(1) First, in order to do justice to the complexity of the identification which Ahmad speaks of, and which, in my opinion, touches on a very sensitive issue in these discussions. As Ahmad points out, in a complex and interesting way, the process of identification involved is, as he sees it, *twofold*: 'identifying *with* the intent of this reconciling', 'identify*ing* that with which Derrida has here set out to reconcile himself'.

(2) Second, because, in both cases (one of which is enveloped in the other, as we have seen), it is assumed that reconciliation is on the agenda (something I contest; I will say how and why in a moment), and that *I* am the one who is doing the identifying. Now the process of identification, which is the object, ultimately, of the trickiest analyses in *Specters of Marx*, is taken up precisely at the point where the book enters into the whole matter of spectral logic; I find that Ahmad rather hastily reduces it to a question of proper nouns, personal pronouns and what he calls 'subjects'. He does so with an assurance that I, as will be imagined, am hard put to share. Thus he writes:

> I mean, rather, the active sense of a process, and of a subject: a *mode* of reconciliation; Derrida in the process of reconciling; and we, therefore, in response to the process Derrida has initiated, participating in an *identification* – an identification also in the positive sense of identifying *with* the intent of this reconciling, as well as in the sense of identify*ing* that with which Derrida has here set out to reconcile himself. It is in this double movement of identification that the pleasures and problems of Derrida's text lie for us, the readers of the text.[18]

Yes, 'pleasures and problems'. When, with imperturbable self-assurance, as if he were sure of what he meant to say ('I mean,' he says), Ahmad associates my name with a process of reconciliation (one I am even supposed to have 'initiated'!), I sigh and smile (for yes, I too take a certain pleasure in this); but when he says 'we' ('we therefore . . .') in the following sentence, my laughter becomes, so to speak, at once frank and serious: 'problems,' I should say! For I wonder where this dogmatic sleep finds such resources. Who is entitled to say 'we' here? We 'Marxists? We readers, etc.? And, above all: does everything in my book not come down to problematizing, precisely, *every* process of identification, or, even, of determination in general (identification of the other, or with the other, or with oneself: X is Y, I am the other,

I am I; we are we, etc.)? – all questions which come under the general heading I have been emphasizing from the beginning of this response: ontology or not, spectrality and difference, and so on. This affects, first of all, the very idea of justice and messianicity that provides *Specters of Marx* its guiding thread, the red thread that runs all the way through it. But the only interest and specificity this idea has, if it has any at all, depends on its being able to elude the sway of that logic of identity and self-identity.[19]

Had my overriding concern been some sort of 'reconciliation', I would have proceeded very differently. I would not have foreseen, as I clearly did, what has in fact occurred more often than not – namely, that *Specters of Marx* would above all fail to please those 'Marxists' who are comfortably installed in their proprietorial positions, and identified by themselves with themselves. Precisely because matters are not simple, and because this book does not come from the enemy. From an identifiable enemy. It was especially by way of anticipation of the reactions – variegated, to be sure, but, on this point, similar and eminently predictable – of possessive Marxists (for example, Eagleton, Spivak and Ahmad), watching over orthodoxy as if over a patrimony, that I announced:

> what we are saying here will not please anyone. But who ever said that some-one ever had to speak, think, or write in order to please someone else? And if one interprets the gesture we are risking here as a belated-rallying-to-Marxism, then one would have to have misunderstood quite badly. It is true, however, that I would be today, here, now, less insensitive than ever to the appeal of the contretemps or of being out-of-step, as well as to the style of an untimeli-ness that is more manifest and more urgent than ever. Already I hear people saying: 'You picked a good time to salute Marx!' Or else: 'It's about time! Why so late?' I believe in the political virtue of the contretemps. . . .[20]

(I would also ask that one read what precedes and follows, at least up to 'I am not a Marxist. . . . And who can still say I am a Marxist?')

In writing the above, without having this or that particular 'Marxist' in mind, I doubtless already saw coming the very predictable displea-sure or outrage of self-proclaimed Marxists like Eagleton or Ahmad.

The chrono-logic of the contretemps was, if I may say so, pre-programmed. Two examples:

(1) *The contretemps according to Eagleton*: '[I]t is hard,' Eagleton says, 'to resist asking, plaintively, where was Jacques Derrida when we needed him?' But do we not have to strain to reconcile this accusation of the 'contretemps' with the charge of 'opportunism', aired by the same author? – for Eagleton accuses me of opportunism and the opposite at the same time, as well as of swimming against the current merely in

order to 'exploit Marxism as critique, dissent...' This incorrigible, paradoxical 'opportunism' would thus seem to make me do precisely the opposite of what it is opportune to do at the appropriate moment, the long-awaited moment. I would appear to be an opportunist with a poor sense of timing! The only possible explanation (a bit thin for a Marxist, it will perhaps be agreed) would seem to be psychological-characterological, or even a matter of my idiosyncrasies or character disorders: my 'adolescent perversity'.[21] This hypothesis makes me smile – and, as Ahmad would say, I almost take a certain pleasure in it. For what, after all, does Eagleton have against adolescent perversity? Is he militating for a return to normalcy before all things? For normalization? Is his model revolutionary the normal adult, cured of all perversity? Of what other sorts of perversity as well? Once one has set to castigating one form of perversity, it is never hard to extend the list. But even supposing that this psychologistic hypothesis accounts for my personal vices, the realm under discussion, as Eagleton is well aware, transcends my person. Even if only one reader took an interest in me, it would be necessary to discuss him too in terms of 'adolescent perversity'. And if so many 'perverse adolescents' in the world incline to this side rather than that, a 'Marxist' ought to wonder what is going on – in the world at large, not in the world of my deranged drives. He ought to look for explanations other than the libidinal deviation of an author who is not growing old with the requisite grace. For I suspect that Eagleton ultimately reproaches me with not growing old fast enough, with growing old à contretemps.

(2) *The contretemps according to Ahmad.* This critic not only regrets the fact that I have been tardy with what he calls (I will come back to this in a moment) my 'affiliation' or 'reconciliation'. He also confesses, for his part, that he has read me too quickly (which is true), indeed, on the plane; 'on,' he confides, 'my flight to Ljubljana'.[22] This is no excuse for contenting oneself with flying through a text. The effects of thus skimming through my text on the fly are not limited to the hastily formed impression that it is a gesture of 'reconciliation' (my book is obviously anything but that, and reconciliation with myself, any other aside, has never been easy for me; I have a painful experience of it which I will not succeed in communicating to the readers I am speaking of at the moment, but which, I am sure, is in theory legible in all that I write).

I am also taken aback by a certain eagerness to speak of *Specters of Marx* or my work in general as if it were merely a species, instance, or example of the 'genre' *postmodernism* or *poststructuralism.* These are catch-all notions into which the most poorly informed public (and, most often, the mass-circulation press) stuffs nearly everything it does not like or understand, starting with 'deconstruction'. I do not consider myself either a poststructuralist or a postmodernist. I have often explained why I almost never use these words, except to say that they are inadequate to what I am trying to do. I have never spoken of 'the announcements of the end of all metanarratives', let alone endorsed them. Ahmad thus contents himself with skimming over my text on a more than routine reconnaissance mission when he writes, on the subject of my critique of Fukuyama, that 'the discussion would have been more fruitful had he offered reflections on the political and philosophical adjacencies between Fukuyama's end-of-history argument and the announcements of the end of all metanarratives that one finds routinely in the work of so many deconstructionists.' Confusion. I do not know what context or routine is being alluded to. But I am certain that there is no necessary relation between these 'announcements' and the 'deconstructions' I know of or carry out myself. So this charge doesn't stand up. I suppose that the 'postmodernists' (Lyotard, for example) who *do* use the word 'metanarrative' (something I have never done in my life, for good reason) would find this amalgam as unsettling as I do. 'Deconstructionists' have occasionally also been accused, quite as unjustly, with having a weakness for – yet another catch-all notion – the grand metanarrative discourses, the *grands récits*, when, for instance, they speak imprudently of 'Western metaphysics' *tout court* or *the* metaphysics of presence, as they sometimes do, and as I too have sometimes done for pedagogical reasons (I have often explained why elsewhere).

One more word about Fukuyama, and three brief reminders.

(1) I have never sought to compete with Perry Anderson, whose then recent text I did not know at the time. I was not out to be more 'original' (Eagleton) or less 'conventional' (Ahmad) than Anderson in my critique of Fukuyama. I note in passing that the two 'Marxists' in this volume who show the greatest inclination toward 'proprietoriality about Marx', those who are, I would say, the most *patrimonial*, are also those who begin by defending and protecting – as if this were in dispute – the copyright, priority and privilege of Fukuyama's 'first' officially Marxist critic: Perry Anderson.

(2) I did not simply offer an *internal* critique of Fukuyama; I also pointed out the contextual effects and political logic governing the reception and exploitation of his book. Moreover, if, as Ahmad says, Anderson is to be credited with recognizing 'what strengths there were in Fukuyama's arguments', I did not, for my part, fail to acknowledge that 'this book is not as bad or as naïve as one might be led to think by the frenzied exploitation that exhibits it as the finest ideological showcase of victorious capitalism in a liberal democracy. . . .'[23]

(3) As to the problematic of the end of history, etc., although I have nothing against Anderson's reading (since when does one have to regret all convergence with a Marxist?), the argument I put forward is, in its overall design and its details, woven into the substance and intent of my book – which, it will be granted, is thoroughly un-Andersonian. My reasoning is tied by so many threads to previous publications (mine, of course – too many for me to be able to mention more than *Of an Apocalyptic Tone . . .* – but, especially, those of untold others as well, from the 1950s on!) that I have n either the stamina nor the space to reconstitute their tangled skein. As I shall have to do again, for lack of time and space, and, alas, more than once, I here content myself with inviting interested readers to reread these texts in order to form their own judgment, if only about the specificity of each argument. But, frankly, I do not think that Anderson's critique of Fukuyama, even if I had read it at the time, would have persuaded me of the futility or conventionality of my own. Let the reader judge.

Ahmad is right, it seems to me, to wonder, 'what *kind* of a text is it that Derrida has composed?' Indeed, one understands nothing about this text if one fails to take into account the specificity of its gesture, of its writing, composition, rhetoric and address – in a word, everything a traditional reader in a rush would have called its form, or tone, but which I, for my part, consider inseparable from its content. Ahmad is right again when, answering his very good question, he says: 'We have, in other words, essentially a *performative* text . . .' Yes, of course. But I am, naturally, no longer in agreement with him when he reduces this performativity to a 'performance', especially to the 'performance' of a 'literary text', especially when this 'performance' is in its turn reduced to conventional, confused notions of 'form of rhetoric', 'affectivity', 'tone', and so forth. Who would deny that there are rhetoric, affect and tone in *Specters of Marx*? I certainly would not; but I lay a different kind of claim to them, and relate them differently to the performativity of the analysis itself. Does Aijaz Ahmad think his text is so very atonal? Does he think that what he writes has been purged of all affectivity, all rhetoric, and, since this too is a matter that seems to bother him, of every gesture of 'filiation and affiliation'? *Specters of Marx* is not only a text which, no more than any other, cannot efface or deny all filiation and affiliation. On the contrary: it assumes more than one, and explains why. This multiplicity changes everything. The book also does something else that can seem contradictory, explaining and justifying the contradition. Yes, it is possible to articulate several apparently contradictory gestures, simultaneously or successively, in one and the same book. For example, I invoke the authority of Marx [*je me réclame de Marx*], but it can also happen that, having spoken 'for him', I also speak 'against him': in the *same* book, without suspecting that this was against the rules! Or that one had to choose: to be 'for' or 'against' Marx, as in a polling booth! Expressly identifying itself as a book on inheritance, *Specters of Marx* also analyzes, questions and – let us say, to save time – 'deconstructs' the law of filiation, particularly patrimonial filiation, the law of the father–son lineage: whence the insistence on *Hamlet,* although this could be justified in many other ways as well. This insistence is not merely the consequence of a taste for literature or mourning, any more than Marx's interest in Shakespeare makes *Capital* a literary work. I have simultaneously marked out the law, effects and ethical-political risks of this filiation. One has to read *Specters of Marx* very naïvely indeed to miss the whole analysis of the paternalistic phallogocentrism that marks all scenes of filiation (in *Hamlet* and in Karl Marx!). The antecedents of this analysis extend too far back in my work, are too explicit and systematic for me to have to review them here. I would merely like to emphasize that the question of woman and sexual difference is at the heart of this analysis of spectral filiation. Specifically, this question of sexual difference commands everything that is said, in *Specters of Marx,* about ideology and fetishism. If one follows this path, which also leads back to my analysis of fetishism in *Glas* and elsewhere, then the scene of filiation and its interpretation, and, especially, the reference to Hamlet, the paternal specter and what I call the 'visor effect', begin to wear a very different aspect. I suggest that Ahmad do some rereading after touching down; he will then see that my gesture is not solely one of filiation or affiliation. No, I do not simply claim to be Marx's heir, and even less to have exclusive rights to the inheritance. In affirming as often as I do that there is more than one specter or spirit of Marx, I acknowledge that there are and must be as many heirs as there in fact are, and that they must sometimes be clandestine and illegitimate, as everywhere. Ahmad, in contrast, seems to complain, as the *presumptively* legitimate 'Marxists' and 'communists' and *presumptively* legitimate sons seem to complain, of having been dispossessed of his patrimony or 'priorprietoriality'. (I emphasize the word *presumptively,* for, in the Marxist family as elsewhere, legitimacy is always *presumptive,* especially when what is at stake is filiation in general, and not only, as people right down to Freud and Joyce have too naïvely believed, paternal filiation as 'legal fiction': for this 'fiction' applies to maternity as well, and did so even before maternity could be supplemented by surrogate mothers.) One can judge this fierce claim to filial legitimacy by, at least, Ahmad's *tone,* as he himself would say, at the moment when he declares that I have a tendency to identify with Hamlet, to 'position' myself like Hamlet, to identify with both Hamlet and the 'Ghost'! even, indeed, with Marx himself![24] As if it were not possible to read and closely analyze a scene of filiation without straight-forwardly identifying with one of the characters! Here again, I fear that the tendency to find me too 'literary' betrays a somewhat naïve experi-ence of what reading, literature and the reading of what is known as a 'poetic' or 'literary' text are.[25] On this point too, the lesson given by Marx, reader of Shakespeare, has not always been well understood by the 'Marxists' or those who are 'generally known as Marxists':

> [H]is [that is, my] initial act of positioning himself within his own text [I already find *every one* of these words comically irrelevant, but never mind] by enclosing his text between two quotations from *Hamlet*, which foreground the Ghost of the dead father (obvious reference to Derrida's *title* – 'Specters of Marx' – [we're in agreement there, the reference is 'obvious', I shall make no further attempt to camouflage it] as well as to the *theme* of the finality of the death of Marxism [agreed, although here, I make bold to say, matters are not quite so simple; but it is from this point forward that things become really disturbing] and to his assertion that *he* and his deconstruction, not communists and those who are generally known as Marxists, are the true heirs of Marx, the dead Father). Here is, then, the opening quotation, with its own repetition of a key phrase:

> > The time is out of joint
> > – *Hamlet*

> > *Hamlet*: . . . Sweare.
> > *Ghost* [*beneath*]: Sweare . . . [26]

I have never maintained, of course, that 'I' and 'my deconstruction' (!) were the 'true heirs' of Marx, the 'dead father'. I do not believe that. Nor does the question much interest me. Moreover, everything I say makes the expression 'true heir' irrelevant to the point of carica-ture. That pretension is, indeed, the subject of the book – I would almost say its *target*. On the other hand, the idea or hypothesis (in fact, the fantasy) that someone is making such an 'assertion' or claim (that of being a true heir of Marx) manifestly sets Ahmad's teeth on edge. He watches jealously over the inheritance. He denounces in advance everything he presumes to be a claim to the inheritance whenever it seems to him to come from someone *he* regards as not belonging to the family or lineage of those he tranquilly calls the 'communists and those who are generally known as Marxists', ranking himself among them, without a doubt – without, I mean, ever being visited by the slightest doubt on this head. Preoccupation with legitimate descent is a feeling that I do not find within myself. I have even learned to cultivate and publicly defend my indifference to this subject, to explain the 'logic' of that indifference, and to go so far as to make of it a kind of ethical and political first principle. As I rule, I analyze and question the fantasy of legitimate descent (fathers, sons and brothers, etc., rather than mother, daughter and sister), attempting to throw it into crisis, whereas, for Ahmad and 'those who are generally known as Marxists', that fantasy plainly continues to be an obsessive one. This is obvious when he criticizes me, but also when, on the strength of a good many points of agreement that I shall not consider,[27] he says that he 'accepts' what I say 'with a sense of comradeship'.[28] This communitarian concern for familial reappropriation, this jealous claim to 'prioprietoriality', here as in other domains, is the very subject of my work: in this book and, for thirty years now, in everything Ahmad calls, in a phrase I shall let him assume the responsibility for, 'his [my] deconstruction'.

In order to think at, if not to rise to, a level above all 'proprietoriality', comrades, *encore un effort*!

Of course, I am grateful to Ahmad for his 'sense of comradeship', especially when he – remarkable, this – congratulates me on my 'very salutary affiliation with what he [I] call[s] a "certain spirit of marxism".' But it is then that I sense, emanating from him rather than me, an insatiable desire for proper genealogy, legitimate filiation and quasi-familial community: unite, all ye legitimate sons of Marx, 'those who are generally known as Marxists', unite as good comrades, as brothers of all countries! If it were not a well-known fact that Marx had a bastard son by his maid (in France, a play was recently written about this; it included extracts from Shakespeare, Marx and *Specters of Marx*); if I were not afraid of sustaining Eagleton's verdict (yet another affair of tone: 'The high humourlessness of Derrida's literary style – French "playfulness" is a notoriously high-toned affair – reflects a residual debt to the academic world he has so courageously challenged');[29] and if, finally, I dared recall the entire deconstructive critique of 'fraternity' I elaborated in *The Politics of Friendship* – which I do not dare do – then I would here speak of the Marx brothers. If I did, the reason would be, more seriously, that *Specters of Marx* is, like *The Politics of Friendship*, also a sort of critique of the genealogical principle, of a certain fraternalism, and of the brother/brother as much as of the father/son couple. The hauntology of Marx himself, his terrified fascination in the face of his own specters, often revolved around the brother (Stirner as a 'bad brother' of Marx, because he was a 'bad son of Hegel').[30] But in the midst of my professions of gratitude, I must, moving too quickly, alas, admit, ingrate that I am, that I do not find myself in agreement with much of anything Ahmad says, very emphatically, about a great many things, and always with a view to accusing me of them, or suspecting me of them. I shall have to step up the pace if I am to avoid making a detailed, attentive response filling hundreds of pages (that is, indeed, what is called for, but I have not been allotted the space).

(1) I do not find myself in agreement with what Ahmad says, first, about the 'tone' of my text. I do not believe one has the right to isolate what he discusses under the confused rubric of 'tone' ('tone of religious suffering', 'messianic tonal register', 'quasi-religious tone', 'this *tone*, part sermon, part dirge', 'virtually religious cadences', etc.). To be entitled to isolate and thus criticize a tone, one would have to have a slightly more elaborate concept of tone, of its fusion with concept, meaning and the performativity I spoke of earlier, in order to lay claim to it and to question it. Above all, one must have, if I may say so without appearing offensive, a finer ear for the differential, unstable, shifting qualities of a tone – for example, the tonal values that signal irony or play, even at the most serious moments, and always in passages where the tone is, precisely, inseparable from the content. Ahmad is as insensitive as Eagleton to variations in tone – to, for example, the irony and humor that I am fond of cultivating in all my texts, without exception. That is his right. By definition, especially given the short time at my disposal, I will not be able to change his mind or modify his taste. But even if one loses something of the meaning when one misses the tremor and the differential vibration of a tone, enough is left in the words, sentences, logic and syntax that one does not have the right to miss *everything*. For, to use only Ahmad's own words, the 'virtually' ('virtually religious') and the 'quasi' ('quasi-religious'), for example, should by themselves suffice to change a great deal, indeed, almost everything, given that what is in question in the book, from first to last, is a subtle but indispensable distinction. Which distinction? That between, *on the one hand*, a certain irreducible religiosity (the one that commands a discourse on the promise and justice, and a discourse on revolutionary commitment, even when such discourses emanate from 'communists and those who are generally known as Marxists', and, in fact, whenever ethical and political discourse bears the stamp of messianicity – as distinguished from messianism, by a precarious dividing-line which is worth whatever it is worth, and which I will come back to, although Ahmad cannot be unaware that it organizes the whole logic of the book); and, *on the other hand*, religion, the religions for which I can justifiably say that *Specters of Marx*, like everything I write, betrays no weakness (Ahmad would seem to acknowledge this).[31] One cannot, as Ahmad does here, dispense with the vast question of religion and the religious by leveling rather muddled accusations about a 'quasi-religious' tone. The religious question should not be regarded as clear or settled today. One should not act as if one knew what the 'religious' or the 'quasi-religious' was – above all if one wants to be a Marxist, or calls oneself that. Between the two there is, yes, the question of ideology (irreducible, indestructible and irreducibly welded to the

religious, according to Marx). I shall come back to this question here as well.

(2) Again, I do not agree with what Ahmad so blandly advances on the subject of metaphoricity in *Specters of Marx* ('metaphor of mourning', 'metaphorical language of "inheritance" and "promise of Marxism"', 'the language of metaphor', 'language of poetic indirection', and so on). I have, in the past, made too great an effort to problematize the concept, and utilization of the concept, of metaphor (in, precisely, its relation to the concept) not to be suspicious of Ahmad's rhetoric here, or of the very dogmatic way he uses this word ('metaphor', 'metaphorical', 'metaphoric'). Doubtless there is, in all mourning work, a process of metaphoricization (condensation or displacement, interiorization or introjection, and thus identification with the dead, re-narcissization, idealization, etc.). But the motifs of mourning, inheritance and promise are, in *Specters of Marx*, anything but 'metaphors' in the ordinary sense of the word. They are focal points for conceptual or theoretical activity, the organizing themes of the entire deconstructive critique that I am attempting to make. Inseparable from one another, they command, among other things, the analysis of the politico-phantasmatic world scene after the alleged death of communism and the putative 'death of Marx'. They also enable me to introduce into the political realm necessary questions of a psychoanalytic type (those of the specter or *phantasma* – which also means specter in Greek) – something the 'Marxists' have rarely succeeded in doing in what I would regard as a convincing and rigorous manner. All this presupposes a transformation of psychoanalytic logic itself, precisely as it bears on the subjects of mourning, narcissism and fetishism. I have, elsewhere, tried to suggest how the transformation might be brought about, and cannot discuss this at length here.[32]

(3) I do not agree with Ahmad when he speaks of 'Derrida's refusal of class politics'. There is a serious misunderstanding here. I am doubtless partly responsible for it, and would like to provide a better explanation of the matter than I have so far. Let us make a transition, then: it is, precisely, the concept of 'transition' which will occupy us now, and will serve me as a passageway between Ahmad's text and others in this volume which, in diverse modes, display a certain uneasiness with what I am supposed to have said or, rather, not to have said about classes, the concept of class and class struggle. This holds for Lewis. In a very different sense, it holds for Jameson too, whom Lewis also invokes, inasmuch as he clearly situates his critical essay in the wake of those by Ahmad and Jameson, whose responses to *Specters of Marx* had already appeared (in *New Left Review*) when Lewis wrote his own. In an attempt to respond simultaneously to Ahmad's and

Lewis's objections (for I do not consider the paragraphs that Jameson devotes to these questions of 'class' to be objections, and I shall say why), I would like to quote a sentence I wrote some time ago; Lewis takes it as one of his epigraphs, as if it ought to constitute the central target of a critique, a critique he does in fact develop in the subsection of his essay called 'On class':

> I felt that the concept of class struggle and even the identification of a social class were ruined by capitalist modernity. . . . Thus any sentence in which 'social class' appeared was a problematic sentence for me.[33]

What, to begin with, is said in these two sentences, which are thus brutally torn from the context of an interview in which I described my relation to the Althusserian project as it developed in the closest possible proximity to me, close in a hundred different ways, in terms of place and of friendship, in the 1960s? In context, these two sentences did not say that what was or still is called 'social class' has no existence in my eyes, that it does not correspond to anything real, any social force capable of generating conflicts, effects of domination, struggles, alliances and so on. They said, very precisely, that the principle of identification of social class as presupposed by the concept of 'class struggle' (it being understood, but this goes without saying, that what is in question is the coded concept as promoted by the dominant Marxist discourse, that of the communist parties – I will come back to the question of the party below) – they said, then, that this principle and this concept had become 'problematic' for me in the sentences I was hearing at the time (I repeat, 'thus any sentence in which "social class" appeared was a problematic sentence for me'). If I had wanted to say that I believed there were no more social classes and that all struggle over this subject was passé, I would have. All I did in fact say was that the concept and principle of *identification* of social class current in the Marxist discourse I was hearing then (in the 1960s) were *problematic* for me. I underscore the word 'problematic', which does not mean either false or outmoded or inoperative or insignificant, but rather susceptible of transformation and critical re-elaboration, in a situation in which a certain capitalist modernity 'ruins' the most sensitive defining criterion of class (for example – but a great deal more needs to be said about this, for everything is hanging in the balance here – the concepts of labor, worker, proletariat, mode of production, etc.). I by no means said, not even in this improvised interview, that I considered the *problem* of classes to be outdated or irrelevant. So little did I say or think it that, immediately after the sentence Lewis cites, I offered the following clarification (which Lewis, if he has read more than three lines of my text, ought to have had the fairness to cite):

> Thus any sentence in which 'social class' appeared was a problematic sentence for me. For the reasons expressed earlier, I could not say [this] *in this form* [today, in 1998, I underscore '*in this form*', the form of Marxist statements of the 1960s]. *I believe in the gross existence of social classes* [again, emphasis added today, in 1998], but the modernity of industrial societies (not to mention the Third World) cannot be approached, analyzed, taken into account within a political strategy, starting off from a concept whose links are so loose. I had the impression I was still seeing models for sociological and political analysis inherited if not from the nineteenth, at least from the first half of the twentieth century. . . . *I believe that an interest in what the concept of class struggle aimed at, an interest in analyzing conflicts in social forces, is still absolutely indispensable.* [Once again, I am underscoring these words today, in 1998; is the sentence sufficiently clear and unambiguous?] But I'm not sure that the concept of class, *as it's been inherited* [again, I underscore these words in 1998] is the best instrument for those activities, *unless it is considerably differentiated* [emphasis added, again, in 1998].

I do not dare quote myself further. I would simply invite interested readers to restore all these contexts, particularly the whole discussion[34] which develops the passage just cited in the direction of the concepts of the 'last instance', 'overdetermination', appropriation and ex-appropriation (this is the best answer I can give here). I would also invite them to restore the other contexts that, in *Specters of Marx*, take determinate shape around these focal points. It should in any event be fairly clear that I took and take very seriously the existence of some 'thing' like that which one calls, since Marx, social classes, and that I take seriously the struggles of which this 'thing' is the field, locus, stakes, driving force, etc. It should be just as clear that I believe, to repeat, that an 'interest' in this thing and this struggle is 'indispensable', but that, consequently, interest in the progress of the analysis which one adjusts in the struggle is also indispensable. What seemed especially problematic to me at the time was the insufficiently 'differentiated' nature of the concept of social class as it has been 'inherited'. What seemed problematic to me at the time, I repeat, was above all the principle of identification of social class, and the idea that a social class is what it is, homogeneous, present and identical to itself as 'ultimate support'.[35] But a certain difference from itself, a certain heterogeneity in a social force, does not seem to me to be incompatible with the movement constituted by a social struggle. *On the contrary.* When, in *Specters of Marx*, I speak of a 'critical inheritance', the questions about this 'ultimate support' and 'the self-identity of a social class' not only do not exclude struggle, antagonisms, or unstable relations of domination, but, *on the contrary*, are formulated with reference to this struggle for hegemony. For example, I say (but, again, I invite interested readers to restore the context in which these propositions occur) that

> at least provisionally, we are placing our trust, in fact, in this form of critical analysis we have inherited from Marxism: in a given situation, provided that it is determinable and determined as being that of a socio-political antagonism, a hegemonic force always seems to be represented by a dominant rhetoric and ideology, whatever may be the conflicts between forces, the principle contradiction or the secondary contradictions, the overdeterminations and the relays that may later complicate this schema . . .[36]

That is my question and my main concern: what I find 'problematic' has to do, first of all, with what comes along to 'complicate this schema'. I admit, of course, that this 'complication' goes very far indeed, in my estimation. It can go so far as to

> lead us to be suspicious of the simple opposition of dominant and dominated, or even of the final determination of the forces in conflict, or even, more radically, of the idea that force is always stronger than weakness. . . . Critical inheritance: one may thus, for example, speak of a dominant discourse or of dominant representations and ideas, and refer in this way to a hierarchized and conflicted field without necessarily subscribing to the concept of social class by means of which Marx so often determined, particularly in *The German Ideology*, the forces that are fighting for . . . hegemony. . . . One may continue to speak of domination in a field of forces not only while suspending the reference to this *ultimate support that would be the identity and the self-identity of a social class* [I add this emphasis today, in 1998, to make it clear that what seems to me problematic is not something like social class as such, but, rather, what is usually attributed to it in a certain dominant Marxist tradition: the status or place of 'ultimate support' and 'identity as self-identity'], but even while suspending the credit extended to what Marx calls the idea, the determination of the superstructure as idea, ideal or ideological representation, indeed even the discursive form of this representation. All the more so since the concept of the ideal implies this irreducible genesis of the spectral that we are planning to re-examine here.[37]

What turns on this program in *Specters of Marx* has not captured the attention of those who here reproach me, I believe unjustly, with, at the very least, taking the problem of class and class struggle lightly. The passage I have just quoted (like many others) is plainly inscribed in a logic open to all possible 'overdeterminations' (in this sense, it is a logic that is at least provisionally coherent with a Marxist – for example, Althusserian – discourse); but it also 'complicates this schema', and, without ceasing to take class formations and class struggles into account, goes so far as to put back on the drawing board, in the 'class struggle', the relations between weakness and strength, between labor, production, the economic and the 'ideological'.

My failing lies perhaps in my unfamiliarity with all the Marxist work that elaborates a *new* concept of class and class struggle while taking more fully into account the new realities of the techno-scientifico-capitalist 'modernity' of world society. I confess that, on this specific point, I do not know of any work I find convincing, although I have made a point of hailing, on more than one occasion, recent work by Marxist theoreticians who have refused to let a rather unpropitious historical climate discourage them in their analyses and commitments. I am, in any case, certain of one thing: among the Marxists I am to respond to here, those who object to what I say, or fail to, about classes and the class struggle do not themselves advance a single new concept – with the exception of Jameson, whose remarks I do not at all take as objections (I shall return to this point without delay). But before coming to Jameson, I would like to clarify a matter which ought to be self-evident, but seems to have been overlooked in Ahmad's and Lewis's hurried and somewhat global readings. Whenever I speak of the New International in *Specters of Marx*, emphasizing that, in it, solidarity or alliance should not depend, fundamentally and in the final analysis, on class affiliation, this in no wise signifies, for me, the disappearance of 'classes' or the attenuation of conflicts connected with 'class' differences or oppositions (or, at least, differences or oppositions based on the new configurations of social forces for which I do in fact believe that we need new concepts and therefore, perhaps, new names as well). What I say about the New International (which is already a reality – I shall return to this too – has nothing abstract or Utopian about it, and is neither demobilized nor demobilizing, quite the contrary) as little presupposes the disappearance of power relations or relations of social domination as it does the end of citizenship, national communities, parties, or fatherlands. At issue is, simply, another dimension of analysis and political commitment, one that cuts across social differences and oppositions of social forces (what one used to call, simplifying, 'classes'). I would not say that such a dimension (for instance, the dimension of social, national, or international classes, of political struggles within nation states, problems of citizenship or nationality, of party strategies, etc.) is superior or inferior, a primary or a secondary concern, fundamental or not. All that depends, *at every instant*, on new assessments of what is urgent in, first and foremost, *singular* situations, and of their structural implications. For such assessment, there is, by definition, no pre-existing criterion or absolute calculability; analysis *must begin* anew every day everywhere, without ever being guaranteed by prior knowledge. It is on this condition, on the condition constituted by this injunction, that there is, *if* there is, action, decision and political responsibility – repoliticization. The 'undecidable' has never been, for me, the opposite of decision: it is the condition of decision wherever decision cannot be deduced from an existing body of knowledge [*un savoir*] as it would be by a calculating machine. Incidentally, I nowhere speak of a New International that 'declares itself without class', as Lewis says; nor do I speak 'in the absence of class considerations'. What I say, precisely, at the end of a long discussion that I cannot reproduce here, but would ask those interested to reread, is that the alliance or 'link' which forms this International can be forged, and is in fact being forged, 'without common belonging to a class'.[38] That has nothing to do with an 'absence of class considerations', with ignorance or neutral-ization of what used to be called a class – in any case, the interests of social and economic forces for which we need, it seems to me, more refined analyses. If I am wrong, from the standpoint of knowledge or political action, if my critics think that every International is forged, must be forged, out of 'common belonging to a class', they should say so and demonstrate what they say (something neither Ahmad nor Lewis does), rather than dogmatically anathematizing every discourse that does not take the traditional code of 'class struggle' for granted, or hold it sacred. Another of Lewis's confusions consists in thinking that he can discern, in what I say about the New International, 'an abstract concern with human rights'. But, aside from the fact that, even if this were as clearly the case as Lewis seems to think, he is obliged to admit that there is nothing anti-Marxist about it ('a commitment [to human rights],' he says, 'that in its concrete forms is not antithetical to classical Marxism, but which revolutionary Marxists insist is unrealizable short of revolution, and which is properly "undecidable" in the absence of class considerations'), it so happens that I make this allusion to 'common belonging to a class' more precise a few lines earlier. As is, alas, all too often the case, this has escaped the impressionistic, intermittent attention of those who have an interest in making what I say over into an abstract formalism insensitive to social determinations (to say nothing of their confusion on the subject of what I term the 'undecidable'). What I in fact wrote was that a

> 'new international' is being sought through these crises of international law; it is already denouncing the limits of a discourse on human rights that will remain inadequate, sometimes hypocritical, and *in any case formalistic* [I emphasize, today, in 1998, the most significant of the many features of my argument that seem to have escaped Lewis's attention, especially when he speaks of 'abstract concerns with human rights'] and inconsistent with itself as long as the law of the market, the 'foreign debt,' the inequality of techno-

scientific, military, and economic development maintain an effective inequality as monstrous as that which prevails today, to a greater extent than ever in the history of humanity. For it must be cried out, at a time when some have the audacity to neo-evangelize in the name of the ideal of a liberal democracy that has finally realized itself as the ideal of human history: never have violence, inequality, exclusion, famine, and thus economic oppression affected as many human beings in the history of the earth and of humanity.[39]

Indeed, I put such little faith in the abstract concept of 'human rights' that, a bit later, the same discussion calls into question, at least programmatically, but in pursuing a trajectory that my work has been following for a very long time, the metaphysical concept of man [*le concept métaphysique de l'homme*] which, precisely, finds itself at the center of these 'human rights' [*droits de l'homme*] (particularly as they are counterposed to an equally 'abstract' concept of the animal).

In the end, I have decided to let remarks of this kind go unanswered, leaving it to the reader to judge Lewis's rhetoric and good faith when, in the same breath, he is moved to write, 'Derrida's International further asserts the desirability of cross-class alliances (bosses alongside workers); its call to membership is addressed most of all to intellectuals – preferably, other deconstructionists.'[40] Even a demagogic candidate in the heat of a nineteenth-century electoral campaign would not have dared indulge in this kind of slur. He would not, at any rate, have had the cheek to submit that as an argument in a debate. I would say much the same about another ridiculous accusation, without replying to it or discussing it, so crude and demagogically polemical is a remark of the following sort: 'it may also surprise many deconstructionists [who? which ones?] to learn that the death Derrida mourns is not Marxism's but rather that of a particular regime of state capitalism [for Lewis, this is the only valid definition of Stalinist Bolshevism]. For Marxists, there is nothing to mourn.' (Ah, is that so?)[41]

I quite agree: 'deconstructionists' (which ones, exactly?) and a good many others are indeed likely to be surprised upon being informed, by Lewis, that I am not wearing mourning for Stalinism. Will they be any less surprised to learn that Lewis, for his part, is not wearing mourning at all? And as I am in the process of identifying the points I will not pause to discuss in Lewis's text, here is at least an initial list:

(1) The allegation that I have criticized 'a deficiency of morality in Marxism by equating Leninism and Fascist totalitarianism'.[42] I have never done so anywhere, and no trace of this 'equation' is to be found anywhere in my text – which does not mean that I consider Leninism to be irreproachable and innocent of all 'totalitarianism'.

(2) The definition of my work as 'postmodernist', which occurs a

hundred times over. This is a gross error, which I have already discussed above. It is exacerbated here by the identification of 'postmodernism, poststructuralism', and the critiques of 'metanarrative'.[43]

(3) The allegation that I claim 'the working class is shrinking in terms of absolute numbers on a worldwide scale'.[44] I have never thought that. Nor have I ever said that 'classical Marxism cannot account for the homeless as a group, excludes them, and ignores their revolutionary potential'.[45] At such moments, I have the feeling that Lewis has a compulsive interest in making me out to be the diabolical last representative, the consummate incarnation of all the real or potential objections, justified or not, that can be directed against Marxism! One ought, rather, to be worried by the increasing rarity of criticism and discussion – and wonder why even those who formulate objections are beginning to be few and far between in this domain.

(4) To say that I seek to 'discredit *revolution* both as a political strategy for the present and as a social aspiration for the future'[46] is a blatant counter-truth. On more occasions than I care to count (so many that I do not even have the time to look up the references, in *Specters of Marx* and elsewhere), I have invested the word 'revolution' with a positive, affirmative value, even if the traditional figure and imageries of revolution seem to me to call for certain 'complications . . .' Everything that I range under the rubric of 'messianicity' 'without messianism' is inconceivable without the reference to *revolutionary* moments that interrupt not only states of conservation, but even processes of reform (I insist on the latter point, because Lewis often describes me as a 'reformist' – which, I grant, I can also be in certain specific contexts, for I refuse to make an abstract choice between two allegories, Reform and Revolution). Suffice it to say that I am hard put to recognize anything at all of what I am or do in diagnoses such as: 'Pessimism about the willingness and the ability of the working class to fight for a better society accounts for a great deal of the kind of postmodern theorizing [*Specters of Marx*] contains.'[47] The discussion of messianicity, as will be clear to anyone willing to attend to it, inclines neither to the past nor to passivity. I could show that it is fundamentally *optimistic*, if I did not find that category as trivial and uninteresting as the category *pessimism*. I will say a word about this later. I have already explained what I think about the 'working class' and the category 'postmodernism'.

(5) I have never said, to cite Lewis's formulation, that 'Marxism leads inevitably to the gulag insofar as Marxism seeks to materialize its critical spirit in a real society.'[48] If I thought so, I would have said so. But, if I thought so, how could I have written *Specters of Marx*? It *is* true – though this is quite the opposite, in my view – that I am inclined to

believe that a certain 'Marxism', an alleged or self-styled 'Marxism', a pseudo-Marxism, was in fact unable to avoid the gulag. But this is not because it sought to 'materialize its critical spirit in a real society'. Quite the contrary! It is precisely because it *did not*, because it failed sufficiently to 'materialize its critical spirit in a real society'. To be sure, I make no specific analysis of what we might call, using a very inadequate term, the Soviet, Bolshevik, Leninist, or Stalinist 'failure'. That was not what my book set out to do, and I admit that I am not yet capable of offering such an analysis. To date, I have not read anything on this terrible subject that I regard as satisfactory. I thank Lewis for the bibliography he provides me on this question, but I do not find it very helpful (for he does no more than sum up a vague doxography, appealing to Bukharin's formula: 'Telegraphically stated, Stalinism *is* the doctrine of "socialism in one country".'[49]) Everything then depends on the way one reads and deploys the telegram. By itself, it is very meager. Lewis says nothing convincing about it. If I understand certain of his allusions, he has in mind a refined version (Tony Cliff's, for example) of the Trotskyist interpretation: the degeneration of a workers' state is in reality supposed to have been due to nothing more than the fact that a bureaucracy replaced a bourgeoisie. The bureaucracy is said to have played the same role as the bourgeoisie in the accumulation process and the production of surplus-value. Perhaps. One would have to ask – since it is Lewis who brings up the gulag – how the substitution of a bureaucracy for a bourgeoisie can by itself account for the gulag (I doubt it can), and, above all, if our role here, in the face of the gulag, should be to 'account for' it. Doubtless we need to work out and mobilize a different problematic. Which one? For instance, the one that, articulating psychoanalysis and politics in a new way – something none of those who respond to me in this book do – takes into consideration the experience of death and mourning, and, therefore, of spectralization. (Need I recall that my book moves in that direction?) This is necessary to approach both the political assassinations and the gulag, and also, precisely, what is so hastily labeled bureaucratization. I am afraid that the concept of bureaucracy, which has been used and abused, is a most abstract phantom; furthermore, it is not, in my opinion, possible to analyze how the bureaucracy could arise, and, precisely, the ghostly abstraction that constitutes it, without a serious, precise and differentiated theory of the effects of spectrality. Moreover, Lewis says nothing concrete, beyond the unjust accusation he throws at me and the words he puts in my mouth without offering a shred of proof (where have I said – something I do not think – that 'Marxism leads inevitably to the gulag insofar as Marxism seeks to materialize its critical spirit in a real society'?); he contents himself with referring the reader to work that has been carried out elsewhere ('It is impossible,' he says, 'to do justice to the richness of the theory of bureaucratic state capitalism in this space. . . . I am aware that a number of important questions and issues remain after the incomplete summary I have offered of how the theory of "bureaucratic state capitalism" explains the rise of Stalinism. It is not possible on this occasion, however, to pursue other matters, such as . . .' – there follows a list of all manner of real problems that are left untouched).[50]

I do not wish to take undue advantage of all of Lewis's alibis, postponements and dodges, but I would like to spell out two points: (1) *on the one hand*, the supposed richness of a theory (*concesso non dato*) does not necessarily imply that it is pertinent or sufficient; (2) and, *on the other hand*, given that matters are stated as schematically and programmatically as they are here, I find it amusing that Lewis is pleased to chide *me* for still being 'metaphysical' ('But enough has been indicated to allow the core of the theory to emerge and to know that we stand here at a far remove from Derrida's metaphysical view of the Bolsheviks' eventual failure'[51]).

Of course – and one could say that this is *where the whole problem lies* – I do not simply find this program and alibi (the theory of the bureaucracy, of which, to boot, Lewis gives a very sketchy account) highly abstract, schematic and *metaphysical* in the form in which they are presented. Not only do I believe that anything one might have to say of interest on the subject of the bureaucracy and state capitalism (incidentally, I have no doubt that others could surely say useful, interesting things on this score – but Lewis's essay only gives the bare bones of an account, in very unconvincing fashion) presupposes thinking 'spectrality' by way, precisely, of that 'hauntology' whose direction and main lines I indicate in *Specters of Marx*; I believe above all that the hauntology I discuss is anything but 'metaphysical' and 'abstract', which is what *all* the contributors to this volume seem to imply, wrongly, because they have not read or wanted to read me – with the exception of Hamacher, and, perhaps, Montag, who, in a perceptive essay with which I am almost everywhere in agreement, clearly notes that: 'To speak of specters, the lexicon of ontology is insufficient.'[52]

For, immediately after denouncing 'Derrida's metaphysical view of the Bolsheviks' eventual failure', Lewis, as if to illustrate what he says, discusses this 'hauntology', which, for him, is only abstraction and metaphysics. I will come back to this, of course, but let me first say here, in a kind of sledgehammer statement of principle, that the spectral logic I appeal to in *Specters of Marx* and elsewhere, is, in my view, not metaphysical, but 'deconstructive'. This logic is required to account for the processes and effects of, if I may be allowed to put it this way, metaphysicalization, abstraction, idealization, ideologization and fetishization. (Incidentally, Jameson quite rightly points out that I have 'consistently demonstrated the impossibility of avoiding the metaphysical'.)[53] For no serious Marxist can shrug his shoulders over, say, abstraction, as if it were nothing to speak of. Nor, for that matter, over 'metaphysics' as an abstraction. Bureaucratization, for example, is also a phenomenon of abstraction and spectralization. That is something else I have learned from reading Marx: namely, that we need to account for the possibility of the process of abstraction. Marx spent a lifetime analyzing the possibility of abstraction in all spheres of existence. And he taught us, among other things, that we should not shrug off abstraction as if it were nothing to speak of ('that's just an abstraction'), as if it were the insubstantiality of the imaginary, and so on. Need I repeat that my book is also a critique of abstraction? Let me quote once again, among a host of similar passages in *Specters of Marx*, the page I have already recommended to Spivak's distracted attention ('It is even more a certain emancipatory and *messianic* affirmation, a certain experience of the promise that one can try to liberate from any dogmatics and even from any metaphysico-religious determination, from any *messianism*. And a promise must promise to be kept, that is, not to remain "spiritual" or "abstract", but to produce events, new effective forms of action, practice, organization, and so forth. To break with the "party form" or with some form of the State or the International does not mean to give up every form of practical or effective organization. It is exactly the contrary that matters to us here.'),[54] in order to spell out the following: I find more 'metaphysical abstraction', more 'bad' abstraction, more demobilizing and depoliticizing abstraction in Ahmad, Lewis, or Eagleton than in myself; indeed, to borrow Lewis's amusing term, I find more 'pessimism' in those Marxists who would like to reproduce the present obsolete forms of organization represented by the state, Party and International. To be sure, I must confess that I simply cannot bring myself to take seriously the trivial opposition between optimism and pessimism as Lewis employs it: the messianicity I speak of, like the 'experience of the impossible'[55] at the heart of messianicity, is the strange alloy [*alliance*] of 'pessimism' and 'optimism' that underlies, it seems to me, all serious revolutionary approaches to the political realm (*la chose politique*]. And since it follows from this that one can just as well say 'optimism' as 'pessimism', I make little use of either of these pseudo-categories.

At the point I have reached in these responses, it is perhaps time to mark out, in Jameson's remarkable response, certain areas of debate, of agreement and disagreement. I will begin with the two themes I just recalled: social classes and the messianic.

Classes. Although Lewis appeals to Jameson against me, I by no means take what Jameson says on this subject[56] as a critique of what I put forward. For I find myself in basic agreement with Jameson; I have, at any rate, the same basic orientation he does vis-à-vis the following proposition, even if I do not subscribe to the letter of all he says (the reader should reread his contribution, which I cannot cite at length here):

> As for class, however, merely mentioned in passing as one of those traditional features of Marxism that can be jettisoned en route by any truly postcontemporary Marxism – 'this ultimate support that would be the identity and the self-identity of a social class' [*Spectres de Marx*, p. 97/*Specters of Marx*, p. 55] – it seems to me appropriate to take this opportunity to show how this very widespread conception of class is itself a kind of caricature. It is certain that – even among Marxists – the denunciation of the concept of class has become an obligatory gesture today . . .[57]

I feel that there is a close proximity of views between Jameson and myself when he writes, a page further on:

> And this is of course exactly the gesture I will myself reproduce here, by reminding you that class itself is not at all this simple-minded and unmixed concept in the first place, not at all a primary building block of the most obvious and orthodox ontologies [I note in passing that it is this ontology and ontologization in general which disturb Jameson as they do me, thus setting him apart from all those who more or less directly hold out an ontology and an ontologism against me, especially and above all Negri; I will come back to this], but rather in its concrete moments something a good deal more complex, internally conflicted and reflexive than any of those stereotypes.[58]

Those stereotypes are all I wish to contest;[59] they have greater currency in discourse of a Marxist type than Jameson seems, or pretends, to think. Otherwise he would not insist as heavily as he does on all these risks. And I subscribe to what he says before and after the passage I have quoted, as well as to all the indications he provides of those complexities and areas of conflict. I am not sure, however, that I understand or, consequently, can accept, the word 'allegory', which he goes on to use a number of times; it doubtless calls for clarifications and a debate that would take us beyond the bounds of this brief discussion[60] (see, in its entirety, the conclusion to the subsection entitled 'Undermining the unmixed', where Jameson and I are obviously in very close agreement, as we are on many other points).[61]

I continue to have reservations concerning the word 'allegory', which Jameson assigns so important a role in the context just evoked, and am still undecided about it. I would, however, firmly reject the use of the words 'aesthetic' on the one hand, and, on the other, 'Utopia', 'Utopianism', or 'Utopian', to characterize my work.

(A) The *aesthetic*. This is a motif on which Jameson places a great deal of weight,[62] with consequences that are all the more serious in that, as the result of a still more unfortunate misunderstanding, he ranges the reference to spectrality under this 'umbrella'. As I have far too much to say about my reasons for regarding this category as inadequate, I will provisionally limit myself to making only three points here. (1) Whether or not I succeed, everything I write tends to show that even where my discourse does not posit any philosophical thesis, and, indeed, expressly refrains from doing so, and even where it questions notions both of thesis and position (*Setzung*), and also of philosophical theme or system, it is nevertheless not an aesthetic affirmation (which would, moreover, be exposed and vulnerable to the same questions: a value or evaluation in the aesthetic realm is a 'position', and my gestures with regard to the value of form or of taste are anything but formalistic or dogmatic). Even less is my discourse the affirmation of a 'minimalist' aesthetic (and I think I can say that this 'even less' is not a 'minimalist' upping of the ante). (2) It is not enough to call the idea of 'systematicity' in philosophy into question (the system is only one form of coherence or 'consistency', a form that, moreover, appears late in the history of philosophy) in order then to take refuge in the aesthetic or in 'personal aesthetic tastes'. I have multiplied 'deconstructive' gestures vis-à-vis the traditional categories 'system' and 'aesthetic'. (3) When Jameson writes that 'what saves the day here is the central formal role of the Heideggerian problematic, which assigns a minimal narrative to the entire project', or, again, when he affirms that Rorty's aestheticism (I am, in fact, not at all, truly not at all in agreement with Rorty, especially where he takes his inspiration from my work) is, as aestheticism, more radical than mine, because I arrange 'to rescue the discipline secretly in this backdoor Heideggerian manner . . .', etc.),[63] I would merely recall that my mistrust of this 'minimal narrative' and Heideggerian axiomatic has been abiding, frequently emphasized and legible. Everywhere. I even have the unpardonable pretension of thinking that, among attentive readers of Heidegger (I cannot say whether there are many of them, but I am trying to be one), I do not know any more reticent than I am in this regard. I will not, then, allow myself to be trapped in the alternative 'aestheticism/Heideggerianism'. I like to think that there are other ways; they are the ones that have always attracted me.

Let me add something that might bring me even closer to Jameson on this point. It is perhaps not uninteresting or irrelevant after all to speak of an 'aesthetic' of my texts; it perhaps does 'make sense to talk about something like an "aesthetic" [the word is in inverted commas, is it not? Jameson puts it in inverted commas] of the Derridean text'.[64] One could perhaps write pertinent, interesting things, even theses, on this point. But I would then simply say, by way of response to Jameson, but also to all those – they are legion – who think they can 're-aestheticize' matters in this book, reducing its concepts (the concept of the 'specter', for instance) to figures of rhetoric, or my demonstrations to literary experiments and effects of style: none of what matters to me, and, above all, may matter to the discussion under way (ever since, precisely, my texts have managed to expose themselves to, or enter into, discussion), can be reduced to, or elucidated by, this 'aesthetic' approach. Even if my protest here is not sufficient to lay the allegation (and, often, accusatory suspicion) of the aesthetic or aestheticism to rest, even if the evidence provided by all I have written on this subject is still not sufficient to disarm this critical interpretation, I may perhaps be allowed to bring the following very unsophisticated argument to bear: the number, duration and, sometimes, vehemence of the discussions which have sprung up around these texts suggests that what is at stake in them is not a matter of aesthetics, and even less of the order of some minimalist aesthetic. At issue is the question of how one writes or argues, of what the norms that apply here are (especially the academic norms). This question is anything but 'aesthetic'; it is particularly, and perhaps above all, political.

(B) Nothing would seem to be at a further remove from Utopia or Utopianism, even in its 'subterranean' form,[65] than the messianicity and spectrality which are at the heart of *Specters of Marx*. Jameson regularly and repeatedly translates everything I say about the 'messianic' as 'Utopianism'. As this is, I believe, at least a twofold misunderstanding, a single sentence of Jameson's will permit me to identify two points of disagreement, one bearing on messianicity itself, and the other on the ostensibly Benjaminian heritage of this concept. Thus Jameson writes: 'indeed we will later on want to see in *Specters of Marx* the overt expression of a persistent if generally subterranean Utopianism, which he himself (shunning that word) will prefer to call "a weak messianic power", following Benjamin.'[66] What does indeed call for explanation, first of all, is, precisely, my reason for wanting to 'shun' the word 'Utopia'. Messianicity (which I regard as a universal structure of experience, and which cannot be reduced to religious messianism of any stripe) is anything but Utopian: it refers, in every here–now, to the coming of an eminently real, concrete event, that is, to the most irreducibly heterogeneous otherness. Nothing is more 'realistic' or 'immediate' than this messianic apprehension, straining forward toward the event of him who/that which is coming. I say 'apprehension', because this experience, strained forward toward the event, is at the same time a waiting without expectation [*une attente sans attente*] (an active preparation, anticipation against the backdrop of a horizon, but also exposure without horizon, and therefore an irreducible amalgam of desire and anguish, affirmation and fear, promise and threat).

Although there is a waiting here, an apparently passive limit to anticipation (I cannot calculate everything, predict and program all that is coming, the future in general, etc., and this limit to calculability or knowledge is also, for a finite being, the condition of praxis, decision, action and responsibility), this exposure to the event, which can either come to pass or not (condition of absolute otherness), is inseparable from a promise and an injunction that call for commitment without delay [*sans attendre*], and, in truth, rule out abstention. Even if messianicity as I describe it here can seem abstract (precisely because we have to do here with a universal structure of relation to the event, to the concrete otherness of him who/that is coming, a way of thinking the event 'before' or independently of all ontology), we have to do here with the most concrete urgency, and the most revolutionary as well. *Anything but Utopian*, messianicity mandates that we interrupt the ordinary course of things, time and history *here–now*; it is inseparable from an affirmation of otherness and justice. As this unconditional messianicity *must* thereafter negotiate its conditions in one or another singular, practical situation, we have to do here with the locus of an analysis and evaluation, and, therefore, of a responsibility. These must be re-examined at every moment, on the eve and in the course of each event. But that that re-examination has to be carried out, and carried out without delay – this is an ineluctability whose imperative, always here–now, in singular fashion, can in no case yield to the allure of Utopia, at least not to what the word literally signifies or is ordinarily taken to mean. Indeed, one could not so much as account for the possibility of Utopia in general without reference to what I call messianicity.

Nor does this *non-Utopian* way of thinking messianicity belong – not really, not essentially – to the Benjaminian tradition that Jameson and Hamacher are, to be sure, right to recall, though they proceed a bit hastily, perhaps, when they reduce what I have to say to that tradition, or re-inscribe it here. I too evoked this Benjaminian tradition, in a note.[67] But, in that note, I discuss the differences as much as I do the consonance ('consonant . . . despite many differences'). For I do not believe, as Hamacher and Jameson *do*, that the continuity between the Benjaminian motif and what I am attempting is determinant – or, above all, that it is sufficient to account for what is going on here. One should not be too quick to recognize and identify things, even supposing that Benjamin's purpose were, in itself, sufficiently clear and identifiable for one to be able to identify something else with it. I do not mention the possibility of this discontinuity with Benjamin in order to lay claim to some sort of originality, but simply to clarify, in programmatic fashion, a number of points.

(1) In the text of Benjamin's to which I referred, the reference to Jewish messianism seems to me to be constitutive – and, to all appearances, ineradicable. That appearances may be deceptive is a possibility I do not exclude, but, in that case, a considerable effort would be required to dissociate the Benjaminian allusion to a 'messianic power', however 'weak', from any and all forms of Judaism, or, again, to dissociate a certain Jewish tradition from the usual figures or representations of messianism, of the kind that can dominate, not only the prevailing *doxa*, but sometimes even the most sophisticated orthodoxies. It may be that what I am attempting to do tends in that direction. But I am not at all sure; for, in principle, my use of the word 'messianic' bears no relation to any messian*istic* tradition. That is why I speak, precisely, of 'messianicity *without* messianism'. And that is why I wrote, if I may insist on the letter of this short sentence, that 'the following paragraph names messianism, or, more precisely, [the] messianic without messianism, a "weak messianic power" [*eine* schwache *messianische Kraft*; Benjamin's emphasis]'. The interpolated phrase, 'the messianic without messianism', is, of course, *my own*, not Benjamin's. It is not, then, an appositional phrase, translation, or equivalent expression; I wanted, rather, to mark an orientation *and* a *break*, a tendency running *from* weakening *to* annulment, from the 'weak' to the 'without' – and, consequently, the asymptote, and *only the asymptote*, of a *possible* convergence of Benjamin's idea with the one I would like to propose. Between 'weak' and 'without', there is a leap – perhaps an infinite leap. A messianicity *without* messianism is not a watered-down messianism, a diminishment of the force of the messianic expectation. It is a different structure, a structure of existence that I attempt to take into account by way of a reference less to religious traditions than to possibilities whose analysis I would like to pursue, refine, complicate, *and* contest – for example, the analysis offered by a theory of speech acts or a phenomenology of existence (in the twofold Husserlian and Heideggerian tradition): the possibility of taking into account, *on the one hand*, a paradoxical experience of the performative of the promise (but also of the threat at the heart of the promise) that organizes *every* speech act, every other performative, and even every preverbal experience of the relation to the other; and, *on the other hand*, at the point of intersection with this threatening promise, the horizon of awaiting

[*attente*] that informs our relationship to time – to the event, to that which happens [*ce qui arrive*], to the one who arrives [*l'arrivant*], and to the other. Involved this time, however, would be a waiting *without* waiting, a waiting whose horizon is, as it were, punctured by the event (which is waited for *without* being awaited); we would have to do with a waiting for an event, for someone or something that, in order to happen or 'arrive', must exceed and surprise every determinant antici-pation. No future, no time-to-come [*à-venir*], no other, otherwise; no event worthy of the name, no revolution. And no justice. At *the point of intersection* of these two styles of thought (speech act theory and the onto-phenomenology of temporal or historical existence), but also against both of them, the interpretation of the messianic that I propose does not, it will perhaps be agreed, much resemble Benjamin's. It no longer has *any* essential connection with what messianism may be taken to mean, that is, at least two things: on the one hand, the memory of a determinate historical revelation, whether Jewish or Judeo-Christian, and, on the other, a relatively determinate messiah-figure. The very structure of messianicity *without* messianism itself suffices to exclude these two conditions. Not that I think we must reject them, or that we must necessarily denigrate or do away with the historical figures of messianism; these are, however, only possible on the universal and quasi-transcendental ground of the structure constituted by this '*without* messianism'.

Here, be it said in passing, everything seems to come down to the interpretation and 'logic' of the little word 'without'. I have treated this question elsewhere at length,[68] in connection with Blanchot, and in his wake. It is well known that Blanchot makes apparently paradoxical use of the preposition 'without', sometimes placing it between two homo-nyms that are virtually synonymous, between two homonyms whose synonymy is broken up at the very heart of the analogy which fuses their meanings (*la mort* sans *mort, le rapport* sans *rapport,* etc.).[69] 'With-out' does not necessarily designate negativity; even less does it designate annihilation. If this preposition effects a certain abstraction, it also accounts for the necessary effects of abstraction in so doing – of the abstraction of the 'there is', of the abstraction *that* 'there is'. Initially, I imagined that I would be able to organize all these 'responses' (responses without response, of course) by subordinating them to an analysis of the word 'without' – and of the way most of the contributors to this volume use that word. Some of them are serenely confident that they can make it serve as a weapon against me (Eagleton, with his usual triumphant air, doubtless assumes that he will spark the plaudits, mirth, or wrath of the crowd by denouncing, starting with the very title of his essay, a 'Marxism without Marxism'! But yes, that is precisely the point!

I am happy to confirm this for him, and to sign and seal my deposition). Others – for example, Macherey – express legitimate misgivings about a 'dematerialized Marx', but in agreeable fashion this time, in intelligent, serious fashion: 'Marx *without* social classes, *without* the exploitation of labor, *without* surplus-value . . .' (my emphasis). Macherey is right to conclude that such a Marx 'risks, in fact, no longer being anything but his own ghost'.[70] But it is obviously riskier to go on to imply that a 'ghost' is nothing, that it is less than nothing, without any materiality, without any body, a pure, illusory appearance – and to suppose that the true, good Marxists have rid themselves of all 'ghosts' and all spectrality. For that brings us back, once again, to the spectral logic that certain of my readers, in this volume, want to exorcize, conjure away, deny, or ignore at any price, in eminently traditional fashion.[71] It goes without saying that if a ghost is a ghost and nothing more, nothing more than nothing, nothing come of nothing, then my book does not deserve a second's attention (a possibility that must never be ruled out; I would be the last to do so). But the same would have to be said of all the possibilities that have something in common with this spectrality, although they cannot be reduced to it (ideology, fetishism, value – both exchange-value and use-value – language, everything produced by mourning work, a negativity, an idealization, an abstraction, a virtualization, etc.). And as I have now come to the allusion to Marx 'without classes', let me briefly recall my response to Lewis, who was also alarmed by the notion of an International '*without* class', and who, in the sentence 'without coordination, without party, without country . . . , without co-citizenship, *without common belonging to a class*', underscores only '*without common belonging to a class*': the point is not to eliminate or deny class affiliations, any more than citizenship or parties, but rather to make an appeal for an International whose essential basis or motivating force would not be class, citizenship, or party. It does not follow that one need not take class, citizenship, or party into consideration – and as rigorously as possible, depending on the determinate context. Moreover, if Lewis is unsettled by the phrase 'without classes', why does he not balk at 'without citizenship'? Because it would be ridiculous to express surprise over the fact that an International (even the old International) should constitute itself 'without' reference to citizenship. The 'without' has nothing negative about it, and does not at all imply that the citizens who make a commitment to this International therefore cease to be, at another level, citizens, or to give due consideration to their citizenship. The same might be said about party and class, even at the moment when 'Party' and 'class' are ceasing to be the major reference or dominant paradigm (something which I do in fact believe, today; here I doubtless part company with

Lewis and a number of other 'Marxists' – not *all* 'Marxists'). All of this is difficult enough not to have anything to do with the 'third way' the old rhetoric of certain Marxists is accustomed to denouncing. Their aim is to convince themselves, or to affect to believe, that they are dealing with something familiar, at a juncture in which, no longer finding the usual landmarks, they cannot, after all, claim to be confronting an enemy from the right, a 'class enemy': this is how Ahmad, with Lewis's staunch approval, seeks to define what I am about: 'third way', but that's old hat! What they really like is the family, authenticated genealogy, family resemblance; it reassures them to recognize the old familiar things, to recognize each other as they reassure each other; that way one knows who's who, who belongs to which family and which family line: 'We are thus on a very *familiar* territory: deconstruction as the Third Way, opposed certainly to the Right but also to "everything", as [Derrida] put it earlier, that the word "International" has historically signified.'[72]

The figures of messianism would have to be (to put matters too hastily here, crisscrossing all the codes in a somewhat confused manner) deconstructed as 'religious', ideological, or fetishistic formations, whereas messianicity without messianism remains, for its part, undeconstructible, like justice. It remains undeconstructible because the movement of any deconstruction presupposes it – not as a ground of certainty, the firm ground of a *cogito* (to cite Macherey's hasty interpretation),[73] but in line with another modality.

What is to be said of this 'quasi-transcendental' supposition? And why maintain the reference to the messianic, even while claiming to rule out all messianism, precisely in describing a universal structure (waiting without awaiting another future-to-come and an other in general; promise of a revolutionary justice that will interrupt the ordinary course of history, etc.)? Why this name, the *messianic* or the *messiah*? I shall come back to this in my third point, where the greatest difficulty resides.

(2) For I wonder if Benjamin does not link the privileged moments of this '*weak* messianic power' (*eine* schwache *messianische Kraft*) to determinate historico-political phases, or, indeed, crises. The hypothesis makes sense, at least, given the political context and the date of his essay (the Hitler–Stalin pact at the beginning of the war), even if that does not suffice to make it certain. Thus there would be, for Benjamin, critical moments (pre-revolutionary or post-revolutionary), moments of hope or disappointment, in short, dead ends during which a simulacrum of messianism serves as an alibi. Whence the strange adjective 'weak'. I am not sure I would define the messianicity I speak of as a

power (it is, no less, a vulnerability or a kind of absolute powerlessness); but even if I did define it as a power, as the movement of a desire, as the attraction, invincible élan or affirmation of an unpredictable future-to-come (or even of a past-to-come-again), the experience of the non-present, of the non-living present in the living present (of the spectral), of that which lives on [*du sur-vivant*][74] (absolutely past or absolutely to come, beyond all presentation or representability, etc.), I would never say, in speaking of this 'power', that it is strong or weak, more or less strong or more or less weak. For, in my view, the universal, quasi-transcendental structure that I call messianicity without messianism is not bound up with any particular moment of (political or general) history or culture (Abrahamic or any other); and it does not serve any sort of messianism as an alibi, does not mime or reiterate any sort of messianism, does not confirm or undermine any sort of messianism.

(3) I must further complicate this schema. By way of objection to the foregoing, one might make the following argument, which I have not omitted to bring foward against myself, between the lines: Since you say that the 'messianic' is independent of all forms of 'messianism' ('without messianism'), why not describe the universal structure in question *without even mentioning* the messianic, without making allusion to any messiah whatever, to the Messiah-figure who so evidently maintains an ultimate affiliation with one language, one culture and one 'revelation'? The objection is legitimate, and obvious enough not to have escaped my attention; here, then, is the response I was constrained to give – to begin with, to myself. An essentially strategic response, it takes account of a complex situation; this calculation can therefore not be summed up in a single word.

(a) *On the one hand*, this word (messianic) is, in my estimation, relatively arbitrary or extrinsic; it has merely rhetorical or pedagogical value. Through reference to a familiar cultural landscape, it makes it easier to understand, in certain contexts, what that which I accordingly call messianicity *resembles* (what it resembles, I hasten to add, *without* identifying itself with it, or reducing itself to it). In a context in which what I intend by messianicity is understood, if it comes to be understood some day, it should be possible to talk about this not only without reference to traditional messianism or a 'Messiah', but even without the 'without'. But by that point, under the old words, all the names will have been changed.

(b) But, *on the other hand*, matters are not so simple. Beneath this arbitrary choice and pedagogical usefulness, there lurks, perhaps, a more irreducible ambiguity. I find it hard to decide whether messianicity without messianism (*qua* universal structure) precedes and conditions every determinate, historical figure of messianism (in which case it would be radically independent of all such figures, and would remain heterogeneous from them, making the name itself a matter of merely incidental interest), or whether the possibility of thinking this independence has only come about or revealed itself as such by way of the 'Biblical' events which name the messiah and make him a determinate figure.[75]

(c) On the latter hypothesis (which I have to leave open, and suspended, because I have no answer to the question posed in this form – and I am for the moment retaining the word 'messianic' *so that* the question remains posed), it is harder to treat the reference to the messianic as a provisional, didactic tool – even if the messianic is strictly determined as 'without messianism'. This for several reasons, of which there are at least *four*; I will lay them out in elliptical, economical, cut-and-dried fashion here.

(i) To begin with, one cannot, it seems to me, ignore or deny the fact that the event named 'Marx' (with all its components, premises and consequences) is rooted in a European and Judeo-Christian culture. What is in question here is not a delimitable empirical sphere. It is necessary to assess all the stakes of Marx's implication in this culture, down to the logic and rhetoric of the discourse inherited from him, even in societies or cultures at a far remove from this Biblico-European tradition. Marx, and every 'Marxism', have appeared in a culture in which 'messiah' means something, and this culture has not remained 'local' or easily circumscribable in the history of humanity. It is always useful to recall this sedimentation, if only to draw diverse political consequences from it.

(ii) For, in the second place, Marxist culture, down to the very letter of its language, has in its way participated, willy-nilly, in the phenomenon I have elsewhere dubbed 'mondialatinization'.[76] It would therefore be difficult (and highly abstract to boot) to purge it of every messianic reference. My essay on Marx – I beg the reader's indulgence for the insolence of this remark – is only an element in a structure [*dispositif*] that is not limited to Marx.

(iii) No critique of *religion*, or of *each determinate* religion, however necessary or radical that critique may be, should or can, in my view, impugn *faith* in general. As I have tried to show elsewhere as well, especially in 'Foi et savoir . . .', the experience of belief, of credit, of faith in the pledged word (beyond all knowledge and any 'constative' possibility) is part of the structure of the social bond or the relation to the other in general, of the injunction, the promise, and the performativity that all knowledge and all political action, and in particular all revolutions, imply. The critique of religion itself, as a scientific or political undertaking, makes appeal to this 'faith'. It therefore seems to me impossible to eliminate all reference to faith. The expression 'the messianic without messianism' appeared to me well suited to translating this difference between faith and religion, at least provisionally.

(iv) Here we touch upon the sensitive point of the 'question of ideology'. What is to be said of the *concept* of ideology? Of the indestructibility of the ideological? What, above all, is to be said of the exemplary – that is, irreplaceable – role which religion plays in the emergence of this Marxian concept? Leaving to one side a historical urgency, namely, the fact that the geopolitical situation *today* requires us to rethink the question of religion (this is a point on which I fully agree with Jameson),[77] I must here ask those who do not want to take my use of the word 'messianic' and my reference to a spectral logic seriously to reread certain pages of *Specters of Marx*. I am thinking, in particular, of everything which seeks to pave the way for a response to the question 'What is ideology?' by insisting on two forms of 'irreducibility': *on the one hand*, 'the irreducibly specific character of the specter', and, *on the other*, 'the irreducibility of the religious model in the construction of the concept of ideology'.[78] 'Only the reference to the religious world allows one to explain the autonomy of the ideological';[79] or again: 'The religious is thus not one ideological phenomenon or phantomatic production among others.'[80]

The consequences of this hypothesis, if one admits it, are formidable: every ideological phenomenon would be marked by a degree of religiosity; and, as it is impossible radically to dissociate the *phainesthai* from the *phantasma*, to dissociate the appearing (of what appears) from the spectrality of the spectral, it follows that, like the ideological, like the religious, the spectral too is, at root, as indestructible as it is non-delimitable. It is just as hard to make of it a circumscribable object or field as it is to separate pure faith from any and all religious determination. We are here in the most difficult zone, that of the 'theory of ideology' (present or absent) in Marx. It is from this vantage point that I have begun to understand, admire and approve of the opening of Rastko Močnik's essay – although I must confess that, for lack of competence, I have been unable to follow, in all their richness, the most highly formalized passages of this text, those which integrate the problematics of Lévi-Strauss, Lacan and Lefort. Nevertheless, I find myself in agreement with what Močnik says to the effect that the very possibility of a theory of ideology is ruined by 'the very idea of ideology'. I would only add that the fact that a theory of ideology is impossible, in the strict sense of the word 'theory' (a formalizable system of objectifying theorems, the formulations of which lie outside the field of objectivity thus delimited; in other words, in the present instance, a *non-ideological theory of ideology*, a theory of ideology or science of ideology, as they used to say in France thirty years ago, divested of all ideologemes), does not necessarily have to be regarded as a negative limit or catastrophe. In the face of this, by now, classical situation, one needs, perhaps, to find a different way of thinking both the 'ideological' (the word has perhaps seen its day, in the history of ideas of the *idea* or *eidos*) and the relationships among thought, philosophy, science and, precisely, 'theory', together with everything that interests all of us here: what still remains to 'be done', what remains irreducible to the constative, to knowledge (which a certain Marx called, sharply limiting the notion, 'interpreting': interpreting the world, when the point is to 'change' it). If I had not already gone on at too great length, I would attempt to show that what I here mean by 'thinking' (which cannot be reduced to philosophy, scientific theory, or knowledge in general, although to say so is not to exclude or denigrate them) calls for the coming of an event, i.e., calls precisely for that which 'changes' (in the transitive and intransitive sense of this odd word).

Let us conclude here, provisionally, with a smile – the smile that the specter of Marx – like *Specters of Marx* – never lost. I owe a debt of gratitude to Antonio Negri for having, in his way, left this smile floating about the lips of a specter – though it is not easy to say which one. After reading, gratefully, 'The Specter's Smile', I would have liked to say to Negri, in brief (for this short response has already gone on too long): I agree, agree about everything with the exception of one word, 'ontology'. Why do you cling to that word? Why do you want to put forward a *new ontology*, after having duly noted the transformation that renders the Marxist paradigm of ontology obsolete? Why do you want to re-ontologize at all costs, at the risk of restoring everything to order? to the grand order, but to order? I was first given pause, in my enthusiastic approval, when, somewhere, I came across a first reference to ontology. To be sure, it was initially included to describe and follow a move of my own:

> Transferred onto the terrain of the critique of political economy, this project [Marx's *The German Ideology*] of a spectral reading of ideology is applied to the categories of society and capital, develops ontologically, and becomes definitively fixed in *Capital* (Derrida speaks of this in *Specters*, pp. 147–58). The specters narrated herein have a particular ontological pertinence: they reveal the complete functioning of the law of value.[81]

Yes, I understand; but, to begin with, the word 'ontological' as such is not to be found in Marx (one should perhaps not be too quick to reinsert it in his text); moreover, I was trying to show in this passage that it is in re-ontologizing the process, in re-philosophizing his concepts, that Marx limits the pertinence and force of his turn toward spectral logic. Negri is certainly a better Marxist than I am, he is more faithful to the spirit of Marx than I am when he describes this movement; but, in doing so, he cedes to what I think is the most problematic aspect of Marx, namely, the unrestrained, classical, traditional (dare I add 'Platonic'?) desire to conjure away any and all spectrality so as to recover the *full, concrete reality* of the process of genesis hidden *behind the specter's mask*. Let me recall that when Negri, in the first part of his essay (in sum, the part devoted to commentary),[82] he reproduces (without, it is true, adopting it) precisely that gesture in Marx which I see as being still metaphysical, *because it is ontological.* Here is what I say in the passage Negri alludes to, of which I will cite only the following lines, while referring the interested reader to the whole discussion that surrounds them and forms the backbone (I dare not say the thesis) of my book:

> In their common denunciation, in what is at once most critical and ontological about it, Marx and Saint Max are also heirs to the Platonic tradition, more precisely to the one that associates in a strict fashion image with specter, and idol with phantasm, with the *phantasma* in its phantomatic or errant dimension as living-dead. The 'phantasma,' which the *Phaedo* (81d) or the *Timaeus* (71a) do not separate from the *eidola*, are figures of dead souls, they are the souls of the dead.[83]

I was attempting to bring out the *phallogocentric* tendency of this metaphysics, the *patrimony* that has always linked it to the question of the father (that is why the title of the present essay, 'Marx & Sons', is anything but a joke). I spelled out, somewhat further on:

> It is doubtless a hypothesis without originality, but one whose consequence can be measured by the constancy of an immense tradition, or rather one must say of the philosophical *patrimony* such as it is handed down, through the most parricidal mutations, from Plato to Saint Max, to Marx and beyond. The lineage of this patrimony is wrought, but never interrupted, by the question of the idea, the question of the concept and the concept of the concept, the very one that harbors the whole problematic of *The German Ideology* (nominalism, conceptualism, but also rhetoric and logic, literal meaning, proper meaning, figural meaning, and so forth).[84]

To this point, it seems to me, there is no fundamental disagreement between Negri and me. Nor is there any disagreement when, wondering what we can do with the 'Marxist specters' 'today', Negri notes that a mutation has occurred, especially as far as 'the labor paradigm' is concerned (I noted this as well). He himself says: 'We agree in deeming the Marxist ontology out of date, and *this* ontological description of exploitation, in particular.'[85]

The disagreement, misunderstanding, or, rather, 'disadjustment' sets in at the point where Negri undertakes to do two things that seem to me to be equally open to question. (1) He believes that he can make out a movement of 'nostalgia', of 'melancholy', a 'work of mourning', in what I am doing; and, above all, he thinks he has detected a fundamental, determinant note here.[86] (2) He believes that he can remedy this sad negativity with the help of, in sum, a new 'ontology' – one he calls 'post-deconstructive'.

(1) First of all, I believe, and have often emphatically stated, that deconstruction, which is affirmative right down to this conception of the messianic without messianism, is anything but a negative movement of nostalgia and melancholy (this is so clearly what I think, and I have said it so often, that I will perhaps not be required to do so again). It is true that this has not prevented me from reflecting, just as insistently, on the work of mourning (or from generalizing this concept – notably in *Glas* – to the point of making it coextensive with work in general). And, of course, I have also done so, massively, in *Specters of Marx*. But one can discuss the work of mourning, analyze its necessity and political effects across the globe (after the alleged 'death of Marx' or of the communist idea) – one can be constrained to do so for all kinds of reasons, without therefore relinquishing a certain gaiety of affirmative thinking. Even without recalling the many texts and talks I have devoted to this possibility, I think it is fair to say that *Specters of Marx* is anything but a sad book: notwithstanding a gravity that I am also not prepared to relinquish, it is, as I see it, a gay, humorous book. It is more light-hearted than I am, undoubtedly, but my books are not necessarily or solely self-portraits; it may be that they transform themselves into a kind of antithesis of myself. What is more, contrary to what Lewis too seems to assume, I do not myself mourn, and feel no nostalgia at all, truly none at all, for what has just vanished from the face of the earth after having usurped the figure of communism. But that does not prevent me from analyzing the paradoxical symptoms of a geopolitical mourning, or trying to articulate them with a new logic of the relations between the unconscious and politics. Spectral logic – I will not go back over this – seemed to me indispensable here. Trying to put it to work in rigorous fashion is, I would like to testify, not a sad experience. I often take a great deal of pleasure in it. And even if this is a rather peculiar pleasure, I do not recognize in it anything of what Negri describes as falling under

the shadow of that melancholic libertinism when, at the end of another revolutionary age, men who were still free testified in refusal of the Counter-Reformation and awaited the martyrdom of the Inquisition. We cannot content ourselves with this, perhaps because our Marxist heritage has already been proven in practice; more likely because – in dealing with specters – the eye, the other senses, and the mind begin to detect delineations of new realities. So is it possible then to proceed beyond the level of moral protest?[87]

I cannot content myself with this, either: not because 'our Marxist heritage has already been proven in practice' (I do not believe that at all; there, my disagreement is sharp and emphatic), but, above all, because the analogy with a paradigm identifiable in another age is one of those reassuring gestures of which, as I have already said, I am always wary, like the 'family resemblances' one thinks one can make out, or like 'familiarity' in general. Even supposing that I suffer from, or enjoy, some sort of 'melancholic libertinism', I do not believe the least trace of it can be found in what I try to think and say in *Specters of Marx*, which concerns, precisely, the 'delineations' of new things – I hesitate to say, for the reasons stated below, 'delineations of new *realities*'. Nor do I think there is any question, in *Specters of Marx*, of simple 'moral protest' or of reducing everything to it, although it is also difficult to expunge every trace of the moral or of 'religion', or, at any event, every 'act of faith', from a revolutionary injunction, even with a view to establishing the new 'post-deconstructive ontology' Negri seems to be in quest of. Negri is unjust when, on the subject of the 'moral', he says: 'There's a word that rarely appears in Derrida's book: exploitation.'[88] I do not know if the word appears there, or, if so, how often, but I am sure that the reference to the 'concept' and the 'thing' is recurrent in the book, and more or less central – at least in the chapter 'Wears and Tears (tableau of an ageless world)' and in the evocation of the ten plagues of the new world order. Doubtless the classic concept of exploitation is subjected to a certain degree of deconstructive turbulence (the question of ontology, again, and therefore that of the *proper*, of the appropriable, of proper or alienated subjectivity and what I call, everywhere, *ex-appropriation* – the logic of which singularly complicates the traditional discourse on exploitation and alienation). But that in no sense means that suffering and oppression, the 'exploitation of man by man', are passed over in silence. To be sure, I also speak of the exploitation of the animal by man (but let us leave this capital question open).

(2) Above all, the re-ontologization Negri proposes is hardly likely to bring back the gaiety he imagines I have been robbed of. Nor will his new ontology – emancipatory or emancipating – persuade me to reconsider, at least for now, in view of the arguments advanced, the

entire deconstruction of the 'ontological' motif itself, at its root. That deconstruction (which, let me point out again, is neither a critique nor a simple delegitimization) is reaffirmed and developed in *Specters of Marx*. But, whether I am right or wrong, this is a point which we could not discuss seriously without engaging in a long, excessively long debate about everything that has occupied me for the past thirty years. I therefore decline, provisionally, to enter into that debate again here. But Negri will perhaps allow me to say that it is *his* concern to rehabilitate ontology, even if the ontology in question is 'post-deconstructive', as he puts it, which seems to me to bear the marks of mourning, nostalgia and, indeed, melancholy. Ontology involves, indeed *is*, on my view, mourning work (sometimes doomed to failure and to melancholy [the well-known theme of the melancholy of Aristotle and Heidegger – who, incidentally, speaks of the melancholy peculiar to philosophers]) – carried out with a view to reconstituting, saving, redeeming a full presence of the present-being, where that present-being, in accordance with what is not merely a lack or flaw [*défaut*], but also an opportunity, appears to be lacking (*faire défaut*): differance.

I do not want to turn Negri's own words against him unfairly; but, at the point in his text where he twice packs me off to prison,[89] I wonder if he does not do so in order to deny that he, for his part, is still confined, out-of-it-in-it, within the walled perimeter of a new ontological fatherland, a liberated ontology, an ontology of self-liberation. In, for example, a Spinozan sense of the word 'liberty'.

As we have neither the time nor the space here for a gigantomachy, in the manner of *The Sophist*, over the essence of being [*l'être de l'étant*] and ontology in general, I offer Negri, so as to conclude with a smile, an armistice based on a compromise: perhaps the two of us could, from now on, agree to regard the word 'ontology' as a password, a word arbitrarily established by convention, a shibbloeth, which only pretends to mean what the word 'ontology' has always meant. In that case we could, between us, use a coded language, like Marranos. In philosophical company, we could act as if we were still speaking the language of metaphysics or ontology, knowing full well, between us, that this was not at all so. For I found the allusions to the Marranos in 'The Specter's Smile' highly seductive. I know that Negri was thinking, as always, of Spinoza. But no matter. He probably does not know that I have often played, as seriously as can be imagined, at secretly presenting myself as a sort of Marrano. I have done so in particular, and openly, in *Aporias, Circonfessions* and *Archive Fever* – and, doubtless, elsewhere as well. And I have done so less openly *everywhere* – for example, in *Le Monolinguisme de l'autre*. But I will not unveil all the other scenes of this simulacrum.

What if, to conclude, we floated the idea that not only Spinoza, but Marx himself, Marx the liberated ontologist, was a Marrano? A sort of clandestine immigrant, a Hispano-Portuguese disguised as a German Jew who, we will assume, pretended to have converted to Protestanism, and even to be a shade anti-Semitic? Now that would really be something! We might add that the sons of Karl himself knew nothing of the affair. And that his daughters didn't either. And now the supreme twist, the abyssal upping of the ante, the absolute surplus-value: they would have been Marranos who were so well disguised, so perfectly encrypted, that they themselves never suspected that that's what they were! – or else had forgotten the fact that they were Marranos, repressed it, denied it, disavowed it. It is well known that this sometimes happens to 'real' Marranos as well, to those who, though they are really, presently, currently, effectively, *ontologically* Marranos, no longer even know it themselves.

Claims have also been advanced to the effect that the question of marranism was recently closed for good.

I don't believe it for a second. There are still sons – and daughters – who, unbeknownst to themselves, incarnate or metempsychosize the ventriloquist specters of their ancestors.

Translated by G.M. Goshgarian

Notes

1. Although the question (apparently abstract and speculative) of Marx's ontology is broached, under that name, only in certain of the texts assembled here (especially Hamacher's, Jameson's and Negri's), I believe it traverses all of them at a crucial moment. It was also, let me recall, a question everything seemed to hinge on in *Specters of Marx*.

2. *Spectres de Marx* (Paris: Galilée, 1993), pp. 166–7; *Specters of Marx*, trans. Peggy Kamuf (New York and London: Routledge, 1994), pp. 101–2. The rest of this passage, not quoted here, expands upon this problematic of the Party, which I shall come back to, and the question of ideology as 'fable' (*Märchen*) – here, the fable of the specter. [Subsequent references to *Specters of Marx* are to the French original, followed by the English translation. – Editor's note.]

3. This thread runs through the whole book, but it also connects two debates – very different, to be sure – which are pursued with Michel Henry on the one hand (ibid., pp. 177 ff./p. 186, n. 7) and Étienne Balibar on the other (ibid., pp. 116 ff./p. 181, n. 8).

4. Ibid., p. 89/p. 50.

5. Ibid., p. 89/p. 51.

6. Ibid., p. 58/p. 29. Again on the following page, and throughout the book, what is in question, if I may put it that way, is Marx's 'ontological response' – not only to the spectral question of the specter (the question of the spectrality that lies beyond any and all ontological determination: life/death, the sensuous/the intelligible, presence/absence, etc.), but also to an injunction that would be older [*plus vieille*] than the question or the question-form of discourse, as if it were the eve of that question [*comme sa veille même*]. Marx's 'ontological response', his response insofar as, and wherever, it is still

ontological, consists, in my view, in suturing the question; the ontological response reduces or denies the abyss of the question, conjures away the threat of the question. On the effects – positive and negative – of this ontological treatment, see especially ibid., p. 150/ p. 91.

7. *Politiques de l'amitié* (Paris: Galilée, 1994), pp. 43–92; *Politics of Friendship*, trans. George Collins (London: Verso, 1997), pp. 26–48.

8. *Spectres de Marx*, p. 58; *Specters of Marx*, p. 29. I underscore 'perhaps' today.

9. On this twofold point, depoliticization and repoliticization, see ibid., pp. 149–51 and *passim*/pp. 91–2 and *passim*.

10. 'Ghostwriting', *Diacritics* 25/2 (Summer 1995), p. 65.

11. Ibid., p. 72.

12. Ibid., p. 69.

13. *Spectres de Marx*, p. 144/*Specters of Marx*, p. 87. I have added the emphasis on 'otherwise' here.

14. I could cite a thousand passages in my book to confirm what I say here. The following is just one that occurs not far from the passage Spivak falsifies, as we have just seen:

> It is even more a certain emancipatory and *messianic* affirmation, a certain experience of the promise that one can try to liberate from any dogmatics and even from any metaphysico-religious determination, from any *messianism*. And a promise must promise to be kept, that is, not to remain 'spiritual' or 'abstract,' but to produce new forms of action, practice, organization, and so forth. To break with the 'party form' or with some form of the State or the International does not mean to give up every form of practical or effective organization. It is exactly the contrary that matters to us here. (Ibid., pp. 146–7/p. 89)

15. Jameson, p. 60. [This and other essays printed and reprinted in this volume are cited as 'Jameson', 'Ahmad', etc. – Editor's note.] Tom Keenan would seem to interpret matters the same way: he too cites this remark of Jameson's in a powerful, courageous book he has just published (*Fables of Responsibility: Aberrations and Predicaments in Ethics and Politics* [Stanford, CA: University of Stanford Press, 1997], p. 224). See esp. his chapter on Marx (first published in 1993), which I have already referred to in *Specters of Marx* (p. 265n./p. 195, n. 35). One cannot, then, err more egregiously than to speak, as Ahmad does, at the risk of seeming to wish to deceive the reader, of the 'anti-politics' of *Specters of Marx* ('. . . the anti-politics he advocates might well bring us not a "new International" but a mere Fortinbras – a "new" order that is a variant of the very old one' [Ahmad, p. 107]).

16. Hamacher, p. 212 n. 40.

17. Ahmad, p. 90.

18. Ibid.

19. See, in its entirety, the chapter entitled 'Injunctions of Marx', together with the 'deconstructive' reading of what Heidegger has to say on these matters; *Spectres de Marx*, esp. pp. 39 ff./*Specters of Marx*, pp. 16 ff.

20. Ibid., pp. 144–5/pp. 87–8.

21. Eagleton, pp. 85–6. 'There is more than a touch of this adolescent perversity in Derrida, who like many a postmodernist appears to feel (it is a matter of sensibility rather than reasoned conviction) that the dominant is *ipso facto* demonic and the marginal precious *per se*. One condition of the unthinking postmodern equation of the marginal with the creative, apart from a convenient obliviousness to such marginal groups as Fascists . . . .'

The balance of the passage also bears rereading: I have cited it to this point in order to underscore – besides the summary, archaic psychologism of the distinction between 'sensibility and reasoned conviction' – the rhetorical effect sought, in this polemic, by way of the analogy-begging [*analogiste*], contaminating reference to 'Fascist' marginality. Let the reader judge: the insinuation is nothing less than that I am insensitive to the threat of Fascism, hence that I am not vigilant vis-à-vis Fascism, and thus that I am inclined to be irresolute in the face of Fascism. But, above all, I have cited this much of the passage in order to recall that the facile, demagogic, grave error of confusing my work (or even 'deconstruction' in general) with postmodernism is indicative, in Eagleton as in Ahmad or Lewis, of a massive failure to read and analyze. This rudimentary misunderstanding might by itself warrant my breaking off all further dialogue until certain 'homework' was done. But that is the road not taken, and it is too late to take it.

22. Ahmad did not consider it worthwhile to go back over what he himself calls a 'quick response' to the lecture he read on the airplane after he had read the book the lecture turned into ('Lengthier comment on the book I have resisted'). This justifies my taking seriously something he himself takes rather seriously, his high velocity notwithstanding, and entitles me to treat his remarks as the fruit of solid reflection, however hard I sometimes find this to do. One can cite other effects of precipitation and the contretemps among a good many Marxists, or those who are, to borrow Ahmad's expression, 'generally known as Marxists'. Thus Gayatri Chakravorty Spivak, for her part, speaks, not of the time it took her to read me (one wonders sometimes), but, rather, of the time she devoted to writing. 'I am writing at speed,' she declares at the outset of her essay ('Ghostwriting', p. 65). This chronology of an acceleration in reading or writing would thus seem to characterize those Marxists in the habit of criticizing me for having been too slow to speak of Marx: Eagleton, whom I have just cited, is a case in point, as are Spivak (see, for example, p. 66) and many others. They and I do, indeed, have different ways of dealing with time and the contretemps. We do nothing at the same speed, which is – I say this quite seriously – the chief source of all these misunderstandings. We do not make up our minds in the same way about which situations call for rapid action and which ones require, on the contrary, that one take one's time – as much time as possible.

23. *Spectres de Marx*, p. 98/ *Specters of Marx*, p. 56.

24. Sharp sleuth that he is, Ahmad believes he can 'detect an identification [mine] with Hamlet', but he espies another as well: 'we detect a similar identification with the ghost' (Ahmad, p. 106), that is – because the series of substitutions, by definition, cannot come to a halt (this, moreover, makes for its interest, and is the nub of the question) – an identification with Marx himself. Thus I would seem to identify with every possible father! And Ahmad does not like that.

25. It is no accident that Eagleton too makes literature a grievance, or a count in his indictment. In the most academic, indeed, the most conservative manner imaginable, he denounces my 'poetic' language, a bit as if one ought not to confuse genres and disciplines or stray into the wrong department. True, what he doesn't like about my 'poeticizing' is that it is 'portentous'. It is 'portentous' because it lends itself to parody. Indeed. I prefer to let the reader judge. To that end, I would invite him to reread what immediately precedes and follows the accusation of 'portentous poeticizing'. To top things off, Eagleton, falling back on a well-known but rather unconvincing tactic, blames me for the 'epigones' to whom he counterposes 'the *maître* himself, who really *is* politically earnest and engaged, whose relevant contexts are Auschwitz and Algeria, Althusser, the ANC and Eastern Europe rather than Ithaca or Irvine.'

How can I respond to this strategy? I find it inadmissible, even if Ahmad, for his part, is so generous as to spell out that I am not to be held 'answerable' for those who 'invoke [my] name'. This strategy is inadmissible not only because the distinction between 'master' and 'epigones' is highly suspect in my eyes (for a thousand reasons, of which some are, precisely, political), but also because I do not know 'who' these 'epigones' are and what they have allegedly said and done; under cover of darkness, they are accused of all the sins in creation, though not a one of them or their sins is named, and we are offered no rational discussion or argument about a text.

I would say the same thing to Ahmad when he berates, not the 'epigones', but the 'Derrideans' ('whatever other reservations I have about Derrida's work and influence [more about Derrideans, actually, than about himself], I have never thought of him as a man of the Right.'). Thank you very much. One should also read the passage that follows; it absolves me of having '*sought* the company of the right-wingers'. The word the author underscores leaves a lurking suspicion to the effect that, if I have not *sought* such company, I may yet have *found* it. Assuming that that could be demonstrated, one would have both to demonstrate it, i.e., to prove it, but also to assure oneself, in the same act, that one has oneself managed to avoid this suspect 'company'. The two tasks are equally difficult. Everywhere, and especially in the academy, a good many 'Marxists' find themselves 'in the company' of the most conservative forces. I would go even further than 'in the company', and speak of an 'alliance', occasionally more than an 'objective alliance', as we used to say not so long ago.

26. Ahmad, p. 91.

27. For example, Ahmad indicates his agreement with me about that which holds together 'this triple structure of political, mediatic and academic discourses' (in my opinion, this presupposes an agreement whose boundaries it would be difficult to establish; if we really do agree about that, we ought to agree about almost everything) (Ahmad, p. 97). Again, he says we agree about 'religious particularism' (the premises of that agreement also have rather far-reaching consequences) (Ahmad, p. 100).

28. Ahmad grants me his pardon, then. Although he says elsewhere that what is at issue is not, as he sees it, my reconciliation 'with Marx', nor a reconciliation 'of Marxism with me', he writes, in a gesture of forgiveness: 'Much of what Derrida says on this account one can accept readily, with a sense of comradeship, the past acrimonies between Marxism and deconstructionism notwithstanding' (Ahmad, p. 101). Although I do not know, and I am quite serious, what deconstructionism is (if not a journalistic fantasy), and although I never speak of it or in behalf of it, and do not feel that I am represented by this 'thing' (I would say the same thing for 'Marxism': who represents 'Marxism'?), and despite all the efforts I keep making to detect signs of acrimony, I have no recollection of any, either on my part, or on the part of those whose work is, in one way or another, close to mine. To be sure, one could find things to say about this or that text by a 'Marxist', but this is not evidence of acrimony against Marxism.

On the other hand, I am, even today, I must confess – this is, moreover, easy to see – rather insensitive to any 'sense of comradeship'. If I had the time and space, I would explain why this is not a reflex on my part, certainly not a class reflex. It is, rather, a carefully considered act, a way of thinking the politics of friendship or friendship in politics. I am therefore deeply touched when Ahmad concludes: 'We are glad to say, as he himself says, that he is one of us.' But I remain mystified despite my emotion. 'One of us'? Where do I say that? And who is 'us'?

29. Eagleton, p. 85. Eagleton is undoubtedly convinced that, with the finesse, grace and elegance he is universally acknowledged to possess, he has hit upon a title ('Marxism without Marxism') which is a flash of wit, an ironic dart, a witheringly sarcastic critique, aimed at me or, for example, Blanchot, who often says – I have discussed this at length elsewhere – 'X without X.' Every 'good Marxist' knows, however, that nothing is closer to Marx, more faithful to Marx, more 'Marx', than a 'Marxism without Marxism'. Need we recall here that this Marxism without Marxism was, to begin with, the Marxism of Marx himself, if that name still means anything?

30. *Spectres de Marx*, pp. 198–9/*Specters of Marx*, p. 122. This is one of the many arguments (decisive, in my estimation) that Hamacher is the only one to single out and take seriously (Hamacher, p. 185). He alludes to this passage, which is, he writes, 'the only passage which strikes an explicitly autobiographical tone'. I am less sure of this than he is, but it does not matter much, in the end. Moreover, what enables one to recognize an 'explicitly autobiographical tone'?

31. 'Not the least refreshing aspect of this passage is Derrida's lucid sense that a certain narrow-minded religious particularism ... is a characteristic not only of some Islamicist countries but also of the West itself, capitalist Europe itself, in its moment of greatest triumph' (Ahmad, p. 100).

32. See 'Freud and the Scene of Writing', in *Writing and Difference*, as well as *Glas, Fors, The Post Card, Résistances – de la psychanalyse* (esp. 'Être juste avec Freud'), etc.

33. 'Politics and Friendship', in *The Althusserian Legacy*, ed. E. Ann Kaplan and Michael Sprinker (London: Verso, 1993), p. 204.

34. With Michael Sprinker, ibid., pp. 204 ff.

35. *Spectres de Marx*, p. 95/*Specters of Marx*, p. 55.

36. Ibid.

37. Ibid.

38. Ibid., p. 142/p. 85.
39. Ibid.
40. Lewis, p. 140.
41. Ibid., p. 157.
42. Ibid., p. 162 n. 15.
43. Ibid., p. 145.
44. Ibid., p. 150.
45. Ibid., p. 152.
46. Ibid., p. 145.
47. Ibid., p. 157.
48. Ibid., p. 153.
49. Ibid., p. 155.
50. Ibid., pp. 154, 156.
51. Ibid., p. 157.
52. Montag, p. 71.
53. Jameson, p. 32.
54. *Spectres de Marx*, pp. 146–7/*Specters of Marx*, p. 89.
55. Ibid., pp. 146 ff./pp.89 ff.
56. Jameson, pp. 46 ff.
57. Ibid., p. 46.
58. Ibid., p. 47.
59. That is why, at the point where it seems to me necessary to complicate certain of the 'stereotypes' that Jameson rightly denounces, I insist on the ongoing transformation of the concepts and problematic, while saluting certain work, for example, Balibar's. See my long footnote on this subject (*Spectres de Marx*, pp. 116 ff./*Specters of Marx*, pp. 181 ff., n. 8), particularly on everything involving 'dialectical materialism' and the concepts of 'transition' and 'non-contemporaneity'. Everything I say is inscribed in the historical and theoretical space of the 'transition', as I suggested above – a transition whose concept is, in its irreducible specificity, harder to think than is generally believed.

60. 'The point to be made, however, is not [just] that all such class mappings are arbitrary and somehow subjective, but that they are inevitable allegorical grids through which we necessarily read the world' (see the rest of this passage up to the point where the word 'allegorical' recurs). 'Class categories are therefore not at all examples of the proper or of the autonomous and pure, the self-sufficient operations of origins defined by so-called class affiliation: nothing is more complexly allegorical than the play of class connotations across the whole width and breadth of the social field, particularly today' (Jameson, p. 49). It is because I find myself in close agreement with what Jameson says (except perhaps for what 'allegorical' is intended to mean here), because I am sensitive to this 'complexity', that I am so prudent and reserved when it comes to references to 'social class', make them so sparingly, and am so concerned to define an International which would no longer depend on a classification whose connotations are so problematic, 'particularly today', as Jameson aptly says. Having signaled my agreement with Jameson, I would like to know what the critics I have just replied to, especially Ahmad and Lewis, think of his argument.

61. For example, on how my work is read in the United States ('Derrida's own philosophical moves have to be grasped as ideological or rather anti-ideological tactics, and not merely as the abstract philosophical discussions as which these texts cross the ocean and become translated here'), and on what distinguishes my trajectory from that of de Man (ibid., pp. 50, 51).

62. Especially ibid., pp. 32–6.
63. Ibid., p. 34.
64. Ibid., p. 32.
65. Ibid., p. 33.
66. Ibid.

67. *Spectres de Marx*, pp. 95–6n./*Specters of Marx*, p. 181, n. 2. Permit me to recall that this long note remains cautious from first to last, pending a forthcoming rereading of these 'dense, enigmatic, burning' pages (p. 96/p. 181).

68. See 'Pas', in *Parages* (Paris: Galilée, 1985).

69. [*Le mort sans mort* means 'death without death'. *Le rapport sans rapport* means 'relation without relation(s)'. *Attente sans attente*, which I have translated 'awaiting without expectation' or 'a waiting without awaiting', depending on the context, exploits the fact that *attente* has a range of meanings that go from 'wait' in the sense of passively marking time to 'anticipation' or 'expectation'. – Translator's note.]

70. Macherey, p. 24.

71. This obviously does not hold for Hamacher. It holds even less for Warren Montag, whose remarkable analysis takes 'the distinction between spirit and specter' seriously (Montag, p. 77). Macherey's move is more disconcerting. Although he describes my book as a 'work of art' (a plainly ambiguous compliment that can easily modulate into a denunciation of a style or rhetoric – a denunciation I have responded to above), he concedes that, in Marx's texts as I reread them, the 'reference to specters intervenes not only as a figure of rhetorical style but as a determination of those texts' content of thought' (Macherey, p. 18). But then why not take into account, in the remainder of the essay and in concluding, the resistance the concept of spectrality offers to any attempt to reduce it to the status of immaterial appearance? Why contrast, on this point, my argumentation with that put forward by Balibar, who, even while taking the appearing of appearance seriously, is supposed to be saying 'the same thing' as I am, but 'in an inverted way, from the perspective of a Marx one could call "rematerialized", which restores to the "appearances" of ideology their weight of reality, instead of denying every appearance of reality to reality, according to the profound inspiration that underlies the enterprise of a deconstruction' (Machery, p. 24)?

It hardly seems necessary to say that this definition of the 'profound inspiration that underlies a deconstruction' seems to me arbitary and extremely misleading. Obviously, a great deal could be said about the words 'body', 'reality', 'materiality', 'appearing' (*Erscheinung*), or 'appearance' (*Schein*), all brought into play here. But, surely, if by 'specter' I had simply meant appearance without reality and materiality, I would have wasted a great deal of my own and other people's time for nothing. The specter (which is, simply, not spirit) is anything but nothing, anything but incorporeal, and anything but mere appearance. My whole book can be read as one long response to that objection. For a more finely honed approach to the problem, which it is not possible to delimit, I would refer the reader to, in particular, chapter V of *Specters of Marx*, 'Apparition of the Inapparent', and to all the notes to that chapter, especially n. 6, p. 189, on *phantasma* and *phainesthai*.

I am grateful to Jameson for not having shrugged off spectrality as if it were nothing at all, even if he reduces it to the 'non self-sufficiency of the living present' – which it does indeed presuppose, but can by no means be identified with.

72. Ahmad, p. 103; Lewis, p. 148; my emphasis.

73. '[W]ouldn't this position of something undeconstructible – which recalls in its own way the Cartesian *cogito* – be itself a ghost, the ghost or the "spirit" of Derrida?' (Macherey, p. 24).

No; what motivates deconstruction – the undeconstructible which, in this context, is given the name justice, as distinguished from law or right [*droit*] – does not take the form of a founding limit where a kind of radical doubt would be arrested, which it would butt up against. It is an injunction which any construction or foundation would be inadequate to. Not that this injunction is an infinite idea in the Kantian sense. Nor is it Utopia (in the sense in which Jameson too quickly assimilates the impossible to Utopia ('the impossible [Utopian] hope', he says on p. 59, whereas everything that I call *the impossible* in numerous recent texts issues from an entirely different logic and calls for an entirely different way of thinking – in many different figures – events that are eminently real. This entire 'project' comes down to thinking what is known as the 'possible' and the 'impossible' in a different way. I cannot expand upon this here, or do more than refer the reader to other publications – indeed, to almost everything I have published in the last ten years at least). This undeconstructible injunction of justice is never gathered up and assembled in a single place, nor does it ever identify with itself (see *Specters of Marx*, pp. 19 ff.), though it very urgently commands, without waiting, here–now; and the inadequation of everything which measures itself against it, of everything it sets into motion, is the possibility, but also the necessity of a history; it is also the possibility and the necessity of a deconstruction. Deconstruction is so little a philosophy of the *cogito* that it begins by taking issue with it, as it were, in its Cartesian as well as its Husserlian forms. For all these reasons, I find it difficult to follow Warren Montag when *he* follows Macherey on the tracks of this *cogito*, suggesting that *Specters of Marx* reverses or contradicts what *Of Grammatology* says on the subject of the letter or the trace. On the contrary, I believe that the effort to think the trace is inseparable, and has from the outset been literally (I could marshal very many explicit indications of this; they have been accumulating for thirty years now) indissociable from an effort to think spectrality.

74. [*Survivant* usually means 'survivor'; *vivant* is the present participle of *vivre*, to live, and so means 'living' or 'alive'; *survie*, a related word, means both survival and life after death. – Translator's note.]

75. This resembles the debate it would be possible to have about *Offenbarung* (Revelation) and *Offenbarkeit* (the possibility of revelation and manifestation). Heidegger always seems to make the possibility of revelation into a deeper, older and therefore independent structure of existence, on the basis of which revelation in the religious sense, and this or that historical religion, become, secondarily, possible, and take determinate form. One is tempted to oppose to this powerful, classical argument at least one question: what if it were only by way of the (historical) event of revelation that the revelation of revealability, as such, manifests itself, etc.?

76. See 'Foi et savoir. Les deux sources de la religion dans les limites de la simple raison', in *La Religion* (Paris: Seuil, 1995); translation by Sam Weber, forthcoming from Stanford University Press.

77. See on this point Jameson's very apt comments on the religious and the theory of religion in Marx (Jameson, pp. 53 ff.).

78. *Spectres de Marx*, pp. 236 ff./*Specters of Marx*, pp. 148 ff. The question 'What is ideology?', like the ensuing discussion, follows the analysis of the ten specters ('the specter of a Decalogue and a decalogue of specters', the Table of the ten commandments, corresponding to the ten plagues, and another table of Aristotle's ten categories in this book about so many tables and so many sets of ten). It also follows a certain familial scene, and the question of the phallogocentrism between the father and the son (the good and the 'bad son' [p. 198/p. 122], which indicates that it is henceforth inseparable from the question of the '*patrimony of the idol*', a phrase I felt it necessary to italicize in order to highlight the question of the father raised by it (p. 236/p. 147).

79. Ibid., p. 262/p. 165.

80. Ibid., pp. 264 ff./pp. 166 ff.

81. Negri, p. 6.

82. 'The phenomenology of capitalist production described by Marx in *Capital* demonstrates therefore how, by way of this spectral movement, a true and proper metaphysics of capital is produced, as well as the autonomy of its power. But because it unfolds itself in a spectral form and autonomizes capital, this phenomenology – Marx maintains – *masks the real genesis of the process* of capital's development' (Negri, p. 7; my emphasis).

83. *Spectres de Marx*, p. 235/*Specters of Marx*, p. 147.

84. Ibid.

85. Negri, p. 10.

86. For example, he writes: 'Why does deconstruction want an aura of nostalgia which renders the ontological consistency of the new spectral dimension elusive and frankly ungraspable?' (Negri, p. 8). Everything that follows – up to 'We do not know how to respond to Derrida's sad sidestepping, nor do we know how to construct a straight line that would cut through his process's agonizing curves' (ibid.) – seems to me to reflect a misreading for which I, perhaps, share the responsibility with Negri, but against which I firmly protest. Similarly, I protest against the words 'mysticism' and 'negative theology à la Blanchot' (Negri, p. 13), I have elsewhere explained why I object to this stereotype, and so refrain from doing so here.

87. Negri, p. 10.

88. Ibid.

89. '[D]econstruction remains prisoner of an ineffectual and exhausted definition of ontology. The reality principle in deconstruction is out of its element. . . . Derrida is a prisoner of the ontology he critiques' (Negri, pp. 12–13).

Even if there were an element of truth in that, why this figure of the *prison*, today? Why would the presupposition of an ontology be carceral? And, above all, is Negri incapable of imagining that one can *also* be the prisoner of ontology in general (old or new)? That one can be imprisoned in a discourse on the *on*, on the present-being as such? And that what is 'exhausted' is not one or another definition of ontology, but ontology itself, at least if one continues to assign ontology the minimal, non-arbitrary sense that is, as it were, inscribed in the word 'ontology': the discourse (or science or *ratio*) bearing on the *present-being as such*? Of course, if one is prepared to question, in all its forms, this reference, in the word 'ontology', to the *present-being, properly present* and as such (real, concrete, actual, etc.), while arbitrarily, or for strategic reasons, deciding to make the word express something entirely different in the hope that this terminological decision will produce some sort of emancipatory effect, then so be it; I have nothing against the word itself. But the result will be a new word, or an encrypted word. I will come back to this point by way of conclusion.

Index